DATE DUE

MY 8 '97		
MY 27 '97		
RENEW		
RENEW		
OC 30 '97		
AP 27 '98		
MY 3 0 '98		
NO 2 '99		
DE 2 0 '00		
DE 6 '01		
NO 2 '04		
FE 1 2 '09		

DEMCO 38-296

THE PEOPLE OF GEORGIA

The People of Georgia

AN ILLUSTRATED HISTORY

Mills Lane

A Beehive Press Book

LIBRARY OF GEORGIA

Savannah · 1992

FRONTISPIECE
Rural family, Greene County, May, 1939
Marion Post Wolcott, Library of Congress

This book was edited by The Beehive Press,
which retains all rights to its contents and design.
This book is published by The Beehive Foundation
without profit or compensation to The Beehive Press.
The Beehive Foundation gives copies of its books
to college and public libraries throughout Georgia
and also sells them to individuals by mail.

Library of Georgia
℅ The Beehive Foundation
321 Barnard Street
Savannah, Georgia 31401

CONTENTS

Introduction:
Southerners and Americans

UNTIL the last few years, American history seemed to be a celebration of national innocence and virtue, generosity and power. This was our inheritance from the ideals of the Revolution, Jeffersonian and Jacksonian Democracy, the Civil War, the Progressives and the New Deal. This was what we called our economic destiny—immigrants coming to the new continent, sweeping through virgin forests, creating a new society free of the constraints of the Old World. Our confidence in this materialistic progress suffused our foreign policy, and clad it with virtuous trappings, from the Open Door in China, to two world wars and the Cold War. But Southerners seemed excluded from this view of American history, for it was hard to reconcile the sad fatalities of our unhappy regional past—the moral guilt of slavery and segregation, the frustrations of military defeat followed by military occupation, the region's social and economic backwardness—with the inherited belief in the American Dream. Like individuals who must find identities for themselves, accepting weaknesses and discovering strengths, before they can face constructively the world around them, so Southerners must come to terms with their past. In the 1990's, when all Americans are facing a crisis of national nerve, an honest look at our history may help reaffirm the essentially hopeful and unifying lessons of the American experience.

From its outset Georgia was the last and poorest colony at the southern extremity of the British empire in America, a rude and crude

7

W. H. Holmes plowing sweet potatoes,
Greene County, November, 1941.
Jack Delano, Library of Congress

place caught in a triangular struggle between France, Spain and England to control that part of North America after 1700, and a near disaster as an imperial enterprise. Georgia's reputation as a haven for weak and impotent persons was established from the outset, though perhaps only a handful of debtors ever came to Georgia, and the colony soon attracted a cosmopolitan assortment of international fugitives. In 1740 Henry Garrett wrote from the struggling military outpost which was then colonial Georgia: "I got into a very bad corner of the world, where poverty and oppression abound to such a degree that it's become proverbial this way to say 'as poor as a Georgian.'" After the Revolution, Georgia remained one of the last seaboard states to establish a stable society, for the removal of the Indians was a slow, difficult experience, not completed until 1838. La Rochefoucauld, an exiled peer of France who came to Georgia in 1796, called frontier Georgians the most barbarous, drunken, disorderly and reckless people in America. After the invention of the cotton gin in 1793, the South's preoccupation with cotton and slaves delayed the creation of a middle-class society of shopkeepers, workers, factories and cities. From his train, as it moved toward Macon during the Civil War, William Howard Russell viewed the social landscape of an enduring frontier: "From the windows of the carriages we could see that the children were barefooted, shoeless, stockingless—that the people who congregate at the wooden huts and grogshops of the stations are rude, unkempt, that the villages are miserable places." The Civil War disrupted Southern life, destroyed property and wealth and brought a social revolution which was not accepted for a century. For the next three generations, Georgians continued to live close to the land, farming, fishing and mining for their livelihood, retreating further toward regional isolation and suffering terribly as their agricultural system collapsed.

By the American standards that "bigger is better," that "nothing

Mrs. Ira C. Brown with her canned goods,
Union Point, November, 1941.
Jack Delano, Library of Congress

succeeds like success," that "change is progress," this Southern history has been a failure. The Puritan ethic, popularized by outspoken American figures from Cotton Mather in the eighteenth century to Horatio Alger in the nineteenth, taught that hard work and virtue were rewarded with success, a doctrine which excluded most Georgians from grace. During the angry controversies leading to the Civil War, Georgians were described as ignorant, rude, bigoted, uncultivated and cruel people who delighted in oppressing their slaves and who had been made lazy and corrupt by a sinful institution. In the aftermath of the Civil War, the victorious side found every evidence of the moral decay, lack of free institutions and Northern enterprise which had foredoomed the Southern cause in its view. In 1865 Sidney Andrews surveyed Newnan, Georgia, where he recognized everywhere the symptoms of Southern inferiority: "Newnan is just like every other Southern town—streets full of mud, holes and wallowing swine, fences in every stage of tumble-down ruin, sidewalks in every condition of break-neck disorder, yards full of sticks and stones and bits of every conceivable rubbish—everywhere a grand carnival of sloth and unthrift and untidiness and slovenliness—everywhere that apathy of shiftlessness so pitiful to the soul of a New Englander!" Carl Schurz wrote from Mississippi after travelling through Georgia in 1865: "I found all of my preconceived opinions verified most full, no, more than that. This is the most shiftless, most demoralized people I have ever seen." In 1908 the *New Republic* called Georgia "a country like Haiti, which must be supervised by a more civilized and enlightened society." In 1920 H. L. Mencken called the South "an awe-inspiring blank . . . of fat farms, shoddy cities and paralyzed cerebrums" and wrote of Georgia in particular: "A self-respecting European, going there to live, would not only find intellectual stimulation utterly lacking; he would actually feel a certain insecurity, as if the scenes were the Balkans or the

Man selling bait, Augusta, August, 1936.
Margaret Bourke-White from You Have Seen Their Faces
(New York, 1937), with permission

China Coast. There is a state with more than half the area of Italy and more population than either Denmark or Norway, and yet in thirty years it has not produced a single idea." Though in 1931 Mencken awarded Mississippi the lamentable preeminence as The Worst American State, he ranked Georgia, out of the then forty-eight states, 45th in wealth, 46th in education, 43rd in public health, 46th in public order. Donald Davidson of Nashville parodied the legend of Southern barbarism portrayed by such sophisticates: "So the tale runs—a region full of little else but lynchings, shootings, chain-gangs, poor whites, Ku Kluxers, hookworm, pellagra, and a few decayed patricians whose chief intent is to deprive the uncontaminated, spiritual-singing Negro of his life and liberty. Over such pictures the East stormed, or shed crocodile tears, in the clever nineteen-twenties." Such criticisms were based partly on Southern problems—and partly on a denial of problems throughout American history and life.

But no longer can Americans from any region afford the luxury of self-satisfied self-righteousness. The American dream of unlimited opportunity and achievement will always be a real ideal and worthy of our pursuit, but it may have been the reality of American life only during the early nineteenth century. Our recent national history has demonstrated that the United States is not the perfect, powerful, innocent nation we had believed. The moral and military failure of the Vietnam War showed how essentially honorable, well-intentioned people could make honorable, well-intentioned mistakes. This was an important lesson for a nation committed to the idea that nothing succeeds like success and that good people win and bad people fail. Scandals in the administrations of presidents Nixon and Reagan—Watergate and Iran Contra—revealed moral failure in high and formerly respectable places. Once the South was obliged to accept black civil rights in the 1960's and 1970's, the greatest racial tensions and injustices, punctuated by explosive violence, remained in cities like Boston, New York, Detroit and Los Angeles. A binge of speculation and spending

Cotton chopper, White Plains, May, 1941.
Jack Delano, Library of Congress

in the 1980's, accompanied by scandals on Wall Street and deficit budgets in Washington, left us poorer and maybe wiser. As our national economic destiny passes to other emerging nations, the environmentalists continue to remind us that bigger is not always better. Riots in Los Angeles in the spring of 1992, followed by unrest in other cities, reminded all Americans of urban decay and problems of racism throughout all America. This crisis of national nerve frees Georgians and Southerners from the burden of an unrealized American dream. Now, at last, we can reexamine our regional past without romanticism or apology.

Beneath the layers of scholarly varnish, the essential history of Georgia is the story of good, simple people, black and white, living close together and close to the land, sharing great hardships and disappointments. Their history is the failure of an agrarian ideal, which James Oglethorpe, Georgia's founder, called "the Agrarian Equality," by which he meant a hope that a society of sturdy, independent yeoman farmers could live there in honest simplicity and self-respecting equality. But this hope was frustrated throughout Georgia's history — by the military preoccupations of the early colony which caused such great distress that most of the colonists fled from the place within the first ten years, by the expansion of slavery and plantations across the frontier which destroyed the foundations of a class of small farmers, by the Civil War debacle, by the development of sharecropping and farm tenancy at the end of the nineteenth century, and by the neglect of rural society in an urban, industrialized era. A tour of the Georgia countryside today, away from gleaming Atlanta and the white concrete ribbons of Federal highways, shows everywhere the abandoned farms, naked land, decayed buildings and languishing towns, which are the ruins of an agrarian world that has died. It is a melancholy scene which W.E.B. DuBois of Atlanta University described in 1901: "A feeling of silent depression falls on one as he gazes on this scarred and stricken land, with its silent mansions, deserted cabins and fallen fences." In this sense, Atlanta, populated in part by displaced rural people who

E. A. Marcus's son, Greene County, June, 1941.
Jack Delano, Library of Congress

could no longer live on the land and supported now by interstate commerce which has little to do with the economic life within Georgia, represents the failure and not the progress of Georgia since the Civil War.

Now, when the nationalizing, homogenizing pressures of our industrialized, urban society are bringing a real conclusion to state and regional history, Southerners had better pause to sift out and preserve the valuable traditions of their experience before they become too "American." Georgia was one of the greatest social and philanthropic experiments during the era of its establishment. The subsequent warts and pimples of Georgia history make us damned interesting. Southerners who now live in busy cities can find needed stability and humane values in the continuity and rhythm of their agrarian history. Southerners who now live in a consumption-oriented, cosmetic world of gratification and salesmanship can find a strong antidote in a plain and bittersweet account of their history. Indeed, Georgia's honest if humble history is important for all Americans, not just for Southerners. Thomas Wolfe wrote to his mother in 1923 that Southern promoters who shouted "Progress, Progress!" only meant more Fords, more Rotary Clubs, more Baptist Ladies Social Unions. After generations of Pollyanna platitudes about national triumph and righteousness, we Americans have become a reckless, selfish people, and we need some tenderness, tolerance, humility and humanity. Americans who have looked at their history superficially as a brittle story of success and reward may learn valuable lessons from the sad experience of Georgians who have already had to accept failure and disappointment. Now every American is called upon to reconcile himself to the reality of the nation's diminished role in world affairs and even her incapacity to solve her own national problems. The South's apparent "backwardness" may be only one obvious example of deep national imper-

Farm boy, August, 1936.
Margaret Bourke-White, Syracuse University Library

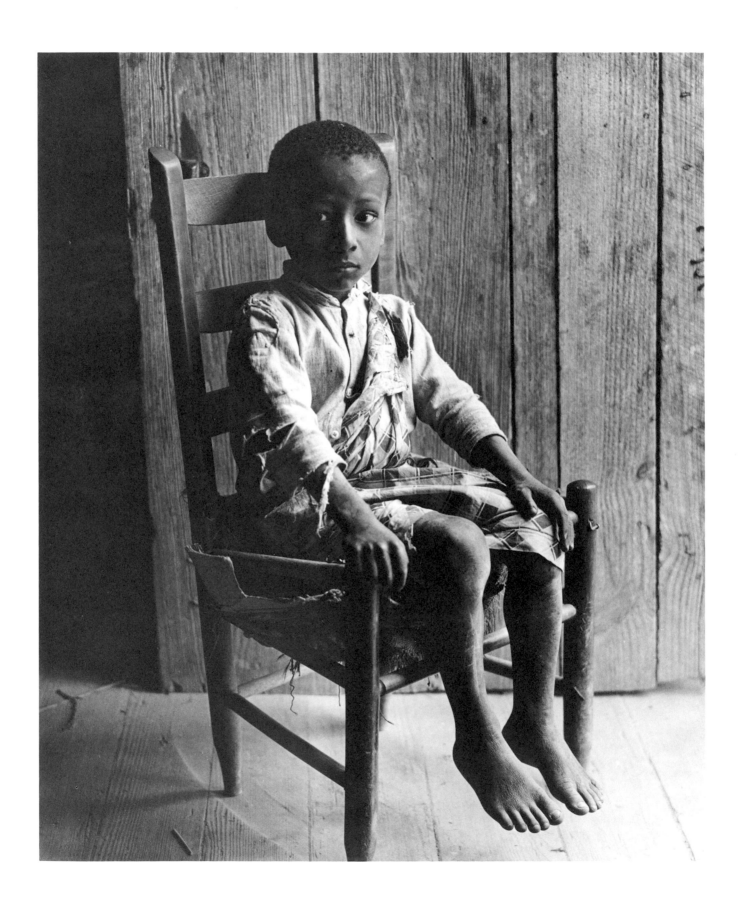

fection; certainly it is a common link to the poor and distressed condition of most people in our troubled world. Americans should understand that good exists beside evil, that poverty does not exclude happiness and that people can fail but still be admirable. In art, the ideal of beauty is based on an acknowledgement of imperfection. The real nobility of human experience is found not in triumph and riches but in struggle, courage, disappointment, perseverance against overwhelming odds and even in failure, itself. This is the great lesson of Georgia history.

This book was written nearly twenty years ago, and now the author, middle-aged and with a bald spot expanding as fast as his belly, returns to it. Though occasionally marred by the overwrought idealism of a young author, the lessons of *The People of Georgia* remain vital. For the urgent problems of the 1990's loom larger, and seem even more insoluble, than those of the 1970's, and our people seem more divided than they have been at any time in their history. It seems to me we have two transcendent problems. First, we have lost "something to believe in." That "something" was once faith in religion, human perfectibility or science and technology—tarnished idols all. The absence of a cohering confidence has contributed to our second problem. We have also lost a sense of community. Everywhere we seem divided by contention, while unifying local traditions are assaulted by a vulgar, homogenized mass-market culture. An honest look at our history can help us to restore a shared idealism, valuing the best and accepting the worst in our shared past. Thus informed, we could more easily forgive ourselves and others for our weaknesses and mistakes—past, present and future. Had our people and our leaders such wisdom, Americans would be less self-righteous and more at peace with themselves and the world.

Frank Cunningham's son, Heard County, April, 1941.
Jack Delano, Library of Congress

1. Georgians and Englishmen

THE first colonists sailed to Georgia in November, 1732. The *Gentlemen's Magazine* reported the historic departure: "The *Anne* Galley, of above 200 Tons, is on the point of sailing from Deptford for the new Colony of Georgia, with 35 Families, consisting of Carpenters, Bricklayers, Farmers, etc. who take all proper Instruments. The Men are learning Military Discipline of the Guards, as must all that go thither, and to carry Muskets, Bayonets and Swords, to defend the Colony. She has on board 10 Ton of Alderman Parson's best Beer, and will take in at the Maderas five Ton of Wine, for the Service of the Colony. James Oglethorpe, Esquire, one of the Trustees, goes with them to see them settled." On the *Anne*, according to one of several conflicting reports, there were forty-four men, twenty women, twenty-five boys and seventeen girls, including a potash maker, two merchants, five carpenters, two wig makers, two tailors, a miller and baker, a writer, a surgeon, one gardener, five farmers, an upholsterer, a basket maker, two sawyers, an apothecary, a vintner, a wheelwright, one stocking maker and a reduced military officer. Aboard ship these colonists slept in thirty-five wooden cradles, one for each family, divided by canvas curtains. Every Thursday and Sunday the colonists were fed pork and peas; every Saturday, stockfish and butter; and every other day, beef and pudding. On calm days the lower decks were washed down with vinegar. The women knitted and sewed, while the men exercised at small arms.

20

James Oglethorpe, the founder of Georgia, c. 1735. *A. E. Dyes after Willem Verelst, National Portrait Gallery, London*

A Plan representing the Form of Setling the Districts, or County Divisions in the Margravate of Azilia.

FIDES ADITV... CREDE... GLEBÆ

During the preceding fifty years, since the last American colony, Pennsylvania, had been chartered in 1681, there had been much talk of new American settlements. Spain had established camps in Florida and what would later become Georgia during the sixteenth century, nearly a hundred years before the first permanent British settlement at Jamestown. When Ponce de León discovered Florida in 1512 he may have come as far north as Georgia; in 1540 Hernando de Soto probably marched across the Georgia frontier; in 1562, French Huguenots under Jean Ribault paused at the coast of Georgia long enough to name some Georgia rivers Seine, Somme, Loire, Garonne, Gironde and Grande; and in 1566 Spanish missions were established on Saint Catherine's and Cumberland islands. In 1713 Thomas Coram, who would later become a Georgia trustee, proposed a "Georgia" which he would have located somewhere between Maine and Nova Scotia. In 1717 Sir Robert Mountgomery, a proud Scot baronet and self-styled genius, designed "Azilia," a feudal barony to be planted on territory that would later become Georgia. But, like Coram's scheme, this was a paper fantasy. In 1724 Jean Pierre Purry of Switzerland appealed to European monarchs to make their colonies a haven for persecuted Protestants throughout Europe, and in 1730 he received a grant from the English Crown to settle on the Carolina side of the Savannah River. In 1729 Joshua Gee proposed sending convicts, vagrants and other useless people who could not support themselves to the border of the southern colonies, where they could buttress the frontier defenses and support themselves on the land, perhaps by raising silk. In 1730 Sir Alexander Cumming brought back to England several Cherokee chiefs from the headwaters of the Savannah River, focussing attention on the unsettled, disputed land between English Carolina and Spanish Florida. Early in 1730 the Board of Trade had been planning an extension of Carolina beyond its southern border, then the Savan-

In 1717 Sir Robert Mountgomery proposed a feudal barony with a turreted fortress on territory that would later become Georgia. *From Mountgomery's* Discourse Concerning . . . a New Colony *(London, 1717), Library of Congress*

nah River. The general notion was that a new English colony in America should be a frontier settlement near Carolina or the West Indies settled by poor people, soldiers or foreign Protestants.

In 1729 a committee of the House of Commons was investigating the condition of several of England's debtor prisons and proposed reform legislation which led to the release of some thousands of prisoners. Inspired by that experience, the committee's chairman, James Oglethorpe, approached another member of the committee, John Viscount Percival, with the idea of sending one hundred vagrants and poor children under the age of sixteen, bound as servants to invalid soldiers, to some place in "the West Indies"—by which he meant anywhere in British America or the Caribbean. "That worthy Gentleman Mr. Oglethorpe opened to me a scheme he had formed, to which I was before a perfect stranger but which I very much supported," wrote Percival, "to settle a hundred miserable wretches, lately relieved out of jail, on the continent of America, and for that end to petition His Majesty for a grant of a suitable quantity of acres, whereon to place these persons." As Oglethorpe, Percival and their philanthropic friends—who later became the Trustees of Georgia—drafted a petition to the King, they adopted many of the ideas about colonies which had been circulating in popular conversation. Oglethorpe had been a veteran of war with Spain, so he recognized that the new colony would become a defense for Carolina from her enemies, especially the Spaniards in Florida. England's poor and foreign Protestants could find refuge in the new colony, which would become a buyer's market for raw materials and a seller's market for manufactured goods. England would no longer have to import silk from France, flax and linen from Russia, wine from Madeira: all would be produced in Georgia. In 1732, King George II, convinced that the venture would be good politics as well as good works, granted the vacant lands lying between the

The Parliamentary committee investigating Fleet Street
Prison in 1729, with its chairman, James Oglethorpe.
William Hogarth, National Portrait Gallery, London

Savannah and the Altamaha rivers, extending from the Atlantic Ocean westward indefinitely to the South Seas, to a group of trustees for twenty-one years and gave it the benefit of his name, Georgia.

This last and poorest of the thirteen colonies was launched by the most elaborate promotional campaign in early American history. Propagandists painted a rosy picture of what they called "the most delightful country of the universe," a land watered with noble rivers, stored with useful minerals, abounding with beasts, birds and fish to an incredible degree of plenty. The trustees suggested that Georgia lay at the same latitude as the Garden of Eden and the Promised Land. The poets invited Britannia to view a sprightly scene of industry and prosperity: "Instant at work a thousand hands appear / These fell the trees, and these the fabricks rear / The vigorous axe resistless wins its way / And bids th' eternal woods admit the day / The sunny hills afar, and prostrate plains / Invite the labours of the lusty swains / Their annual stores already seem possest / And future harvests wave in ev'ry breast." The future visitor to Georgia would witness a panorama of pastoral plenty: "Let him see those who are now a prey to all the calamities of want, living under a sober and orderly government, settled in towns, which are rising at distances along navigable rivers; Flocks and herds in the neighbouring pastures, and adjoining to them plantations of regular rows of mulberry trees, entwined with vines, the branches of which are loaded with grapes; Let him see orchards of oranges, pomegranates, and olives; In other places extend fields of corn, or flax and hemp. In short, the whole face of the country changed by agriculture, and plenty in every part of it." Phillip Thicknesse recalled his coming to the colony in 1736: "The truth was that I had been so poisoned by the glaring colours in which Oglethorpe had in his printed books displayed the prospects of his new colony of Georgia, that I was determined to go thither. This project had filled me with

Among the persecuted and impoverished colonists recruited for Georgia were the Salzburgers, the exiled Protestants of Austria. *Elias Bach, Royal Library of Denmark*

OVERLEAF:
The Trustees' propaganda suggested that it would be easy to cultivate and settle the rich lands of Georgia. *From Benjamin Martyn's* Reasons for Establishing the Colony of Georgia in America *(London, 1773), Library of Congress*

infinite delight, for I then considered myself as one setting out to begin the founding of a new world." "In a word," wrote Joseph Fitzwalter, another of the early colonists, "I take it to be the promised land."

The trustees promised to transport poor people to Georgia and support them with cattle, land and supplies until the first harvest. In the colony there was to be a public store full of all the tools and provisions the people would need. Each colonist was to receive for equipment a watch coat, a musket and bayonet, a hatchet, a hammer and handsaw, a shod shovel or spade, a broad hoe, a narrow hoe, a gimlet, a drawing knife, an iron pot, a pair of pothooks and a frying pan. Each colonist was to receive for food 300 pounds of beef or pork, 114 pounds of rice, 114 pounds of flour, 114 pounds of peas, 44 gallons of strong beer, 64 quarts of molasses for brewing more beer, 18 pounds of sugar, 5 gallons of vinegar, 30 pounds of salt, plus 12 quarts of lamp oil and 12 pounds of soap. These charity colonists were to have possession of fifty acres of land in Georgia, including a small house lot in town, a garden in the city common and a distant 45-acre farm in the woods. In return for this charity, the colonists agreed to follow the trustees' orders to work at communal labor for the first year and to stay in Georgia for at least two more years. The trustees also offered to grant up to five hundred acres to independent colonists who would come to Georgia at their own expense with at least one servant for every fifty acres of land.

The trustees' promotional campaign attracted a cosmopolitan complexion of colonists to Georgia. The first 114 colonists were followed by five hundred more during the first year and by some five thousand more hopeful people during the next decade. Petitions were sent to the trustees from Rotterdam, The Hague, Genoa and other places where persecuted people had paused in search of permanent asylum. Some Lutherans, exiled by the Catholic archbishop of Salz-

Flying to Georgia in an airship propelled by wild geese, from Grady's *Description of the Famous New Colony of Georgia* (Dublin, 1734). *University of Georgia Library*

The ship *London Merchant*, carrying the Salzburgers, passed the white chalk cliffs of the Isle of Wight as it began the voyage to Georgia in the fall of 1735. *Drawing by Philip G. F. von Reck, Royal Library of Denmark*

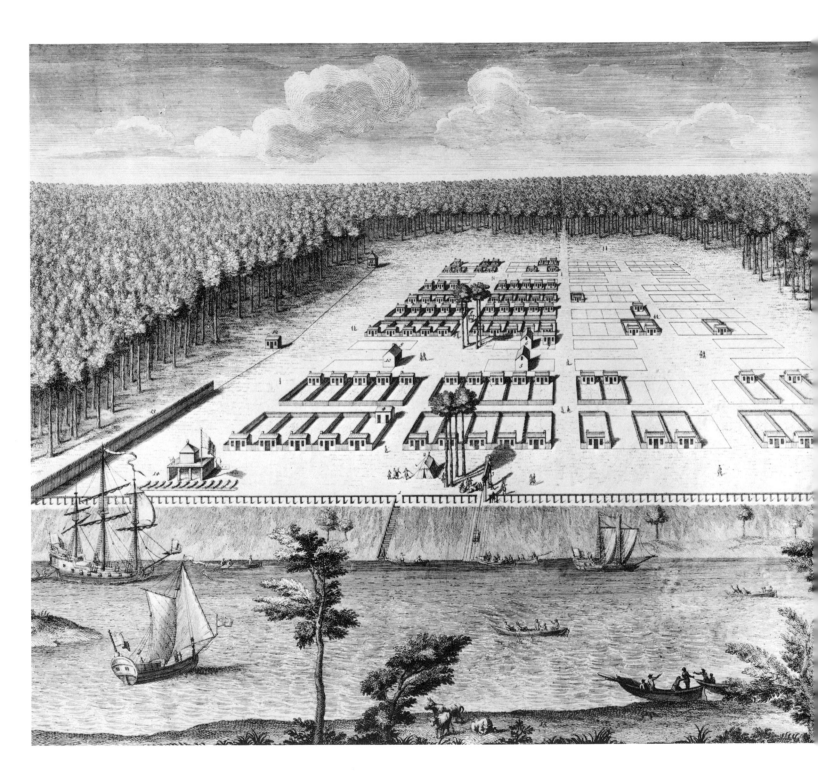

A View of Savannah, a small village on the sandy river bank,
surrounded by endless pine forests, March, 1734. *Engraving
after Peter Gordon, Library of Congress*

burg in 1731, had already gone to Maryland and Virginia, and Swiss Protestants had settled on the Carolina side of the Savannah River at Purrysburg in December, 1732. In March, 1734, seventy-eight Lutherans came to Georgia and settled twenty-five miles upriver at Ebenezer. Between 1735 and 1738 some forty-five Germans of another Protestant sect, the Moravians, arrived. In January, 1736, the Scot Highlanders, fleeing the abortive Jacobite rebellion of 1715, founded New Inverness, later called Darien, on the Altamaha River. During the colony's first ten years the trustees sent to Georgia at their expense 1,847 colonists, of whom 1,008 were British people and 839 were foreigners. In Georgia, a visitor could hear Gaelic spoken at Darien, German at Ebenezer, French at Highgate, Spanish at Hampstead, Creek among the Indians in the forest.

The first colonists reached the new settlement of Savannah in early February, 1733. Oglethorpe reported to the trustees from the place: "I went myself to view the Savannah River. I fixed upon a healthy situation about ten miles from the sea. The river here forms a half moon, along the South side of which the banks are almost forty foot high and on top flat, which they call a bluff. Ships that draw twelve foot water can ride within ten yards of the bank. Upon the river side in the center of this plain, I have laid out the town." On top of the steep, sandy bluff, the colonists hastily pitched four tents. Except for the cries of birds in the woods, the movement of lazy alligators on the muddy banks of the river and smoke from the campfires of a nearby Indian village, the scene was still, silent and undisturbed.

At the northern end of the bluff, Oglethorpe found a trading house of John and Mary Musgrove, who became invaluable interpreters, and a scraggly Indian village called Yamacraw, about forty Creek Indians recently reduced by smallpox. Mark Catesby, a pioneering naturalist who had come in 1722 to territory which would later become Georgia, reported that these Indians had good teeth and sweet breath, since he had been "necessitated to sleep with them." Phillip Thicknesse, who came to Georgia in 1736, acknowledged that the Indians were gentle and civilized men, no matter how singularly savage their "rude dress, painted faces, sliced ears, nose bobs! and tattooed skin rendered their external appearance to us Britons." Sixteen-year-old Thicknesse purchased the pleasures of an Indian squaw for the price of a pair of boots, some paint, a looking glass, a comb and a pair of scissors. By 1737 a young ensign in Oglethorpe's regiment counted four hundred half-breed children in Georgia. In May, 1733, Oglethorpe signed a formal treaty with fifty chiefs of the Lower Creek Nation. In May, 1734, Oglethorpe returned to England, carrying with him the Yamacraw chief Tomochichi, his nephew Toonahowi and other noble savages from the new world. Colonial agents found little difficulty securing enough land from the Indians, and later treaties of 1763 and 1773 gave the British a further considerable territory that makes up about one-eighth of present-day Georgia.

Military discipline stamped Savannah and Georgia with stern regimentation. On the bluff of the Savannah River, Oglethorpe organized his town to face emergencies, just as any good field commander would plan temporary encampments to preserve order, control and discipline among his troops. The town was laid out in four wards, each made up of four tythings. Each ward was run by a constable to whom four tythingmen reported for the welfare and good conduct of the families in each tything. Ten men in each tything were ready to bear arms at all times and, until other colonists arrived, they would take turns standing watch every fourth night. Oglethorpe inspired good marksmanship by putting up wild turkeys as targets, which then became prizes for the best shot. He gave muskets to orphan boys, so they would become accustomed to habitual guard duty and

The chief of the Creek Indians at Savannah, Tomochichi, with his nephew Toonahowi, c. 1735. *Mezzotint after Willem Verelst, Private Collection*

Senkaitschi, a Yuchi chief, 1736. *Drawing by Philip G. F. von Reck, Royal Library of Denmark*

become good soldiers. Savannah was to be protected by a circle of fortifications, each manned by ten families, and these settlements were established during the first months around Savannah. In December, 1735, Oglethorpe planted a frontier military garrison at Frederica, a village of huts thatched with palmetto leaves and a fort faced with sod, on Saint Simon's Island.

During the first year the new outpost at Savannah was laid out, forty houses were built and a municipal government of courts and magistrates was organized. The colonists were busy clearing land, cutting timber and planting corn, peas and potatoes. In March, 1733, colonist Thomas Causton wrote his wife from the place where Savannah was rising: "It is impossible to give a true description of the place because we are in a wood, but I can't forbear saying it is a very pleasant one." By mid-March two clapboard houses were built and three sawed houses were framed, also a crane to lift heavy loads over the bluff, a battery of cannon and a magazine. By June there were nine framed houses and a smith's forge. Georgia's first houses were the simplest clapboard cottages, raised on log foundations. Thomas Causton, storekeeper at Savannah, described them: "Of one floor, only a cock-loft over it sufficient to hold two beds, the lower part will make one large room and two smaller ones." Francis Moore, recorder at Frederica, described them: "A frame of sawed timber, 24 by 16, floored with rough deals, the sides with feather-edged boards unplaned and the roof shingled." The colonists built a log jail, a well twenty feet deep and a gloriously large oven. The river bluff was fenced, new stairs were built up the sandy bluff. At Tybee Island, a lighthouse, twenty-five feet wide and ninety feet high, was begun, constructed of pine and cedar. Savannah was fortified by a stockade of pine logs, eighteen feet high, facing the forest, and by a battery of twelve cannon, facing the sea. In July the colonists met to name the wards and squares of their little city. By January, 1734, Oglethorpe reported that there were already 437 people receiving the trustees' support in Georgia. Phillip Thicknesse settled on an isolated spot four miles from Savannah, where he shot squirrels and wild birds, bartered venison from the Indians and ate that meat dipped deep in honey. He wrote his mother happily in November, 1736: "The country seems to agree with me very well, for every coat and waistcoat I have is so much too small for me that it will not button within four inches, and I am grown tall and tanned with the sun." Altogether it was, Thicknesse wrote rapturously, "a true Robinson Crusoe line of life!"

The trustees had selected as colonists weak people who were the least able to face the adversities of frontier life. Skidaway Island was settled by a peruke maker, a clogmaker, a ropemaker, a weaver, a dyer, a victualler, a bookbinder and an ex-soldier, most of them city-slickers. Though perhaps no more than a dozen debtors came to Georgia, the trustees were flooded with applications from self-acknowledged failures in England, and the trustees had expressly designed to select only those applicants who were not useful at home and who could not support themselves in England. In January, 1733, the trustees interviewed eight carpenters and found them "miserable objects most of them: One had by sickness been obliged to sell his bed, and another was to sell his tools to pay his creditors." In July, 1733, there were further interviews: "Persons noted down for a future embarkation, reduced to the last extremity of want."

  The first colonists on the *Anne* were surprisingly old men 35–50 years of age, evidence that they had decided to resort to Georgia in middle age after early disappointment and failure. William Stephens, secretary of the colony after 1737, characterized the colonists as "poor unfortunate men, who were render'd incapable of living at

The Trustees of Georgia, with a delegation of Indians, a bear cub and eagle from America. *Painting by Willem Verelst, The Henry Francis duPont Winterthur Museum*

home . . . a parcel of poor people." Samuel Penseyre, who fled to Georgia to escape from his bitchy, drunken wife, knew very well how "Nobody would leave his native country if they had not some crosses or misfortunes to bear."

The colonists found themselves in a strange land of alligators, deer, snakes, bears, bugs, sandy beaches and palm trees. The climate was hotter than expected: an eighteenth-century visitor, La Rochefoucauld, complained that he could cook an egg in just twelve minutes by putting it into the Georgia sand on a hot summer day. The climate was colder than expected: William Stephens, who came to Georgia to report to the trustees in 1737, said ice formed in the chamber pot under his bed on cold winter nights. Thomas Causton wrote his wife in 1735: "Every insect here is stronger than in England. The ants are half an inch long and, they say, will bite desperately." Edward Kimber, who came to Georgia in 1743, reported "an abundance of torments, as Cock-roaches, Wood-ticks, Sand-flies, Moskettos, and other Vermin." Francis Moore in 1736 said that the alligators at Frederica were "terrible to look at, stretching open an horrible large Mouth, big enough to swallow a man, with rows of dreadful large sharp teeth, and feet like dragons, armed with great claws."

The charity colonists had agreed to accept elaborate prescriptions in return for the trustees' benevolence, a smothering paternalism that would weigh heavily on the colonists in Georgia. A typical colonist who had been shipped to Georgia at the trustees' expense had to be twenty-one years old, so he could be strong enough to plow his land and carry a musket. He had to agree to remain in Georgia for at least three years, so he could contribute to the stable defense of the place. He had to agree to plant one hundred white mulberry trees on every ten acres of his land to feed silk worms—a Georgia industry which never materialized. He could claim no more than fifty acres of land, so the population would not be too spread out. He could not sell or mortgage his

"MacDonnel, Piper to the Highland Regiment . . . Tried in the Tower for Desertion in June 1743 [and] sent to Georgia" by John Bowles. *Private Collection*

The first houses built by Englishmen on Saint Simon's Island were a tent-like hut of cruck construction and another of puncheons or upright logs buried in the ground, 1736. *Drawing by Philip G. F. von Reck, Royal Library of Denmark*

land and only his son could inherit it. He could not purchase slaves, because they might overturn the government or create inequality among the settlers. South Carolina, which had three times as many blacks as whites in 1734, was considered weak and unstable. The Georgia colonist could not drink rum, which would lead to weakness and indolence. The idea behind all these restrictions was what Oglethorpe called "the Agrarian Equality," by which he meant the design of building a population of small farmers capable of supporting and defending themselves.

These benevolent, aggravating regulations made ambitious and propertied colonists frustrated and unhappy. They could see how Carolinians owned and sold their land, not merely had possession of it, how they profited from slave labor, drank rum and joined in the lucrative molasses and timber trade with the West Indies. Ships stayed away from Georgia because people were too poor to buy a shipload of merchandise and could not afford to hire labor and then ship cheap raw materials which competed with those produced by slave labor. There was no cash in the public store in 1737 to pay workers building a fort at Savannah, so the project was abandoned. At different times there were no munitions, physicians, candles, meat or money at Savannah. In February, 1737, hunger was so great that people began stealing vegetables from neighbors' gardens and the trustees' cattle were killed secretly in the woods at night. Distracted by their obligations to perform communal labor, building their houses and fighting the Spaniards in Florida, the colonists were not able to support themselves, and the trustees' subsistence, intended for only the first year, had to be extended indefinitely until the public store was closed in 1738.

In Oglethorpe's absence there was dispute instead of leadership in the colony. Thomas Causton, the storekeeper, was accused of

A.Haupt Straßen B.Markt Plätz
rer ein jeglicher Zehen Wohnungen
welcher ebenfals eingezaint.P.Hölt
Land wo die Saltzburger ihre Vieh

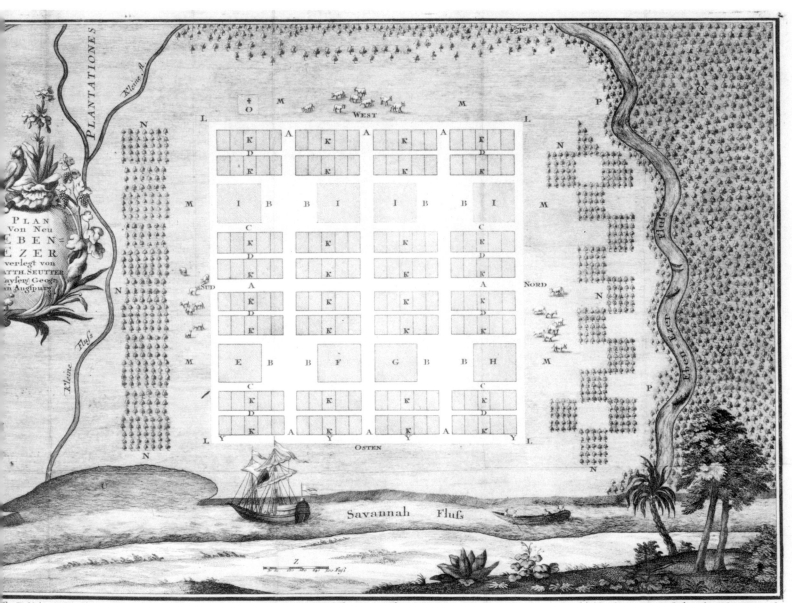

In February, 1736, the Salzburgers began building the town of New Ebenezer, some ten miles north of Savannah near the Savannah River. A 1747 engraving after Matthew Seutter. *Library of Congress*

starving the people and enriching himself. The workmen at Tybee in 1735 were said to be continually drinking instead of building the lighthouse. John Wesley, the minister at Savannah, was run out of the colony, accused of improper relations with one of his communicants, Sophia Hopkey. In 1735 a group of unhappy indentured servants and others conspired to overthrow Savannah and murder the magistrates. Paul Amatis, the silkman, came to Savannah in 1734, found the trustees' garden with trees and stumps where he should have seen carefully tended rows and weedless furrows, and he threatened to shoot Joseph Fitzwalter, the public gardener, if he ever tried to return. There were gossips, horse stealers, cattle rustlers, jail breakers, counterfeiters and murderers among the first people of Georgia. Alice Riley drowned weak old Mister Wise in a bucket of water. Mrs. Bland who came from Charleston in 1735 was considered to be quite mad. Joseph Watson, the Indian trader, would run around drunk and lie naked with the Indians. Some colonists lived openly with mistresses and had bastard children, like Thomas Christie and his housekeeper who shared only one bed "which they made use of together." Brides at Purrysburg in 1734 were suspected of being ready to bear children in less than the usual nine months, "whether by reason of the fruitfulness of the Air or of some Tryal of Skill beforehand." John Terry wrote Harman Verelst, the trustees' accountant, in 1741: "I long very much to get out of Savannah, for there are here Human Snakes, much more dangerous than the Rattle ones."

The vocal malcontents in the colony complained that Georgia's prospects had been misrepresented in England, that the land restrictions were a hardship for people without sons and that prosperity would never come to Georgia without slaves. When two representatives of the unhappy colonists, Peter Gordon in 1735 and Thomas Stephens in 1739, tried to present these complaints in person before

Oarsmen, women with waterbuckets on their heads, men offering handshakes and the first houses at New Ebenezer in the spring of 1736. *Drawings by Philip G. F. von Reck, Public Record Office (top), Royal Library of Denmark (bottom)*

the trustees in London they were dismissed unsympathetically. From their office in Old Palace Yard, Westminster, and warm suppers at the Castle Tavern, the trustees could not appreciate the real hardship of life in Georgia. The trustees felt unfairly maligned by ungrateful people. Peter Gordon wrote what he thought the trustees wanted to hear, when he warned that the idle colonists in Georgia might "return like a dog to his vomite, to gratify those vicious habits of idleness & drinking, which brought them to that unhappy state before." The trustees believed that the colonists were men who had been useless in England and who were again useless in America. The prohibitions against slaves and rum, proposed and drafted by Oglethorpe, reflected the trustees' belief that the colonists were weak and needed a healthy dose of discipline. When Oglethorpe, a stern disciplinarian, was asked what laws were intended for Georgia, he reportedly replied, "Such laws as the Trustees think proper, what business have poor people to do with laws?"

Oglethorpe returned to Georgia in September, 1738, with five transports of nearly seven hundred soldiers and a commission from the King as Captain General of the combined forces of South Carolina and Georgia. He discovered that there had been no money for months to pay the soldiers and sailors at Frederica. He faced a mutiny of soldiers at Fort Saint Andrews on Cumberland Island, during which the general was himself grazed by a bullet. Oglethorpe journeyed to Savannah and dismissed many of the public officers and, finding the colony nearly bankrupt, closed the public store. In October, Spain and England declared open war. In November, Oglethorpe reported sarcastically the gloomy situation of the colony: "I am here in one of the most delightful situations as any man could wish to be. A great number of debts, empty magazines, no money to supply them, numbers of

George Whitefield's Bethesda Orphan House, outside Savannah, 1740–42, was the largest and most famous building of early Georgia, seen in a promotional tract by the evangelist. *Library of Congress*

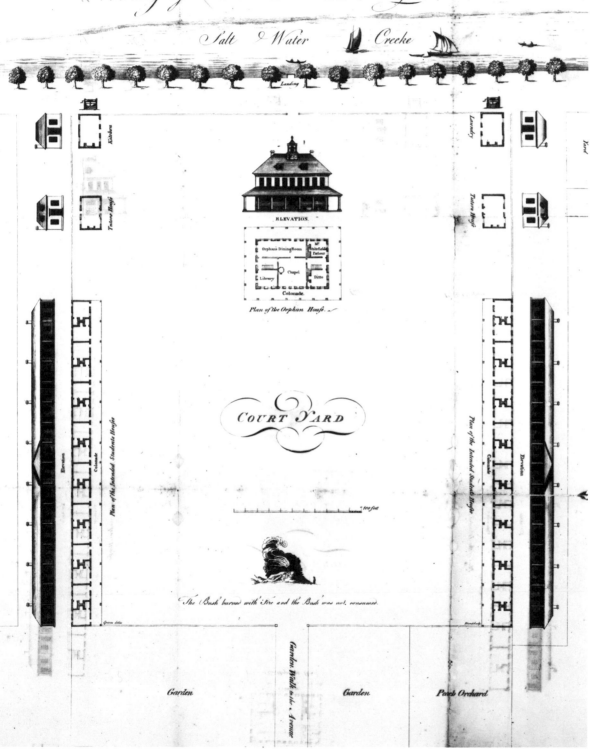

The Plan and Elevation of the Present and Intended Buildings of the

Georgia ORPHAN HOUSE & Academy

Salt Water Creeke

Landing

Kitchen

Laundry

Tutors House

Tutors House

ELEVATION.

Orphans Dining Room

Mr Whitefields Parlour

Library

Chapel

Ditto

Colonade.

Plan of the Orphan House.

Plan of the Intended Students House

Plan of the Intended Students House

Colonade

Colonade

Elevation

Elevation

COURT YARD

100 feet

The Bush burned with Fire and the Bush was not consumed.

Garden Walk to the Avenue

Garden.

Garden.

Peach Orchard.

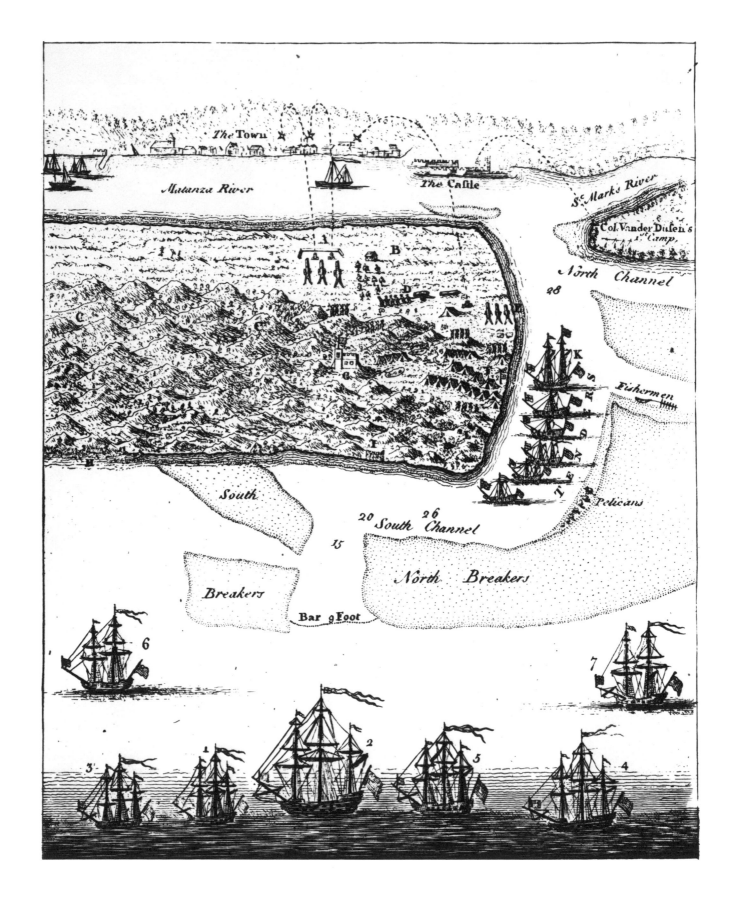

The Town

Matanza River

The Castle

St. Marks River

Col. Vander Dusen's Camp

North Channel

A

B

D

C

K

Fishermen

I

Pelicans

South

28

South Channel

15

20

26

Breakers

North Breakers

Bar 9 Foot

6

7

3

1

2

5

4

people to be fed, mutinous soldiers to command, a Spanish claim and a large body of troops not far from us."

In November, 1739, the Spaniards fell on Amelia Island and killed two Georgians. In retaliation Oglethorpe marched into Florida, ravaging the countryside. During the winter of 1740 Oglethorpe collected nine hundred British troops and eleven hundred Indians for an attack on Saint Augustine. Two Spanish forts, Diego and Moosa, capitulated, but the great fortress of Saint Augustine withstood the British assault. The Georgians did not receive the prompt support expected from Carolina, the attack was delayed long enough for Augustine to receive reenforcements and the hurricane season was approaching. So Oglethorpe abandoned the siege in July, 1740. In May, 1742, a Spanish armada, sailing from Havana to Augustine, launched an invasion of Georgia. In July at Bloody Marsh on Saint Simon's Island, the Georgians repulsed the Spaniards within only a mile of Frederica. In March, 1743, Oglethorpe made another unsuccessful advance on Augustine.

The general's aggressive behavior, establishing Frederica and southern forts beyond Georgia's chartered limits, had provoked the Spaniards to retaliate and imposed a great economic burden on the Georgia colonists. Men who were needed to support the colony were drawn off to fight in Florida. When strange, swarthy men appeared from the woods or privateers appeared on the horizon, men were called from their fields to face frequent false alarms. Facing impending invasion in February, 1737, the alarmed citizens of Savannah raised an uncontrollable clamor for a new and stronger fort to which they might flee in the last extremity and all productive work was stopped while it was being built. In 1737 the common at Savannah was still littered with logs and cluttered with weeds, evidence of neglect and unfinished work. By the summer of 1738 only one quarter of the plantations in the

In 1740 General Oglethorpe, in a reckless defense of Georgia's southern border, marched his army into Florida and attempted without success to capture the Spanish citadel of Saint Augustine. *A view by Thomas Silver in* London Magazine *of 1740, University of Georgia Library*

vicinity of Savannah had been cleared. In the summers of 1740 and 1742 the terrified women and children of Savannah evacuated their town, and the public records were shipped to more remote Ebenezer for safe-keeping.

The inhabitants of the colony were dispirited and heartbroken. Elisha Dobree wrote from Frederica in February, 1737: "When people are driven to poverty, distress or expectation of, they will drink to get up their courage. For we always have observed that the people in England will either be quite forlorn without hopes or mad with liquor. Our people are almost mad and I am obliged to drink with them." In August, 1740, Henry Garrett wrote: "I got into a very bad corner of the world, where poverty and oppression abound to such a degree that it's become pro-verbial this way to say 'as poor as a Georgian'." Unhappy Georgians realized that by crossing the Savannah River and entering Carolina they could get the land, slaves, peace and prosperity missing in Georgia. Between 1737 and 1741 the population of Georgia may have dropped from five thousand to only five hundred. In 1741 there were only 80 people left at Darien and 161 civilians at Frederica. In 1742 there were 287 people at Savannah. When Oglethorpe's regiment was disbanded in 1749, of more than 650 soldiers and their families, only 151 decided to remain in the colony. From their refuge in Charleston, the Georgia malcontents cried bitterly: "The inhabitants of Georgia are scattered over the face of the earth, her plantations a wild, her towns a desert, her villages in rubbish, her improvements a by-word, and her liberties a jest; an object of pity to friends and of insult, contempt and ridicule to enemies!"

Many people believed that Georgia was a miserable corner of the world not worth saving. There was talk in Parliament in 1741 of making Port Royal in Carolina the southernmost extent of Britain's "plantations" in America and retreating. Sir Robert Walpole considered re-

St. Paul's Church at Augusta, a center of Indian trade established in 1736, seen in the builder's drawing in 1749. *Society for the Promotion of the Gospel, London*

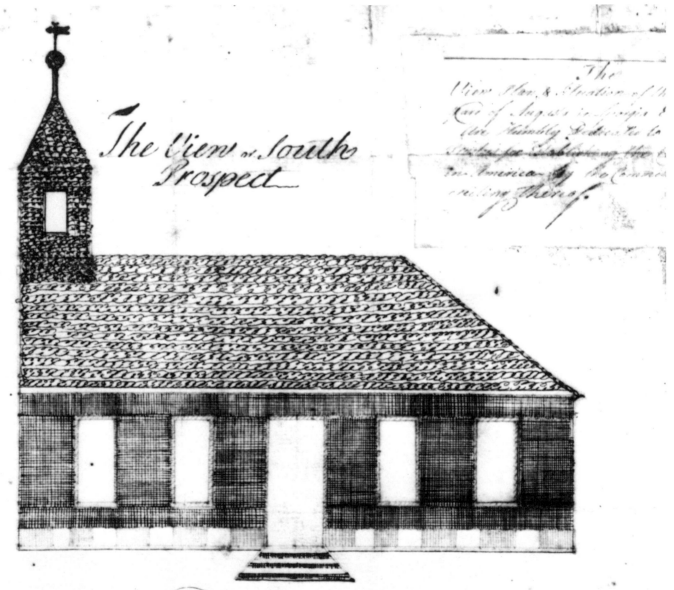

The View or South Prospect

The Frame of the Church is of Wood So Strong that it will last for many Years between
the Studs is a Wall of Clay Eight Inches thick, Supported in the Center of that Clay with
pieces of Wood three Inches thick, let into the Studs by a Groove. The Outside is rough-
cast with Lime & Gravil appearing like Stone, The inside Plaistered white wash'd and
Arch'd the roof Supported by two Columns as p. Plan which we propose to have
handsomely Ornamented. We do likewise, when we are able, intend to underprop
the Church with Brick as it appears by the Plan but at present it is only Supported
with loggs of lasting Oak, which is the only part that does not answer the View.

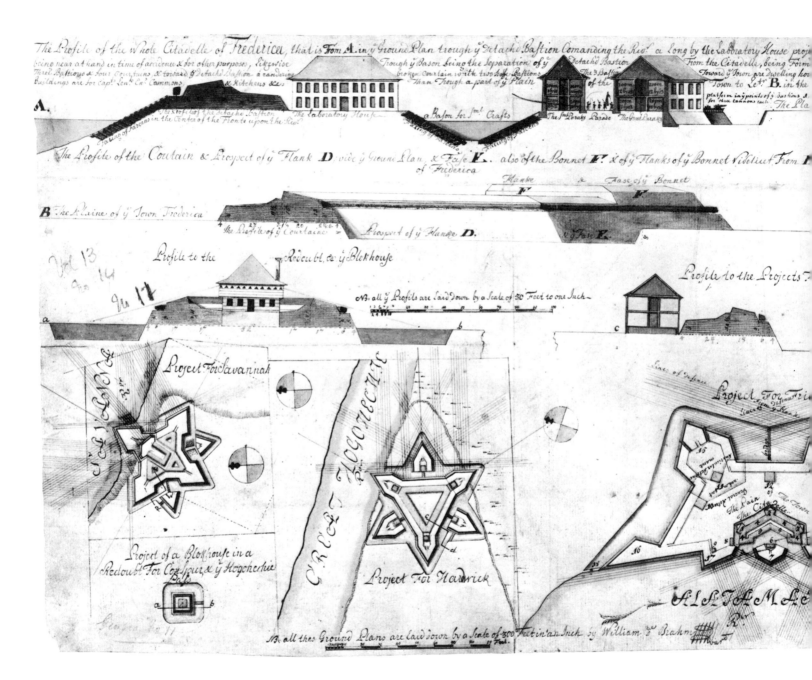

Under the able, stable administration of Georgia's Royal governors, plans for fortifications at Savannah and along the coast were prepared by the military engineer William De-Brahm, c. 1761. *Public Record Office, London*

turning Georgia to Spain as a peace offering. There was slack attendance at Georgia trustees' meetings: "It is a melancholy thing to see how zeal for a good thing abates when the novelty is over and when there is no pecuniary reward," Oglethorpe's friend Egmont wrote. In 1742 for the first time Parliament refused to vote money for Georgia, and Egmont resigned as a trustee in unsuccessful protest. In July, 1743, Oglethorpe sailed back to England, saying farewell to the colony he had founded. John Dobell wrote bitterly to the trustees in July, 1743: "There is such an odium cast upon Your Honours and the scheme you have formed for the colony that both you and it are detested by all!"

Georgia's second decade was an anticlimax after the colony's exhausting, exciting early years. There were further threats of Spanish invasions during 1744 and 1745, for the war with Spain did not end until 1748. Some people continued to expect Oglethorpe to return and rescue the colony, but he finally married in 1744 and settled down to a comfortable literary life. Meetings of the trustees were held very seldom after 1744–45. The land inheritance restrictions had never been strictly enforced, in 1742 the act prohibiting rum was repealed, and in 1750 the slave prohibition was also revoked. In 1750, the trustees allowed a provincial assembly to convene in the colony.

In 1751 Parliament again refused money to the Georgia trustees. In June, 1752, the trustees surrendered their charter to the King. They had sent to Georgia about twelve hundred British people and one thousand foreigners and spent £153,000 of public and private money. Two-thirds of the charity colonists had eventually left the colony. Perhaps six thousand people came to Georgia in the 1730's; probably all but one thousand had left by 1743. By 1752 there were still only two thousand whites and one thousand blacks in Georgia. Military preoccupations had made the early colony an unhappy and unsuccessful endeavor. The province, a mere pimple at the southern extremity of the British empire in America, was not a very significant project compared with the great wars taking place in Europe. Georgia could not be, in the words of the trustees' promotional slogans, both a Garden of Eden and the Gibraltar of America. Great expectations had led to great disappointments in Oglethorpe's Georgia.

John Reynolds, the first of three governors appointed by the King to govern Georgia before the Revolution, reached the colony in December, 1754, and found the province miserably poor. Savannah, he wrote, was a mere village of 150 houses, "all wooden ones, very small, & mostly very old," and the Savannah River was blocked with sunken wrecks and old trees. Frederica was "entirely in Ruins, the Fortifications entirely Decayed and the Houses falling down." At Augusta only a ruined wooden fort remained, "so rotten that great part of it is propt up, to prevent its falling." When the governor and his council tried to meet for the first time to transact business, the government building collapsed at one end, forcing them to retreat to a shed behind the courthouse. Governor Reynolds estimated the colony's diminished population to be 4,500 whites and 1,855 blacks in 1755. In July, 1757, the colonial assembly summarized the distressed condition of Georgia: "To find ourselves in a Country surrounded with most cruel & insolent Savages; absolutely destitute of every means of defending ourselves from their barbarities in case of a Rupture; without any Forts that are not utterly in ruins or funds to erect them; Without any Troops stationed here save twenty odd Rangers yet unestablished, unpaid & undisciplined; without any Vessels of War for the protection of our Coast; with but few Inhabitants & those poor & widely dispersed over the Province; open on one Side to every possible insult from the most inconsiderable of the Enemy's Vessels: In such a situation our all is precarious!" Life in the colony continued unhappy under Reynolds,

The entrance to the Savannah River was marked by a wooden lighthouse and protected by a small fort on Cockspur Island, seen in anonymous drawings dated December, 1764. *University of Georgia Library*

The Royal governors who administered the colony after
1752 spent most of their time negotiating with the Creek
Indians, whose settlements are seen in William Bonar's
1757 "Draught of the Creek Nation." *Public Record
Office*

an arrogant man who played favorites in the provincial government and who was removed from office in 1756.

Georgia made considerable and rapid progress under the squire-ship of Henry Ellis, governor between 1757 and 1760, and James Wright, governor after 1760. After its idiosyncratic beginnings as a charitable trust, Georgia was now cradled in the lap of the British imperial system. Georgia was governed by a royal governor and council appointed in England and by a Commons House of Assembly elected by the colonists. After 1750, slaves had been allowed in the colony, and Georgia's first slave codes were passed in 1755 and 1765. In 1758 the Anglican church became the established religion of the colony, and Georgia was divided into eight parishes, administrative units christened with religious names—Saint Paul (Augusta), Saint George (Waynesboro), Saint Matthew (Ebenezer), Christ Church (Savannah), Saint Philip (Hardwick), Saint John (Midway), Saint Andrew (Darien), Saint James (Frederica). In 1763 James Johnston, Georgia's first printer, established the *Georgia Gazette*, the first newspaper published in the colony. In 1763 the Treaty of Paris, ending the Seven Years' War, compelled Spain to cede Florida to Britain, removing the greatest threat to the tranquility and prosperity of Georgia.

Significantly, the Georgia governors spent most of their time approving land grants and greeting Indians, whom James Wright called "most Troublesome, disagreeable & Expensive Guests." Always there was the threat that Cherokees and "frenchified" Creeks would become allies of the French colonials in Mississippi and Alabama against the English in Georgia and Florida. The decade of the 1760's became a period of border barbarities between eager settlers and embattled Indians. For every enemy scalp they would bring in, Governor Ellis in 1760 promised the Indians a trading gun, three pounds of powder, six pounds of shot, a blanket, a pair of boots and a four-gallon keg of rum. Indian presents ordered from England included nests of tin kettles, tin pots, looking glasses, checked shirts, striped shirts, ruffled shirts, cloth, knives, hats, coats, razors, scissors, ivory combs, hatchets, brass wire, trading guns and fowling pieces, best and common flints, saddles and bridles, paint, gunpowder and bullets, bags of tobacco. A great conference of Creek, Cherokee, Choctaw, Chickasaw, Catawba Indians and provincial governors from Georgia, the Carolinas and Virginia was held at Augusta in 1763 and succeeded in opening up to settlement nearly two and one-half million acres of Indian land, lying between the Oconee and the Savannah rivers in the northwest and between the Altamaha and Saint Mary's rivers in the south, tripling the size of the colony. In 1773 Governor Wright offered to assume debts owed by the Indians to white traders, in return for a "New Purchase" which added two million more acres in the northwest. Altogether Wright succeeded in adding some six million acres of land to the one million inherited from the trustees in 1754.

Early in the 1760's the first tide of transcontinental migration reached Georgia. The end of the Spanish war opened the southern coast near Florida for settlement, and the establishment of slavery encouraged ambitious, substantial people to come to Georgia for the first time. Along the coast, a group of Puritans from Connecticut and Massachusetts, who had lived for more than a generation in South Carolina in the early eighteenth century, settled in 1752 at Midway, a place "midway" between the Savannah and Altamaha rivers. In 1761 they established Georgia's second port, Sunbury, a city of great promise in the eighteenth century. The lands at the southern border of Georgia were becoming so attractive that the government of South Carolina tried to claim the territory south of the Altamaha River, arguing that King George II had granted to Georgia's original trustees only lands stretching to that place and no further south. Both Governors

The Three Cherokees, came over from the head of the River Savanna to London 1762.
1. Their Interpreter that was Poisoned.

The Royal governors negotiated Indian treaties that
opened to settlement one-eighth of present-day Georgia.
These Cherokee chiefs were brought to London in 1762.
University of Georgia Library

The emerging merchants and planters of Georgia prospered under the Royal governors and were, like the Tannatt family of Savannah seen here in 1770, deeply divided by pre-Revolutionary agitation. *Painting by Henry Benbridge, The National Gallery of Canada, Gift of Jasper H. Nicholls*

Ellis and Wright considered shifting the capital of Georgia from Savannah to a new city farther south, Hardwick. Some 160 Germans under William DeBrahm settled at Bethany, west of Savannah, in 1751; in 1768 Irish Protestants settled at Queensbury on the Ogeechee; in 1768 Quakers from North Carolina settled at Wrightsboro, north of Augusta. In 1761 Governor Wright complained that the colony was already being overrun with "a Parcel of Runagates from Virginia & North Carolina, a kind of Vagrants who live like the Indians by Hunting & Stealing other Men's Cattle & Horses." By 1761, 394,944 acres of land in Georgia had been granted to new settlers. From three thousand whites and two thousand blacks in 1754, Georgia's population swelled to fifty thousand people, half free and half slave, by the end of the Revolution.

The able, stable administration of the royal governors, the pacification of the Indians and the opening of their lands to white settlement, the expansion of plantations and slavery along the coast and up the Savannah River, the end of the Spanish war and the flood of immigration into the southern frontier were all leading Georgia to prosperity for the first time. Rice, wheat and indigo were the main crops, and there was a busy trade in provisions, lumber and naval stores. In 1754 the colony exported 1,899 tons of goods worth £15,744 on 9 square-rigged vessels and 43 sloops and schooners; in 1770, the colony exported 10,514 tons of goods, worth £99,383 on 83 square-rigged vessels and 113 sloops and schooners. In 1755, 2,200 barrels of rice had been shipped from Savannah; in 1768, 17,783 barrels were exported. In 1762 Georgia exported 417,783 feet of timber, 325,477 staves and 683,265 shingles; in 1772 the colony exported 2,163,582 feet of timber, 988,791 staves and 3,525,930 shingles, an increase of five hundred percent in ten years. With good justification then, Governor Wright reported with sanguine confidence in December, 1768, that Georgia was at last making "a very rapid progress toward being an Opulent & Considerable Province."

Still Georgia was a young and weak colony, whose areas of settlement extended, at the deepest point, only some thirty to fifty miles inland from the Atlantic coast and along the banks of the Savannah River. Of the one and one-half million people who lived in the American colonies in 1760, fewer than ten thousand lived in Georgia and thirty-six hundred of those were slaves. Inevitably, this little colony was more dependent on England than the older and richer northern settlements. The provincial government and the colonists shared a common interest in making Georgia a prosperous and contented place. James Wright, who owned nineteen thousand acres of Georgia land, twelve plantations, five hundred slaves, was the natural leader of the new class of rice planters and shipping merchants.

All the good works of the governors had, however, contributed to the wealth, self-confidence and ambitions of Georgia's merchants and planters. The provincial assembly, composed of some twenty-five prominent planters, traders and professionals, began to assert its prerogatives during the 1760's. In 1767 the assembly refused to provide barracks and other necessities for the British soldiers stationed in Georgia. In 1768 the assembly disobeyed instructions from the governor, endorsed a circular letter from northern colonies protesting against the Townshend Acts, which imposed import duties on the American trade, and Governor Wright dissolved it. During 1771–72 the assembly three times elected Noble Wimberly Jones, a famous radical, as its speaker against instructions from the governor, who again dissolved it. In 1774 the assembly claimed the exclusive right to nominate Georgia's colonial agent to England. But these were political contests, unclouded by complicating moral issues, for Governor Wright was always a popular man and he did not have the resources

George Washington, when he visited Savannah in 1791, stayed at Stephen Miller's house, built c. 1785–90, seen in a 19th-century view. *Georgia Historical Society*

Less than a handful of pre-Revolutionary buildings has
survived in Georgia, and most of these have been altered.
Charles Oddingsells Cottage, Savannah, 1798–99.
Frances Benjamin Johnston, Library of Congress

with which to threaten the Georgians. During the 1760's and early 1770's, conservatives tended to be officials and clergymen from England, older and wealthy Savannahians, Indian traders, recent immigrants, the Germans at Ebenezer, all those who were most dependent on Britain; and radicals were younger Savannahians, frontiersmen and residents of two southern coastal parishes. Noble Jones and James Habersham were conservatives, while their sons Noble W. Jones, James Habersham, Jr., and John Habersham were radicals. In Georgia, where there were no moral controversies, it is easy to understand how the Revolution was a political struggle among the Americans.

At best reluctant rebels, Georgians were led toward revolt by pressures and propaganda from outside the colony. In 1765 the Stamp Act was passed by Parliament to provide income for imperial defense by requiring that legal documents and publications be written or printed on special paper sold by public officials. Georgia was so far away from the center of action that the stamped paper did not reach Savannah until a month after the tax was to go into effect. But Georgians' objections were so weak that the stamps were used to clear vessels for about two months, one of the rare instances of the use of the stamps in America. South Carolina voted to stop all trade with Georgia in retaliation. Georgia sent no delegates to the Stamp Act Congress, held in October, 1765. In December, 1773, Bostonians dumped a shipload of tea into their harbor rather than allow it to be landed and taxed. In the spring of 1774 the port of Boston was closed, protest meetings were held in Savannah during July and August, 1774, against these "intolerable acts" by Parliament. In 1774 the northern colonies resolved to boycott British manufactures and organize a nonimportation association, which Georgia was reluctant to join. Again South Carolina voted to cut off trade with Georgia and Rhode Island, the only two colonies still trading with England. Two Georgia parishes on the southern coast—Saint James and Saint Andrew—adopted that Continental Association independently at the end of 1774, and Saint James tried to secede from Georgia and join South Carolina. Georgia sent no delegates to the First Continental Congress, held at Philadelphia in September, 1774. A Georgia provincial congress in 1774 was attended by representatives from only four of Georgia's eight parishes, reflecting widespread public apathy; and the three delegates elected by that assembly to attend the Second Continental Congress declined to serve, saying they could not speak for a majority of the province.

During the year 1775, however, revolutionary sentiments spread through Georgia, as rumors and reports filtered south from other colonies, and mobs began to flout public law and demonstrate the weakness of royal officials at Savannah. In February, a crowd of some twenty people outside Savannah, costumed as sailors and with their faces blackened, tarred and feathered a guard who was protecting some goods seized by the government for nonpayment of duty. In May news reached Georgia that a sanguinary battle had taken place at Lexington, Massachusetts, between rebels and redcoats, and the public magazine at Savannah was robbed of six hundred pounds of gunpowder. In June the first liberty pole was set up at Savannah. In July a second provincial congress met at Savannah, this time attended by 102 delegates representing all but two of Georgia's eight parishes. Joachim Zubly, a Presbyterian minister from Savannah and member of the Continental Congress from Georgia, expressed his colony's sentiments of 1775: "I shall briefly state the immediate causes that have given rise to this Provincial and a general American Congress: To enforce some Acts for laying on a duty to raise a perpetual revenue in America, which the Americans think unjust and unconstitutional, which all America complains of, and some provinces have in some measure opposed. A fleet and army has been sent to New England, and after a long series of hardships by that province patiently endured, it is

George Spencer House, Savannah, c. 1791. *Frances Benjamin Johnston, Library of Congress*

New Englanders began to immigrate to the Georgia coast
in the late 18th century, among them settlers from Connecticut and Massachusetts who built a Congregational
Church at Midway about 1792. *Carolyn Carter*

now out of all question that hostilities have been commenced against them; blood has been shed, and many lives have been taken away; thousands, never as much as suspected of having any hand in the action which is made the pretence of all the severity now used against that province have been and still are reduced to the greatest distress. How far and wide the flame so wantonly kindled may be permitted to spread, none can tell. . . . The Americans have been called 'a rope of sand,' but blood and sand will make a firm cementation, and enough American blood has been already shed to cement them together into a thirteen fold cord, not easily to be broken. . . . My Lord, the violence of the present measures has almost instantaneously created a continental union, a continental currency, a continental army. . . . The most zealous Americans could not have effected in an age what the cruelty and violence of administration has effectively brought to pass in a day.''

Four provincial congresses were elected between July, 1775, and June, 1777. These became Georgia's first revolutionary government, electing Archibald Bulloch the first president and delegating to a Council of Safety the power to act when the provincial congress was not in session. The Council of Safety collected and purchased provisions and war materials, bribed and negotiated with the Indians, improvised taxes and elections, raised and spent money, censored the newspapers and did all the everyday business of a functioning revolutionary government until May, 1777, when the state's first constitution went into effect. In June and September, 1775, regular shipments of gunpowder to the Indian traders were captured at the mouth of the Savannah River and some of it, according to tradition, was dispatched to aid the Continental Congress and was used at the battle of Bunker Hill. In July the revolutionaries in Savannah removed stores, cannon and powder from the royal magazine, while the governor and his loyal councillors watched powerless to stop them. During the summer, the rebels took control of the provincial militia by electing their own officers sworn to revolutionary loyalty, and Wright was helpless to punish or resist the street mobs. In August, a crowd forced open the royal jail and freed a man who had been imprisoned for recruiting troops for a Carolina regiment. In September, Governor Wright lamented: "It is really a Wretched State to be left in . . . the government totally annihilated and assumed by Congresses, Councils and Committees, and the greatest Acts of Tyranny, oppression, gross Insults Committed and not the least means of Protection, Support or even Physical Safety." In December armed men occupied the Savannah courthouse and royal law enforcement was abandoned.

In January, 1776, the governor wailed that with "No Troops, no Money, no Orders, or Instructions and a Wild Multitude gathering fast, what can any Man do in Such a Situation?" Almost immediately Wright was arrested, but, breaking his parole, he escaped to the H.M.S. *Scarborough*, a man-of-war anchored in the Savannah River, during February and returned to England. In July, the Continental Congress at Philadelphia adopted the Declaration of Independence, signed by Georgia's three delegates, Button Gwinnett, George Walton and Lyman Hall. In May, 1777, a new constitution went into effect, replacing the old colonial parishes with counties named for English politicians who had supported the American cause—Wilkes, Burke, Effingham, Glynn, Chatham, Camden, plus one named for the ideal cause of Liberty. In late 1777 Loyalists were expelled from the state. The military situation remained quiet in Georgia during 1777 and 1778, except for intermittent invasions by English Loyalists who had taken refuge in Florida and for three unsuccessful American expeditions against East Florida and Saint Augustine. Meanwhile, the British were busy concentrating their forces in New York, New Jersey and Pennsylvania.

But in 1778 Sir Henry Clinton, British commander in America, decided to mass an expedition of some twenty-five hundred to thirty-

de Savannah, du Camp, des Tranchées et de L'attaque Octobre 1779.

In October, 1779, French and American forces attacked Savannah, which had been held by the British since December, 1778. The attack failed, and Savannah and much of the Georgia coast remained in British hands until 1782. *Drawing by Pierre Ozanne, Library of Congress*

five hundred troops under Archibald Campbell to recapture Georgia. This force reached the southern coast in December, 1778, and recaptured Savannah easily when a slave showed the British a secret passage behind the American lines. Then General Augustine Prevost, commander at Saint Augustine, brought forces from Florida, recaptured Sunbury and occupied Savannah, while Campbell's army captured Augusta. In March, 1779, the British government was restored in territory occupied by the King's forces, and Governor Wright returned to Savannah during the summer and continued to administer his part of Georgia until July, 1782.

The British controlled Savannah and the area about forty miles around it, and the rebels controlled the interior and lower coast. The American Congress was too poor to fortify Georgia after 1778 and the British were preoccupied with military problems in Florida and the Carolinas. In the backwoods of Georgia, the Revolution settled into a guerrilla war. William Lee, who moved to Georgia in 1780, found that there was no safety in the countryside, for both loyalists and rebels were plundering and killing all who joined the opposite party. In February, 1779, a rebel militia under Andrew Pickens, John Dooly and Elijah Clarke defeated redcoats at Kettle Creek. In March, Lieutenant Colonel Mark Prevost, brother of Augustine Prevost, massacred rebel troops at Briar Creek. In October, 1779, a French fleet of twenty-two vessels and four thousand soldiers, commanded by Charles Henri Comte d'Estaing, attempted to recapture Savannah from the British. After a four-day bombardment and a furious direct assault, in which Sergeant William Jasper and Count Casimir Pulaski were mortally wounded, the Allies were compelled to abandon the siege and retire in humiliation. During 1780–81 the important fighting in the South was between Cornwallis and Greene in the Carolinas, and two governments, rebel and royal, continued to govern Georgia until the Peace of Paris in 1783.

James Oglethorpe, aged 102, sketched from life at the sale of Dr. Johnson's books in 1785 by P. Ireland. *Private Collection*

2. Indians and Settlers

AFTER the Revolution Georgia was one stage for the American epic of exploration across a virgin land, the mass migration of eager settlers into Indian territory and the creation of a new society deep in the wilderness. King George II had granted the colonial trustees an immense domain which extended from the Atlantic Ocean indefinitely to the South Seas, and until 1802 the new state of Georgia continued to claim lands stretching to the Mississippi. Even after the state surrendered its western claims to the United States, Georgia remained the largest state east of the Mississippi, some sixty thousand square miles, about the same size as England and Wales. During the debates at Philadelphia in 1787 to revise the Articles of Confederation, Georgia's delegates voted for a strong central government, because they wanted national help to fight the Indians, and voted with larger states for the concept of unequal representation in the new national union, because they expected Georgia to become a rich and populous state someday.

But before 1800 the only part of Georgia which had been populated was a narrow strip of settlement along the Atlantic coast and up the Savannah River to Augusta, perhaps no more than fifty miles deep at most. Georgia was still a vast, virgin land, possessed by deers, panthers, wolves, bears, polecats, wildcats, buffaloes, elks, turkeys, eagles and Indians. William Bartram, who came to Georgia in 1773, described sylvan scenes of enchanting innocence: "A vast expanse of

74

After wandering through the Southern colonies during the Revolution, William Lee, seen here in his Indian dress in 1780, settled in Georgia. *From Lee's* True and Interesting Travels *(York, 1782)*, *University of Georgia Library*

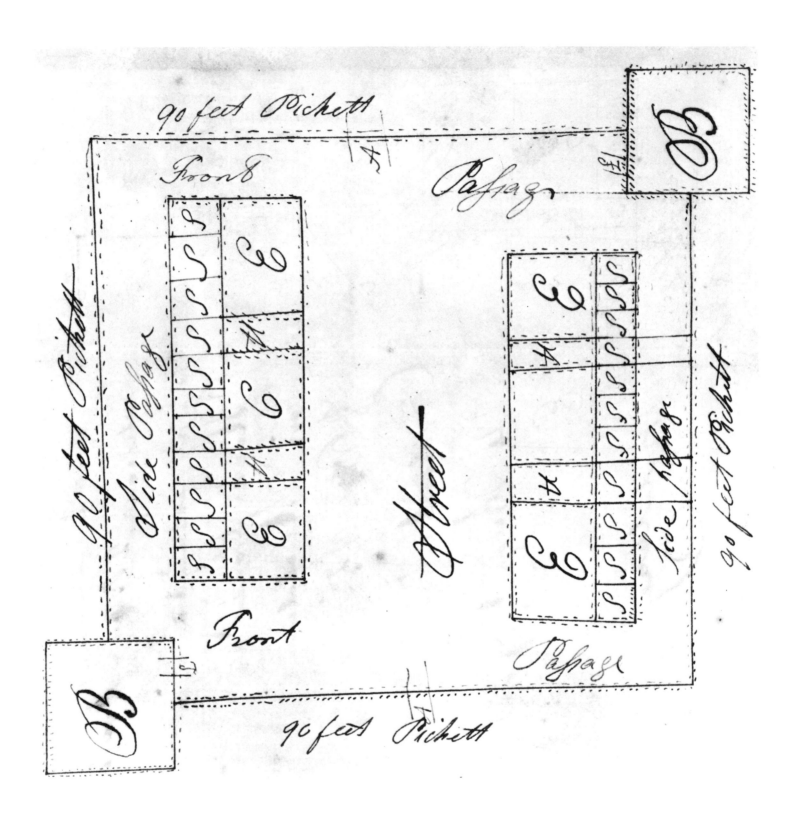

The plan of a frontier stockade presented by the builders
Isham Williams and Thomas Kemmerley in 1797. *Georgia Historical Society*

green meadows and strawberry fields; a meandering river sliding through, saluting in its various turnings the swelling, green turfy knolls, embellished with parterres of flowers; flocks of turkeys strolling about them, herds of deer prancing in the meadows or bounding over the hills; companies of young, innocent Cherokee virgins, some busy gathering the rich fragrant fruit, others having already filled their baskets, lay reclined under the shade, disclosing their beauties to the fluttering breeze, and bathing their limbs in the cool fleeting streams." Bartram recognized, with the rare historical insight of a man who loved universal nature more than the British empire of which his native Philadelphia was then a part, that this formerly secure and tranquil scene was now threatened by a torrent of invading settlers.

At the very time Bartram was in Georgia, during the 1770's, a wave of immigrants, settlers from North Carolina and Virginia, began to move into the state, forced south because tobacco farming had exhausted the soil of their old homesteads. The Indians called all the strangers on their lands "Virginians," signifying that these were new men from outside the state, not merely old Georgia colonists moving into the interior from the coast. All three signers of the Declaration of Independence from Georgia were born outside of the state: George Walton, born in Virginia, came to Georgia in 1769; Button Gwinnett, born in England, came to Georgia in 1765; Lyman Hall, born in Connecticut, came to Georgia in 1756. An army of Virginians came to fight in Georgia during the Revolution and remained there. Georgia granted land after the Revolution to nine thousand veterans, of whom only two thousand were native Georgians. Abraham Baldwin, the founder of the University of Georgia, was a Connecticut man and a graduate of Yale College, after which the new Georgia university was modelled. A North Carolinian who came to the new state in 1782 wrote home: "Georgia must in a few years be one of the Richest States in the Union,

Two Revolutionary veterans from Virginia who claimed lands in Georgia in the 1780's, Oliver Porter and his brother, seen in a silhouette by Francis Chapman. *Georgia Department of Archives and History*

and Where I've no doubt you may live happy and secure a lasting and Valuable Estate for your self & family." Even before John Pope reached Augusta in 1791, he had already heard that a great proportion of the people who lived there were "insolvent Refugees from the northern states." James Jackson wrote John Milledge in 1797: "Some thousands of people are now moving into this State. They will rush like a torrent in search of subsistence." Between 1790 and 1800 the population of Georgia nearly doubled, from 82,548 to 162,686, and by 1820 the state counted 340,989 people.

The old, established society of coastal Georgia, settled generations earlier by direct colonization from England and closely tied to her still by commercial and personal relations, viewed the new up-country settlers with much disdain and some fear. James Habersham of Savannah wrote in August, 1772, of these new immigrants along the northern frontier of Georgia: "I have lately received Advice from Mr. Barnard of Augusta, that several idle People from the Northward, some of whom, he is told, are great Villains, Horse Stealers, etc. have settled and built Hutts on the Lands proposed to be ceded by the Indians to His Majesty, and that more might be expected to join them, and if not drove off and they should be suffered to encrease, it might here after be attended with Difficulty to do it. The present Intruders, I am informed, are Persons who have no settled Habitations, and live by hunting and plundering the industrious Settlers, and are by no Means the sort of People that should settle these lands . . . idle and disorderly Vagrants." During the Revolution, the low-country plantations had been devastated and the government run by British soldiers, while the up-country people had run their own insurgent government. In 1783 Anthony Stokes, former chief justice of the colony, reporting on the condition of the British plantations at the time of the Revolution, wrote: "The Southern colonies are overrun with a swarm of men from

Scenes of hunting and dancing in frontier Georgia, a child's sketchbook, 1793. *Georgia Department of Archives and History*

April the 11 day Anno Domini 1793

The Hunter and the Buck &c

Two women and the Bear, April 12th day 1793

the western parts of Virginia and North Carolina, distinguished by the name of Crackers. They are the most abandoned set of men on earth, few of them having the least sense of religion. When these men are routed in the other provinces, they fly to Georgia, where the winters are mild, and the man who has a rifle, ammunition, and a blanket, can subsist in that vagrant way which the Indians pursue; and as the Indians dwindle away before them, they certainly threaten ruin to the civilized parts of the rice colonies." The earliest political contests in Georgia came between the party of James Jackson, William Crawford and George Troup, expressing the view of property owners from the coast and settlers from Virginia, and the party of John Clarke and later Wilson Lumpkin, representing the poorer settlers from North Carolina.

It was, recalled James Lamar, whose family moved from Augusta to then remote Columbus during Georgia's frontier settlement, "a time when to move was in the blood of everyone." Augusta Harris Hansell, born at Thomasville in 1817, remembered that her relatives suffered from the same nomadic itch and were "always ready to sell out and move on the frontier, being fond of the rather wild and often dangerous life of those living close to the warlike tribes of Creek indians." Gideon Lincecum's father spent thirty years wandering back and forth between South Carolina and Georgia, finally settling in Texas: "My father loved a border life, and the place he had purchased on the Ocmulgee, as the people had already commenced settling on the opposite side of the river, was no longer looked upon as a border country. He sold his place and was soon equipped and geared up for the road, and so was I. I had been reared to a belief and faith in the pleasure of frequent changes of country, and I looked upon the long journey, through the wilderness, with much pleasure." Charles Lyell in 1845 recorded how a middle Georgia farmer complained of "a want of

A camp by moonlight near Fayetteville, 1819–21.
Aquatint by Shaw and Hill, New York Public Library

elbow room," although his nearest neighbor was six or seven miles distant. John R. Vinton, sent on a mission to Georgia by President Adams and the Secretary of War in 1827, found himself "amidst a rude homely people, full of pride & high-toned republicanism."

The Georgia frontier beyond the area of established plantations was being overrun by caravans of land-hungry men, most of them before the 1830's small farmers from the northern states. Gideon Lincecum recalled such a journey, another relocation across the western frontier of Georgia into Alabama in 1818: "The journey, the way we travelled, was about five hundred miles, all wilderness; full of deer and turkeys, and the streams were full of fish. We were six weeks on the road; and altogether it was, as I thought and felt, the most delightful time I had ever spent in my life. My brother Garland and I 'flanked it' as the wagons rolled along and killed deer, turkeys, wild pigeons; and at nights, with pine torches, we fished and killed a great many with my bow and arrows." The Augusta *Chronicle* described a similar migration in 1819: "Passed through this place from Greenville District, bound for Chattahoochee, a man and his wife, his son and his wife, with a cart but no horse. The man had a belt over his shoulders and he drew in the shafts—the son worked by the traces tied to the end of the shafts and assisted his father to draw the cart, the son's wife rode in the cart, and the old woman was walking, carrying a rifle and driving a cow."

Georgia was a tough territory, swarming with drunken, brawling men, who were scrambling and struggling for land. Florida was the refuge of freebooters, outlaws, adventurers, runaway slaves, for it remained Spanish territory until 1819. Alabama was a place where the marauding Indians came from and where the latest line of settlers disappeared to. The South Carolinians always looked on Georgians as crude "westerners." La Rochefoucauld, an exiled peer of France who

A frontiersman, "Mr. Ricks, a native of the interior of the State of Georgia," sketched in his hunting dress by Basil Hall, 1828. *Lilly Library, Indiana University*

Mr Ricks in his hunting dress —
24th March 1838
A notice of the interior
of the State of Georgia

Mr Webb
Emanuel Co
Georgia
24th March

/138/

came to Georgia in 1796, called Georgia the worst-regulated part of the Union and her inhabitants the most idle, drunken and disorderly anywhere in the new United States. In 1787 the young wife of a frontier tavern keeper at Washington, Georgia, wrote to her father in distant Massachusetts: "All of the State of Georgia would be no inducement to me to bring my dear little Lambs in this flock of Wolves, as I may properly call many of the inhabitants of this State. The people in general are the most profane, blasphemous set of people I ever heard of. Sometimes ... they look like a flock of blackbirds, and perhaps not one in fifty but what we call fighting drunk. It is impossible for you to conceive what language is used." At Washington, when parties were held at the log courthouse, this is how they would call out the dances: "Gentlemen, lead out your partners. Them that's got on shoes and stockings will dance the cotillion; them that's got on shoes and no stockings will dance the Virginy reel; them that's got on nairy shoes nor stockings will dance the scamper-down." George Gilmer, an early settler, remembered how his family breakfast depended on someone's catching a 'possum overnight or shooting a rabbit early in the morning. Peter Remsen, a New York trader passing through Milledgeville in 1818, viewed the state legislators at the capital city of Georgia: "Their conduct was beneath that of any crew of sailors that was ever seen. Cursing, quarrelling, hollowing, drinking, getting drunk. Disputing landlords' bills. Drunken men hugging sober ones. Illiterate, mean appearances, readiness for rasseling, etc." Columbus, at the extreme western frontier of Georgia, was especially notorious for its drunken Indians and young prostitutes. It was a world of hunting, drinking, gambling, fighting which A. B. Longstreet captured in his classic *Georgia Scenes*, a volume of stories first published at Augusta in 1835. It was an era which gave Georgia some wonderful place names which evoke the wild frontier—Guinea Nest, Rabbit Trap, Snake Rag, Sugar Tit, Wolf Skin, The Lick, Devil's Half Acre, Red Bone, Hello!

Another frontiersman, Mr. Webb of Emanuel County, sketched by Basil Hall, 1828. *Lilly Library, Indiana University*

Fierce fighting was a conspicuous element of frontier life, invariably noted by Georgia travellers and a reflection of the state's primitive society. The state legislature in 1787 complained against Georgians who would "willfully or maliciously cut out or disable the tongue, put out an eye, slit the nose, bite or cut off the ear, nose or lip, or cut off or disable any limb or member of any person." Charles Wilson Janson came to Georgia about 1807 and observed a gouging match: "We found the combatants fast clenched by the hair, and their thumbs endeavoring to force a passage into each other's eyes, which several of the bystanders were betting upon the first eye to be turned out of its socket. At length they fell to the ground, and in an instant the uppermost sprung up with his antagonist's eye in his hand!!! The savage crowd applauded, while, sick with horror, we galloped away from the infernal scene." Anthony Stokes, Georgia's colonial chief justice, marvelled how a small weakling could disable a lusty, muscular fellow by grabbing his opponent's head, putting a thumb into his eye, strangling his throat and biting his left cheek, all in one swift, dexterous operation. William Butterworth, a young sailor at the Georgia coast before 1830, expecting frontier settlers to fight a classic English boxing match, was horrified at the appearance of the victim of a typical brawl: "A shocking spectacle, part of the skin of his forehead, with his eyebrow, hanging upon his face, and the blood streaming down his cheeks. His antagonist informed me it was bit, assuring me that a quantity of hairs were then sticking in his teeth." Isaac Weld, who came to Georgia in 1798, reported: "Whenever these people come to blows, they fight just like wild beasts, biting, kicking and endeavoring to tear each other's eyes out with their nails. To perform the horrid operation, the combatant twists his fore-fingers in the side locks of his adversary's hair, and then applies his thumb to the bottom of the eye, to force it out of the socket." In some parts of the state, he said, every third or fourth

Sketches by Basil Hall of Joseph Collins, his son George Washington Collins and others of Tatnall County and the "Embryo Town" of Columbus in 1828. *Lilly Library, Indiana University*

Tykes ?

Jabine ?

Mr Joseph Collins & his son George Washington Collins
Tatnall County — Gergia. C.L.
22nd March
1828.

Vol IX
p 147

Embryo Town of Columbus on the banks of the
Chatahouchie in Gergia 31st March 1828
C.L.

Country
The Houses in Georgia consist generally of two parts
or wings with an open space between them, covered by one
common roof. There is consequently no outer door
as those for the rooms open from this enclosed space, or
passage. Sometimes there are there are two rooms
at each end, but generally only one.

Unfinished Sketch of a
House near Mercer
in Georgia
28th March
1828
C.L.

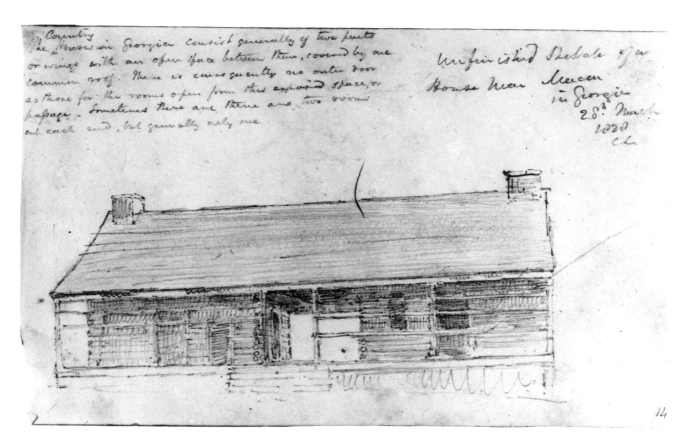

14

Log House on ....
River 29th March 1828
C.L.

144

man appeared with just one eye. Louis Milfort, a supercilious French traveller to the back country about 1780, said that Georgia was the home of a unique race of men, "Anglo-Americans of a peculiar sort, called Gougeurs, who are nearly all one-eyed." At Jacksonborough it was said that in the mornings after drunken frolics and fights you could see the children picking up *eyeballs* in *tea saucers*! In the gold-mining district of north Georgia, when Cynthia Hyde, an American of the Georgia wilds, was brought to trial for assaulting Polly Hefling, the lady declared with passion that she was "as supple as a lumber-jack, strong as a jack-screw, and savage as a wildcat."

When he left the immediate vicinity of Savannah in 1828, Basil Hall was quickly lost: "If required to give the localities with any precision in such a route, it would have been necessary to carry sextants and chronometers in the carriage. For we were fast sinking into the wild and little known parts of the continent, on which the traces of man were as yet but feebly impressed." When Charles Lyell landed on the Georgia coast in the 1840's to hunt fossils, it seemed to him "as if we had been dropped down from a balloon, with our baggage, in the midst of a wilderness." The itinerant minister Francis Asbury wandered among remote Savannah River rice plantations in 1793 and prayed for deliverance: "Oh, how dreadful to be here in the dark!" Places to eat and rest were hard to find and then were generally unsatisfactory. Along the isolated frontier, where there were few public taverns, it was customary for travellers to take room and board in private homes. In 1783 Joshua Clifford instructed his daughter in the fine arts of innkeeping, Georgia-style: "Let your bedsteads be cleansed every March, and you will be seldom troubled by multipedes. Let your water bucket stand so high that your children shall not dabble in it. Keep a spit box in each room: this will teach vulgar people that the floors were not made to spit on. Don't allow your children to examine

Sketches by Basil Hall of a dog-trot house near Macon and a log house near the Flint River, 1828. *Lilly Library, Indiana University*

the baggage of your guests; nor to belch upwind at the table." There were few single beds or private rooms. George Featherstonhaugh wrote with philosophical calm from the Georgia-Tennessee border in 1835: "We stopped for the night at another dreadful dirt hole. The fatigue of the day made me sleep well, although on the floor." Sheets were changed only when they began to smell. Always, Margaret Hall lamented in 1828, there was the usual complement of fleas and bugs: "But we have ceased to expect anything else. Every night I am awakened by Mrs. Cownie striking a light to commence her search for her tormentors. When I undress, I find them crawling on my skin, nasty wretches." James Buckingham summed up the sorry tourist situation at Sparta in 1839: "The dirty state of the room in which the table was laid, the filthy condition of the table-cloth, the coarse and broken plates, rusty knives and forks, and large junks of boiled pork, and various messes of corn and rancid butter, added to the coarse and vulgar appearance and manner of most of the guests, made the whole scene the most revolting we had yet witnessed in the country."

After the Revolution there were just 50,000 citizens of English Georgia, while there were perhaps 35,000 Indians, Creek tribes in the western and southern parts of the state and the Cherokee tribes in the northern parts. The colonial agents had found little difficulty securing enough land from the Creeks, and early treaties made in 1733, 1763 and 1773 gave the English a considerable territory which represents about one-eighth of present-day Georgia. But during the first four decades of the nineteenth century, the population of Georgia swelled from 162,000 to 691,000. From 1800 to 1809, fourteen new counties were created; from 1810 to 1819, nine more counties; from 1820 to 1829, twenty-nine; from 1830 to 1839, seventeen. Milledgeville was laid out at the head of navigation on the Oconee River; later Macon and Columbus were

The dog-trot cabin at Elijah Clarke State Park is a recreation of the most popular house form of the American frontier. *Van Jones Martin*

Travellers' Rest, a tavern outside Toccoa, was built about 1815–25 and enlarged about ten years later. *Van Jones Martin*

established on the Ocmulgee and Chattahoochee. The state capital was moved from Savannah to Augusta in 1785, to Louisville in 1796, to Milledgeville in 1806, each time farther northwest, following the center of population. The Creek tribes, who had occupied the banks of the Savannah River when Oglethorpe landed, were forced to retreat to the Oconee River in 1802, to the Ocmulgee in 1804, to the Flint River in 1821, to the Chattahoochee in 1826. The Cherokees, living in mountainous north Georgia, where they were less in the way of expanding settlements, were not removed from the state until 1838.

Anthony Stokes reported in 1783 that during the Revolution the Americans lost much of their fear of the Indians, "for the Crackers [the new settlers], who are destitute of every sense of religion, which might withhold them from acts of perfidy and cruelty, have been discovered to outdo the Indians in bearing hunger and fatigue; and as they lead a savage kind of life, they are equally skilled in the arts of bush-fighting, and discovering the enemy by their tracks." If an immigrant were not scalped by an Indian in a dispute about territory, said Stokes, then he would probably be cheated out of his land by "profligate white men called Crackers, who are much addicted to exercise the Rights of Man, when they see a good horse, or any other article they like, having abolished the institutions of their Ancestors, forbidding theft, and other crimes, which the Crackers find it convenient to commit." In 1742 William Stephens called Indian traders "a Parcel of loose debauched Fellows." Benjamin Hawkins, Washington's Indian agent in the South, bluntly characterized some of the white traders he met among the Upper Creeks: "a hard drinker," "an indolent, careless man," "an active man of weak mind, fond of drink and much of a savage when drunk," "an enemy to truth and his own character," "a man of infamous character, a dealer in stolen horses." These men were building trade routes, establishing new settlements and slowly de-

94

Georgia gold miners, from William Phillips's *Essay on the Georgia Gold Mines* (New Haven, 1833). *University of Georgia Library*

priving the Indians of their ancestral hunting lands. La Rochefoucauld in 1796 carped that, in the continual quarrels between the whites and Indians, the settlers were in the wrong four times out of five: "It is admitted by everybody that there cannot be a more vicious set of people than the whites who dwell on the boundaries; they rob, murder and betray the Indians."

The excitement of new opportunities and new lands at the time of the Revolution, a rush to plant cotton lands in middle Georgia during the flush times after the invention of the cotton gin, the scramble for land in northwestern Georgia, after gold was discovered there in 1829, all contributed to the frontier land fever. Samuel Butler, who moved from Virginia to the back country above Augusta in the Broad River Valley in 1784, complained in homemade rhyme: "New Georgia is a pleasant place / If we could but Enjoye it / Indians & Rogues they are so great / But allmost have destroyed it. / Could but the Indians be subdewd / And Rogues could have their portion / There could be no better place / On this side of the ocean." Francis Asbury, that travelling minister who came to Georgia on several tours between 1791 and 1815, observed sadly the disappointing effects of his preaching: "I have ridden about two hundred and fifty miles in Georgia, and find the work, in general, very dead. The peace with the Creek Indians, the settlement of new lands, good trade, buying slaves, etc., take the attention of the people." In 1794 Elijah Clarke, who had led an expedition against the Indians during the Revolution, took unilateral possession of some unceded Creek lands on the Oconee River, constructed forts, settled on soil that had been previously guaranteed to the Indians and proclaimed an independent republic, which he occupied with some land-hungry followers until President Washington ordered the Georgia governor to intervene. In the lawless spirit of the time, the settlers looked on the Indians as trespassers on their own land.

Four of the Creek Indian chiefs who came from Georgia and other Southern states to meet with President George Washington at New York in 1790, sketched by John Trumbull. *Yale University Art Gallery (tl, br) and Smithsonian Institution (tr, bl)*

Bad relations between Indians and settlers in south Georgia were aggravated by troubles in north Florida, seen in this melodramatic "Massacre of the Whites by the Indians and Blacks in Florida," c. 1836. *Library of Congress*

This land fever was stimulated by public policy and private speculation. Georgia, hoping to encourage settlement of her territory, gave away the land virtually without cost. After the Revolution, the state government promised two hundred acres of open land, plus fifty additional acres for each family member, to any American soldier who could produce evidence of his wartime service. The state granted some three million acres of this bounty land to nine thousand veterans. After 1802, the state ran a lottery, and each white male adult citizen was entitled to draw for new land. Between 1803 and 1833 eight great distributions were made, totalling 22,404,250 acres. Speculators bought up and resold much of this land, with advertising which a wag satirized in 1787: "Halloo, Halloo, Halloo. The subscribers will sell on most moderate terms: Ten millions of acres of valuable pine barren land in the province of Utopia, on which there are several very sumptuous air castles, ready furnished, that would make commodious and desirable habitations for the gentlemen of the speculative class." In 1795 four companies acquired a vast territory from the state of Georgia, some forty million acres of what is now Alabama and Mississippi, near the Yazoo River, paying a very small price. It was revealed that all but one member of the state legislature had been bribed in the bargain, a terrific public outcry was raised and the act was rescinded by the next legislature.

During the Revolution the Creeks, although they tried to remain neutral, were forced by an English embargo to fight against the Americans. In the following years, each episode of border warfare ended with further Indian cessions. In 1782 at Augusta and in 1785 at Galphinton, certain Creek tribes ceded lands between the Altamaha River and the Florida boundary to the Georgians. These treaties were disputed by other Indians, led by Alexander McGillivray. In 1786 these tribes made a reprisal raid against the settlers, which provoked the

OVERLEAF:
In 1813 General John Floyd and the Georgia militia from Fort Hawkins attacked and killed some two hundred Indians at Autosse in Florida. *University of Georgia Library*

Georgians to dispatch fifteen hundred militiamen against them. At Shoulderbone the Indians were compelled to accept the two disputed treaties and to cede still more territory. During 1787–89, the Creeks reportedly killed 82 people, captured 30 whites, 110 blacks, 642 horses, 984 cattle and 387 hogs and burned 89 houses. In 1790 President Washington invited Alexander McGillivray to New York, where he was flattered and bribed into accepting a compromise treaty. But this treaty was repudiated by other Creek factions in Georgia led by William Augustus Bowles, a former English soldier who was living with the Indians, and denounced by the Georgians, because the treaty seemed to guarantee indefinitely Indian occupation of some Georgia territory. Georgia proceeded to make its own treaties in 1785 and 1786 with sympathetic factions of the Indians.

In 1802 Georgia traded her western claims to territory of Mississippi and Alabama in return for the United States government's promise to remove all the Indians as soon as possible on reasonable, peaceful terms. Though most of the Lower Creeks in Georgia remained friendly to the Americans during the War of 1812, the Upper Creeks in Alabama took that opportunity to assert their independence. In 1813–14 Andrew Jackson and his Tennessee army, with John Floyd from Fort Hawkins and his Georgia militia, attacked the Creeks at the Georgia border. The Georgians objected that the Treaty of Fort Jackson, which ended this war, left the heart of Georgia—from the Ocmulgee to the Chattahoochee—in Indian possession. In 1823 Georgia Governor George M. Troup condemned the federal government for not removing the Indians, and President Monroe appointed two Georgians as Indian agents. These agents made a treaty at Indian Springs, which ceded all Creek lands in Georgia. But the new President, John Q. Adams, declared the treaty illegal and forbade Georgia's surveying this land. But Governor Troup proceeded to survey the land and even

George Lowery was one of several Cherokee chiefs who petitioned Congress to protect their lands from the avaricious Georgians in 1824. *Painting by George Catlin, Thomas Gilcrease Institute of American History and Art, Tulsa*

to commence preparations for war with the United States. At the last minute, the United States negotiated treaties with the Creeks in Washington during 1826 and 1827, averting war and purchasing the last Creek territory in Georgia.

In mountainous north Georgia, the Cherokee tribes were less in the path of settlement, so there was less pressure to remove them from the state. Tutored by Moravian missionaries from North Carolina, the Cherokees had become a civilized nation, with an alphabet, a newspaper, a written constitution and a capital city at New Echota. In fact, they even owned slaves. But gold was discovered at Dahlonega (the Indian name means "the place of yellow metal") in 1829, and by 1830 some three thousand Georgians were digging for gold in Indian territory. In 1830 the Cherokees sued against the Georgians' violations of Indian rights, but the Supreme Court ruled that the Indians were not citizens and therefore could not apply to the Court. When the Court ruled in another case, brought by an Indian missionary who had been jailed by the Georgians, that Georgia could not extend its laws over the Indians, the Georgia governor, Wilson Lumpkin, stated that his state would ignore the judges, and President Jackson, a determined Indian fighter, did not attempt to enforce the Court's decision. Without any treaty giving them rights to Cherokee lands, Georgians surveyed the Indian territories in 1831, granted them to Georgians in a lottery in 1832, and in 1834 settlers were allowed to take possession and the Cherokees were ordered to get out within two years. In the ensuing confusion, different Cherokee factions accepted, rejected and again accepted a final cession of their last Georgia lands. In 1838 General Winfield Scott and the U.S. Army rounded up the last sixteen thousand Cherokees who remained in Georgia and herded them to the West. The Indians had no horses, they had to march on foot; it was winter, and five thousand of them died.

William McIntosh, a Creek chief, was shot to death by other Indians because he assented to the final cession of Creek lands in Georgia in 1824. *Alabama State Archives*

3. Masters and Slaves

HUMANITARIAN feelings had little to do with the decision to make Georgia the only one of the thirteen colonies which prohibited slavery at its founding. The trustees of Georgia wanted to make their southern outpost strong against Britain's Spanish and Indian enemies, by compelling the colonists to feel a responsibility for productive work, by preventing the development of large plantations financed with cheap labor, keeping the landholdings small, compact and easily defensible and by maintaining a cohesive equality among the settlers. Peter Gordon, one of the first colonists who came to Georgia on the *Anne* in 1733, wrote with unconscious irony: "It is morally impossible that the people of Georgia can ever get forward in their settlements or even be a degree above common slaves without the help and assistance of negroes." In 1743 Thomas Stephens, a vocal malcontent who argued that the prohibition against slavery was another hindrance which had retarded the progress of the colony, complained: "It is clear as light itself, that negroes are as essentially necessary to the cultivation of Georgia as axes, hoes, or any other utensil of agriculture." Only with the adoption of slavery after 1750, and the end of the Spanish war in 1763, did Georgia prosper for the first time. Once they were legalized, slaves became deeply woven into the fabric of Georgia life. In 1751 William DeBrahm, provincial surveyor of the southern colonies, found "scarce three Dozen of African Servants," but by 1771, when he finally

104

Two former slaves, Jack and Abby Landlord, were photographed by J. N. Wilson in Savannah about 1875. *New-York Historical Society*

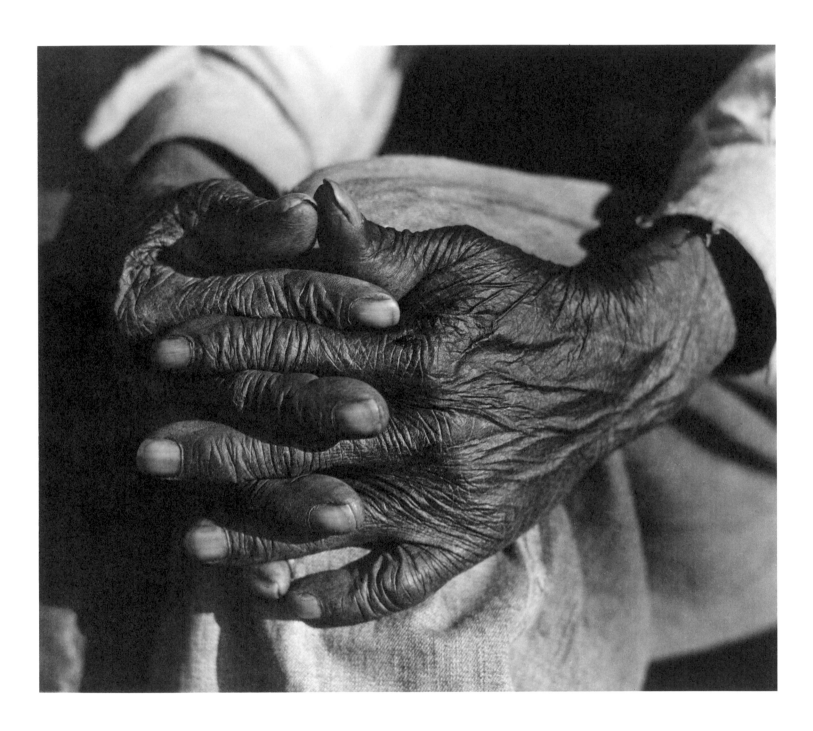

The hands of Henry Brooks, an aged former Georgia slave, were photographed by Jack Delano in Greene County in 1941. *Library of Congress*

sat down to write his account of Georgia, there were already 13,000 of them. By the time Georgia was founded, slavery had evolved as a labor system in the United States, and the Englishmen who came to Georgia adopted the caste system already built into American life. La Rochefoucauld, who visited Georgia in 1796, noted that Savannah employed no ships in the slave trade and that bondsmen were carried to Georgia on ships from New England, especially Rhode Island. In 1784 Joseph Clay, a merchant in Savannah, wrote to London: "The Negro business is a great object with us, both with a view to our Interest individually, & the general prosperity of this State & its Commerce. It is to the Trade of the Country, as the Soul to the Body." In 1776 there were 16,000 slaves in Georgia, compared with 15,000 in New York, 80,000 in Maryland, 75,000 in North Carolina and 110,000 in South Carolina. In 1793 Eli Whitney, a young graduate of Yale College who had come to Georgia as a plantation tutor, invented the first commercial cotton gin and transformed the social and economic life of the region. Cotton now replaced the desultory cultivation of rice and indigo on the coast and wheat and tobacco in the interior. In 1800 there were 59,406 slaves in Georgia, 148,656 in 1820, 280,944 in 1840 and 462,198 slaves in 1860. In 1860, of the fifteen slaveholding states, Georgia was second only to Virginia in the number of slaves and slaveowners.

It will never be possible for anyone to present a final and complete portrait of slavery, a complex and always changing institution which has been perceived very differently by succeeding generations of historians. But the memories of bondsmen and travellers, instead of plantation apologists or Northern abolitionists, seem to be the most reliable source. And these indicate that slavery was not an inhuman system, but an intensely human situation, not a perfect order of laws and economics, but a very imperfect accommodation between men who lived together as individuals as well as masters and slaves and

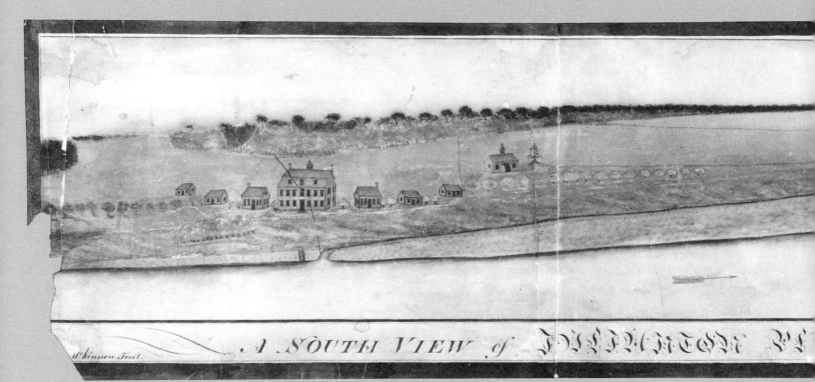

A SOUTH VIEW of PILLINGTON Pl

M.Kinnen Fecit.

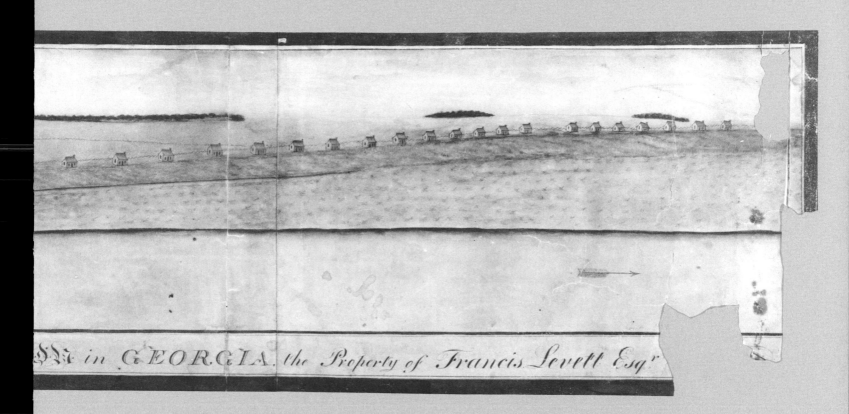

...in GEORGIA the Property of Francis Levett Esq.

Though slavery was outlawed in early Georgia, the institution was legalized in the 1750's and spread rapidly, especially along the coast. The surveyor John McKinney drew this view of Francis Levett's Julianton plantation in McIntosh County about 1796. *Duke University Library*

who had to get along together because they were ultimately dependent on each other. Like most human institutions, slavery had possibilities for benevolence and malevolence. A fugitive slave from Georgia acknowledged: "If there are hard and cruel masters in the South, there are also others of a contrary character. The slave-holders are neither more nor less than men." Fredrika Bremer, a Swedish lady who rode up the Savannah River on a steamer loaded with slaves in 1850, reflected: "There are good and there are bad masters—happy and unhappy slaves." At times, as U. B. Phillips pointed out fifty years ago, slavery may have been harsh and oppressive despotism, resented and resisted; at times it may have been cooperative and affectionate paternalism, received with gratitude and loyalty.

Travellers who came to Georgia before the Civil War recognized that slavery was inconsistent with the professed ideals of American life, but, comparing it with the nasty, brutish and short lives of Europe's laboring poor, they found Georgia's slaves surprisingly content and secure. They acknowledged the moral righteousness of the abolitionists but found unexpected freedom within the slave system. They saw efforts at compulsion and repression, but found the slaves often leading an uncontrollable, underground existence all to themselves. They acknowledged the ties of common experience and even common interests which could bind master and slave together, but found the South suspicious of outsiders and fearful of slaves and freedmen. The travellers viewed immense plantations and hustling cotton centers, but they felt that the condition of the great mass of white people was retarded rather than advanced by slavery.

Immense plantations were not the mainstay of Georgia agriculture before or after the Civil War, despite the moonlight and magnolia mythology which has since obscured the plain realities of southern life. In 1860, there were 2,858 planters, 4,909 overseers, 67,718 farmers

Beverley—House. Country seat of Robert Habersham, Esq?

Near Savannah,

Jan 8. 1844.

Though this drawing of Robert Habersham's "country seat" at Beverley is dated 1844, the house appears to date from the late 18th century. *Private Collection*

On a swamp Plantation

19 March
1821
C.

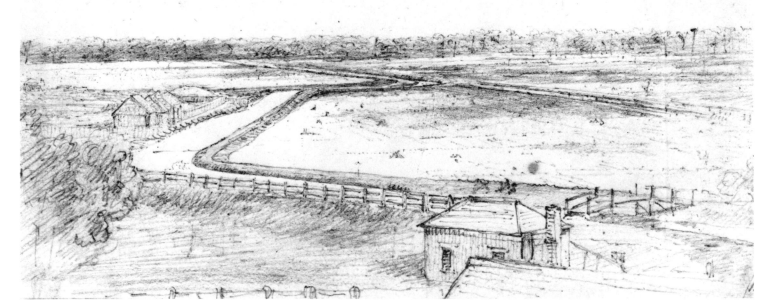

and 19,567 white farm laborers in Georgia. Of the 53,887 farm-owning families in Georgia in 1860, only 901 cultivated more than 1,000 acres of land with 60–500 slaves, while 2,692 families cultivated 500–1,000 acres with 30–60 slaves, 18,821 families cultivated 100–500 acres with 6–30 slaves, 14,129 families cultivated 50–100 acres with 2–6 slaves, and 13,644 families cultivated 20–50 acres with one slave. The portrait of an average Georgia "planter" which emerges from these statistics is a small proprietor, who works alongside his dozen slaves on his hundred acres of land and shares with them a simple, strong and rather difficult life. Blacks and whites lived in the same backwoods, depended on the same weather and harvests, ate the same cornbread, bacon and molasses, attended the same camp meetings, received the same burials. Letters from planters were preoccupied with three things: the weather, the crops and the health of the slaves. Daily journals of planters record a life of monotonous, unending chores: splitting rails, sowing oats, planting potatoes, cutting sugar cane, spreading manure, chopping the cotton.

The vast majority of Georgia planters lived in modest comfort but without much display or leisure time. Thomas Richardson of Wilkes County died owning four slaves, eleven head of cattle, a dozen hogs, three horses, probably a log house, four pewter dishes, a frying pan, a churn, an iron pot and hooks, one piggin, two axes, a handsaw, a drawing knife and two or three hoes. There were few glass window panes, a paucity of furniture and books. George Womble, a Georgia slave, recalled that there was no real coffee for anyone on the plantation where he grew up. Basil Hall described a plantation house in 1828: "Almost all these forest houses in the interior of the State of Georgia consist of two divisions, separated by a wide, open passage, which extends from the front to the back of the building. They are generally made of logs, covered with a very steep roof. The apartments, at the

The house and rice fields of James Couper's plantation near Darien, drawings by Basil Hall, 1828. *Lilly Library, Indiana University*

end of these dwellings, are entered from the open passage which divides the house in two, the floor of which is raised generally two or three feet from the ground. This opening being generally ten or twelve feet wide, answers in that mild climate the purpose of a veranda, or sitting-room during the day." James Stuart described a similar house in 1830: "The common form of the planters' houses, and indeed of all houses that you meet with on the roadsides in this country, is two square pens, with an open space between them, connected by a roof above and a floor below, so as to form a parallelogram of nearly triple the length of its depth. In the open space the family take their meals during the fine weather. The kitchen and the places for slaves are all separate buildings, as are the stable, corn-houses, etc. About ten buildings of this description make up the establishment of an ordinary planter with half a dozen slaves." Fanny Kemble described her family's house on Butler's Island in 1838: "Three small rooms, and three still smaller, and a kitchen detached from the dwelling—a mere wooden outhouse. Of our three apartments, one is sitting, eating and living room, and is sixteen by fifteen. The walls are plastered indeed, but neither painted nor papered; it is divided from our bedroom by a dingy wooden partition covered all over with hooks, pegs, and nails, to which hats, caps, keys, etc. are suspended in graceful irregularity. The doors open by means of wooden latches, raised by means of small bits of thread. The third room, a chamber with sloping ceiling, immediately over our sittingroom and under roof is appropriated to a nurse and my two babies. Of the closets, one is the overseer's bedroom, the other his office." John Newland spent the night at a planter's house near Macon in 1843: "We were shown into the best room, which was a smooth boarded room, with large crevices in every direction. In one corner was a bed, in another a piano, sofa, marble centre-table, etc., no carpet, and a broken chair put against the door to keep it shut. Our dinner

John MacDonald's house, outside Ringgold in north
Georgia, was built in 1797 and photographed in 1864. It
was a fairly typical Georgia farmhouse. *George Barnard,*
Private Collection

Robert Smith House, Atlanta, c. 1840, is also typical of
Georgia's 19th-century farmhouses. *Van Jones Martin*

consisted principally of bacon and hoe-cake which made me delight-fully sick." Emily Burke, a New England schoolmarm who came to Georgia in 1840, described another planter's house: "The house stood upon four posts about five feet from the ground, allowing a free circulation of air beneath, as well as forming a fine cover for the hounds, goats, and all the domestic fowls. It was divided into four apartments below, and two in the roof, and furnished with two broad piazzas, one in front of the building, where is always the gentleman's sitting room, and one on the back of the house, where the servants await their master's orders. The building was slightly covered with boards, arranged like clapboards to shed the rain. This was the entire thickness of the walls, there being no ceiling, lathing or plastering within. The floors were all single and laid in so unworkmanlike manner, I could often see the ground beneath. The roof was covered with log shingles nailed to the timbers, to save the expense of the boards beneath. Two chimneys, one upon each end, built of turfs, sticks, blocks of wood, and occasionally a brick, plastered over with clay, ornamented the outside of the house." J. T. Trowbridge slept one night at the close of the Civil War at the home of a planter: "It was a plain, one-and-a-half story, unpainted, weather-boarded frame dwelling, with a porch in front and two front windows. The floors were carpetless but swept clean. The rooms were not done off at all; there was not a lath, nor any appearance of plastering or white wash about them. The rafters and shingles of the roof formed the ceiling; the undisguised beams, studs and clapboards of the frame composed the walls. The dining-room was a little detached frame box, without a fire-place. There was a cupboard, a wardrobe, and a bed in the sitting-room; a little bedroom leading off from it; and two beds in the garret."

Harrison Berry, a Georgia bondsman who published a unique defense of slavery by a slave in 1861, chastised the self-righteous

Nancy Hart, servant in the family of Tomlinson Fort of Milledgeville. *Georgia Department of Archives and History*

abolitionists: "You must recollect, fanatical sirs, that the slave children and their young masters and mistresses are all raised up together. They suck together, play together, go a hunting together, go a fishing together, go in washing together, and in a great many instances, eat together in the cotton-patch, sing, jump, wrestle, box, fight boy fights, and dance together; and every other kind of amusement that is calculated to bolt their hearts together when grown up." Frederick Law Olmsted, the New England landscape architect, creator of Central Park in New York and a professed critic of slavery, recognized these ties of long family association, common tradition, common memories and even common interests which could bind master and slave together. Tyrone Power, the Irish comedian who came to Georgia in 1836, saw the special rapport which could exist among the members of a slaveholding family: "My days were passed at the hospitable home of Mr. G——n, where I was attended by the sleekest, merriest set of negroes imaginable, most of whom had grown old or were born in their master's house; his own good-humoured, active benevolence of spirit was reflected in the faces of his servants." When Sir Charles Lyell, the renowned geologist, visited Hopeton, a coastal Georgia plantation, in 1841, he saw slavery as a benign anachronism in democratic America: "There is an hereditary regard and often attachment on both sides, more like that formerly existing between lords and their retainers in feudal times of Europe, than to anything now to be found in America. The slaves identify with the master, and their sense of their own importance rises with his success in life." John Davis, another traveller, recorded the affectionate greetings received by a Georgia planter when he returned to his family after a trip: "The negroes of the plantation beheld the coming of Mr. Wilson with joy; old and young of both sexes came to the landing place to welcome his approach. The air resounded with exclamations." Fanny Kemble,

A slave family picking cotton outside Savannah, a photograph of the 1850's by Pierre Havens. *New-York Historical Society*

though uncompromisingly hostile to slavery, reported how gratefully she had been received as the new mistress at Butler's Island in 1838: "No sooner had I disembarked and reached the house, than a dark cloud of black life filled the piazza and swarmed up the steps, and I had to shake hands, like a popular president, 'till my arm ached at the shoulder joint."

Private records reaffirm these published reports of real human relations between masters and slaves. The certificate of freedom for a Georgia slave, dated 1761: "This is to satisfy to whom it may concern that this Black Man, Mr. Moses Handlin is a Free man. . . . This very black Moses Handlin is a very onnis Black Man. I knowed him from a Boy." James Habersham wrote to New York in 1764: "Oronoko's wife died last Night, and the poor fellow is inconsolable, and she nursed two of my daughters. I must own the sight of her has affected me more than all the negroes I have ever lost. I have really been obliged to lay down my pen several times." When John Kell of Griffin went off to school at Savannah in 1838, a slave wrote to him: "My dear Master– I hope you are doing well. I know you wont be in bad company though. Your horse is very fat. I always feed him every night & morning. I cried very much the night you went but I hope to see you again my dear master. & be well & hearty. Has your room got a fire place? I hope so, Your boy Ben." When slave Kate's baby died in 1860, her mistress wrote: "My husband and I went out in the morning to select the spot for its burial. We chose a portion of ground and will have it inclosed with a railing. The rain seems to fall on my bare heart." Charles Ball, a fugitive slave, described parting with his dying master: "Tears came in his eyes as he talked to me, and said, that as he could not live long, he hoped I would continue to be faithful to him whilst he did live. This I promised to do, for I really loved my master."

Living was hard work for Georgia's slaves, chopping cotton with backs bent for long hot hours under the naked sun or planting rice

Slaves ploughing fields outside Savannah, a photograph of the 1850's by Pierre Havens. *New-York Historical Society* with swollen feet immersed for long winter days in cold water. Slaves worked every day of the year, from sunrise to sunset, except Saturday afternoons, Sundays and the week before Christmas and New Year's. They were given assigned tasks each day, which they could complete at their own rate of work, or they were supervised by a driver for a prescribed period of work each day. Houses were small cabins, one for each family. Slaves were provided with one or two suits of clothing for winter and another for summer, one pair of heavy shoes each autumn, a new blanket every two years. Food consisted of pork, corn meal and molasses. Punishments were often severe, and laws delineated a very narrow path for their lives. As personal property, slaves could not own property, make legal contracts or enjoy the rights of citizenship. But laws were often not enforced in the isolated privacy of the Georgia forest. Although the slave codes provided that slaves could not be taught to read, George Womble recalled that on a nearby plantation the owner caught his own son teaching a little slave boy to write. Though Georgia laws gave no legal sanction to slave marriages, the rights of husbands and wives and family life were generally respected, including during slave auctions, when families might be sold only as family groups. A slave could not own firearms, but Charles Ball and William Grimes, two fugitive slaves, were both given old hunting rifles by their masters.

Slaves who were not overtasked could complete their assigned work early in the day and devote some time to pleasure or to raising vegetables or livestock which they could sell for pocket money. Olmsted noted how the slaves were often victimized by "a swarm of Jews" in Southern towns, who sold the simple bondsmen cheap clothing, trinkets or nauseating whiskey diluted with water and tobacco juice. Celestia Avery, a former slave, danced in her cabin at night to the tune of fiddles which she had purchased with money from selling her chickens. In the cities, a slave might be allowed to hire himself out to a

Slaves and their houses on Fort George Island, at the Georgia-Florida border, in the 1850's. *New-York Historical Society*

The best slave houses were made of tabby, a concrete-like mixture of lime, oyster shells, sand and water. Two views of slave quarters on Saint Catherine's Island, photographed about 1870 by J. N. Wilson. *University of Georgia Library*

white man other than his master. This system allowed the slaves to select their own work, keep most of the proceeds of their labor and to be generally responsible for their own lives. When William Grimes's master left Savannah, the slave was left behind to hire himself out; he was able to earn one dollar a day, so, after paying his master three dollars a week, he could keep four dollars for himself. In the woods around plantations and in their own quarters of towns, the blacks seem to have led an uncontrollable, underground life of their own. In 1763 Patrick Mackay complained about the Negroes who wandered to his plantation at night, stealing livestock and vegetables and creating "very great disorder amongst his slaves by debauching his slave wenches." William Grimes could go out and pay twenty-five cents to have his future predicted by a black fortune-teller, a fascinating glimpse of slave life in Southern cities. The existence of patrollers, white men who served as sentries to maintain law and order among the slaves at night, was proof that the blacks were accustomed to doing what they wanted after dark.

Ultimately, however, slaves were always dependent on the disposition of their masters. Cecily Cawthorn, a former slave, recalled: "I had a cousin to run away, and they got her back from Charleston. The overseer gave her a hundred licks. One lick cut the blood, and my mistress got so mad, she quarreled at Marster. He said he had to make an example for the other slaves. Mistis said it injured the woman to whip her that a way, so then Marster made 'em be more careful." An overseer reported how one slave tried to flee in 1861: "George (big) attempted to run off in presents of the entire force and in my presents. He was caught by Driver John. I give him sixty straps in presents of those he ran off in presents of." William Grimes told of begging to escape punishment: "Mr. Sturges was a very kind master, but exceedingly severe when angry. He had a new Negro, by the name of Cato, with whom I got a fighting and bit off his nose, just as my master was

A "badly whipped slave" from Frances Anne Kemble, *The Views of Judge Woodward and Bishop Hopkins on Negro Slavery at the South* (New York, 1863). *University of Georgia Library*

going to sell him, which injured the sale of Cato very much. For this I had to beg very hard to escape being whipped." Leah Garrett, a former slave, recorded: "Everybody always stripped you in them days to whup you, 'cause they didn't care who seed you naked. Some folks' chillun took sticks and jabbed you all while you was bein' beat. Sometimes these chillun would beat you all 'cross your head, and their Ma's and Pa's didn't know what stop was." The regulations on Pierce Butler's plantation set limits to the beating of slaves: field drivers could administer only twelve lashes, the head driver no more than thirty-six, the overseer as many as fifty. Mollie Kensey remembered her slave sister: "They'd make her go out and lay on a table and two or three white men would have intercourse with her before they'd let her up. She was just a small girl." John Brown, a fugitive slave, claimed to be the victim of eccentric medical experiments at the hands of a neighboring planter to test sunstroke remedies by baking him in the sun, to discover the effects of fastings and bleedings, to learn the depth of a Negro's dark skin by blistering and peelings. Georgia laws against "unnecessary and excessive whipping, beating, cutting or wounding, or cruelly and unnecessarily biting or tearing with dogs" were cool evidence that such abuses did exist.

Travellers saw signboards and placards announcing slave auctions and found slave pens surrounded by high walls where the bondsmen were kept for inspection. A typical advertisement might read: "A Cargo consisting of about 170 Young and healthy New Negroes, Chiefly Men, all of whom have had the Smallpox, from Gambia." John Brown, a Georgia slave, was sold by the pound. Moses Roper, another fugitive slave, was put up for auction along with the other valuable property of his late master's estate, including a carriage, horses, a gold watch and cigars. For a time Roper worked for a slave trader in Georgia, and his job was to grease the bodies of the blacks every morning with sweet oil before they were put up for sale, to make

Advertisements for the return of runaway slaves and slave auctions at Savannah, 1787 and 1788, Campbellton, 1846, and Lumpkin, 1859. *Duke University Library (top), Private Collection (bottom)*

24 DOLLARS REWARD.

RAN AWAY from the subscriber, on Friday the 3d instant, about 12 o'clock in the day,

FRIDAY,

A very stout likely Negro Man, about 23 years of age, 5 feet 9 or 10 inches high, marked with *African* marks on his cheeks, and small eyes; he had on when he went away an oznabrig shirt and trowsers, but, as he has a number of other clothes, will probably soon change his dress; he was lately the property of Col. Pannell, of Wilkes county, and it's believed he is now gone to Washington.

S. TUFT.

Savannah, 6th *August*, 1787.

Run away from the Subscriber,

About eight days ago,

The following Negroes, viz.

  CHARLES, a thin fellow, about 5 feet 9 or 10 inches high, of a yellowish complexion, has a very sour look, and is about 23 or 24 years old.

 FRANK, a pretty stout fellow, about 5 feet 8 or 9 inches high, 25 or 26 years old, has had one of his eyes hurt, which is generally weak, has remarkable broad flat feet, a big mouth, and thick lips.

LONDON, about 5 feet 8 or 9 inches high, 23 or 24 years old; is pretty well made, except his feet, which are very broad and flat, had on when he went away a purple negro cloth jacket and trowsers very much worn.

They are all smooth faced, and none of them have any beard, speak good English, and are very artful. *London* can also speak German; he carried off with him a small BROWN BAY MARE, about 12 and an half hands high, 5 years old, with a long switch tail and bushy mane; no brands.

Whoever will deliver the said Negroes to me on Savannah river, or to the Warden of the Workhouse in Savannah, shall receive a *Reward of Three Guineas* each for *Frank* and *London*, and *One* for *Charles.*

GEO. P. READ.

April 2, 1788.

EXECUTOR'S SALES.

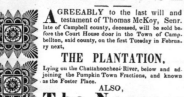

AGREEABLY to the last will and testament of Thomas McKoy, Senr. late of Campbell county, deceased, will be sold before the Court House door in the Town of Campbellton, said county, on the first Tuesday in February next,

THE PLANTATION,

Lying on the Chattahoochee River, below and adjoining the Pumpkin Town Fractions, and known as the Foster Place.

ALSO,

The Negroes

Belonging to said estate—consisting of MEN & WOMEN, BOYS & GIRLS; Among them are 2 House Carpenters; and between Thirty and Forty in Number.— *Terms of Sale.*—The Purchaser will be required to pay one half cash, and the balance due on the first day of January, 1848, with good personal security, in sums not exceeding Thirty Dollars. Property sold for a division among the legatees.

JOHN BOWEN, Exec'r.
November 25, 1846.

EXECUTOR'S SALE.

ON the 2nd Monday in January next, will be sold at the residence of Thomas McKoy, Senr., late of Campbell county, deceased, all the Perishable Property of said deceased—consisting of Corn, Fodder & Wheat, Horses, Mules, Cows & Calves, Pork and Stock Hogs, and other articles not now recollected. Terms made known on the day of sale.

JOHN BOWEN, Exec'r.
Nov. 18, 1846.

Notice To Debtors & Creditors.

ALL Persons indebted to the estate of Thomas McKoy, senr., late of Campbell County, dec'd, are requested to make immediate payment—and those having demands against the estate will present the same, properly attested, for payment, within the time prescribed by law, to

JOHN BOWEN, Exec'r.
Nov. 18, 1846.

NEGROES, NEGROES.

The undersigned has just arrived in Lumpkin from Virginia, with a likely lot of negroes, about 40 in number, embracing every shade and variety. He has seamstresses, chamber maids, field hands, and doubts not that he is able to fill the bill of any who may want to buy. He has sold over two hundred negroes in this section, mostly in this county, and flatters himself that he has so far given satisfaction to his purchasers. Being a regular trader to this market he has nothing to gain by misrepresentation, and will, therefore, warrant every negro sold to come up to the bill, squarely and completely. Give him a call at his Mart.

J. F. MOSES.

Lumpkin, Ga., Nov. 14th, 1859.

them glow with apparent health and vigor. Charles Ball, later a fugitive slave, realized that he would soon be sold from South Carolina into Georgia and reflected: "I was now in a country where the life of a black man was no more regarded than that of an ox, except so far as the man was worth more money in the market." The general rule, in fact, was that an able-bodied field hand was worth $100 for every cent cotton was bringing; thus, a planter figured he could afford to pay $1,000 for a slave when cotton was selling for ten cents a pound. A traveller named Nason in 1848 left work to attend a sale of slaves and horses at Savannah: "Saw fifty-four men, women and children sold as chattels, but not without emotion, to see the serious look, the falling tear, and the submissive will. There are three auctioneers selling at the same time. Sometimes one man is up [for sale], sometimes three or more. Sometimes a woman and children, called 'an interesting family of negroes.' Now a plantation – now, a gun – now, an old man, wife and daughter – now, a young man, etc. etc. The time for this traffic in slaves, and the souls of men, is the first Monday in each month." Former Georgia slaves spoke with affecting simplicity about sales. Willis Cofer: "We used to hear tell of big sales of slaves, when sometimes mammies would be sold away from their chilluns. It was awful, and then they would just cry and pray and beg to be allowed to stay together. At them sales they would put a nigger on the scales and weigh him, and then the bidding would start." George Womble: "I never saw my father as he was sold before I was old enough to recognize him as being my father." Mollie Kensey: "They sold my father in 1858. I never 'member seein' him. See, chile, I was three years old. They sold him from ma and five chilluns." Sally Brown: "I was given away when I was just a baby and I never did see my mama again." Traveller George Lewis met a Georgia slave bound for the New Orleans market

Slave market, Whitehall Street, Atlanta, photographed by George Barnard, 1864. *Library of Congress*

OVERLEAF:
A view of Savannah, through Monterey Square and down Bull Street toward the river, by J. Smith, 1856. *Private Collection*

who told him: "Master promised I should die in his service. It is mighty bad to sell me. I is heart-break, and I think I will die."

In 1793 Eli Whitney invented the first commercial cotton gin on a plantation near Savannah and transformed the social and economic life of the region. When Whitney came to Georgia, the main crops were rice and indigo on the coast and wheat and tobacco in the interior. Travellers navigating the Savannah River at the time of the Revolution saw only tobacco and corn on the river banks and on the pole barges heading downriver to the sea. In 1773 William Bartram had observed that cotton was planted only by the poorer class of people and then just enough for their family consumption. In 1791 George Washington reported that rice and tobacco were Georgia's most important exports. F. A. Michaux reported at the turn of the century: "The culture of rice has diminished very much within a few years; it has been, in a great degree, replaced by that of cotton, which yields greater profits to the planters." During the next thirty years prices were high and the profits were terrific. Cotton plantations and slaves moved into the lands along the Savannah River and just beyond Augusta by 1800, swept into the rich lands of the central interior by 1820 and proceeded into the newly acquired Indian territory of southwestern Georgia after 1830. Cotton production in Georgia soared from 1,000 bales in 1790 to 90,000 bales in 1820, to 408,481 bales in 1840 and 701,840 bales in 1860.

Now Savannah, a village of sandy, littered streets, was changed by the cotton bonanza into a world port, a real international city to be traded with and reckoned with. Augusta, a frontier fort which had been a depot for the Indian traffic and tobacco trade in the eighteenth century at the falls of the Savannah River, became a busy market for cotton headed downriver to Savannah and the sea. Athens, a hillside village, was established as the new home for the University of Georgia

George Washington Lay and his cousin James Berry Lay, Gordon County, c. 1855. *Georgia Department of Archives and History*

by its governing body, the Senatus Academicus, in 1801. Milledgeville, a raw town at the headwaters of the Oconee River named for Governor John Milledge, was designated the state capital in 1804, only a year after its founding and before even a dozen houses had been built there. In October, 1807, fifteen wagons carried the state's public records from Louisville, the old capital, to Milledgeville. This was a quiet but significant event, which symbolized the shifting of Georgia's population, wealth and power from the coast to the cotton belt. By 1830 two-thirds of the population of Georgia lived within ninety miles of Milledgeville. Macon was laid out in 1823 on the Ocmulgee River near old Fort Hawkins, and Columbus was laid out in 1828 on the Chattahoochee River near old Fort Mitchell. In 1838 Roswell King moved from a coastal plantation to the interior uplands, where he established a cotton factory and a town named in his own honor, Roswell.

Travellers were struck by the passionate preoccupation of the Georgia people with cotton. John Davis dined at Dillon's boarding house, Savannah, about 1800: "There was a large party at supper, composed principally of cotton manufacturers from Manchester, whose conversation operated on me like a dose of opium. Cotton! Cotton! Cotton! Cotton! was their never-ceasing topic. Oh! how many travellers would have devoured up their discourse; for my part, I fell asleep, and nodded till a negro offered to light me to my room." Ebenezer Kellogg sighed at Savannah in 1818: "I hear nothing but talk of the price of cotton. The Georgians are madly devoted to cotton." Adam Hodgson came to Georgia in 1827: "I arrived in Augusta and when I saw the cotton waggons in Broad Street, I whistled! but said nothing. There was more than a dozen tow boats in the river, with more than a thousand bales of cotton on each; and several steam boats with still more. And you must know, that they have cotton warehouses covering whole squares, all full of cotton; and some of the knowing ones told me, that there were then in the place from 40,000 to 50,000

Thomas Jefferson Ruslin of Georgia, 1861.
Library of Congress

bales. It puzzled me to tell which was the largest, the piles of cotton or the houses." William Cullen Bryant came to Savannah in 1843: "One should see the multitude of bales of it accumulating in the warehouses and elsewhere, in order to form an idea of the extent to which it is produced in the southern states—long trains of cars heaped with bales, steamer after steamer loaded high with bales coming down the rivers, acres of bales on the wharves, acres of bales at the railway stations." John Lamar, a planter from Macon, wrote to Howell Cobb in 1845: "The whole world of planters, buyers, etc. are on tiptoe for the news by the steamer which left Liverpool on the 4th February. My prayers are fervent for advices of a ha'penny advance and large sales, great demand for cotton goods, spinners prosperous, corn plenty and all that sort of parlance, so interesting to us poor toads under a harrow, planters of cotton." Fredrika Bremer cruised up the Savannah River in 1850 and saw: "On deck, a few gentlemen, planters, who were polite and wished to talk, but talked only of 'cotton, cotton, cotton.' I fled away from these worshippers of cotton." A traveller of 1856 summed up the popular feeling: "A kind of cotton insanity appears to affect all classes. To their distempered imaginations, cotton is the pabulum that nourishes and sustains the rest of mankind; cotton, the 'open sesame' to wealth, honor, and personal and national aggrandizement; cotton, the Atlas which upholds and the lever that moves the entire world."

People, commerce, steamboats and railroads followed the advance of cotton planting across Georgia. Like fingers stretching from the sea, the Savannah, Altamaha, Oconee and Chattahoochee rivers reached from the coast toward the new plantations. In 1819 a steamboat commenced regular runs between Milledgeville in the interior and Darien on the coast, and soon a fleet of steamers replaced the pole barges which had been carrying cotton from Augusta to Savannah, from Milledgeville to Darien, from Columbus to Appalachicola in

Richard Richardson House, Savannah, 1817–19.
Van Jones Martin

Nicholas Ware House, Augusta, 1818.
Van Jones Martin

Florida. In 1826 Wilson Lumpkin surveyed the route for a proposed railroad, to be towed by mules, over the north Georgia mountains. In 1836 construction was commenced on the Georgia Railroad west from Augusta, and in 1837 the Central of Georgia began laying rails from Savannah toward the northwest. Early factories, most of them cotton mills, were established in places like Augusta, Athens, Roswell and Columbus, where water power and cotton plantations came together. Meanwhile, the University of Georgia had been chartered in 1785 and opened in 1801. A Medical Academy was founded at Augusta in 1828. Adiel Sherwood founded Mercer Institute at Penfield in 1831, later supported by the Baptists; Emory College near Covington was established by the Methodists in 1834; Oglethorpe College near Milledgeville was founded by the Presbyterians in 1838.

For the first thirty years after Whitney's invention, the land was cheap, the soil virgin, the slaves prime and the harvest bountiful. But by 1830 the land was becoming dearer, aging slaves a greater burden and abused soil less productive. In the early 1820's and before, a small planter could buy slaves and raise cotton at a substantial profit, but after 1835 he could no longer do so. The cost of land and slaves was rising, while the price of cotton was declining, making it necessary for planters to raise larger and larger crops to survive. Cotton prices ranged from twenty to forty cents per pound in the early nineteenth century and from ten to twelve cents per pound during the 1850's, while the cost of prime field hands rose from $300 in 1790 to $1,600 and $1,800 in 1860. Expressed in terms of cotton, slave prices were soaring from 1,500 pounds of cotton in 1800, to 3,000 in 1810, to 5,000 in 1820, to 7,000 in 1830, to 8,000 in 1840, to 10,000 in 1850 and to 18,000 in 1860. It was symptomatic of the economic stress that planters had to abandon their old practical rule, that they could afford to pay for a field hand a price in hundreds of dollars equal to the price of cotton in cents. Borrowing money to buy more land and more slaves,

James Stirling observed from Macon in 1850, made the indebtedness of Southern planters notorious. John Melish saw indications of this desperate dependence on the price of cotton: "The staple commodity of this state is cotton, and it had so fallen in value, as to cut off upwards of one third of the income. I accordingly found that all the people in the interior of the country were clothed in homespun."

Meanwhile, cotton cultivation was exhausting the farms of Georgia. Many planters had to face an inevitable choice: a few years more, going on at that rate, they must either remove West, be sold out by the sheriff to pay their debts, or live in extreme poverty. Emily Burke wrote in 1840 that Georgia planters had poor houses because they had to move frequently: "One often meets deserted plantations. A plantation is cleared, and a sort of temporary hut erected, then covered with slaves who cultivate the soil as long as it will produce any thing, then left for another to be used in the same way." John Lamar of Macon wrote his cousin Howell Cobb in 1847, giving us a rare insight into the planter's mind: "Lord, Lord, Howell, you and I have been too used to poor land to know what crops people are making in the rich lands of the new counties. I am just getting my eyes open to the golden view. On these good lands, when cotton is down to such a price as would starve us out, they can make money." The new territory was, he said, a veritable promised land. "Buy we must! That is a fixed fact, there is no getting around it. It must be done." As planters tried to buy more land to plant more cotton and weather the economic squeeze, the enlarged plantations pushed out any foundations of a substantial class of independent farmers in Georgia after 1830. In Wilkes County in 1820 there had been 1,057 farmers who owned 8,921 slaves, but by 1857, 469 farmers owned 7,587 slaves, a reflection of the expansion of great plantations and the exclusion of small farmers. James Silk Buckingham recorded this interview in the Georgia cotton belt in 1837: "One of the

Nathan van Boddie House, LaGrange, 1836.
Frances Benjamin Johnston, Library of Congress

Georgia State House, Milledgeville, as remodelled in 1827.
Eberhardt Studio, Milledgeville

farmers, who was upwards of sixty-five years of age, told me that he had made up his mind to migrate next year, to the valley of the Mississippi; and when I asked him what could induce him, now so far advanced in life, and with a large family, to move so far from his home, he replied, that there was too much aristocracy here for him! I asked him who or what constituted the aristocracy of which he spoke. He said they were the rich men of these parts, who bought up all the land at extravagant prices, and left none for the poorer citizens to purchase." By 1850 there were already fifty-nine thousand Georgians in Alabama and seventeen thousand in Mississippi. Cotton land speculators on the western borders of Georgia were said to be swarming thicker than the locusts in Egypt.

By the 1830's, then, people were again on the move across the Georgia frontier, but this time most were leaving rather than entering the state and searching in other places for opportunities which were no longer open for them in Georgia. In 1820 Adam Hodgson observed the first stages of this secondary migration of excluded small farmers and distressed planters from Georgia: "In the course of the day we passed some Indians with their guns and blankets, and several waggons of emigrants from Georgia and Carolina to Alabama. We also saw many gangs of slaves whom their masters were transporting to Alabama and Mississippi, and met one party returning from New Orleans to Georgia. We were astonished to meet this solitary party going against the stream. Often a light carriage, of a sallow planter and his lady, would bring up the rear of a long cavalcade, and indicate the removal of a family of some wealth, who, allured by the rich lands of Alabama, or the sugar plantations on the Mississippi, had bidden adieu to the scenes of their youth and undertaken a long and painful pilgrimage through the wilderness." In 1834 Tyrone Power described other caravans of wagons moving toward Georgia's western border, "each laden, first with the needful provisions and such household gear as may be considered indispensable; next, over this portion of the freight is stowed the family of the emigrant planter, his wife, but commonly a round squad of white-haired children, with their attendants; on the march these vehicles are surrounded by slaves, varying in numbers from half a dozen to fifty or sixty, according to the wealth of the proprietor; a couple of mounted travellers commonly complete the cavalcade, which moves over these roads at the rate of twelve or fifteen miles a day." Power said the numbers of immigrants leaving Georgia for the Southwest were incredible. Georgians had become again nomads passing across an unsettled land.

The economic drain of cotton planting perpetuated an undeveloped agricultural economy. Daniel Turner, a young Rhode Island doctor at Saint Mary's in southernmost Georgia in 1805, wrote his family about the land-poor planters: "I suppose in all Camden County there is scarcely a planter with a hundred dollars by him & perhaps his plantation & Slaves worth a hundred thousand." George Lewis, who travelled through Georgia in 1844, observed: "Nothing was attended to but the rearing of cotton and slaves. The more cotton the more slaves, and the more slaves the more cotton!" This meant that there was little capital used to develop a balanced economy or build a society of shopkeepers, artisans, factories and cities. Charles Lyell in 1846 was struck by the difficulty of raising money in Georgia for building cotton mills: " 'Why,' they say, 'should all our cotton make so long a journey to the north, to be manufactured there, and come back to us at so high a price?' It is because all spare cash is sunk in purchasing negroes." James Stirling wrote: "What capital they save, and that is not much, they lay out in niggers. Niggers and cotton—cotton and niggers; these are the law and prophets to the men of the South." In 1860 forty-six percent of Georgia's wealth was invested in slaves and

Executive Mansion, Milledgeville, 1838–39.
Van Jones Martin

not in the comforts of civilized life or in banks, machinery and ships. Frederick Law Olmsted noted that the cart wheels in Georgia came from the North, that the plows came from New York. According to Charles Lyell, the wife of Georgia's governor did not realize that people outside the South could buy soap in shops instead of always having to make it for themselves at home. James Silk Buckingham proclaimed rhetorically that had Southern capital not been tied up in slaves, it could have been used to advance the region by at least a century.

The undeveloped industrial economy, the region's reputation for slavery and the few opportunities for skilled workers all discouraged the migration of ambitious artisans to Georgia, another element of a cycle of limited growth and diminished opportunity. The work of skilled craftsmanship was done by the slaves, who held a privileged position in the labor market, subsidized, trained and employed by their owners. Charles Lyell visited Columbus in 1846: "Several New Englanders have complained to me that they can not push on their children here as carpenters, cabinet makers, blacksmiths, and other such crafts, because the planters bring up the most intelligent of their slaves to these occupations." In 1855 Frederick Law Olmsted reported: "New England factory girls have been induced to go to Georgia to work in the newly-established cotton factories, by the offer of high wages, but have found their positions so unpleasant — owing to the general degradation of the laboring class — as very soon to be forced to return." A white carpenter at Rome in 1849 complained that the competition of cheap black laborers made it impossible for him to be paid a living wage for his skills. It was reported that some planters hired Irish laborers to do unhealthy work too dangerous for their valuable slave property.

Georgia, like a tender sapling girdled at its trunk, was being strangled by its devotion to cotton and slaves. Town life was eclipsed

Barrington Hall, Barrington King House, Roswell, 1840.
Van Jones Martin

OVERLEAF:
Oglethorpe University, Milledgeville (tl); Georgia Female College, Macon (bl); Medical College of Georgia, Augusta (tr); and Brownwood Female Institute, LaGrange (br); from W. C. Richard's *Georgia Illustrated* (Penfield, 1842). *University of Georgia Library*

by the predominance of the plantation system. Because of the sparse population, caused by Georgia's considerable territory and the maturing enlargement of plantations after 1830, it would have been difficult for the state to become a cohesive, stable society. Between the Revolution and the Civil War, Georgia's white population increased about eight times, but the land area also increased, by cession from the Indians, about eight times, so the population remained spread out over a large territory. In 1860 the population density in the coast-planting states, an area which included Georgia, was 15.25 persons per mile compared with 50.47 in New England and 69.83 in the Middle Atlantic states. Forty-four percent of those people in the South were slaves, for whom education was forbidden, so it was doubly difficult for Georgia to establish a coordinated system of public education. The original plan for the University of Georgia, product of the idealism of the Revolution, had included a college at Athens and preparatory schools in each county. But the college struggled with difficulty during its early years, when state officials were preoccupied with Indian troubles. At this time the president of the college was its only faculty member, and the college was saved only by selling its land endowment. The system of academies was never built, and no public school system was created until after the Civil War. In 1860, 19.6 percent of all white adult Georgians could not read or write. Between 1802 and 1865 Georgia publishers started more than fifty literary magazines, but most of them, like the famous, fated *Orion*, which was started at Penfield in 1842 and which expired in 1844, were quick failures.

In the eighteenth century, when Habersham and Stokes complained with seaboard snobbery about "crackers," they meant the vigorous men coming into Georgia from North Carolina and Virginia in search of new land. After 1830, when travellers wrote about "crackers," they meant passive poor people living on marginal land deep in

Bulloch Hall, James Bulloch House, Roswell, 1840.
Van Jones Martin

the Georgia forest. In 1860 most white families in Georgia owned no slaves and no land. There were 118,000 white families in Georgia, but only 41,084 families owned slaves, which meant that 75,000 families owned no slaves. With 118,000 white families in Georgia, there were only 53,887 farms, which meant that some 65,000 Georgia families were landless. Notably, these statistics reveal that only some 12,000 farms were cultivated without the use of slave labor, evidence that no class of sturdy, independent farmers had survived the expansion of larger plantations after 1830. It was difficult for these landless families to find work on the land, for the slaves tilled the soil, or to find work in the few cities, where there were few industrial operations and where slaves had become the skilled artisans. Without good land or good jobs in Georgia, those families who were able moved to the West. Some of those who were not able, struggled for subsistence on the poorest land as squatters or renters. So nearly one-half of the white families in Georgia lived a landless, slaveless life in a society based on land and slaves.

Fanny Kemble described the lives of these people in 1838: "Have you visions of well-to-do farmers with comfortable homesteads, decent habits, industrious, intelligent, cheerful and thrifty? Such, however, is not the yeomanry of Georgia. The scattered white population, too poor to possess land or slaves, and having no means of living in the towns, squat on other men's land till ejected. They are hardly protected from the weather by the rude shelters they frame for themselves in the midst of these dreary woods. Their food is chiefly supplied by shooting the wildfowl and venison, and stealing from the cultivated patches of the plantations nearest at hand. Their clothes hang about them in filthy tatters, and the combined squalor and fierceness of their appearance is really frightful." George Featherstonhaugh saw them in the countryside of northern Georgia in 1835: "tall, thin, cadaverous-

Andrew Low House, Savannah, 1850.
Van Jones Martin

looking animals, looking as melancholy and lazy as boiled cod-fish." James Silk Buckingham saw them near Macon in 1839: "The appearance of nearly all the men we saw from the country was reckless, dirty, dissipated, and vulgar." Fredrika Bremer saw them in 1850: "One day I went to see, in the forest, some of the poor people, a kind of wretched white people, who live in the woods, without churches, without schools, without hearths, and sometimes, also, without homes." John Brown, a fugitive slave from Georgia, remembered poor whites, too proud or unable to work, who induced the slaves to steal corn and chickens from plantations for them. Charles Ball, another fugitive slave, wrote about the poor whites of Georgia: "There is no order of men in any part of the United States who are in a more debased and humiliated state of moral servitude than are those white people who inhabit that part of the southern country, where the landed property is all, or nearly all, held by the great planters." These people were still leading frontier lives.

Considering the state's slow material and social progress, the handful of rich and accomplished men who built Georgia's cities, railroads, its agricultural, medical, historical and literary societies were truly exceptional men. Thomas Spalding of Sapelo was an inventive genius of truly Jeffersonian dimensions who lived on an island off the coast of Georgia. James Hamilton Couper dispensed urbane hospitality and read from a great private library at Hopeton, his remote property on the Altamaha River in the middle of a tropical swamp. The family of Charles Jones in Liberty County were genteel, cultivated people, with a fluent and literate correspondence, despite their primitive isolation. Crawford Long, a physician who pioneered the use of anesthesia in 1842, did it in a sleepy village of Jefferson, Georgia. William Crawford emerged from the brawling politics of frontier Georgia and nearly became President of the United States. These people,

Dinglewood, Joel Hurt House, Columbus, c. 1855.
Van Jones Martin

who might take holidays at Madison Springs, Tallulah Falls or Stone Mountain, or Clarkesville in north Georgia, who imported English manners and New York furniture, who sent their sons to Princeton, Yale or, less likely, Harvard, were not a considerable number. Cities like rich Savannah, aristocratic Augusta or bustling Columbus were extraordinary urban developments in a frontier land of forests and widely dispersed plantations.

From the Revolution to the Civil War, Georgia remained a wilderness country, an undeveloped and rather primitive place. People were poor, not from the rigors of pioneer life, but from persistent failure. The land was still undeveloped and unpopulated. James Stirling wrote from Macon in 1857: "Every step one takes, one is struck with the rough look of the whole face of civilization. The country is nowhere well cleared; towns and villages are few and far between, and even those which you see have an unfinished look." William Howard Russell, a London newspaper correspondent, viewed the social landscape from his train as it moved toward Macon during the Civil War: "From the windows of the carriages we could see that the children were barefooted, shoeless, stockingless—that the people who congregate at the wooden huts and grogshops of the stations are rude, unkempt, that the villages are miserable places." The most dramatic signal of Georgia's falling outside the mainstream of American life was that the national frontier had far outdistanced Georgia and crossed the Mississippi. That national frontier, the hopeful threshold of opportunity and confidence that Southern people had glimpsed after the Revolution, had now progressed thousands of miles across the continent, leaving Georgia behind, more and more isolated for another seventy-five years.

William B. Johnston Villa, Macon, 1855.
Van Jones Martin

4. Soldiers and Civilians

THOUGH Georgia's political leaders had led the Compromise of 1850 in Congress, during the last decade before the Civil War the South's political frustrations had forged a truly regional party and the South's social fears had united white Georgians—people who really had very diverse and conflicting interests—to defend slavery. In 1860 no Republican electors appeared on the ballot in Georgia, and no votes were cast for the Republican candidate. But even before the news reached Georgia, it was recognized that Abraham Lincoln would be elected President. The political frustrations and social fears of a generation now exploded. In November, the state legislature appropriated one million dollars for military purposes, authorized a small army of ten thousand troops and called a convention of the people to decide what response Georgia should make to Lincoln's election. By the time that convention assembled at Milledgeville in January, 1861, four states—South Carolina, Mississippi, Florida and Alabama—had already seceded. The governor, two of the three justices of the State Supreme Court, the two senators and six congressmen from the state and four of the five living former governors favored immediate secession. On January 19, 1861, Georgia became the fifth state to secede from the United States. In February, the state sent delegates to form a provisional regional government at Montgomery in Alabama. Alexander Stephens of Georgia became Vice-President of the new Confederacy, and Robert Toombs of Georgia,

By defending his state's interests at the expense of the united Confederate policy, Georgia's Civil War Governor Joseph E. Brown helped undermine the Southern war effort. *University of Georgia Library*

The first flag of Georgia's independence was raised in
Johnson Square, Savannah, in November, 1860. *Lithograph by R. H. Howell, Private Collection*

THUNDERBOLT. BATTERY.

There was little military action in Georgia early in the Civil War. These soldiers at Thunderbolt Battery outside Savannah in 1861 idle away their time by fishing, sailing and sunning themselves. *Drawing by W. D. Grant, Private Collection*

who had expected to become its President, was made Secretary of State. Georgians and Southerners were gripped by thrilling but contradicting emotions of excitement and fear, patriotism and selfishness which they could not perhaps understand.

In January, 1861, a cheerful band of Georgia volunteers sailed down the Savannah River to capture Fort Pulaski, on Cockspur Island at the mouth of the river, before the federal government could fortify it, and their happy, holiday mood demonstrated sadly that they did not foresee the bitter, bloody war ahead of them. William Plane of Baker County expressed the mock-heroic spirit: "'Tis glorious to die for one's country and in defense of innocent girls and women from the fangs of the lecherous Northern hirelings!" Eddie Neufville of Savannah, then a student at Princeton, wrote home: "Won't it be glorious to meet once more in the Republic of Georgia to fight for our Altars and our fires, God and our native land!!! By God that's bully!!! If those infernal Yankees don't get more hot lead than they can digest in a year, then I don't know anything about Southern pluck and shooting!" J. A. Hardee wrote: "I bet, by George, it won't be long before we give the Yankees *hell*!" The South was rushing to secession, confident that a strong show of force would push the other side to compromise and that any war would be brief.

The plain people of the South were also demonstrating that they valued something more than their own lives by, literally, dying to fight. A Georgia volunteer fighting in Virginia, Shephard Pryor, wrote to his wife in July, 1861: "If I fall in this struggle, I feel that I fall in a good cause." K. T. Pound wrote his parents from camp in September: "I tell you, I shall feel like I am fighting for home, sweet home." Benjamin Moody wrote in October: "The sweeter the country will seem to us when we gain our independence. I think when we gain our independence and get back home we will have a jubilee and say truly, 'Our country!' and live a happy people." Shephard Pryor wrote his wife in February, 1862: "As for myself, I expect to live in a noble country, my native South, and [see] her free or die in her cause. It is for my country, for you and for our children that I enlist to fight in this war." William Stillwell wrote his wife from the front in August, 1863: "I may fall in the next engagement, God only knows. But if I do, I hope I am ready. I feel that I will die in a just cause. If I die, it will be in defense of my country and the liberty of my people." In April, 1861, the Cuthbert Rifles were drilling day and night with eighty-four volunteers—"some very awkward ones," including the local music teacher. Theodore Fogle and other recruits at Tybee Island were as happy and excited as "a pasul of schoolboys on a holiday." Sentiment in favor of secession was strong throughout the state, except in mountainous north Georgia.

After gathering at railheads, Georgia volunteers, armed with an odd assortment of old muskets, hunting rifles and English pistols, and often uniformed in red or blue cloth or local militia outfits (the official gray never became universal because of shortages), carrying sermons against gambling, swearing, drinking and whoring, were ready to go to the Virginia front. Benjamin Mobley confessed to his mother in August, 1861: "Do you think hard of me [for] not telling you good-by? I did not wish to bid you and Sue farewell weeping." All along the route from Georgia to Virginia, excited crowds were waiting to see and cheer the soldiers. In South Carolina, William Batts of Smithville found ladies waiting at the railroad station with large tubs, jars and cans full of buttermilk and teacakes by the baskets full. Ivy Duggan saw demonstrations of affection and patriotism everywhere from Sandersville to Manassas: "Ladies waved their handkerchiefs, bonnets, flowers, secession aprons, flags with both hands. Little boys stand beside the road and [shout], 'Hurrah for Jeff Davis and the Southern Confederacy!'"

B. E. Yerby found the streets of Richmond crowded with people: "When we marched through there, they poked their heads out of the windows and doors and squalled out, 'Hurray for Georgia! Bring me

Josh, a slave, went to war with his master. *Georgia Department of Archives and History*

Volunteer soldiers from Floyd County, c. 1861. *Georgia Department of Archives and History*

a scalp when you come back!" In Virginia the volunteers were greeted with brass bands, parades in front of pretty girls, inspections by generals dressed in splendid uniforms, inspiring speeches by prominent officials. Soldiers from Georgia could see their leaders at close range. Theodore Fogle described President Davis as "a dried-up specimen of humanity . . . the God of famine." John Wood described Robert E. Lee as "a gray-and bald-headed, wise-looking old man." New horizons were opening to farm boys who had been drawn from routine lives in isolated communities to help make history and create a new nation. Hundreds of miles from home, visiting cities with fancy shops and strange people, rubbing elbows with soldiers from every state in the new Confederacy, watching long trains of wagons and horses wind 'round and through Virginia mountains, surveying horsemen splash into shimmering silver water as they forded a river, with colors flying and gun barrels flashing in the sunlight, Georgia "boys" suddenly realized, perhaps for the first time in all the confusion, that a new Southern nation was being born.

The people of Georgia embraced secession hastily and without preparation, because they did not expect any war. Georgia simply lacked the population, capital and experience of manufacturing industry necessary to wage a war. During the 1820's the state legislature had laid out inland towns at the headwaters of the major rivers, the most interior places where ships from the coast could navigate. The first steamers did not travel to Macon until 1829 and regular service did not commence until the early 1830's. The new cities, Columbus and Macon, with older Augusta, were centers for local cotton markets. They became manufacturing towns only incidentally, putting to good use the water power and cotton supplies close at hand. The major railroads in Georgia were chartered in the 1830's, their main routes completed in the 1840's and short routes added in the 1850's. But these railroads merely replaced the steamboats, which had replaced the pole

Harrison Nations of Whitfield County bristled with the weapons of war—a rifle, bayonet, a pistol and a knife.
Georgia Department of Archives and History

barges, serving the needs of agriculture and not diversified commerce. The rapid economic expansion of Georgia during the 1850's was limited to grain milling, lumbering and cotton manufacturing.

Three generations of Georgians had invested almost everything in land, slaves and cotton. Georgia was the largest state east of the Mississippi, but its population was small and sparsely settled. Agriculture had meant a static economic tradition. The undeveloped industrial economy, the region's reputation for slavery and the few job opportunities all discouraged the migration of skilled artisans and workers to Georgia, another element of a cycle of limited growth and opportunity. The cheapness of labor made inventiveness and machinery unnecessary. In 1860 there were only four cities in Georgia with more than 5,000 people, and only 4.9 percent of the people of Georgia lived in them. Only 11,575, or 1.9 percent of Georgians worked at manufacturing jobs. In 1860, only $10,890,975 was invested in industry, while $202,694,855 was invested in slaves. At the war's outbreak there was no heavy industry in Georgia, except three foundries in Macon which made railroad supplies, so the state found herself engaged in a war without the means to wage it. Governor Brown appealed to the people to turn in their hunting guns for the state's defense. The difficulty of securing firearms became so great that the governor raised a battalion of troops armed only with wooden pikes. Because they were so poorly equipped, many of Georgia's first recruits were not accepted by the Confederate government. At Savannah, Josiah Tattnall took command of a "mosquito fleet" of four ships —an old paddle-wheeled passenger steamer and three remodelled tugboats—Georgia's entire "navy" in 1861 and a further reflection of the state's economic situation.

The self-imposed isolation of secession compelled Georgia to become more self-sufficient. All kinds of miscellaneous products which

Fort McAllister, on the Ogeechee River outside Savannah, 1864.
Library of Congress

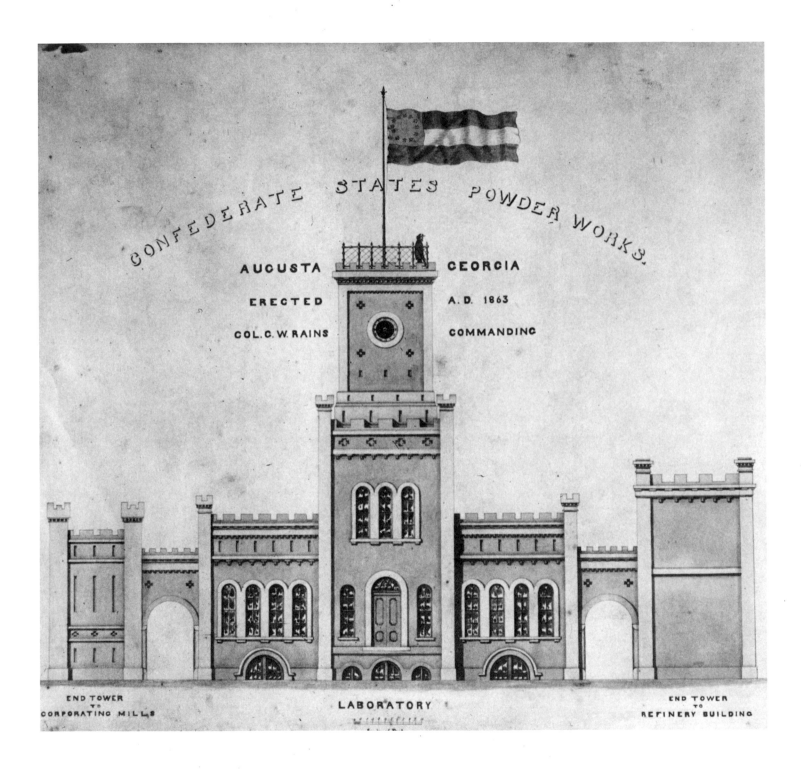

Georgia, an agrarian and rural state, hastened to industrialize. The Confederate States Powder Works was built at Augusta. *Private Collection*

had been imported—like furniture, coffins, matches, ink and paper, glass, medicines and farm machinery—now had to be produced within the state. The tremendous public spending of the war stimulated Georgia's economic development. Mechanics and factory workers were exempt from the Confederate draft. The state government established a powder mill and gunshop at Augusta, a cannon factory at Rome, others at Athens, Milledgeville, Columbus and Macon. In 1861 the legislature offered ten thousand dollars to anyone who would build a cannon factory. Arsenals were set up in Atlanta, Savannah, Macon, Augusta and Columbus, and the state penitentiary at Milledgeville was converted into a rifle factory in 1862. Confederate quartermasters built garment shops at Augusta, Atlanta and Columbus. There was not only more economic development during the war but also a different quality of growth. Significantly, while no new cotton mills were opened in Georgia, eight new iron mining companies were chartered during 1861–63. True industrial products were made in Georgia for the first time. Factories which had made only the simplest railroad supplies before 1861 now produced other machinery and equipment. Atlanta's rolling mill, no longer just reworking railroad iron, began making heavy plate for gunboats. The Athens Foundry became a cannon factory. The static inertia of agrarian life close to the land was disrupted by the war, as people moved to the cities and turned to factory work. Georgia society became more specialized with professionals, producers and consumers. The Civil War, the first "modern war," brought the industrial revolution to Georgia.

The war stimulated production of farm products across the Georgia countryside, and wartime restrictions on cotton planting prodded reluctant farmers to diversify their crops. From the mountains to the coast, Georgia became a vast harvest land of corn, wheat, sugar, lumber, rice and livestock. The well-filled corn, wheat and oat cribs which Sherman's army found proved Georgia's agricultural productivity, even while distant Virginia was suffering. Fenwick Hedley, who marched with Sherman, called Georgia "literally a land overflowing with milk and honey." Nineteen-year-old Jezze Dozer of Illinois wrote from Big Shanty, Georgia: "I went and got some apples and kooked them for supper. The wheat is getting nearly ripe. Corn knee high. Our teemsters are reeping the wheat and feeding it to their teems. The Citizens here think the yankees are harvesting their wheat too soon." Dolly Lunt Burge faced the bluecoat invasion at Covington: "Like demons they rush in! To my smoke-house, my dairy, pantry, kitchen, and cellar, like famished wolves they come, breaking locks and whatever is in their way. The thousand pounds of meat in my smoke-house is gone in a twinkling, my flour, my meat, my lard, butter, eggs, pickles, wine are all gone. My eighteen fat turkies, my hens, chickens, and fowls, my young pigs are shot down in my yard." John Van Duser, a Union officer, recorded: "I have never seen a country better supplied than this—Turkeys Chickens Geese beef Cattle Sheep & swine in abundance. The story of starvation in the South is played out." From Savannah George Hanger wrote his family in Ohio: "Does every body talk of starving out the rebel army? If so, I think that if they had of been on this trip it would make converts of them. Of all the sweet potatoes and molasses that I ever saw, this state beats them all."

The future site of Atlanta had been uninhabited Indian territory until 1821, but the economic impact of the war transformed the place into a boom town with the prospect of future greatness. During the early 1840's three converging railroads—the Western and Atlantic to Chattanooga and the Midwest, the Georgia Railroad to Augusta and South Carolina, the Macon and Western Railroad south toward the coast—came together at a village first called "Terminus." Before the W&A was built and attention was riveted on the new town of Atlanta,

Fort Pulaski, built by the Federal government on Cockspur
Island near Savannah over a prolonged period 1828–47,
was ocupied by Georgia volunteers in January, 1861. *Fort
Pulaski National Monument*

The Federal fleet had come to the Southern coast in late 1861, and their gunboats began roaming up the Savannah River and, here, the Ogeechee River, where the Union ironclad *Montauk* attacked the Confederate steamship *Nashville* in February, 1863. *Lithograph by Currier and Ives, Museum of the City of New York*

most people in Georgia expected Macon, at the center of the state, to become the state's great city and next capital. Robert Somers, who came to Atlanta in 1870, caught the spirit of Atlanta's birth: "The various railroads which meet at this crowded point do not go to the town; the town is gathering in thick and hot haste about the railways." One local citizen boasted, "I guess the railways were here before the people came to Atlanta . . . the new city rising up around the place where it was convenient for the locomotives to be fed with wood and water." In 1847 Atlanta was still a shanty town of twenty-five hundred inhabitants, thirty stores, two hotels, surrounded by woods, the streets filled with stumps but alive with people and progress. There were no churches then and preaching was held, prophetically, in the railroad depot. Charles Olmstead remembered Atlanta in the 1850's as "a sorry-looking place, always associated in my mind with rain and a super abundance of red-clay mud." Felix DeFontaine, war correspondent of the Charleston *Courier*, complained in March, 1862, that Atlanta's sea of mud was "six inches deep and rising." Pedestrians were cautioned to cross streets only on stepping-stones which rose above the mire, and gentlemen were obliged to tuck their trousers into their boots. In 1861, Atlanta's promoters made a determined, though unsuccessful, effort to make their city the capital of the new Confederacy. There were so many strangers coming to Atlanta during the busy war years that street signs had to be put up for the first time. Atlanta's population increased from 11,468 in 1860 to more than 16,000 before the war's end. In a new era of interstate commerce inaugurated by the Civil War, Atlanta would become the great regional distribution center of the South. Significantly, railroad mileage in Georgia increased thirty percent during the decade of the Civil War, despite the considerable destruction at the close of that struggle. Sherman's burning of Atlanta in 1864 was the most dramatic possible recognition of the city's growing importance.

There was no sustained military action in Georgia until Sherman entered the state in May, 1864, though the war had raged in Virginia, Tennessee and Mississippi for three cruel, destructive years. The uncooperative, independent policies of Georgia's Governor Joseph E. Brown were, for the Confederate government at Richmond, nagging and insulting evidence of Georgia's wartime isolation and prosperity: Brown interfered with Confederate conscription agents trying to raise troops in Georgia, he withdrew Georgia troops from Confederate service, he forbade the transportation of firearms beyond state lines, he insisted on naming the officers in Georgia's units of the Confederate Army, he exempted large numbers of persons from Confederate military service so he could keep them within Georgia to defend his own state, he instigated abortive peace negotiations with General Sherman near the end of the war, he led a fierce personal attack on Jefferson Davis.

In October, 1861, a fleet of forty-one federal ships had sailed to Port Royal in South Carolina and, after forcing the Confederates to a hasty retreat, the invaders landed just twenty-five miles from Savannah. By December the Federal forces had surrounded the mouth of the Savannah River and enemy gunboats began cruising around the coastal islands of Georgia. In April, 1862, Fort Pulaski was captured, sealing the blockade of the port of Savannah. But the Federals never tried to attack the city from the sea. There were minor military episodes along the coast. In April, 1862, Federals and Confederates tangled at Whitemarsh Island; in March, 1863, Northern troops tried without success to dislodge the Confederates at Fort McAllister, an earthenwork fortification on the Ogeechee River outside Savannah; in June, 1863, the Federals destroyed a bridge over the Turtle River near Brunswick; and in July, 1863, the coastal town of Darien was burned. In north Georgia there were two attempts to cut the Western and Atlantic Railroad. In

In April, 1863, after surrounding the garrison, the Federal forces bombarded Fort Pulaski. Modern rifled cannon ripped open the walls of the supposedly impregnable brick fortification. *Library of Congress*

April, 1862, Captain James Andrews led twenty soldiers disguised as civilians in the daring theft of a train parked outside Marietta. The raiders fled toward Tennessee, destroying bridges and tracks behind them, until their engine ran out of fuel and they were captured. In April, 1863, Abel D. Streight and his cavalry of sixteen hundred men were repulsed near Rome and captured just across the Alabama line by Nathan Bedford Forrest. In September, 1863, a terrible battle was fought at Chickamauga Creek, but it was part of the Tennessee campaign around Chattanooga and took place only incidentally in Georgia. In the early spring of 1865, months after Sherman had left Georgia and a week after Lee's surrender, General James M. Wilson made a cavalry raid from Columbus to Macon.

But the people of Georgia did join in the war and suffer, if from a distance. About 125,000 Georgians fought in the Civil War, and about 25,000 of them were killed. In 1870 there would be 10,000 *fewer* young white men in Georgia, twenty to twenty-nine years of age, than there had been in 1860. Richard Malcolm Johnston wrote to Alexander Stephens in 1861: "It is a sad sight to see our young men go away to war, and to hear the lamentations of mothers, wives and sisters. I have seen three companies go away already." A Butts County wife, named Mollie Evans, wrote her husband in 1863: "I am very lonesom evry Sunday since you left. I am lonesom all the time but I am worse evry Sunday. I wish you was her to go to meeting with me to morrow and next day. I had rather you were home and I and you living in A doll house then to live in the finest house in the state with out you present. I think of you often in the day and my last words at night is A prayer in behalf of you." William Fisher of Baker County wrote his wife in June and July, 1862, from Virginia: "I cannot describe the battle field. I would to God it could be the last & our country saved. . . . The dead lying all around, your foes unburied. The stiffened bodies lie, grasping

Top: More than two thousand slaves were conscripted from nearby plantations to build emergency fortifications around Savannah in 1863. Bottom: Hundreds of slaves straggled behind Sherman's army as it marched across Georgia in 1864. Woodcuts from pictorial newspapers. *New York Public Library (top), Private Collection (bottom)*

in death the arms they bravely bore, with glazed eyes and features blackened by rapid decay. The air is putrid with decaying bodies of men & horses. My god, My God, what a scourge is war."

Angus McDermid, a farmer's son from Adel, Georgia, entered the army in 1861, with the girls waving handkerchiefs as he marched in parade. At training camp he tasted barracks life: "We are all hear in a house some fiddling and some playing cards and some cussing. . . . Cussing I never did hear the like in all my life." In November, 1861, he heard the mutter of federal cannon at Sapelo Island and shuddered: "I am willing to dy on the battle field if it is my lot. A many a por fellow died on the battle field las Thursday but it is an honerable death to them." Hospitalized in July, 1862: "Now I will tell you what a sick man gets to eat hear. They get one cracker and a cup of coffee and a sick man cant eat that for I cant when I am well. You may no that we fair like dogs hear." The war brought Angus maturity, April, 1863: "Oh father, your letter how sad I felt after I red it. I could not read it without crying for it put me in remembrance of what a bad boy I hav bin in my life and is yet but I have quit a heepe of my wayes and is more sturdy than I was." In July, 1863, there was a bombardment: "I was in five foot of Major Lain when he was killed. His whole head was shot off. His brains flew all over several of us. I never got hit with any ball but a miner ball went through my hair and Mother let me tell you I was hid behind a house one time when the shells was a falling thicker than hail." After the battle of Chickamauga Angus was homesick, September, 1863: "I never did want to go home so bad in all my life as I do now. I think while I was at home I thought that it was a bad place, but I was a fool for thinking so. Home is the best place in this world that I ever hav seen." In November, 1863: "I was glad to get the sox but I cant ware them til I get shoes." In March, 1864, desertions increased: "The Jeneral . . . had a man Branded yesterday on the left hip with a letter D

Union soldiers pose proudly with the cannons in captured Fort Pulaski, 1863. *New-York Historical Society*

Over 13,000 Union prisoners died at Andersonville Prison, outside Macon. *Lithograph by John Walker, Library of Congress*

for deserting." Near Marietta, June, 1864: "I am so black and dirty the clothes that I hav got on me I hav had on 7 weeks. I haint got no cloths only what is on me." After the battles for Atlanta in September, 1864: "I went over the Battle ground since the fite. I tell you the men is their thick and a little dirt put on them. It smells awful shore. I cant stand hardly to smell a dead man and dead horses." Marching in October, 1864, northwest of Atlanta: "In these 3 days march we have lost some where a bout 6000 our men deserted. . . . Mother I am a heep harder hearted than I ought to be but I hav seen so many men killed and wounded till I dont care for it no more than if it was a chicken." Angus died in December, 1864, fighting in Alabama.

By the end of 1864, the Civil War was rushing to a conclusion and the Confederacy was fast disintegrating. During the autumn, General William T. Sherman with sixty-two thousand men, thirty-five thousand horses, mules and cattle, twenty-five hundred wagons, six hundred ambulances and a horde of stragglers marched across the heart of Georgia. His purpose was to destroy the enemy's economic system and to demoralize the civilians. Already Union forces held the Mississippi River and territory north of Vicksburg and St. Louis in the West and everything north of the Tennessee River and most of Tennessee and Virginia in the East. All the Confederate seaports had been blockaded and outside Atlanta Sherman heard first news that Farragut had entered Mobile Bay. While Sherman was penetrating into Georgia, Grant was advancing on Richmond. In the North, Sherman's triumphant procession through Georgia in the bosom of the South strengthened the war party at a critical time and insured President Lincoln's reelection in November. In the South, the march brought an apocalyptic revelation that the war had been lost.

In May, 1864, General Sherman's army left Tennessee and crossed into Georgia. Chauncey Cook, a seventeen-year-old soldier from Wis-

General William T. Sherman, c. 1865.
Library of Congress

consin, wrote from north Georgia, explaining the situation to his parents: "If we can take Atlanta, now the strongest fortified city in the South, we can march to the sea, and then [say] good-bye to the rebellion." The march would follow the Western and Atlantic Railroad from Chattanooga to Atlanta, the Macon and Western Railroad from Atlanta toward Macon and the Central Railroad to Savannah. In the north Georgia mountains, the Union army of ninety-nine thousand faced an inferior Confederate force of forty-four thousand. The Confederate commander, Joseph E. Johnston, tried to avoid direct tests of strength, carefully choosing well-defended ground, fading and dodging back behind destroyed bridges and railroads, while Sherman's greater force was able to outflank the rebels and push them back relentlessly toward Atlanta. On June 27 Sherman launched a costly and unsuccessful direct assault on Kennesaw Mountain, which was held by the Confederates, but by again outflanking them he forced Johnston's men into Atlanta's trenches, the final retreat. On July 17, Johnston was relieved of command by President Jefferson Davis. The new commander, John B. Hood, attempted to regain the initiative with two disastrous, impulsive offensives at Peachtree Creek and Ezra Church during the last days of July. After Sherman had bombarded Atlanta for forty days, part of the federal force swung around south of the city, threatening the Confederate supply routes leading to Macon. When Hood found he could not check this Union force at Jonesboro, he was compelled to evacuate Atlanta on September 1.

These mountain campaigns brought the terrible horror of the Civil War home to Georgia. The soldiers faced wild, desperate dashes across picket lines, under screaming artillery shells and shrapnel, struggling through obstructions, tripping, falling, rising to fall again, rushing on toward more intense gunfire and the probability of death. Theodore Upson, a nineteen-year-old Indiana volunteer, recorded the action in mid-August: "Yesterday the Johnnies attacked us with a

On June 27, 1864, General Sherman launched a costly
and unsuccessful assault on Kennesaw Mountain, but by
flanking the Confederates he forced them to make a final
retreat into Atlanta. *Drawing by William Waud, Library
of Congress*

The Confederate lines outside Atlanta, 1864.
George Barnard, Library of Congress

heavy force. They charged our works. We could see them plainly. Orders were given to hold our fire till they got close. When we did open up their lines seemed to melt away. Time after time those brave desperate men tried to advance their line, but it was of no use." The troops, many of them boys, were offered liquor to stiffen their courage before battle. Union veterans remembered how the Confederates, like men who knew they were throwing away their lives, would charge with their hats pulled down low over their eyes, so they could not see the certain destruction awaiting them. At Dalton in April, Benjamin Smith of Illinois found unburied Union dead, lying naked in the hot blistering sun, stripped of clothing by the retreating rebels. Near Marietta, Sherman wrote his wife at the end of that brutal summer: "It is enough to make the whole world start at the awful amount of death and destruction that now stalks abroad. I begin to regard the death and mangling of a couple of thousand men as a small affair, a kind of morning dash—and it may be well that we become so hardened." From May to September, 4,988 Union soldiers and 3,044 Confederates were killed in Georgia. In July and August, 62,750 northern and 46,332 southern soldiers were hospitalized—one in every two Confederates and one in every three Federals each month. Malaria, typhoid fever, diarrhea, dysentery, exposure, measles, chicken pox did the work which battle wounds could not accomplish.

As Sherman's army advanced, the Georgians fell back in dismay. From Marietta, Sherman wrote his wife: "We have devoured the land. All the people retire before us and desolation is behind. To realize what war is one should follow our tracks." In Marietta there was confusion and panic, the Sisters of Charity loading hospital bedsteads and mattresses into wagons, slaves staggering under burdens of hastily assembled belongings and locomotives steaming up and down the tracks. Minerva McClatchey, who chose to remain at Marietta while her husband fled to south Georgia, saw alarmed citizens with slaves,

A panoramic view of Atlanta, seen from the top of the
Female Seminary, showing the area from the Medical
College on the left to Peachtree Street on the right, in
October, 1864. *Library of Congress*

horses, cows, hogs and sheep racing ahead of Sherman, heard picket guns and skirmishing in the surrounding woods, with the shrieks and cries of wounded soldiers who passed on ambulances, and finally faced an invasion of rough, strange men. The roads into Atlanta were lined with carcasses of horses, hogs and cattle, and the air was heavy with the stench of death and gunpowder. As Sherman's triumphant army passed, the sallow, defeated poor whites watched from the sides of the roads. When Chauncey Cook of Wisconsin tried to offer people Confederate money, they merely smiled sadly and shook their heads. James Patton, an Indiana doctor who had joined Sherman at Chattanooga, saw a young woman on the roadside before Atlanta, skinning a dead cow, while her starving little girl tore at the raw, bloody meat with both hands. Jezze Dozer, that Illinois boy, wrote from outside Atlanta in July: "I could see a sad heart in every man's face."

As refugees and soldiers began to fall back into beleaguered Atlanta, emergency hospitals were set up in the streets. Kate Cumming, a Confederate nurse, found herself surrounded by hundreds of dirty, bleeding and weary soldiers. At times physicians had only old tent cloth to bandage wounds, and the soldiers were eating with their fingers because there were no dishes, knives or forks. Rufus Mead of Connecticut described such a frantic hospital scene on the Union side after the battles for Atlanta: "The poor fellows lay there wounded in every part of the body, some crazy & raving and others suffering all that mortals can. Doctors were busy cutting off limbs which were piled up in heaps to be carried off and buried, while the stench even then was horrible. Flies were flying around in swarms and maggots were crawling in wounds before the Drs could get time to dress them." In Atlanta, ten-year-old Carrie Berry huddled in her basement, while exploding shells fell in the garden outside. As trainloads of wounded soldiers fled Atlanta, the Female College and most of the churches in

Federal pickets outside Atlanta, 1864.
George Barnard, Library of Congress

The ruins of central Atlanta, 1864.
George Barnard, Library of Congress

Macon were turned into hospitals, and when there was no more shelter in Macon, more hospitals were established at Milledgeville. When Macon was evacuated a few weeks later, Eliza Andrews would see houses boarded up, ragged foot soldiers ready to march but not knowing where, fearful civil officials emptying liquor into the gutters.

General Hood abandoned Atlanta on September 1, after destroying eighty-one carloads of ammunition. Outside the city, Sherman's soldiers could hear the blasts and see the red glow of fire from these explosions. In a few weeks the city's population had dropped from more than sixteen thousand to less than three thousand. General W. P. Howard reported to Governor Brown how he had discovered two hundred and fifty wagons of deserters, stragglers and country people plundering Atlanta during that quiet interlude, like the eye of a hurricane, between the Confederate retreat and the federal advance. Sherman's army found the houses perforated with shells and trees splintered with cannon balls. Sherman ordered the civilians to leave the city, offering them transportation to the North or to a neutral camp, called Rough-and-Ready, if they were determined to flee farther south. On November 15, as his army was preparing to leave the city, Sherman ordered his chief engineer to destroy by powder and fire the depot, storehouses and machine shops of Atlanta. Buildings which would not burn were demolished with battering rams. Drunken soldiers, flanked on both sides by burning buildings, raced up and down the streets on foot or horseback. Sherman's aide George Nichols recorded the scene: "The heaven is one expanse of lurid fire; the air is filled with flying, burning cinders; buildings covering two hundred acres are in ruins or in flames; every instant there is the sharp detonation or smothered burning sound of exploding shells and powder concealed in the buildings, and then the sparks and flame shoot away up into the black and red roof, scattering the cinders far and wide." Henry Hitchcock, Sherman's adjutant, saw "the grandest and most awful scene . . . immense and raging fires, lighting up the whole heavens. First bursts of smoke, dense, black volumes, then tongues of flame, then huge waves of fire roll into the sky; presently the skeletons of great warehouses stand out in relief against and amidst the sheets of roaring, blazing, furious flames. Now and then there are heavy explosions; it is a line of fire and smoke, lurid, angry, dreadful to look upon." Most of the central part of the city, but not all of Atlanta, was burned. James Patton glanced back toward the city as the federal army departed on November 15, and, in the brilliant glow of the flaming ruins: "We could see Atlanta burning. I looked at my watch and could see the time very plainly at a distance of ten miles."

Sherman abandoned his supply lines in Tennessee, cut the telegraph wires and moved boldly into the interior of Georgia. For nearly a month the people of the North knew what his army was doing only from reports in Confederate newspapers. From Atlanta the Union army marched in three parallel columns, five to fifteen miles apart, forming a thirty- to sixty-mile front, making good ten to fifteen miles each day across country. The right wing, commanded by Major-General Oliver Howard, moved through Jonesboro, Monticello, Gordon, Irwinton. The left wing under Major-General H. W. Slocum headed to Covington, Madison, Eatonton, Milledgeville. Brigadier-General Judson Kilpatrick led cavalry which struck toward Macon, fell back to Gordon and rejoined Sherman at Milledgeville. The governor and legislature, then in session, hastily abandoned the state capital. The governor pardoned all prisoners in the penitentiary who would join the militia. Sherman's army entered Milledgeville on November 22, burning the depot, arsenal and penitentiary and blowing up the magazine, but not destroying the capitol itself or the governor's mansion. Federal soldiers held a mock session of the legislature and repealed the secession ordinance. The army marched to Sandersville, Louisville and Millen, where the railroad depot was burned on

On December 13, 1864, the Federal forces captured Fort McAllister, the last impediment to Sherman's entry into Savannah. *A. S. Cooley, Library of Congress*

Sherman entered Savannah in late December, 1864, and
reviewed his triumphant troops in front of the U.S. Custom House on Bay Street. *Drawing by William Waud,
Library of Congress*

December 3. On December 13, federal forces under General W. B. Hazen attacked and captured Fort McAllister, a simple earthenwork fortification on the Ogeechee River which separated Sherman's army from the federal fleet off the Georgia coast. During the dark night of December 20, the Confederates abandoned Savannah, retreating silently across the river on pontoon bridges which had been strewn with rice straw to muffle the sound of horses and wagons. Early the next morning the citizens of Savannah surrendered their city without vain resistance, and Sherman dispatched his famous wire to President Lincoln: "I beg to present to you as a Christmas gift the city of Savannah, with one hundred and fifty heavy guns and plenty of ammunition, also about twenty-five thousand bales of cotton."

For the federal army, the march through Georgia was, as one soldier described it, "one big picnic." Sherman's men had tramped from Atlanta to the sea without opposition. There had been only women and children, most of them hiding. There had been plenty of food, the war seemed to be ending and the mood of the victorious army was jubilant. George Bradley, a Wisconsin chaplain, wrote from the outskirts of Milledgeville in late November: "The soldiers seem cheerful and happy, and all, or nearly all, are pleased to have a part in this, the *grandest affair* of the whole war. I heard one say, a day or two since, that he would not have missed it for fifty dollars." George Sharland, an Illinois private, saw his comrades burden themselves with reckless bounty, unskinned pork meat speared on the points of their bayonets, meal and flour filling their haversacks, and frying pans, coffee pots and kettles tied to their knapsacks. Rufus Mead of Connecticut summed up the march from Savannah in December: "We had a glorious old tramp right through the heart of the state, rioted and feasted on the country, destroyed all the RR, in short found a rich and overflowing country filled with cattle hogs sheep & fowls, corn sweet potatoes & syrup, but left a barren waste for miles on either side of the

Two views of the eerily still and silent river-front at Savannah, after Sherman's capture of the port in December,
1864, seen from the steeple of the City Exchange.
Library of Congress

road, burnt millions of dollars worth of property, wasted & destroyed all the eatables we couldn't carry off and brought the war to the doors of the Georgians so effectively, I guess they will long remember the Yankees. I enjoyed it all the time we had pleasant weather & good roads, & easy times generally."

The march brought disaster and the profound sorrow of defeat to the people of Georgia. Civilians saw their own troops steal and plunder. Confederate deserters and stragglers preceded and followed Sherman's army. The newspapers of Georgia and Confederate leaders called upon the people to destroy their supplies and stock to keep the invaders from getting them. Sherman estimated the destruction in Georgia at $100,000,000, of which $80,000,000 was mere waste. General Howard estimated that his wing of the army had burned 3,523 bales of cotton, carried off 9,000 head of cattle, 931 horses and 1,850 mules, consumed or destroyed 9,000,000 pounds of corn and fodder, taken up 191 miles of railroad. General Slocum estimated his wing of the army had captured or consumed 919,000 rations of bread, 1,217,527 rations of meat, 483,000 rations of coffee, 581,534 rations of sugar, 1,146,500 rations of soap, 137,000 rations of salt, 4,090 horses and mules, 11,000,000 pounds of grain and fodder, 119 miles of railroad, 17,000 bales of cotton. General Kilpatrick added 14,000 bales of cotton, 12,900 bushels of corn and 160,000 pounds of fodder. Mary Jones and her pregnant daughter faced invading bluecoats in Liberty County for a month, at times barricading themselves inside the house while strangers killed sheep, hogs and cattle outside. "Clouds and darkness are around us. The hand of the Almighty is laid in sore judgement upon us," she wrote. "We are a desolated & smitten people."

For Georgians, Sherman's march was the most famous and terrible event of their state's history, the last great act of war, the first act of Reconstruction and the symbol of more than a decade of human distress. But Sherman's "march from Atlanta to the sea" was really

General Sherman set up his headquarters at the mansion
of Charles Green, an English-born cotton merchant, built
in 1853. *Library of Congress*

General Sherman's guards and visitors loll in the entrance
hall of Charles Green's mansion in Savannah, December,
1864. *Drawing by Alfred Waud, Library of Congress*

only one part of a more important expedition which began at Chattanooga, Tennessee, in May, 1864, and which ended near Durham,
North Carolina, in April, 1865. Indeed, Sherman's army faced sustained resistance only in the mountains of north Georgia before it
reached Atlanta, and Sherman's men were able to march beyond
Atlanta to the coast without opposition. Despite the celebrated destruction of Georgia, the federal force inflicted greater damage, with
far greater personal vindictiveness, in South Carolina, the hated birth-
place of secession. In fact, the damage done by Sherman's army
extended over only a small part of Georgia, and most of the state
remained untouched by physical warfare. The march was most important as a political triumph, conceived by a military man who
distrusted politicians all his life, and as a glimpse of ruthless twentieth-
century total war, directed by a man who was himself insecure and
plagued with failure. Though the effects of Sherman's march were
computed in terms of miles and tons of physical destruction, the
greatest effects of the march were upon the people of the South and
Georgia in particular. Though the march caused Georgians to remember the years of civil war and Reconstruction as a depressing,
destructive time, Sherman's march was really the pivot point for an
era which brought the industrial revolution to Georgia and which
gave political power to the middle class for the first time, two exhil
arating, constructive social developments.

On January 21, 1865, General Sherman's army crossed the Savannah
River into South Carolina and left Georgia behind in a sea of confusion. After the fall of Richmond, the Confederate government fled
south, held its final meeting at Washington, Georgia, and Jefferson
Davis was arrested near Irwinville on May 10. Governor Brown, Vice-
President Stephens, Senator Benjamin Hill, General Howell Cobb were
also arrested. Major Henry Wirz, commander of Andersonville Prison,

was hanged at Washington. Robert Toombs fled to Europe until it was safe to return. Defeated soldiers were straggling home on foot, eating raw turnips, meat skins, parched corn, anything they could find. John Kennaway, who followed Sherman's tracks in 1865, found ruins of homes at Calhoun, blank walls and skeleton houses at Marietta, a landscape littered with broken wagons, spent ammunition, abandoned breastworks, graves and carcasses of rotting horses. But he reflected that the greatest evidence of disaster was not the ruined property or ravaged countryside, but the faces of the ruined, ravaged people of Georgia: "I do not remember to have seen a smile upon a single human face."

On April 30, General Johnston telegraphed Governor Brown that hostilities with the United States had ceased, and federal authority, already established at Macon and Savannah, was extended over the whole state during April, May and June. In May, President Johnson proclaimed James Johnson, a Columbus lawyer, the provisional governor and instructed him to call a convention of "loyal Georgians" to form a new government. In October the convention met, repealed the secession ordinance, abolished slavery and repudiated the Confederate war debt. In November, Charles Jenkins, a judge who had been a Unionist before the war, was elected governor, and a new state legislature ratified the Thirteenth Amendment and passed laws which guaranteed the civil equality of freedmen. In March, 1867, Congress passed, over the President's veto, the military reconstruction act. Georgia's first government was abolished and the state was returned to military rule. Again the state government was reorganized, with more blacks included and more whites excluded. In April, 1868, Rufus Bullock was elected governor, and in July the new legislature ratified the Fourteenth Amendment. In 1869 the Republican governor quarrelled with the conservative legislature. In December, 1869, the United States Congress again imposed military control over Georgia and the

Henry Wirz, the commander at Andersonville Prison, was hanged at Washington in 1865. *Library of Congress*

Truce boats exchanging prisoners on the Savannah River,
April, 1865. *Drawing by William Waud, Library of
Congress*

state government was reconstructed for a third time. The new legislature, which included many Negroes and Republicans who had been excluded formerly, finally ratified the Fifteenth Amendment, which guaranteed Negro suffrage. Georgia was formally readmitted to the United States in July, 1870.

Though it took more than five years for Georgia to return to the Union, Georgians had quickly regained control of their own affairs. Georgia was reconstructed three times precisely because the conservatives in the state were so powerful. The very first legislature in 1865, in a daring demonstration of strength, elected Alexander Stephens, former Vice-President of the Confederacy, and Herschel V. Johnson, former Confederate senator, to the United States Senate and seven former Confederate military officers to the U. S. House of Representatives. In October, 1866, the legislature refused to ratify the Fourteenth Amendment, which would have secured Negro civil rights. In the April, 1868, legislature, radicals and Democrats were about equally represented, and relatively few white voters had been disfranchised at this time. In September, the legislature expelled its Negro members, three state senators and twenty-five representatives. In November, the Republicans were not able to carry Georgia for Grant. In March, 1869, the state senate rejected the Fifteenth Amendment, although the house narrowly ratified it. Though the freedmen exercised a political voice briefly in 1867 and 1868, the vigilante activities of the Ku Klux Klan subdued any political revolution by blacks in Georgia. Freedmen wandered to the cities to test freedom in 1866 and 1867, but they returned to plantations as renters and croppers, and social life resumed its accustomed pace and place. In the December, 1870, election the Democrats won overwhelming control of the state legislature. Faced with probable impeachment by an angry conservative legislature, Governor Bullock resigned his office and fled from Georgia in October, 1871.

5. Farmers and Businessmen

WHAT a radiant and charming and accomplished man he was!" exclaimed Josephus Daniels, the famous North Carolina journalist, after he had met Henry Grady, the aggressive young editor of the Atlanta *Constitution* during the prosperous 1880's. Grady was a public-spirited journalist and builder of one of the great newspapers of the South. A brilliant orator, Grady became the most acclaimed southerner of his day to plead for sectional reconciliation and regional reform after the Civil War. For nearly a decade, between 1880 when he purchased an interest in the *Constitution* and 1889 when he died unexpectedly, Grady wrote and spoke of economic achievement in a poverty-stricken land, of political harmony to a generation of Georgians who had suffered conquest and occupation, and he spoke of justice for the Negro in a society where slavery had been ended only recently and reluctantly. He was a compelling representative figure, a young Southern man who stood on the threshold of maturity and faced a world which had been transformed since his childhood against the wishes of his society. Grady was, indeed, a true regional patriot, for he voiced the deep, frustrated hopes of Southern people to rejoin the mainstream of American life. The New York *Times* called him "the great interpreter of a new spirit which was awakening the South, exhorting the people to concern themselves no longer about what they had lost, but to busy themselves with what they might find to do, to consecrate the past if they would, but to put

Henry Grady, editor of the Atlanta *Constitution* and spokesman of the industrialized, liberalized New South in the 1880's. *Atlanta Constitution*

206

The commercial center of Atlanta, pictured in *Harper's Weekly*, February 19, 1887. *New York Public Library*

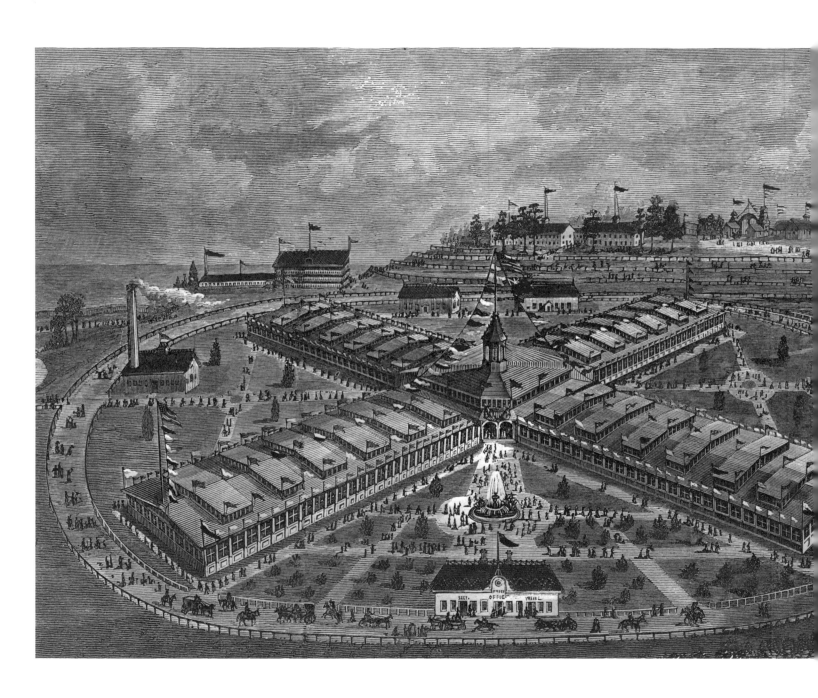

International Cotton Exposition at Atlanta, 1881, from
an illustrated newspaper of the period.
Private Collection

the whole strength of their minds and bodies into the building up of a New South."

A real social and political revolution had taken place in Georgia during the years of war and reconstruction. The Civil War had brought the industrial revolution to the South, and Reconstruction brought power to the middle class. In 1857 Joseph E. Brown, a pugnacious lawyer, once a farmer from north Georgia, had been elected governor and subsequently was reelected three more times during the war, an achievement unprecedented in the state's history. A self-made, professional man from a part of Georgia populated by independent mountaineers, who appealed to the common people for support, Brown's political success represented a shift of power from the old planters of middle Georgia. The vote for secession had been not only a defense of slavery but an assertion of economic independence for a region struggling to advance beyond a frontier, colonial status in national life. The reorganization of state government after 1865 specifically eliminated most of the old leading class—military officers above the rank of colonel, Confederate officials and men whose worth exceeded twenty thousand dollars.

The course of events during the war strengthened this new middle class at the expense of the planter class. The rapid inflation and depreciation of the currency benefitted people with debts and penalized people with money in the bank. The war destroyed the value of bank stock, railroad shares, land, slaves and Confederate bonds and currency, the wealth of rich men during the war. In the aftermath of Sherman's march, the planters were left without liquid capital or reliable labor. During the late 1860's the acreage under cultivation, the size of farm units, the value of land and crop production all declined in Georgia. At the same time, the value of taxable property in towns and cities increased from $38,000,000 to $55,000,000 between 1867 and 1872. Between 1860 and 1870 the value of farms in Georgia decreased from $157,072,803 to $94,559,468, and the value of farm machinery and equipment decreased from $6,844,387 to $4,614,701. During the same interval, the number of industrial establishments increased from 1,890 to 3,836, invested capital rose from $10,890,875 to $13,930,125, yearly industrial production expanded from $16,925,564 to $31,196,115. While the planters had been weakened, a new class of rich men whose wealth did not rest on land and slaves was strengthened.

Atlanta, which had been created and destroyed by the war, was a scene of amazing recovery. In the midst of crumbling walls, solitary chimneys and charred timbers, the city was fast rebuilding. Sidney Andrews described the scene in November, 1865: "From all this ruin and devastation a new city is springing up with marvellous rapidity. The streets are alive from morning 'till night with drays and carts and hand-barrows and wagons, hauling teams and shouting men, with loads of lumber and loads of brick and loads of sand, with piles of furniture and hundreds of packed boxes, with mortar-makers and carpenters and masons, with rubbish removers and house-builders, with a never-ending throng of pushing and crowding and scrambling and eager and excited and enterprising men, all bent on building and trading and swift fortune-making." People were living in shacks and tents, establishing stores in half-roofed houses. In 1867 a Milledgeville newspaper complained: "Atlanta is certainly a fast place in every sense of the word, and our friends in Atlanta are a fast people. They live fast, and they die fast. They make money fast, and they spend it fast. To a stranger, the whole city seems to be running on wheels, and all of the inhabitants continually blowing off steam." The center of Atlanta was described in December, 1865, by a visitor: "The middle of the city is a great open space of irregular shape, a wilderness of mud, with a

A bustling, and somewhat messy, Atlanta in 1908.
Atlanta Historical Society

confused jumble of railway sheds, and traversed by numberless rails, rusted and splashed, where strings of dirty cars are standing, and engines constantly puff and . . . resounds with the noise of carpenters and engines." Elizabeth Sterchi, a middle-aged Swiss schoolteacher who found herself in Georgia in 1868, called Atlanta "the great Babylon," overrun at night with rowdy men and bawdy women. "Atlanta is crowded with poor people piled one on another, perfect heathen in a civilized country. . . . The God of Atlanta," she wrote, "is money." Atlanta's business leaders were a new breed of middle-class industrialists and professional men, while the older generation of agrarian statesmen were aristocrats and conservative landowners. Atlanta was promoted as "a new place— modern, democratic—a fresh production, wholly practical, without antiquities or prejudices." Atlanta's population increased from thirty-seven thousand in 1880 to ninety thousand in 1900. Early in its history, during the Civil War and New South, Atlanta had already become the confident, progressive, boastful and materialistic city that it remains today.

Joseph E. Brown urged the people to accept each new plan of Congressional Reconstruction, no matter how repugnant or severe the terms and no matter how expedient the cooperation, on the grounds that recovery in the future was more important than loyalty to a lost past. The new promoters conspired with the Republicans who brought power with them to Atlanta. In 1867 the governor of the Third Military District brought his headquarters from Montgomery to Atlanta. In 1868 the Republican administration moved the state capital from Milledgeville to Atlanta. The city's industrialists were financial partners with political leaders who were hated by most Georgians. Hannibal Kimball, who came to Georgia from Chicago in 1866, became the city's most famous tycoon, constructing a new state capitol and an elegant hotel in Atlanta. Republican Governor Bullock issued state bonds worth more than thirty million dollars to finance Kimball's

The market place of a Georgia village during the cotton season, *Harper's Weekly*, February 12, 1887. *Private Collection*

railroads. The new leaders of Atlanta welcomed the return of Republicans to the city after the end of Reconstruction, and even Bullock was able to return to Atlanta and resume his business career in later years, despite charges of corruption which forced him to flee Georgia in 1871. Joe Brown announced in the North that his state wanted a great importation of "Yankee energy, Yankee enterprise, Yankee education, and Yankee business sense." In 1881 Atlanta became the scene of an International Cotton Exposition, designed to promote industry and investment in Georgia. The most famous stockholder of that enterprise, the man most celebrated and lionized when he reached Atlanta, was former General William T. Sherman. At last, the forces of economic and social change which came to Georgia during the Civil War and Reconstruction years had produced this happy, if ironic, reconciliation.

Money meant power, and power meant money. Grady's *Constitution* moralized: "Business is the biggest thing in this country. When the princes of commerce and industry say to the politicians that they must let dangerous experiments alone they will be heard and obeyed. Politicians may talk, but businessmen will act, control and dominate the destinies of this common sense country." Grady expressed this philosophy another way when he said, "The New South represents a perfect democracy, the oligarchs leading in the popular movement." "Atlanta is now the political power of the state concentrated in the hands of a few men," their critics cried. "Is Atlanta the state? And are the people willing to submit to the concentration of power in Atlanta and to the monopoly of all the important offices in the hands of a few men?" The new Atlanta ring was led by former Governor Joseph E. Brown, Confederate General John B. Gordon and planter-businessman Alfred H. Colquitt, with Henry Grady their spokesman. Colquitt and Gordon each served two terms as governor; between 1872 and

Cotton market scene, probably Marietta, c. 1900.
Georgia Department of Archives and History

Unidentified rural Georgia family, c. 1900.
University of Georgia Library

1890 Brown or Gordon held one of Georgia's Senate seats and, after the end of his second term as governor in 1882, Colquitt held the other. Two splinter political groups—the Independents of the 1870's, led by William H. Felton, and the Populists of the 1890's, led by Tom Watson—challenged but failed to upset this domination of Georgia politics by the Atlanta machine. Although Brown and Colquitt died in 1894 and Gordon retired in 1895, they were followed by other politicians devoted to cities and industries. In 1904 opposition to the Atlanta machine reached a low when Governor Joseph M. Terrell was reelected without opposition. So great was the concentration of power in Atlanta during these years that a small Georgia newspaper complained: "As we are so far out here in the backwoods, we never hear what is going on at the capital until the thing is over with." Georgia humorist Bill Arp chided gently: "Our folks don't know what we are doing. Now Joe Brown is building a railroad right along in front of my house, and nobody knows it but me and him and his partners."

Henry Grady promised that the South was progressing confidently toward a bright rainbow of economic success and social stability just beyond a beckoning horizon: "A vision of surpassing beauty unfolds before my eyes. I see a South, the home of fifty millions of people, who rise up every day to call from blessed cities, vast hives of industry and thrift; her countrysides the treasures from which their resources are drawn; her streams vocal with whirring spindles; her valleys tranquil in the white and gold of the harvest, her rulers honest and her people loving, her homes happy and their hearthstones bright, her wealth diffused and poor-house empty; her two races walking together in peace and contentment; sunshine everywhere all the time." But Grady's words, no matter how sincere or well intentioned, were not the reality of Georgia life after the Civil War. If Grady's fame rests on unfulfilled promises, that was because he was sincerely optimistic by nature and because he died before he could put his words into action. Woodrow Wilson, that young lawyer in Atlanta, challenged Grady's credibility in 1886: "Papers like the *Constitution*, though they may represent fairly well the opinion of the politicians, do not represent anybody else." Tom Watson, spokesman for the unhappy farmers of the 1890's, cursed what he called "the splendid phraseology of silver-tongued orators from the city . . . the inspired clap-trap of some of its politicians and editors." The opposition in Georgia cried out against widespread poverty, demoralization, crime and misery. Frustrated veterans remembered these years, not as a time of pride and hope, but as an era when the great mass of Georgia people, both black and white, suffered most desperately on the land, when the state government was manipulated by cynical city politicians, when these cumulative frustrations and disappointments turned human relations toward an embittered crisis.

When Sidney Andrews visited Atlanta in 1865, he found the attitude of its citizens recklessly independent: "They point to the railroads centering here and say that if the country around was poorer and less productive, the mere storage and trans-shipment of freight would suffice to make Atlanta a great city." Truly, for the next seventy-five years Atlanta would continue to grow and prosper, not because of Georgia's wholesome social and economic development, but in spite of the state's languishing condition. Northern cotton mills did not come to Georgia in significant numbers until after 1900, and industrial diversification did not arrive until after World War II. Between 1880 and 1900, the number of people working at manufacturing jobs in the South rose only from 4.6 percent to 6.3 percent of the population. Like Jeeter Lester in Erskine Caldwell's *Tobacco Road*, most Georgia people remained on the land, farming, mining or fishing: "The spring-

A country girl coming from the market, from *Outing*,
October, 1903. *New York Public Library*

time . . . knows you got to stay on the land to feel good. God made the land. I stay where God made a place for me." In 1900, eighty-five percent of Georgia's population still lived on farms or in small villages, and sixty percent worked in agriculture. The farm force in Georgia actually increased from 336,000 in 1870 to more than 500,000 in 1900. In 1930 for every Southerner engaged in manufacturing and mechanical pursuits, there were still three in Southern farming. And most of these farmers—at least three-quarters of them in Georgia —continued to raise cotton by a primitive technique which had not changed since the early nineteenth century, one man and his family and a mule devoting all their energies to raising a small patch of cotton. As soon as one crop had been picked, it was time to prepare the ground for a new crop. Despite the new South's preaching about agricultural reform, Southern farmers continued to raise cotton and too much of it. Edward King's observations at Savannah in 1875 were a troubling echo of the cotton preoccupation which had impoverished the South before the Civil War: "We were amazed at the masses of cotton bales piled everywhere. They lined the commercial avenues for hundreds and hundreds of rods; down by the waterside they were heaped in mammoth piles, and the procession of drays seemed endless. The huge black ships swallowed bale after bale; the clank of the hoisting crane was heard from morning till night. At the great stone Custom House the talk was of cotton; at the old Exchange cotton was the theme; and in all the offices from end to end of Bay Street, we encountered none save busy buyers and factors, worshipping the creamy staple and gossiping rapturously of profits possible."

After the deaths of white soldiers and emancipation of black slaves, the greatest practical effect of the Civil War in the South was a shortage of capital and labor. All of the assets of Southerners—Confederate bonds and currency, bank stock, slaves and land—had been

Georgia villagers at a country store, from *Outing*, October, 1903. *New York Public Library* depleted or destroyed by the war. Over the countryside of Georgia, landowners did not have the cash money to hire laborers, and farmers did not have the means to rent farms. So a new system of share-cropping evolved naturally to serve the mutual needs of these people. If a farmer had no money and few implements of agriculture, his land-lord could furnish him not only land and a house to live in, but also food, tools, mules. And at the end of the planting season they would share the harvest between them. The worker would be credited with his share of the cotton and charged with all supplies he had received during the year plus the rent of the land. By 1870 sharecropping had already become common in middle Georgia, and the system spread with agricultural distress across the cotton belt of the Old South, first among the blacks and later among the whites. In 1880, 36.2 percent of all Southern farms were operated by sharecroppers. By 1920, 55 percent of all Southern farms in the ten chief cotton states were farmed by tenants; in 1925, 57.7 percent were tenants; by 1930, 61.5 percent were tenants. Of the 255,598 farm operators in Georgia in 1930, 70,596 owned their land, 9,206 were part owners, 1,406 were managers, 27,533 were cash renters and 146,857 were sharecroppers. The cash renters and sharecroppers, people who did not own the land which was the only means of their support, represented 68.2 percent of Georgia farmers in 1930.

Erskine Caldwell looked into the faces of these Southern share-croppers during the Depression and saw a look of desperate hope in their eyes: "Every one of them was waiting for the cotton to mature. They believed in cotton. They believed in it as some men believe in God. They had faith in the earth and in the plants that grow in the earth. Even though they had been fooled the year before, and for many years before that, they were certain the fields would soon be showered with tumbling, bursting bolls of glistening white cotton." Perversely,

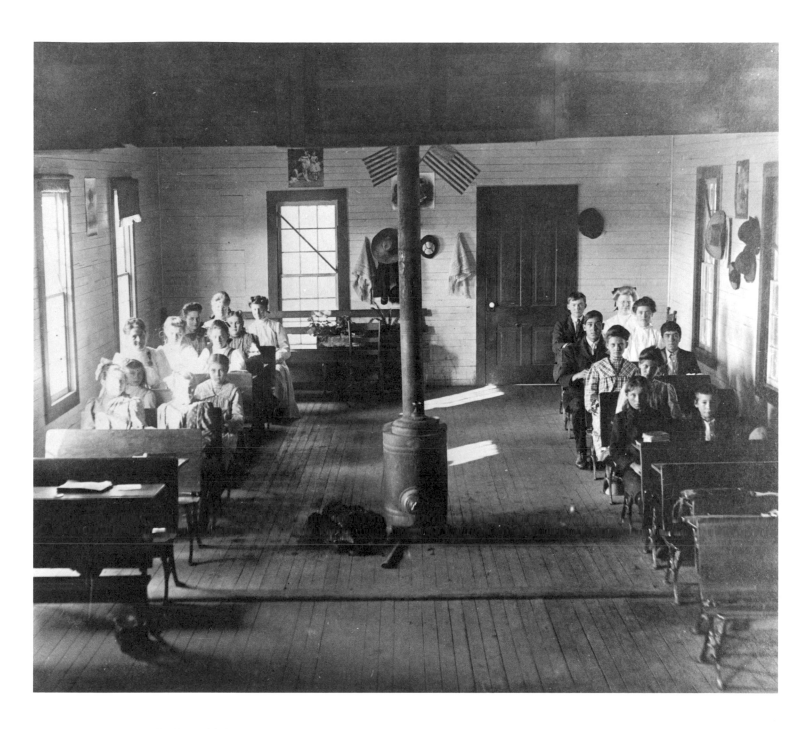

A one-room school, Randolph County, c. 1900.
Georgia Department of Archives and History

cotton was the one staple crop raised in America which contributed nothing directly consumable to the farm family, and the preoccupation with cotton meant that the necessary foods were not being raised. The farms of the New South tended to be less and less self-supporting, compared with the farms and plantations of the Old South, which produced most of their subsistence needs. In 1920 Georgia farm families purchased more than one-half of their food and feed stock from outside of the state. One-crop cotton cultivation contributed to soil erosion. People who rented other people's land would make few improvements on property they did not own; instead, they would squeeze all they could from the soil each year, hoping to move the next season to more fertile fields. A sample study made in 1933 suggested that one-third of all Southern land was eroded and that at least one-half of all eroded land in the United States was in the South.

The one desperate hope of these sharecroppers was to raise a little more cotton, somehow, and sell it at a little higher price and get out of debt. But new, cheap and more productive cotton-producing areas were opening up in the southwestern United States and other parts of the world. From 1860 to 1900, aided by the Homestead Law and the general movement of the American people, total farm acreage in the United States increased 400,000,000 acres. Georgia and the Old South, with worn-out land, little capital and a rigid tradition of one-mule farm cultivation, could not compete in a glutted market, where the only way to survive was to produce large quantities of cheap cotton. Cotton prices continued to decline from a dollar a pound after the Civil War, to twenty-five cents in 1868, to twelve cents in the 1870's, to nine cents in the 1880's, to seven cents in the 1890's. Debts that could have been repaid with ten bales of cotton in 1889 had to be repaid with eighteen bales of cotton five years later. By 1892 there would be a worldwide surplus of 13,000,000 bales of cotton which could not be

Blacksmith, Irwin County, 1935.
Arthur Rothstein, Library of Congress

sold. A further catastrophe for the cotton farmer was the boll weevil, an insect which appeared in Texas in 1894 and began travelling eastward at the rate of seventy-five to a hundred miles per year. The weevil, which destroyed cotton bolls, reached Georgia about 1915. Cotton production, which had been 1,660,000 bales in 1919, plummeted to only 588,000 bales in 1923. This crisis, with the coming of the Depression, was a final disaster from which the small farmer could not recover. Ironically, New Deal farm programs tended to benefit the owners of land and large farmers, not sharecroppers. Acreage or production controls just put farm laborers out of work, while the landowners pocketed federal aid.

For Georgia's suffering cotton farmers, a larger harvest might mean only a smaller income, further accumulating debts and ultimate disaster. Farmers became dependent from harvest to harvest on credit at any terms. A farmer might secure his loans with his farm land until, after years of mounting debts, he would be compelled to sell the land. Then the farmer, now working on another man's land, would have to borrow money secured by his future crop. Creditors, who knew that cotton was not perishable, valued it as loan security, and, perversely, an indebted farmer would find his credit measured by how much more cotton he could produce. This crop lien system encouraged farmers to raise more one-crop cotton, despite its falling price in a glutted market; to sell it immediately even if higher prices could be found by delaying the sale; and to continue credit purchasing from the local merchant or plantation owner at inflated prices and high interest rates. So at the end of this credit conundrum, an unfortunate cotton farmer might find himself without land and, mortgaged to more cotton production, without even the free will to abandon his farm or cotton cultivation. These poor men were slowly, inevitably sinking in the economic quicksand of one-crop cotton, sterile and eroded soil, overproduction, de-

Plowing an eroded field, Heard County, 1941.
Jack Delano, Library of Congress

Unidentified couple, August, 1936.
Margaret Bourke-White, Syracuse University Library

clining prices, small cash incomes, cumulative debts, ultimate impoverishment.

By the Depression the cotton belt of the South would become, as it was described at the time, "a miserable panorama of unpainted shacks, rain-gullied fields, straggling fences, rattle-trap Fords, dirt, poverty, disease, drudgery and monotony that stretches for a thousand miles." A New Deal study portrayed with statistical coolness the life of a tenant family during the Depression: most tenants lived in unpainted four-room shacks; sanitation was most primitive; eighty percent of the homes were supplied with water from wells; the average income per capita was $73 per year, $309 for the average family; one-third of this income was in the form of foods raised for the family, chickens, eggs, pigs, syrup, corn, peas, sweet potatoes; another third of the income was used, $13 monthly, to buy food, flour, lard, salt pork, kerosene, medicines; the last third of the family income was spent for clothing; there was no money left for household improvements or repairs. In 1930, 2.1 percent of Georgia farms had tractors, 2.9 percent had electric lights, 3.1 percent had piped water. In 1934, there were 3,344 licensed midwives in Georgia, mostly black women, who delivered 42 percent of Georgia's children. Between 1920 and 1940, the large majority of southerners, black and white, lived barely above the minimum subsistence level on a diet of meal, molasses and meat, reminiscent of slavery days. All of these raw facts define a world without adequate sanitation, doctors or hospitals, secure homes. They define a confining world of malnutrition, pellagra, rickets, hookworm, unnecessary sickness, lassitude, large families, further distress, frustration and greater misery.

Georgia's farmers had, since the colony's early dependence on England, produced raw materials for outsiders, who sold them manufactured goods in return. Over two hundred years the natural resources of the frontier "colony" had been depleted with no capital accumulated within the South to replace the potential productivity which was being extracted from the land and forests of the region. The only way the people of the exhausted frontier could maintain their standard of living would be to become pioneers and blaze their way into new territory. It was exactly this crisis at the end of the eighteenth century which had brought settlers to Georgia from North Carolina and Virginia, where their lands had been exhausted by tobacco farming. Another similar crisis during the early nineteenth century had forced many small farmers of Georgia to move to Alabama and Mississippi, the new frontier of the 1830's. Between 1865 and 1875 some fifty thousand small farmers, half white and half black, had left Georgia for the fresh cotton fields of Arkansas and Texas, the latest frontier. Each time—1780, 1830 and 1870—the farmers of frontier Georgia had been able to support themselves, after the depletion of the natural resources, forests cut down and land wasted, by moving to a new territory. But after the 1890's, when the American frontier finally closed, the farmers who remained in Georgia and the other states of the Old South were truly stranded at last, with no place to go except to the cities. A great exodus of blacks to Northern cities began during World War I, and whites began moving to Southern cities during the 1920's and the Depression. Between 1920 and 1930, some 266,000 people abandoned 55,000 farms, or 3,400,000 acres of farm land, in Georgia.

The depleted South, still after, as before, the Civil War, remained a "colony" of the industrialized North. Outsiders with accumulated capital even took over control of the marketing of the precious cotton crop—farmers were indebted to planters who were indebted to seaport factors who were really agents of these men. The South continued to produce cheap raw materials and buy costly manufactured goods. Henry Grady told a famous story of an elaborate Southern funeral,

Unidentified Southern family, August, 1936.
Margaret Bourke-White, Syracuse University Library

Family at Dahlonega, August, 1936.
Margaret Bourke-White, Syracuse University Library

where only the corpse and the hole in the ground had been produced in Georgia. The greatest inducement for Northern industry to come to the South in the late nineteenth century was to exploit the region's raw materials and low wage scale. The "industries" which came to Georgia were cotton and lumber mills, the simplest kind of work which paid the lowest wages and depleted the natural resources. Symbolically, the ships coming to Savannah at the end of the nineteenth century often arrived in ballast, because there was no great consumer demand, but the ships steamed away low in the water with cotton, lumber and turpentine. Suggestively, in 1929 Southern industrial workers earned $844 compared with $1,364 in New England and $1,447 in the Middle Atlantic states. In 1940 Southern industries employed 17.3 percent of the nation's factory workers but paid them only 11.8 percent of the national factory wages.

The great enterprises of the region—coal, iron, steel, utilities, newspapers, chain stores, insurance companies—were largely controlled or owned outside the South. J. P. Morgan dominated the Southern Railway System, which he had created in 1894 from thirty separate corporations, one of which was the Central Railroad of Georgia. In 1900, the ten largest railroads in the South were controlled by Northerners, and seventy percent of their directors came from the North. More than ninety percent of the mileage of the thirty-one major Southern lines was controlled by Northern interests in 1900. Under a system of differentiated freight rates, which had grown up during the late nineteenth century and continued until a ruling by the Interstate Commerce Commission in 1939, it cost about thirty-nine percent more to ship manufactured goods in the South than in New England, a practice which tended to keep the South producing raw materials and discouraged the establishment of new small manufacturers in the region. Under a similar system of differentiated prices for iron and steel products—like the famous Pittsburgh Plus, by which Southern consumers paid a premium price, representing the cost of making steel at Pittsburgh plus the theoretical cost of shipping it to Georgia—the established manufacturers were protected from cheap regional competition, Southern prices for steel and iron hardware and plate were raised, and Southern industrialization was effectively retarded. Like British aristocrats visiting their Crown colonies in another era, some of the nation's most wealthy and powerful industrialists spent their winter holidays in Georgia, completing this impressionistic sketch of the state's colonial status after the Civil War: the Vanderbilts and Morgans at their private hunting preserve on Jekyll Island, the Carnegies at their splendid stone castle on wilderness Cumberland Island, Henry Ford at his Richmond Hill plantation, Mark Hanna at Thomasville, a fashionable retreat where he offered William McKinley the chance to become President in 1896.

By the end of the nineteenth century, most of the people of Georgia, who remained unhappy farmers living close to the land and outside the industrial system, who had heard so much propaganda about big business but still lived impoverished lives across the undeveloped countryside, sensed vaguely that they had been swindled by the business promoters and politicians. During Henry Grady's lifetime, Henry Watterson of Louisville, another Southern journalist and New South publicist, had cautioned: "All the robber baron theories, which have amassed unequal and ill-gained fortunes in the East, are dinned in the ears of the honest, but impoverished, South. Mr. Grady should throw himself across the bridle path of this fallacy. If he does not, he will see the day when the best blood of the South will feed the factories which grind out squalor to millions and millions for masters as cruel and rapacious as ever trod New England soil." Tom Watson, the spokesman for Georgia's unhappy farmers during the 1890's, rejected the

Tom Watson, U.S. Congressman and reformer-turned-reactionary. *University of Georgia*

A farm couple at Locket, August, 1936.
Margaret Bourke-White from You Have Seen Their
Faces *(New York, 1937) with permission*

A farm couple at Maiden Lane, August, 1936.
Margaret Bourke-White from You Have Seen Their
Faces *(New York, 1937) with permission*

New South leaders' faith in industrialization and nationalism: "Ever since the close of the Civil War there has been heard the cry, 'We must encourage Northern capital to come South.' We have got down on our knees to the Northern capitalist, and in almost every instance he has been enabled to dictate his own terms. All over the South, when Northern capital puts up a factory, builds a railroad, opens a bank, develops a quarry, sinks a shaft of the Oil Trust, it has been shrewd enough to take into copartnership a sufficient number of Southern men eager to make money. It has taken in Southern editors, whose newspapers need financial support; leading lawyers hungry for good fees, ambitious politicians who need campaign funds, and thus a fictitious sentiment has been created in our midst which sanctions the system under which we suffer."

In 1906 these discontented Georgia farmers at last staged a successful political revolt, when Hoke Smith, the self-proclaimed representative of the common rural folk against the city politicians and industrialists, was elected governor. His election signalled a victory for the farmers and inaugurated a half century, until 1962, during which rural politicians would dominate Georgia government. In 1908 the state Democratic party adopted a county unit system, which gave small rural counties a commanding voice in the choice of governors and senators. Under this system of indirect nomination, each county had a specified number of votes; nominations would be determined by unit, not popular, votes; unit votes of a county would go to the candidate with a popular plurality in the county; the eight most populous counties were entitled to six unit votes, the next 30 largest counties were entitled to four each; and the other 121 counties were entitled to two each. A few votes in a sparsely populated county could nullify thousands of votes in an urban county. A unit vote could represent 938 people in a small county or 92,721 in a large one. So the successful politicians of Georgia between 1908 and 1962 made their appeal to rural voters, playing on their fear of change, big government, cities, industries and Negroes.

In April, 1913, the raped and battered body of thirteen-year-old Mary Phagan was found in the basement of the Atlanta pencil factory where she worked. Her employer, Leo M. Frank, a Northerner from Brooklyn, a Jew and an industrialist, was arrested, convicted and sentenced to death. After two years of unsuccessful appeals, Governor John M. Slaton commuted the death sentence to life imprisonment. Meanwhile, Tom Watson and others had been calling for Frank's death. In August, 1915, a mob took Frank from the state prison at Milledgeville and hung him from an oak tree in Marietta. (Many years later, a witness came forward exonerating Leo Frank.)

After the death of Tom Watson in 1922, a young lawyer from McRae named Eugene Talmadge, who sported red suspenders and white shirtsleeves as his badge of identity with the common man, became the spokesman and representative of the rural people and farmers of Georgia. A candidate for every statewide Democratic party nomination except one between 1926 and 1946—three times for commissioner of agriculture, two for U.S. senator, five times for governor— he was elected four times governor, more than any other man except Joseph E. Brown. Talmadge, who boasted that he would never campaign in a town large enough to have trolley cars, said that God made grass for cows to eat and not for city people to chop off with lawn mowers. In 1932 Talmadge received 118 more unit votes than his seven opponents, though they received 43,000 more popular votes. In 1946 he received more county unit votes but fewer popular votes than his rival, James V. Carmichael, an Atlanta attorney and industrialist. Talmadge preached the old-fashioned virtues of thrift, hard work, individualism, low taxes, small government. The effect of the county

Gene Talmadge, four-term Governor of Georgia in 1930's and 1940's and representative of the common man. *Atlanta Constitution*

The lynching of Leo Frank in August, 1915, reflected Georgians' fear of outsiders and businessmen. *Georgia Department of Archives and History*

Hull, Georgia, August, 1936.
Margaret Bourke-White, Syracuse University Library

unit system, which gave him power, was to make Georgia politics unresponsive to the needs of the city people, with the new ideas they were adopting in their mobile, middle-class lives. Talmadge in the depths of the Depression prevented Georgia from participating fully in New Deal relief programs, because he feared big government and social programs for Negroes.

Lester Maddox, a cafeteria owner who refused at pistol-point to serve two Negro divinity students in his eatery the day after President Johnson signed the Civil Rights Act of 1964, was another spokesman for the fears and insecurities of rural people. Maddox, whose father had moved to Atlanta from the devastated Georgia countryside to labor in an Atlanta steel mill, was a hard-working, self-made man, proud of his property rights and resentful of welfare programs for people who could not, or in his view would not, make it on their own. In 1966, running for governor, Maddox ran second to his Republican opponent but became governor when, no candidate receiving a majority of the votes, the Democrat-controlled legislature selected him. Like Watson and Talmadge, Maddox was a backward-looking reactionary who believed devoutly and sincerely in Thomas Jefferson's eighteenth-century system of sturdy farmers and bucolic pastures, and so could not lead the people of Georgia smoothly into a twentieth-century world of cities and industries. Significantly, Georgia's three most progressive modern governors—Ellis Arnall in the 1940's, Carl Sanders in the 1960's and Jimmy Carter in the 1970's— were not particularly popular throughout the state, perhaps because they were unwilling to indulge the prejudices and fears of rural voters. Halfway through the twentieth century, Georgia was still more isolated and not more united with the main currents of national life, and the South still the poorest and least progressive section of the land. It had not yet become the Georgia and New South of Henry Grady's noble vision in the 1880's.

Lester Maddox, segregationist Governor, 1968. *UPI/Bettmann*

6. Blacks and Whites

THE late 1860's were years of change, confusion and turbulence that would aggravate the inevitable fears and resentments between the defeated whites and long-enslaved blacks. During the first year or two after the war, freedmen wandered into towns to test their independence. Despite efforts of the Freedmen's Bureau to feed and clothe them and protect their rights, the blacks soon discovered that the government would give them little work or land. After a winter or two of homelessness and starvation, most freedmen returned to plantations. Now they were paid monthly wages, but they were often living in the same cabins, working in the same fields under the same drivers from slavery days — and again dependent upon a white man's good will.

Protected for a time by a Republican state government and agents of the Freedmen's Bureau, the blacks had two or three years to exercise their new right to vote. The state government was thrice reorganized by the U.S. Congress, each time with the participation of more blacks and fewer whites. In the summer of 1868, with the approach of the presidential election, political agitation among blacks seemed particularly alarming to the whites. Ella Thomas of Augusta, the wife of a failed planter, predicted an uprising among the blacks: "The South feels instinctively that she is standing upon the mouth of a volcano. Four or five colored men said that the white folks are scared of the niggers, that things wasn't like they used to be and that they was gwine to have fine times and burn up every house along the road!"

242

Unidentified plantation scene, c. 1900.
From Rudolph Eickemeyer's Down South *(New York, 1900), University of Georgia Library*

By 1868 masked patrollers—calling themselves "regulators," "jay-hawkers," "black horse cavalry" or "Ku Klux Klan"—began to frighten ignorant and superstitious freedmen into obedience by breaking into their houses at night, disguised with blackened faces or masks, blowing horns and waving guns. Uncooperative blacks who argued with whites, wanted to buy land a white wanted, courted a white woman, taught school to freedmen or voted for Republicans might be threatened, beaten or killed. Charles Smith of Walton County complained of a Klan visit in 1871: "I heard my wife hollering, 'Ku-Klux! Ku-Klux!' They knocked one door down. They beat me as long as they wanted to with rocks and pistols, and then they took a hickory and whipped me. Eight men struck me eight licks apiece on my bare back. They made my wife get down on her knees and stripped her dress down about her waist. They stripped my sister stark naked!" Back at work on plantations and their vote restricted by intimidation, blacks had already lost much of their new independence, uncertain even when protected by Federal soldiers.

After the end of Reconstruction the people of Georgia and the South were left to themselves to work out their social relations. The Freedmen's Bureau was closed in 1872, when a regular Democrat was elected governor of Georgia. Soon the social idealism of wartime was tarnished by the nation's industrialization, faith in laissez-faire, Social Darwinism, Anglo-Saxon nativism and foreign expansionism justified in part by "the white man's burden." In 1876 the U.S. Supreme Court ruled that the right of suffrage was not necessarily a part of American citizenship as provided in the Fifteenth Amendment. In 1883 the Court declared parts of the Civil Rights Act of 1875, guaranteeing equal accommodations to all regardless of race, as unconstitutional. In 1891 the defeat of Henry Cabot Lodge's bill for U.S supervision of national elections signalled an end of efforts to preserve black voting. In 1896 the Supreme Court ruled that public facilities could be separate

After the Civil War, most blacks returned to the same plantations, fields and houses where they had lived and worked during slavery days. Laborers at the Hermitage plantation, outside Savannah, c. 1890. *Library of Congress*

but equal. In 1895, 1897, 1902, and 1903 the Court refused to hear disfranchisement appeals from black citizens in the South. The sudden emancipation and enfranchisement of nearly one-half of Georgia's population, unprepared by no fault of their own for responsible citizenship, was a serious social problem. White Georgians wished to return the freedmen as much as possible to a productive, and humble, position. In 1879, the traveller Sir George Campbell, an Englishman who was not unsympathetic to the practical problems of rapid social and political change, quoted a Georgian who stated this determination more bluntly: "He thinks the negro first-rate to 'shovel dirt,' a function for which he was made, but no good for much else. He must be 'kept in his place,' as it is the fashion to say in Georgia."

Segregation laws had not, of course, been necessary during slavery days, and there was no rigid segregation in Georgia life and law until the 1890's. Though public schools, started just after the Civil War, had always been segregated, in most areas of daily living custom and choice regulated relations between blacks and whites. Across the state, inconsistency seemed to be the rule. In 1875 blacks could ride street-cars in Augusta and Atlanta but not in Savannah. Railroads usually provided one car for ladies and nonsmokers and another for blacks and smokers. By 1900 blacks could legally still do everything in Georgia except be buried in a white cemetery, marry a white girl, ride or sleep in white railroad cars or work on an integrated chain gang. As long as there was no pressure or opportunity for blacks to cross accepted lines and as long as old traditions of social life prevailed, there was no need for rigid segregation laws.

Emancipation was a fact and black people were making substantial progress between 1865 and 1900. By 1900 seven Negro colleges had been established in Georgia. Illiteracy among Georgia blacks dropped from 92.1 percent in 1870, to 81.6 percent in 1880, to 67.3 percent in 1890, to 52.4 percent in 1900. In Dougherty County landholding

Cotton porter at Savannah, c. 1885.
J. N. Wilson, Private Collection

steadily increased from none in 1870, to 2,500 acres in 1880, to 10,000 acres in 1890, to 15,000 acres in 1898. By 1906 Georgia Negroes owned 1,400,000 acres of land and were assessed for $28,000,000 property. You could express all of these raw statistics by saying that 470,000 freedmen in Georgia increased their landholding by over a million acres and reduced their rate of illiteracy by fifty percent in one generation, a remarkable accomplishment.

During these same years, while the condition of blacks was advancing, the living standard of whites was regressing. Agents from Alabama and Mississippi plantations came to Georgia after the Civil War to hire Negro laborers, whose places on Georgia farms were filled by whites. As cotton prices declined and debts mounted, more and more whites were compelled to sell their land, then rent another man's land and, finally reduced to the last extremity, to become farm tenants or sharecroppers like the Negroes. A tenant cabin might house a Negro family one year and a white family the next. By 1900 there were more white tenant farmers than black tenants in Southern agriculture. By 1920 in the thirteen cotton producing states of the South, 61.2 percent of all tenants were white, and only 38.5 percent were black. After World War I the blacks abandoned the Southern countryside and moved to Northern cities, but the whites remained until the final collapse of Southern agriculture during the Depression. Between 1920 and 1935, 325,000 more whites became tenants in the South, while during the same interval 94,000 Negroes left their sharecropper farms. In Georgia, the number of white tenants increased from 63,317 in 1900, to 98,754 in 1930, to 101,649 in 1935; the number of black tenants increased from 71,243 in 1900 to 113,938 in 1920, decreased to 75,636 in 1930 and to 62,682 in 1935. By 1935 in the South nearly two-thirds of all farm tenants, renters and sharecroppers, were whites. Tenant farmers in the cotton belt of the South were computed in 1932 to be

Woman sifting rice, Saint Simon's Island, c. 1895.
Private Collection

OVERLEAF:
Cotton fields outside Savannah, c. 1885.
J. N. Wilson, University of Georgia Library

1,091,944 whites and 698,839 blacks. Thus a land tenure system which had helped to control Negro labor and keep him in his place after the Civil War had by the 1930's come to dominate nearly twice as many Southern whites as blacks.

In the face of their own alarming retrogression, the whites observed and feared this considerable Negro advancement in ownership, education and future prospects. Before his death in 1885, Robert Toombs pronounced: "As long as a Negro keeps his place I like him well enough. As a race, they are vastly inferior to whites and deserve pity. This pity I am willing to extend to them as long as they remain Negroes, but the moment a nigger tries to be a white man, I hate him like hell." A white man wrote during 1910 about the incipient crisis: "The differences between the races are growing more intense and troublesome. A few years ago the Negro was the laborer and the white men were 'bosses.' That has all changed now, and the two races are coming into close competition as renters and day laborers. The Negro has almost gone out of certain sections of our county, while whites have filled in and are doing the work." Forrest Pope, a working man in Atlanta, wrote in 1906: "All the genuine Southern people like the Negro as a servant, and so long as he remains strictly in what we choose to call his place, everything is all right. But when ambition, prompted by real education, causes the Negro to grow restless and bestir himself to get out of that servile condition, then there will be sure enough trouble . . . and I will kill him." Governor Allen Candler in 1901: "Do you know that you can stand on the dome of the capitol of Georgia and see more Negro colleges with endowments than you can see white schools? I do not believe in the higher education of the darky. He should be taught the trades, but when he is taught the fine arts he gets educated above his caste and it makes him unhappy."

The development of rigid segregation at the end of the nineteenth

Woman grinding rice, Saint Simon's Island, c. 1895.
Private Collection

century was really an admission that the lives of most whites and blacks were converging and that hard lines would have to be drawn for the first time to separate them. In 1890 the Farm Alliance elected 160 of 219 members of the Georgia legislature, and in 1891 the legislature passed the state's first segregation law, a comprehensive bill which separated whites and blacks on railroads. This made Georgia the ninth state to adopt such a law. Further laws passed in 1891, 1897 and 1908 separated convicts on the chain gang and at penal camps. The Separate Parks Law of 1905 was the first state legislation seeking to segregate public amusements and recreation. This was the fulfillment of Henry Grady's own prescription voiced during the 1880's, that the two races must "walk in separate paths in the South. These paths should be made equal—but separate they must be now and always. This means separate schools, separate churches, separate accommodations everywhere . . . separate but equal, as near as may be." This separate but equal doctrine was affirmed by the Supreme Court in 1896.

Negroes had been granted the vote in 1867, but they never dominated the government of Georgia during Reconstruction. Only one black representative served the state in Congress, 1869–71. During the 1860's and 1870's, the black vote was largely eliminated or made ineffective by the Ku Klux Klan, night riders who flogged and threatened uncooperative freedmen. The election of a recognized Democrat as governor in 1872 signalled the conservatives' return to power, and the state legislature in 1873 changed residency requirements for voting from six months to a year in state elections and from thirty days to six months in county elections, a law directed against the transient Negro vote. Nevertheless, for the twenty-five years after 1880, the first post-Reconstruction election in which the Negro vote played a significant part, the black vote was alternately courted and cursed by every white

"The Freedmen's Bureau at Dr. Fuller's Plantation" from Whitelaw Reid, *A Southern Tour* (New York, 1866). *University of Georgia Library*

Coastal Georgia woman with her pipe, c. 1920. *Carl Julien, University of South Carolina Library*

faction. Each political contest threatened to divide the white voters and throw the balance of power to the blacks. This was more than theory in a state with 816,906 whites and 723,133 blacks in 1880. During the late nineteenth century, the conservative whites, who controlled the powerful newspapers and had money to buy the most votes, usually received the Negro vote. For example, in 1880 most Negroes voted for Alfred Colquitt, the machine candidate, and not the reform nominee, Thomas Norwood.

Georgia's unhappy farmers cried out in an angry crescendo of political revolt in the 1890's. In the 1890 elections, in six of the ten Congressional districts, conservatives lost their seats to candidates supported by the Farmers' Alliance. The Alliance took control of the state party convention, chose the governor, wrote the platform, elected three-fourths of the state senators and four-fifths of the state representatives. The state legislature proposed bills to extend the powers of the railroad commission, prohibit monopolistic business practices, regulate banking, reform the crop lien laws, prohibit speculation in farm products, extend the public school system. In 1894 these farmers, now calling themselves Populists, bolted the Democratic Party and appealed to the common interests of all poor Georgians, black and white. Their leader, Congressman Tom Watson, became their spokesman: "The colored tenant is in the same boat with the white tenant, the colored laborer with the white laborer. . . . The accident of color can make no difference in the interests of farmers, croppers and laborers. If you stand up for your rights and for your manhood, if you stand shoulder to shoulder with us in this fight . . . wipe out the color line and put every man on his citizenship irrespective of color."

This radical program, which recognized for the first time the essential mutual dependence of all poor Georgia farmers, was a revolutionary challenge, to which the machine Democrats responded with

A former slave woman learning to read, c. 1900. *From Rudolph Eickemeyer's* Down South *(New York, 1900), University of Georgia Library*

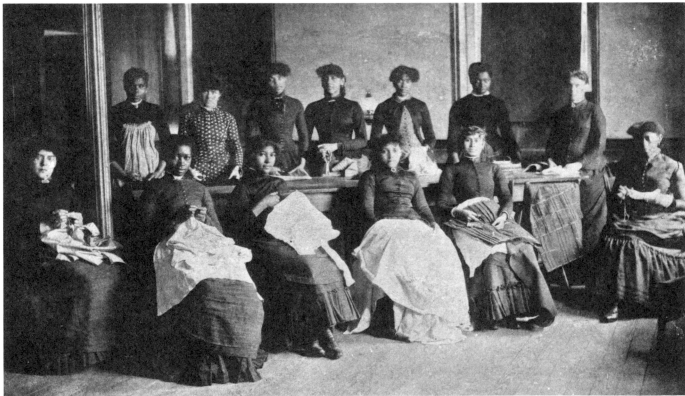

extreme defenses. Whites were told that if they did not vote a straight Democratic ticket, the Negroes would wield the balance of power. But those same Democrats corralled Negroes like sheep, bribed them with liquor and barbecue and herded them into voting places. Sandy Beaver remembered the famous election frauds of 1894: "I remember seeing wagon loads of Negroes brought into the wagon yards, the night before the election. There was whiskey for them, and all night many drank, sang and fought. But the next morning they were herded to the polls and openly paid . . . each man as he handed in his ballot." A Negro, paid ten cents a ballot, could make six dollars by voting sixty times. In the Tenth District the Democratic candidate for Congress received a majority of 13,780 votes out of a total possible poll that should have been no more than 11,240. The total vote cast in Augusta was twice the number of registered voters. Watson lost his seat in Congress, thanks to the cry of "Negro domination," the fear of Negroes which justified these election frauds, and he retired from politics for a decade. One good Democrat exclaimed after the 1894 elections: "We *had* to do it! Those damned Populists would have ruined the country!"

Henry Grady had written years before: "The worst thing, in my opinion, that could happen is that the white people of the South should stand in opposing factions, with the great mass of ignorant and pur-chasable Negro voters between them. If the Negro were skillfully led, it would give them the balance of power, a thing not to be considered. If their vote were not compacted [bought or suppressed], it would invite the debauching bid of factions and drift surely to that which was most corrupt and cunning." The Augusta *Chronicle*, like Grady's *Constitution* a voice for the regular Democrats and the industrialists, said it was a thousand times better for Georgia people to suffer the ills of the present than by division to open the South to a Negro menace.

Cooking and sewing classes at Atlanta University, c. 1890.
From Photogravures of Atlanta University *(Boston, 1900), University of Georgia Library*

Always dissident political groups were accused of inflaming a sea of black passion and violence, and fear of the Negro had been used to justify cheating in elections. So for two generations the Negro had become the effective, though passive, ally of the Democratic political machine against the unhappy farmers of Georgia, the great mass of the white people. Rebecca Felton, whose husband was run out of Georgia politics when he tried to champion Negro rights in the 1870's, reflected in later years: "The Negro and his future in politics became a bugbear—a scarecrow used by crafty office-seekers to infuriate the minds of Southern men and women. It was the clamp that held thousands of good men to the Democratic party after it was known to be dominated by industrial grafters." Tom Watson, frustrated and embittered by the election frauds of 1894, cursed them: "The fear of the Negro has hypnotized the Democratic voters into abject submission to the Corporation Ring. Negro Domination is their mainstay, their chief asset, their pet mascot, their never-ending means of striking terror into the souls of the whites and compelling them to swallow the Ring pill no matter how nasty. The argument against the independent political movement in the South may be boiled down to one word —niggers!"

For most white people in Georgia, the black man had become by 1900 the single most repugnant symbol of the false expectations and cruel frustrations of the New South era. As farm tenants and sharecroppers, the common white farmers had become powerless to alter the direction of their lives, sinking under the pressure of one-crop cotton, sterile and eroded soil, overproduction, declining prices, low incomes and cumulative debts. They grew alarmed when they observed Negro progress after emancipation and compared it unfavorably with their own deteriorating lives. Rigid segregation evolved in the 1890's to protect these fearful whites who were losing their place in

The minstrel show, with white performers in blackface, mingled affection and ridicule of the black man. Terrell County in the 1920's. *Georgia Department of Archives and History*

Le Petit Journal

Le Petit Journal
CHAQUE JOUR — 6 PAGES — 5 CENTIMES
Administration : 61, rue Lafayette

Le Supplément illustré
CHAQUE SEMAINE 5 CENTIMES

5 Centimes **SUPPLÉMENT ILLUSTRÉ** **5** Centimes

Le Petit Journal Militaire, Maritime, Colonial..... 10 cent.
Le Petit Journal agricole, 5 cent. ✳ LA MODE du Petit Journal, 10 cent.
Le Petit Journal illustré de La Jeunesse..... 10 cent.
On s'abonne sans frais dans tous les bureaux de poste

ABONNEMENTS

	SIX MOIS	UN AN
SEINE ET SEINE-ET-OISE	2 fr.	3 fr. 50
DÉPARTEMENTS	2 fr.	4 fr. »
ÉTRANGER	2 50	5 fr. »

Les manuscrits ne sont pas rendus

Dix-septième année   DIMANCHE 7 OCTOBRE 1906   Numero 829

LES « LYNCHAGES » AUX ÉTATS-UNIS
Massacre de nègres à Atlanta (Georgie)

society, at the same time that most blacks and whites were converging in direct competition. The New South leaders had appealed for reform but had stifled any true popular reform, with cries against an exaggerated Negro menace which maintained party orthodoxy and justified cheating in elections. An entire generation had been told they must endure patiently or suffer at the hands of the Negro. These white people now felt, with understandable though perverse logic, that subordination of the Negro would be essential to a recovery of freedom and independence for themselves.

In 1906 the distressed white people of Georgia at last staged a successful political revolution in the state. Tom Watson, the frustrated and embittered farm leader of the 1890's, returned to politics and promised to support the election of any candidate who would pledge to disfranchise the Negro. The Negroes became the central issue of the campaign, attacked as brutes, rapists, criminals: by rejecting the Negro, the people would be rejecting the politics and economics of the New South industrialists who had dominated state government since Reconstruction. Hoke Smith, representative of the common people, defeated Clark Howell, publisher of the Atlanta *Constitution* and representative of the state's business leaders, for governor. Smith's election was viewed at the time as a celebration of the people's freedom from corporation rule, and Smith's platform included true Progressive reforms. But during the election, the Atlanta newspapers had featured inflammatory attacks against the Negroes, as criminals unfit for citizenship; as a tragic sequel to the election, Atlanta exploded in a four-day race riot in September, 1906, during which a mob of five thousand people killed ten Negroes and two whites, wounded sixty blacks and ten whites. Smith had pledged to disfranchise the Negro, and this was done in 1908 by constitutional amendment, making Georgia the sev-

The Atlanta riot of 1906, on the front page of a French newspaper. *Atlanta Historical Society*

enth state to disfranchise the Negro. To vote, a person would have to be a Confederate veteran or descended from one, a person of good character and citizenship, a person who could read and write any part of the U. S. or Georgia constitutions, or the owner of forty acres of land or property worth $500, with all poll taxes paid back to 1877.

The revival of the Ku Klux Klan at Atlanta in 1915 was further evidence of Georgia's social distress. For the Klan offered a mystical world of knight-hawks, ghouls, king kleagles, klaliffs, klokards, kludds, klabels, kladds, klorogoes, and klexters, the thrill of power and an illusion of importance to frustrated and impotent white people who had been unable to shape their own secure place in the world for nearly two generations since the Civil War. Patrollers of whites had scouted the plantation districts of the South before the Civil War to keep an eye on the slaves, and during Reconstruction a Klan had regulated the conduct of freedmen between 1867 and 1869, visiting the houses of idle or troublesome blacks, terrifying them with ghostly scenes, whipping them into subordination and warning them of future visits. Sporadic floggings of Negroes had been common during the late nineteenth century across the Georgia countryside. In 1915 William Simmons, a sometime Alabama minister and salesman, claimed that he was reviving the old Klan. But the new organization was a busy fraternal order with elaborate paraphernalia, gimmickry, rituals. Negro proscriptions were only part of a dogma which included attacks on Catholics, Jews and foreigners, a reaction to great national changes— the world war, rising tides of immigration from central Europe, shifting patterns of industry and cities—many of the same impulses which had created, more positively, the Progressive movement. The new Klan was stronger in Texas, Oklahoma and Arkansas than in the states of the Old South, most of whose major urban daily newspapers kept up a running attack on it. The Klan was perhaps more of a curi-

The Ku Klux Klan, revived at Atlanta in 1915, offered a thrill of power to frustrated white people. Jones County in the 1950's. *AP/Wide World Photos*

osity than a powerful force, but nevertheless it was a threatening statement of social distress.

Another wild symptom of the frustrations of Georgia people was the dramatic rise of lynchings after the 1890's, a development which paralleled the collapse of the cotton economy and the political disappointments of radical reform by the Populists. Scholars have shown a direct relationship between the per acre value of cotton and the number of lynchings in nine cotton states of the South between 1900 and 1930: when the price of cotton was high, the lynchings were few; when the price was low, the lynchings increased. The Panic of 1893, when cotton prices declined to less than five cents a pound, below the cost of production, was followed by the political debacle of 1894, with violent results. Between 1889 and 1918 Georgians lynched at least 386 people —more than any other state—of whom 360 were Negroes. In the dullness and insecurity of rural Southern life, frustrated people were lashing out spastically, desperately against the weakest people in their local neighborhoods, the Negroes on whom they were blaming their political frustrations and whose material progress threatened their place in society. In 1921, Governor Hugh M. Dorsey published a list of 135 examples of alleged mistreatment of Negroes in Georgia during the preceding two years, which included lynchings, peonage, floggings, cruelty. "In some counties," the governor reported, "the negro is being driven out as though he were a wild beast. In others he is being held as a slave. In others, no negroes remain."

As the distressed poor whites and blacks moved into Georgia cities after 1900 from their impoverished farms, these cities began to pass municipal ordinances against blacks. Augusta was the first city to segregate its street cars in 1900. Canton, population 847, allowed no Negroes except nurses to enjoy the public park in 1906. Savannah did not establish segregated streetcars until 1906, though such laws had

Lynching of Lint Shaw, Royston, 1936.
AP/Wide World Photos

been proposed earlier. In 1905 the Southern Bank of Savannah began labelling its teller windows by race, and in 1906 Ray Stannard Baker found elevators in Atlanta marked: "This car for Colored Passengers, Freight, Express and Packages." Atlanta, billed by its promoters as a liberal national city, enacted more segregation laws than any other Georgia town, because its population was large and more fluid, composed of displaced whites who resented the urban blacks who had been freed from the traditional social patterns of their rural communities. In 1925 Negro barbers in Atlanta were forbidden to serve white women and children. In 1931 it became illegal for a member of one race to move into a house previously occupied by a member of the other race, when the house was within fifteen blocks of a public school. In 1942 Albany required separate ticket booths and waiting lines for whites and blacks at theaters. In 1932 it was illegal for amateur sports teams of one race to play within two blocks of a playground set aside for members of the other race, in Atlanta. In 1940 Atlanta's parks were all segregated, except for the city zoo. In 1945 Atlanta officially segregated all theaters, arenas and public halls. Segregation, a relatively recent development, paralleled the final collapse of the South's agricultural empire and the movement of displaced whites and blacks into Southern cities. The system became so complete that white Southerners practically never saw Negroes except in formalized circumstances, since they were excluded from most places of amusement for whites and from most employment except agriculture and personal service. Blacks moved into a separate world, which included separate Bibles for court swearings, side entrances to railroad stations and separate waiting rooms, having to sit at the back of buses, stand at the end of lunch counters or at the kitchen entrance, watch a movie only in a Negro theater or from the second balcony of a white one.

In 1948, Lillian Smith, an ardent feminist and defender of civil rights in Georgia, recalled her Southern childhood: "I can almost touch

Segregated water fountains, Georgia, the 1950's.
Elliott Erwitt (top), Danny Lyon (bottom), Magnum Photos

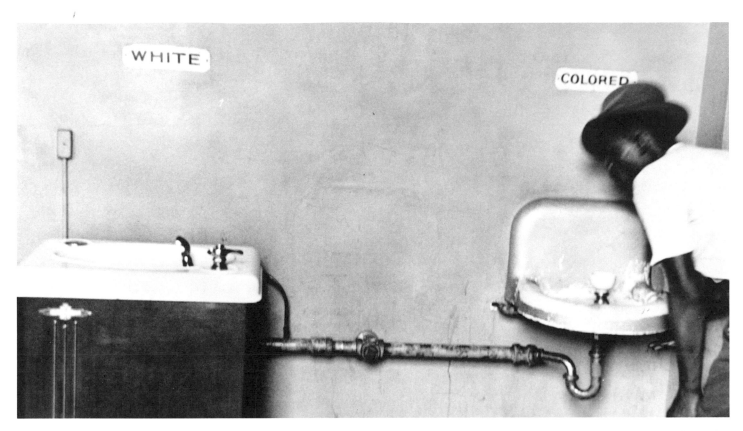

Black school, Greene County, 1941.
Jack Delano, Library of Congress

that little town, a little white town rimmed with Negroes. There it lies, broken in two by a strange idea, segregation. There are signs everywhere. White . . . colored . . . white . . . colored . . . over doors of railroad and bus stations, over doors of public toilets, over doors of theaters, over drinking fountains. There are signs without words: big white church, little unpainted colored church, big white school, little ramshackly colored school, big white house, little unpainted cabins; white graveyard with marble shafts, colored graveyards with mounds of dirt. There are the invisible lines: places you go, places you don't go; white town, colored town; white streets, colored streets; front door, back door; places you sit, places you cannot sit. Little Southern children learn their ritual." However accurate in part, impressions became stereotypes that became prejudices; however understandable historically, customs became rules that became rigid segregation.

Since all Georgians were poor, blacks tended to receive less than their separate but equal share of education. Until January, 1961, no Negro had ever attended a white school or college in Georgia. In Columbus in 1877–78, the school system enrolled 1,485 whites and 1,387 Negroes: the whites received $7,219 for teacher salaries, the blacks $1,530 for teacher salaries; the whites received $147.30 for heating fuel, the blacks $36. In 1874, Macon had 492 whites and 400 blacks in schools: there were six white schools and one black school, fourteen white teachers and eight Negro teachers. In 1900 Athens had the only high school for Negroes in all of the state of Georgia. In 1901 Jefferson County reported 1,703 whites and 2,036 Negroes in its schools, with forty-six white teachers and thirty Negro teachers. In 1906 the Georgia Equal Rights Commission proclaimed that of every one dollar of state school funds, only twenty cents was spent for Negro education. In all Georgia in 1926, only 1.9 percent of the black schools were made of brick or stone; sixty percent of the Negro schools were rented, compared with only twenty-one percent of the white schools;

78.5 percent of Negro schools were one-room buildings, compared with 32.8 percent for the whites. In 1930 the state of Georgia expended for each white child in school $35.42, but only $6.38 for each black child. In 1937–38 Negro teachers, principals and supervisors were paid $352, while white employees were paid $876.

In September, 1936, J. A. Lee of Albany wrote to Mrs. Franklin D. Roosevelt in the White House about the inequality of schools in Albany: "The population is equally divided between white and colored. Seventeen hundred colored pupils were enrolled during the school year 1935–36, but this number could not be accommodated on account of inadequate buildings. The school buildings for colored children are three frame buildings, aged, in need of repair, one condemned by [the] building inspector, another a temporary structure formerly used for housing tools during the construction of a $250,000 white high school. The white buildings are four elementary and two high schools, all brick or stucco. Funds have been used in improving playgrounds for white children, constructing a large football stadium. . . . Nothing as yet has been done to relieve the inadequate facilities for colored schools. Progress in education will be impeded as long as such conditions exist."

Disfranchisement closed the door of hope to half of Georgia's people, for inevitably the whole system of public service, government and justice would become unresponsive to the needs of people who could not vote. In law, Negroes tended to be more harshly punished than whites, for they did not generally serve on juries. In the aftermath of the Civil War, Georgia decided to lease its convicts to private work camps instead of building new prisons. John B. Gordon and Joseph E. Brown, two leading industrialists of that era, leased large numbers of convicts to work in their mines, lumber camps and brickyards. Most of these chain gang prisoners were Negroes: in 1873, there were 524 blacks and 90 whites in Georgia's chain gangs; in 1894, 2,137 blacks

Chain gang, Hood's Chapel, August, 1936.
Margaret Bourke-White from You Have Seen Their Faces *(New York, 1937) with permission*

Black convicts and white guard, Oglethorpe County, 1941.
Jack Delano, Library of Congress

and 191 whites; in 1911, 2,167 blacks and 180 whites. Vagrancy laws,
contract labor laws, lien laws surrounded and encumbered the indebted, uneducated freedmen and their descendants. In 1911 W. J. Northen, former governor of Georgia, proposed with sincerely good intentions that the state "confine at some helpful service" all idle, incorrigible and vicious Negroes and keep them "until they become fit to put upon the community again." At worst, a confused Negro might work himself deep into debt as a sharecropper; then, realizing that he was only getting more indebted each year, he might try to run away from his landlord; the landlord would then have him arrested for evading his debts and then pay him out of jail, with the court compelling the Negro to continue working for his landlord; the landlord might even offer to "sell" the indebted Negro to another white man. A different code of justice for Negroes had evolved. Sporadic floggings of Negroes in rural Georgia continued at least until the late 1940's.

These disadvantages, closing the doors for advancement, tended to make blacks more and more into what many whites had always believed—ignorant, childlike, shiftless, immoral, criminal and unfit for full citizenship. In 1947 Katherine Lumpkin recalled the petty and profound injustices unthinkingly inflicted: "We knew the streets were the white man's wherever he chose to walk, that a Negro who moved out into the gutter to let us pass was in our eyes a 'good darkie.' I could have been hardly more than eight when a little Negro girl of our age, passing a friend and me, did not give ground. Her arm brushed against my companion's. She turned on the Negro child furiously. We were whites! 'Move over there, you dirty black nigger!' We often spoke of the peculiar inborn traits of this so peculiar race. White men stole, but not 'as a race.' We believed that a Negro could not help but steal. In their mental development none could ever go beyond, say, a child of ten or twelve. We used phrases such as 'thieving propensities,' 'innately irresponsible,' 'love of finery,' 'not to be trusted' and a dozen more."

Arthur Raper, a North Carolina-born social worker who went to Putnam County in 1934, was run out of Eatonton by whites angered at the arrival of his black assistants who were educated, well-clothed, addressed by titles and employed by the Federal government: "Many white farmers and mill workers were disturbed over seeing these prosperous, strange Negroes in good cars when so many whites were hard up and on relief. A drunk man announced that he didn't like 'dressed-up niggers' being here. It didn't make any difference how well trained they were, the white people needed the jobs. 'Do you mean to tell me that any nigger, however much education he has, can do a better job than a white man can do, even if he didn't have no training?'" Lillian Smith recalled: "Little Southern children learn their ritual. Some, if their faces are dark, learn to bend, hat in hand; others, if their faces are white, learn to hold their heads high. Some bending, genuflecting, giving in, some shoving, ignoring, demanding, avoiding. Children moving through a labyrinth made by grown-ups' greed and guilt and fear. . . . These ceremonials, performed from babyhood, slip from the conscious mind and become difficult to tear out." Thus, segregation, and the discrimination and neglect that followed in its wake, though a relatively recent development from the 1890's, was woven into the fabric of Southern life.

Tom Watson had predicted in 1907: "The great mass of negroes would gradually reconcile themselves to the condition of a recognized peasantry—a laboring class—within whose reach, as human beings, is every essential of happiness. The negro politician would migrate, the over-educated negro gravitate to the other side of Mason and Dixon's line; the more ambitious and restless of the race would leave the South. Those of the negroes who would remain, would know upon what terms they did so; would occupy the position of laborers simply; and thus the negro would cease to be a peril." One afternoon a white

Henry Mitchell wearing shoes made of old automobile tires, Greene County, 1941. *Jack Delano, Library of Congress*

Child selling "Baits such is miners, crickets, roches, tarket worms," Augusta, 1936. *Margaret Bourke-White from* You Have Seen Their Faces *(New York, 1937) with permission*

merchant in Albany scolded a black customer: "Why, you niggers have an easier time than I do!" To which the Negro replied: "Yes, and so does yo' hogs."

During the Depression, the American government became committed to the idea of using the State as an instrument of social change. The Southern states, too poor to reject Federal relief even with guidelines attached, became channels for this social legislation and for new governmental services which were the permanent outgrowth of relief. During World War II, America and "the democracies" had asserted a worldwide moral leadership, and, during the subsequent Cold War, the United States had to demonstrate to the world how all of its citizens were free and possessed equal opportunities for life and the pursuit of happines. Since World War I, significant numbers of Negroes had migrated from the South; during the 1940's alone, the number of blacks living outside the South jumped from 2,360,000 to 4,600,000. And so the South's peculiar problem became a national one, to which Northern politicians were now responsive.

In the South, other forces were also at work reviving the people who lived in the region's quiet countryside. The final collapse of cotton planting, ending an agricultural system dating back to Eli Whitney's invention of the cotton gin, was perhaps the most important factor in Georgia's future social and economic progress. In 1930, 3,426,000 acres of cotton were harvested in Georgia, but in 1970 only 380,000 acres were harvested. The migration of Negroes away from Georgia altered the composition of the society and reduced the potential threat which whites might feel toward them: in 1890 Negroes made up 47 percent of Georgia's population; in 1930, they were 37 percent; in 1960, 29 percent; in 1970, only 26.1 percent. During the Depression, whites at last abandoned their ruined farms and that traditional, slow-moving world and migrated to busy, progressive cities. The number of farm tenant operators in Georgia declined from a high 62.8 percent in 1930 to 9.2 percent of the farm population in 1969. Cotton had been eliminated as the dominant source of Southern wealth, and one machine could now do the work of eighty men; with these developments there was no longer an economic need to maintain a cheap labor supply, to keep the Negro in his place. During World War II and immediately afterwards, industrialization had really come to the South. During the decade 1940–1950, the South's industrial capacity grew 40 percent and its urban population increased 35.9 percent. As the Atlanta *Constitution* prophesied correctly in December, 1945: "When the history of this time is written some thirty to fifty years from now, it is likely that the first postwar years will be recorded as the years in which the South made its greatest strides toward a way of living that balanced agriculture with industry." In 1950 there were 3,800,000 farm jobs and 2,400,000 manufacturing jobs in the South; in 1972, there were 1,500,000 farm jobs and 4,400,000 factory jobs in the region. Georgia per capita income, which had been $340 in 1932, was $3,332 in 1970. Median income, which had been $1,902 in 1949, was $4,208 in 1959. The median years of schooling completed by Georgians twenty-five years or older increased from 7.8 years in 1950 to 10.8 years in 1970. In 1910 only 20.6 percent of Georgia was "urban," compared with 55.3 percent in 1960 and 60 percent in 1970. In short, each year Georgians were becoming more white, more urban, more industrialized, more educated, "more American."

Meanwhile, the Depression and World War II had given Southerners, isolated by the Civil War, an opportunity to enlist in two great national crusades. Hundreds of thousands of Southerners had expanded their horizons during the war years. Radio and television broke down the isolation of rural life, a process begun a half century earlier by rural free mail delivery and rural electrification. A new

Display window of commercial photographer, Savannah, 1936.
Walker Evans, Library of Congress

283

generation was growing up in the South. Both Roosevelt and Eisenhower, national heroes of the Depression and World War II, were personally beloved in Georgia, where they spent much time, Roosevelt at Warm Springs and Eisenhower at Augusta and Thomasville. During the 1950's, Georgians were chairman of the Senate Foreign Relations Committee, president of the World Bank, president of the Rockefeller Foundation, winner of a Pulitzer prize, president of the American Bar Association. In 1945 the Georgia legislature, prodded by liberal Governor Ellis Arnall, eliminated the poll tax and all other qualifications for voting, and in 1946 the Supreme Court upheld the right of Negroes to vote in white primaries. So in April, 1946, Georgia became the first state in the Deep South to have neither a poll tax nor a white primary. Some 100,000 Negroes voted in 1946. By 1952, 23.3 percent of Georgia blacks were registered to vote; by 1960, 29.3 percent were registered; by 1966, 44.4 percent were registered; by 1970, 64.4 percent were registered. The last surviving Confederate veteran died in Texas in 1959.

Between World War II and the early 1950's the Supreme Court asserted its authority to equalize civil rights, without confronting the specific, significant issue of school desegregation. In June, 1944, the Court ruled that a state could not require segregation of white and Negro passengers on buses and trains which crossed state lines. In February, 1948, President Truman proposed a ten-point civil rights program, including legislation against lynching, the poll tax and Jim Crow laws in interstate commerce, and creation of a fair employment practices commission and a commission on civil rights. In May, 1948, the Court ruled that no persons who purchased or rented property could be bound by restrictive covenants designed to exclude Negroes. In July, 1948, President Truman ordered fair employment practices throughout the federal government, including desegregation of the armed forces. In June, 1950, the Supreme Court ruled in three separate decisions that segregated Pullman dining cars violated the Interstate

Assembling airplanes, Warner Robins, 1943.
Library of Congress

Commerce Act, that the University of Texas should admit a Negro to its law school and that the University of Oklahoma should admit a Negro to fully integrated class life.

Ellis Arnall, governor of Georgia 1943–46 and the youngest governor in the United States at the time, was a rare progressive voice in the South and the only prominent public official in Georgia to defend Negro rights until after 1960. He prodded the state legislature to revise the state constitution, eliminating restrictions on Negro voting. Whether because of conviction or expediency, all prominent politicians in Georgia between 1946 and 1960 condemned the Supreme Court and the Negro. In 1946 former Governor Eugene Talmadge ran for governor, campaigning for the preservation of the white primary, which had been outlawed by the Court in April, 1946. When the Supreme Court ruled that states could not enforce segregation on interstate commerce, Talmadge proposed maintaining Jim Crow in Georgia by requiring passengers to purchase new tickets as they entered the state. In 1948, when Eugene Talmadge's son Herman was campaigning for governor, he vowed to uphold states' rights and obstruct FEPC legislation which had been proposed by President Truman. During the 1948 and 1950 campaigns, Herman Talmadge promised to preserve segregation.

In May, 1954, the Supreme Court ruled that separate schools were inherently unequal and directed that where school segregation existed —in seventeen states, the Old South, some border states, Oklahoma, Delaware and Missouri—it must end. In November, 1955, the Court ruled that segregation was illegal in public parks, playgrounds and golf courses. In late 1955, Negroes in Montgomery, Alabama, boycotted public buses, trying to end segregation on the local transit system. In December, Atlanta's white golf courses, but not pools and playgrounds, were opened to Negroes. In April, 1956, the Court ruled in a South Carolina case that segregation in intrastate transportation

Assembling cardboard boxes, Union Point, 1941.
Library of Congress

was also unconstitutional. In November, 1956, the Court ruled that an Alabama law and Montgomery city ordinance segregating buses were illegal. In January, 1957, a group of Negro ministers in Atlanta was arrested trying to desegregate city buses. In September, 1957, over objections from the Arkansas governor, a federal judge ruled that immediate desegregation of Little Rock schools would have to proceed, and President Eisenhower sent U. S. troops to back up that order. In September, 1958, after plans had been drawn to lease Little Rock's public schools as "private schools," the Supreme Court ruled that such evasive schemes could not nullify the Court's desegregation instructions. In Arkansas, the President and Court had demonstrated in 1958 their determination to enforce desegregation. By December, 1958, suits had been filed in Atlanta against segregation of city buses and schools, in the local state college, at the restaurant of the city airport, but, although five years had passed since the original Court ruling, no desegregation had taken place in Georgia. In June, the U. S. district court at Atlanta ordered the school board to cease segregation and present a plan for desegregation. In August, 1959, integration of Little Rock schools took place. In December, the Atlanta board of education prepared a desegregation plan and submitted it to the district judge, who accepted the proposal with minor changes.

In the fall of 1954, Marvin Griffin had been elected governor, proclaiming, "Come hell or high water, races will not be mixed in Georgia schools!" In November, a constitutional amendment was passed which gave the governor and legislature the power to abolish the public schools and create a system of private schools. In September, 1955, Herman Talmadge and Governor Griffin helped organize a states' rights council of Georgia, loosely affiliated with white citizens' councils in other states, to preserve segregation. In December, Governor Griffin attempted to order the University of Georgia's board of regents, its governing trustees, to prohibit any state college from

Making socks, Union Point, 1941.
Library of Congress

playing with a nonsegregated sports team or before a nonsegregated audience. In April, 1956, the state parks director announced that nine Georgia parks would be leased to private citizens to perpetuate segregation. In April, the Georgia attorney general said he would recommend enactment of laws making it a capital crime for any public official in Georgia to enforce the U. S. desegregation rulings. When Negroes began to apply to white colleges in the late 1950's, the board of regents tightened entrance requirements to keep them out, and Southern governors agreed to finance regional graduate schools for Negroes so they would not enter state schools. In February, 1957, Senator Talmadge introduced legislation in Congress to deny federal courts jurisdiction over school integration cases. In January, 1958, Governor Griffin promised to close Atlanta's public schools rather than integrate them. When Ernest Vandiver was sworn in as governor in January, 1958, he pledged to preserve segregation, and in July he hired a special team of lawyers to figure how to do it. In 1960 Herman Talmadge spoke for six hours in the U. S. Senate—the longest speech of his senatorial career—against civil rights.

So in the spring of 1960 Georgia faced a critical choice: accept the rulings of the federal court to desegregate Georgia schools or close them. In February, 1960, the general assembly created a school study commission which toured ten cities in each congressional district to learn the people's feelings about the issue. While politicians wanted defiance, moderate and pragmatic business and professional men spoke out for compliance. The president of the Georgia Bar Association publicly urged the repeal of segregation laws. In April the commission made the momentous decision to recommend keeping Georgia's schools open. In 1961 the first integration of Georgia schools took place, when two students entered the University of Georgia at Athens and eight Negroes entered four Atlanta public schools. In 1962, pressed by court action, boycotts, demonstrations and an ICC

Police struggling with anti-segregation demonstrators, Atlanta, c. 1963. *Danny Lyon, Magnum Photos*

ruling, all segregated travel facilities in Georgia were ended, and the four major cities desegregated their bus systems.

In 1961, Ivan Allen, a progressive businessman, was elected mayor of Atlanta, defeating Lester Maddox, reactionary segregationist. In 1962, the U.S. District Court enjoined Georgia's Democrat party from using the county unit system, ending an anachronism that had allowed rural legislators to dominate city voters for fifty years. In the same year, a strident segregationist, Marvin Griffin, who appealed to the lingering prejudices of rural voters, was defeated for governor by a self-proclaimed moderate, Carl Sanders, who appealed to city voters. In 1963, Martin Luther King, Jr., the black minister from Atlanta who became arguably the most influential Georgian who ever lived, proclaimed on the steps of the Lincoln Memorial at Washington: "I have a dream, I have a dream that one day on the red hills of Georgia the sons of former slaves and the sons of former slaveowners will be able to sit down together at the table of brotherhood." In 1963 LeRoy Johnson became the first black state senator in ninety-two years, and the galleries of the Georgia Capitol were desegregated. That industrialization and economic expansion coincided with the civil rights movement helped insure its success. During the decade 1960–70, for the first time since the Civil War more people moved into the Southern states than left them. In the decade 1980–90, for the first time since the exodus of blacks to Northern cities began about 1900, their descendants began returning to the South. And so the people of Georgia entered a new era of progress and opportunity, which became possible only when they broke the continuity and abandoned the traditions of their agrarian past.

Martin Luther King, Jr., with his wife, at the Atlanta airport, on his way to Alabama to serve a five-day jail sentence for anti-segregation protests, 1967. *UPI/Bettmann*

Bibliography

This selected list of materials—monographs, articles and published documents—has been arranged chronologically by subject. It is intended as a guide to further reading and also as an acknowledgement to other writers in the absence of footnotes. The reader is reminded that this bibliography was prepared in 1975 and does not include publications of the last seventeen years. Abbreviations: *GHQ* (*Georgia Historical Quarterly*); *MVHR* (*Mississippi Valley Historical Review*); *JSH* (*Journal of Southern History*); *GR* (*Georgia Review*); *GHS* (*Georgia Historical Society*).

I. COLONY, 1733–82

1. Studies and Articles

W. B. Stevens, *The History of Georgia* [1859], Savannah, 1972

Trevor R. Reese, *Colonial Georgia*, Athens, 1963

James R. McCain, *Georgia as a Proprietary Province*, Boston, 1917

Larry E. Ivers, *British Drums on the Southern Frontier, Military Colonization of Georgia, 1733–49*, Chapel Hill, 1974

Milton Ready, "An Economic History of Colonial Georgia, 1732–54," unpublished Ph.D. dissertation, University of Georgia, 1970

Verner W. Crane, "Promotional Literature of Georgia," in *Bibliographical Essays*, Cambridge, 1924

E. M. Coulter, "Was Georgia Settled by Debtors?," *GHQ*, LIII, 1969

H. B. Fant, "Picturesque Thomas Coram, Projector of Two Georgias and Father of the London Foundling Hospital," *GHQ*, XXXII, 1948

Kenneth Coleman, "The Southern Frontier, Georgia's Founding and the Expansion of South Carolina," *GHQ*, LVI, 1972

Kenneth Coleman, "Life in Oglethorpe's Georgia," *GR*, XVII, 1963

Trevor R. Reese, "Britain's Military Support of Georgia in the War of 1739–48," *GHQ*, XLIII, 1959

Randall M. Miller, "The Failure of the Colony of Georgia under the Trustees," *GHQ*, LIII, 1969

Percy Scott Flippin, "Royal Government in Georgia, 1752–76," *GHQ*, VII, 1924, et seq.

W. W. Abbot, *The Royal Governors of Georgia, 1754–75*, Chapel Hill, 1959

Jack P. Greene, "The Georgia Commons House of Assembly and the Power of Appointment to Executive Offices, 1765–75," *GHQ*, XLVI, 1962

C. Ashley Ellefson, "James Habersham and Georgia Loyalism, 1764–75," *GHQ*, XLIV, 1960

Randall M. Miller, "The Stamp Act in Georgia," *GHQ*, LVI, 1972

C. Ashley Ellefson, "The Stamp Act in Georgia," *GHQ*, XLVI, 1962

Spencer B. King, "Georgia and the American Revolution: Three Shades of Opinion," *GR*, XXIII, 1969

Kenneth Coleman, *The American Revolution in Georgia, 1763–89*, Athens, 1958

L. Van Loan Naiswald, "Major General Howe's Activities in South Carolina and Georgia, 1776–79," *GHQ*, XXXV, 1951

Patrick J. Furlong, "Civilian-Military Conflict and the Restoration of the Royal Province of Georgia, 1778–82," *JSH*, XXXVIII, 1972

Kenneth Coleman, "Restored Colonial Georgia, 1779–82," *GHQ*, XL, 1956

Alexander A. Lawrence, "James Jackson: Passionate Patriot," *GHQ*, XXXIV, 1950

Alexander A. Lawrence, *Storm over Savannah*, Athens, 1951

Robert S. Lambert, "The Flight of the Georgia Royalists," *GR*, XVII, 1963

2. Printed Sources

Mark Catesby, *The Natural History of Carolina, Florida and the Bahama Islands* [1731–51], Savannah, 1974

Trevor R. Reese, ed., *The Most Delightful Country of the Universe: Promotional Literature of the Colony of Georgia*, Savannah, 1972 [Contents: Mountgomery, *Discourse Concerning the design'd Establishment of a New Colony*, 1717; *A Description of the Golden Islands*, 1720; Jean Pierre Purry, *Memorial . . . to His Grace the Duke of Newcastle*, 1724; *Some Account of the Designs of the Trustees for establishing the Colony of Georgia*, 1732; *Select Tracts relating to Colonies*, 1732; James Oglethorpe, *A New and Accurate Account of the Provinces of South Carolina and Georgia*, 1732; Benjamin Martyn, *Reasons for Establishing the Colony of Georgia*, 1733; T. Rundle, *Sermon Preached . . . to recommend the Charity for establishing the New Colony of Georgia*, 1734]

E. M. Coulter, ed., "A List of the First Shipload of Georgia Settlers," *GHQ*, XXXI, 1947

E. M. Coulter and A. B. Saye, eds., *A List of the Early Settlers of Georgia*, Athens, 1949

Robert G. McPherson, "The Voyage of the Anne, A Daily Record," *GHQ*, XLIV, 1960

Mills Lane, ed., *General Oglethorpe's Georgia, Colonial Letters 1733–43*, 2 vols., Savannah, 1975

"Letters from General Oglethorpe to the Trustees and Others 1735–44," in GHS *Collections*, III, Savannah, 1873

Allen D. Candler, comp., *Original Papers, 1734–52, Colonial Records of the State of Georgia*, XX, XXI, XXII, pts. 1 and 2, XXIII, XXIV, XXV, XXVI, XXXV, XXXVI; volumes XX, XXXV and XXXVI unpublished manuscripts; others Atlanta, 1910–16

Allen D. Candler, comp., "Letter Books of the Trustees 1732–52," CRSG, XXIX, XXX, XXXI, unpublished manuscripts, State Dept. of Archives and History, Atlanta

Trevor R. Reese, ed., *Our First Visit in America, Early Reports from the Colony of Georgia*, Savannah, 1974 [Contents: journals of Peter Gordon, 1732–35; Von Reck and Bolzius, 1734; Francis Moore, 1735; Benjamin Ingham, 1735–36; John Wesley, 1735–38; Thomas Causton, 1737; George Whitefield, 1738–40]

Trevor R. Reese, ed., *The Clamorous Malcontents, Criticisms and Defenses of the Colony of Georgia*, Savannah, 1973 [Contents: *A State of the Province of Georgia . . . 1740*; Patrick Tailfer, *A True and Historical Narrative of the Colony of Georgia*, 1741; Benjamin Martyn, *An Impartial Enquiry into the State and Utility of the Province of Georgia*, 1741; *An Account Shewing the Progress of the Colony of Georgia in America*, 1741; Thomas Stephens, *The Hard Case of the Distressed People of Georgia*, 1742; Thomas Stephens, *A Brief Account of the Causes that have retarded the Progress of the Colony of Georgia*, 1743]

William Stephens, *Journal of the Proceedings in Georgia* [1737–1740], I–III, London, 1743

E. M. Coulter, ed., *Journal of William Stephens, 1741–45*, I–II, Athens, 1958–59

Robert G. McPherson, ed., *Journal of the Earl of Egmont*, Athens, 1962

Allen D. Candler, comp., *Journal of the Earl of Egmont*, CRSG, V, Atlanta, 1908

Historical Manuscripts Commission, *Diary of Viscount Percival*, I–III, London, 1922–23

Allen D. Candler, comp., *Journal of the Trustees 1732–52*, CRSG, I, Atlanta, 1904

Allen D. Candler, comp., *The Minutes of the Common Council of Trustees 1732–52*, CRSG, II, Atlanta, 1904

Lilla M. Hawes, ed., "A Description of Whitefield's Bethesda" [1748], *GHQ*, XLV, 1961

George F. Jones, ed., *Henry Newman's Salzburger Letterbooks*, Athens, 1966

George F. Jones, ed., *Detailed Reports of the Salzburger Emigrants*, I– , Athens, 1968–

George F. Jones, ed., "Commissary Von Reck's Report on Georgia" [1734], *GHQ*, XLVII, 1963

George F. Jones, ed., "John Martin Bolzius Reports on Georgia in 1739," *GHQ*, XLVII, 1963

George F. Jones, ed., "The Secret Diary of Pastor Johann Martin Bolzius" [1736], *GHQ*, LIII, 1969

Lothar L. Tresp, tr., "August, 1748, in Georgia from the Diary of John Martin Bolzius," *GHQ*, XLVII, 1963

Robert G. McPherson, "The Mutiny of St. Andrews, 1738, A Letter," *GHQ*, XLVII, 1960

Patrick Sutherland, *An Account of the Late Invasion of Georgia*, London, 1742

The Spanish Official Account of the Attack on the Colony of Georgia, GHS *Collections*, VII, pt. III, Savannah, 1913

Report of the Committee Appointed to examine into the Proceedings of the People of Georgia, Charlestown, 1736

The Report of the Committee of Both Houses of Assembly of the Province of South-Carolina . . . on the Late Expedition against St. Augustine, London, 1743

Don Manuel de Montiano, *Letters Related to the Siege of St. Augustine*, 1740, GHS *Collections*, VII, pt. I, Savannah, 1909

Isaac Kimber, *A Relation of the Late Expedition Against St. Augustine under General Oglethorpe*, London, 1742

George Cadogan, *The Spanish Hireling Detected*, London, 1743

A Full Reply to Lieutenant Cadogan's Spanish Hireling, etc. and Lieutenant Mackay's Letter, London, 1743

Allen D. Candler, comp., *Proceedings of the President and Assistants, 1741–54*, CRSG, VI, Atlanta, 1906

Lilla M. Hawes, ed., "Proceedings of the President and Assistants 1749–51," *GHQ*, XXXV, 1951

W. W. Abbot, ed., *King George's Georgia, Letters of the Royal Governors of Georgia, 1754–82*, Savannah, in press

Allen D. Candler, comp., *Proceedings and Minutes of the Governor and Council, 1754–82*, CRSG, VII–XII, Atlanta, 1906–07

Allen D. Candler, comp., *Journal of the Commons House of Assembly, 1755–82*, CRSG, XIII–XV, Atlanta, 1907

Allen D. Candler, comp., *Journal of the Upper House of Assembly, 1755–74*, CRSG, XVI–XVII, Atlanta, 1907–08

William Logan, "Journal of a Journey to Georgia, 1745," *Pennsylvania Magazine of History and Biography*, January, 1912, et seq.

G. Taylor, *A Voyage to North America in 1768 and 1769*, Nottingham, 1771

Thomas Raspberry, *Letterbook 1758–61*, GHS *Collections*, XIII, Savannah, 1959

James Habersham, *Letters 1756–75*, GHS *Collections*, VI, Savannah, 1904

Joseph Clay, *Letters 1776–93*, GHS *Collections*, VIII, Savannah, 1913

Louis DeVorsey, ed., *DeBrahm's Report of the General Survey in the Southern District of North America* [1771], Columbia, 1971

John J. Zubly, *The Law of Liberty*, Philadelphia, 1775

Benjamin Kennedy, ed., *Muskets, Cannon Balls and Bombs: Nine Narratives of the Siege of Savannah, 1779*, Savannah, 1974

Proceedings of the First Provincial Congress, 1775, Proceedings of the Georgia Council of Safety, 1775–77, in GHS *Collections*, V, pt. 1, 1901

Order Book of Samuel Elbert, 1776–78, and *Letter Book of Samuel Elbert, 1785*, in GHS *Collections*, V, pt. 2, 1902

C. C. Jones, ed., *The Siege of Savannah in 1779*, Albany, 1874

An Account of the Siege of Savannah, 1779, from a British Source, in GHS *Collections*, V, pt. 1, 1901

Anthony Stokes, *Desultory Observations*, London, 1792

Anthony Stokes, *A View of the Constitution of the British Colonies*, London, 1783

Anthony Stokes, *A Narrative of the Official Conduct of Anthony Stokes*, London, 1784

Lilla M. Hawes, ed., "Papers of Lachlan McIntosh, 1774–99," *GHQ*, XII, 1957

Lilla M. Hawes, ed., "Minutes of the Executive Council and Other Documents, 1777," *GHQ*, XXXIII, 1949

Lilla M. Hawes, ed., "Some Papers of the Governor and Council of Georgia, 1780–81," *GHQ*, XLVI, 1962

II. FRONTIER, 1782–1835

1. Studies and Articles

James Etheridge Callaway, *The Early Settlement of Georgia*, Athens, 1948

E. M. Coulter, *Old Petersburg and the Broad River Valley of Georgia*, Athens, 1965

U. B. Phillips, *Georgia and States' Rights*, Washington, 1902

Henry T. Malone, *Cherokees of the Old South*, Athens, 1956

Kenneth Coleman, "Social Life in Georgia in the 1780's," *GR*, IX, 1955

C. Burton Adams, "Yale Influence on the Formation of the University of Georgia," *GHQ*, LI, 1967

George R. Lamplugh, "Farewell to the Revolution: Georgia in 1785," *GHQ*, LVI, 1972

Ralph C. Scott, "The Quaker Settlement of Wrightsborough, Georgia," *GHQ*, LVI, 1972

Homer Bast, "Creek Indian Affairs, 1775–78," *GHQ*, XXXIII, 1949

Randolph C. Downes, "Creek-American Relations, 1782–90," *GHQ*, XXI, 1937

J. Leitch Wright, Jr., "Creek-American Treaty of 1790," *GHQ*, LI, 1967

Randolph C. Downes, "Creek-American Relations, 1790–95," *JSH*, VIII, 1942

Richard K. Murdoch, "Elijah Clarke and Anglo-American Designs on East Florida, 1797–98," *GHQ*, XXXV, 1951

Doyle Mathis, "Chisholm v. Georgia: Background and Settlement," *Journal of American History*, LIV, 1967

Henry T. Malone, "The Cherokee Phoenix: Supreme Expression of Cherokee Nationalism," *GHQ*, XXXIV, 1956

Henry Prentice Miller, "Significance and Background of Major Jones's Courtship," *GHQ*, XXX, 1946

U. B. Phillips, "Historical Notes on Milledgeville, Georgia," *Gulf States Historical Magazine*, II, 1903

2. Printed Sources

Albert B. Saye, ed., "Journal of the Georgia Constitutional Convention of 1798," *GHQ*, XXXVI, 1952

John Bartram, *Diary of a Journey through the Carolinas, Georgia and Florida* [1765–66], Philadelphia, 1942

William Bartram, *Travels to North and South Carolina, Georgia, East and West Florida* [1773–77], Savannah, 1973

Mills Lane, ed., *The Rambler in Georgia*, Savannah, 1973 [Contents: Georgia travel accounts by La Rouchefoucauld-Liancourt, 1796; John Melish, 1806–09; John Lambert, 1808; Adam Hodgson, 1820; Basil Hall, 1828; James Stuart, 1830; C. D. Arfwedson, 1833; Tyrone Power, 1834; George Featherstonhaugh, 1836; James Silk Buckingham, 1839; George Lewis, 1844; Charles Lyell, 1845–46; Frederick Law Olmsted, 1853–54]

G. Melvin Herndon, "Samuel Edward Butler of Virginia Goes to Georgia, 1784," *GHQ*, LII, 1968

G. Melvin Herndon, ed., "The Diary of Samuel Edward Butler, 1784–86," *GHQ*, LII, 1968

Lilla M. Hawes, ed., "Miscellaneous Papers of James Jackson, 1781–98," *GHQ*, XXXVII, 1953

Lilla M. Hawes, ed., "Papers of James Jackson, 1781–98," *GHQ*, XXXVIII, 1954

Lilla M. Hawes, ed., "The Letter Book of General James Jackson, 1788–96," *GHQ*, XXXVII, 1953

John K. Mahon, ed., "Correspondence between General James Jackson and Captain William Ross," *GHQ*, XXXV, 1951

Harriet Milledge Salley, ed., *Correspondence of John Milledge* [1785–1818], Columbia, 1949

Marion A. Boggs, ed., *The Alexander Letters*, Savannah, 1916

Louis Milfort, *Memoirs, or My Sojourn in the Creek Nation* [1802], Savannah, 1972

Lilla M. Hawes, ed., "The Frontiers of Georgia in the Late 18th Century: Jonas Fauche to Joseph Vallance Bevan," *GHQ*, XLVII, 1963

Benjamin Hawkins, *Letters 1796–1806*, GHS *Collections*, IX, 1916

Benjamin Hawkins, *Sketch of the Creek Country in 1791–99*, GHS *Collections*, III, pt. II, 1848

Marion Hemperley, ed., "Benjamin Hawkins' Trip across Georgia in 1796," *GHQ*, LV, 1971

Marion Hemperley, ed., "Benjamin Hawkins' Trip across Western and Northern Georgia" [1798], *GHQ*, LVI, 1972

John Davis, *Travels of Four Years and a Half in the United States of America* [1799], London, 1803

Virginia Steele Wood and Ralph Van Wood, eds., "The Reuben King Journal, 1800–06," *GHQ*, L, 1966

Elmer T. Clark, ed., *Journal and Letters of Francis Asbury*, London, 1958

Raymond A. Mohl, ed., "A Scotsman Visits Georgia in 1811," *GHQ*, LV, 1971

Sidney Walter Martin, ed., "A New Englander's Impressions of Georgia in 1817–18: Extracts from the Diary of Ebenezer Kellogg," *JSH*, XII, 1946

Charlotte Newton, ed., "Ebenezer Newton's 1818 Diary," *GHQ*, LIII, 1969

William B. Hesseltine and Larry Gara, eds., "Across Georgia and into Alabama, 1817–18," *GHQ*, XXXVII, 1953

James C. Bonner, ed., "Journal of a Mission to Georgia in 1827," *GHQ*, XLIV, 1960

Achille Murat, *The United States of North America* [1826], London, 1833

John Hammond Moore, ed., "Jared Sparks in Georgia, April, 1826," *GHQ*, XLVII, 1963

Una Pope-Hennessy, *The Aristocratic Journey* [1828], New York, 1931

T. Conn Bryan, ed., "Letters concerning Georgia Gold Mines, 1830–34," *GHQ*, XLIV, 1960

James W. Covington, ed., "Letters from the Georgia Gold Region," *GHQ*, XXXIX, 1955

John H. Goddard, ed., "Some Letters of James Eppinger, 1832–46," *GHQ*, XLVII, 1964

John C. Dann, ed., "A Northern Traveller in Georgia, 1843," *GHQ*, LVI, 1972

III. PLANTATIONS AND SLAVERY, 1835–60

Thomas P. Govan, "Was Plantation Slavery Profitable?," *JSH*, VIII, 1942

James C. Bonner, "Genesis of Agricultural Reform in the Cotton Belt," *JSH*, IX, 1943

Thomas B. P. Govan, "Banking and the Credit System in Georgia, 1810–60," *JSH*, IV, 1938

Bowling C. Yates, "Macon, Georgia, Inland Trading Center, 1826–36," *GHQ*, LV, 1971

L. E. Roberts, "Educational Reform in Ante-Bellum Georgia," *GR*, XVI, 1962

R. P. Brooks, "Howell Cobb and the Crisis of 1850," *MVHR*, IV, 1917

2. Published Sources

U. B. Phillips, ed., *Plantation and Frontier Documents, 1649–1863*, Cleveland, 1909

James Ewell, *Planter's and Mariner's Medical Companion*, Philadelphia, 1807

Richard K. Murdoch, "Letters and Papers of Dr. Daniel Turner, 1804–08," *GHQ*, LIII, 1969, et seq.

John Livingston Hopkins, *Messalina's Questions; or, a Vindication of Slavery*, Liverpool, 1821

J. Jacobus Flournoy, *An Essay on the Origin, Habits, etc. of The African Race*, New York, 1835

William J. Hobby, *Remarks upon Slavery, occasioned by Attempts made to Circulate Improper Publications in the Southern States*, Philadelphia, 1835

Bondage a Moral Institution Sanctioned by the Scriptures by a Southern Farmer, Macon, 1837

Frances Anne Kemble, *Journal of a Residence on a Georgian Plantation* [1838–39], London, 1863

Emily P. Burke, *Reminiscences of Georgia* [1840–41], Oberlin, 1850

Slavery, A Treatise showing that Slavery is Neither a Moral, Political, nor Social Evil, Penfield, 1844

Moses Roper, *Narratives of the Adventure and Escape of Moses Roper from American Slavery*, Berwick-upon-Tweed, 1846

A. B. Longstreet, *A Voice from the South*, 1847

Samuel Dunwoody, *A Sermon upon the Subject of Slavery*, Marietta, 1850

Lewis W. Paine, *Six Years in a Georgia Prison*, New York, 1851

C. G. Memminger, *Lecture . . . Showing African Slavery to be Consistent with the Moral and Physical Progress of a Nation*, Augusta, 1851

Robert Toombs, *An Oration delivered before the Few and Phi Gamma Societies*, Augusta, 1853

Robert Collins, *Essay on the Treatment and Management of Slaves*, Boston, 1853

Charles Ball, *Slavery in the United States*, Pittsburgh, 1854

Nehemiah Adams, *A South-Side View of Slavery* [1854], Savannah, 1974

L. A. Chamerovzow, *Slave Life in Georgia* [1855], Savannah, 1972

William Grimes, *The Life of William Grimes, The Runaway Slave*, New Haven, 1855

Charles Grandison Parsons, *Inside View of Slavery* [1855], Savannah, 1974

Philo Tower, *Slavery Unmasked*, Rochester, 1856

John W. Park, *An Address on African Slavery*, Atlanta, 1857

Fifty Years in Chains or the Life of an American Slave, New York, 1858

Thomas R. R. Cobb, *An Historical Sketch of Slavery*, Philadelphia and Savannah, 1858

William Tappan Thompson, *The Slaveholder Abroad; or, Billy Buck's Visit with his Master to England*, Philadelphia, 1860

Marcus A. Bell, *Message of Love; South-Side View of Cotton is King; and the Philosophy of African Slavery*, Atlanta, 1860

E. N. Elliott, *Cotton is King and Pro-Slavery Arguments*, Augusta, 1860

Joseph R. Wilson, *Mutual Relation of Masters and Slaves as Taught in the Bible*, Augusta, 1861

Harrison Berry, *Slavery and Abolitionists as Viewed by a Georgia Slave*, Atlanta, 1861

E. W. Warren, *Nellie Norton; or, Southern Slavery and the Bible*, Macon, 1864

Ronald Killion and Charles T. Waller, *Slavery Time When I Was Chillun down on Marster's Plantation: Interviews with Georgia Slaves*, Savannah, 1973

C. A. L. Lamar, ed., "A Slave-Trader's Letter Book," *North American Review*, 143, 1886

Robert Manson Meyers, *Children of Pride*, New Haven, 1973

U. B. Phillips, ed., *Correspondence of Robert Toombs, Alexander H. Stephens and Howell Cobb*, Washington, 1913

R. Q. Mallard, *Plantation Days Before Emancipation*, Richmond, 1892

James Z. Rabun, ed., "Alexander H. Stephens's Diary, 1834–37," *GHQ*, XXXVI, 1952

IV. CIVIL WAR AND RECONSTRUCTION, 1861–72

1. Studies and Articles

T. Conn Bryan, *Confederate Georgia*, Athens, 1953

Michael P. Johnson, "A New Look at the Popular Vote for Delegates to the Georgia Secession Convention," *GHQ*, LVI, 1972

Ellen Louise Sumner, "Unionism in Georgia, 1860–61," unpublished M.A. thesis, University of Georgia, 1960

McWorter S. Cooley, "Manufacturing in Georgia during the Civil War Period," unpublished M.A. thesis, University of Georgia, 1929

Richard W. Griffin, "The Origins of the Industrial Revolution in Georgia: Cotton Textiles, 1810–65," *GHQ*, XLII, 1958

John F. Stover, "The Ruined Railroads of the Confederacy," *GHQ*, XLII, 1958

Alexander C. Niven, "Joseph E. Brown, Confederate Obstructionist," *GHQ*, XLII, 1958

Joseph H. Parks, "State Rights in a Crisis: Governor Joseph E. Brown versus President Jefferson Davis," *JSH*, XXXII, 1956

Virgil Sim Davis, "Stephen Elliott: A Southern Bishop in Peace and War," unpublished Ph.D. dissertation, University of Georgia, 1964

Earl Schenck Miers, *The General Who Marched to Hell*, New York, 1951

Ralph B. Singer, "Confederate Atlanta," unpublished Ph.D. dissertation, University of Georgia, 1973

James C. Bonner, "Sherman at Milledgeville in 1864," *JSH*, XXII, 1956

Robert C. Black III, "The Railroads of Georgia in the Confederate War Effort," *JSH*, XIII, 1947

James O. Breeden, "A Medical History of the Later Stages of the Atlanta Campaign," *JSH*, XXXV, 1969

C. Mildred Thompson, *Reconstruction in Georgia* [1915], Savannah, 1972

Alan Conway, *The Reconstruction of Georgia*, Minneapolis, 1966

2. Printed Sources

Richard B. Harwell, ed., "Louisiana Burge: The Diary of a Confederate College Girl," *GHQ*, XXXVI, 1952

Spencer B. King, ed., "Rebel Lawyer: The Letters of Lt. Theodore W. Montfort, 1861–62," *GHQ*, XLVIII, 1964

Charles H. Smith, *Bill Arp, so called, a Side Show of the Southern Side of the War*, New York, 1866

A. M. Cook, *Journal of a Milledgeville Girl, 1861–67*, Athens, 1964

Lilla M. Hawes, ed., "The Memoirs of Charles H. Olmstead," *GHQ*, XLII, 1958, et seq.

Willard E. Wight, ed., "The Diary of Rev. Charles S. Vedder, May–July, 1861," *GHQ*, XXXIX, 1955

T. Conn Bryan, "Letters of Two Confederate Officers: William Thomas Conn and Charles Augustus Conn," *GHQ*, XLVI, 1962

Benjamin Rountree, ed., "Letters from a Confederate Soldier," *GR*, XVIII, 1964

S. Joseph Lewis, Jr., ed., "Letters of William Fisher Plane to his Wife," *GHQ*, XLVIII, 1964

Edmund Cody Burnett, ed., "Letters of a Confederate Surgeon: Dr. Abner Embry McGarity, 1862–65," *GHQ*, XXIX, 1945, et seq.

William Irvine, "Diary and Letters of William N. White," *Atlanta Historical Bulletin*, X, 1937

Clyde C. Walton, *Private Smith's Journal*, Chicago, 1963

James M. Merrill, "Personne Goes to Georgia: Five Civil War Letters," *GHQ*, XLIII, 1959

Martin Abbott, ed., "Irrepressible Optimism of a Georgia Confederate Soldier in 1864: A Letter," *GHQ*, XXXVII, 1953

Andrew Forest Muir, ed., "The Battle of Atlanta as Described by a Confederate Soldier," *GHQ*, XLII, 1958

Charles Brockman, Jr., ed., "The John Van Duser Diary of Sherman's March from Atlanta to Hilton Head," *GHQ*, LIII, 1969

Donald W. Lewis, ed., "A Confederate Officer's Letters on Sherman's March to Atlanta," *GHQ*, LI, 1967

George W. Murray, *A History of George W. Murray and his Long Confinement at Andersonville, Georgia*, Northampton, 1865

Robert H. Kellogg, *Life and Death in Rebel Prisons*, Hartford, 1865

A. O. Abbott, *Prison Life in the South*, New York, 1865

Mills Lane, ed., *"War is Hell!" Sherman in Georgia*, Savannah, 1974

David P. Conyngham, *Sherman's March through the South*, New York, 1865

John H. Kennaway, *On Sherman's Track*, London, 1867

George Sharland, *Knapsack Notes of Sherman's Campaign through the State of Georgia*, Springfield, 1865

G. S. Bradley, *The Star Corps; or Notes of an Army Chaplain*, Milwaukee, 1865

George C. Osborn, "Sherman's March through Georgia: Letters from Charles Ewing to his Father, Thomas Ewing," *GHQ*, XLII, 1958

Henry Russell Hitchcock, *Marching through Georgia*, New Haven, 1927

James A. Padgett, "With Sherman through Georgia and the Carolinas: Letters of a Federal Soldier," *GHQ*, XXXII, 1948

"An Indiana Doctor Marches with Sherman," *Indiana Magazine of History*, XLIX, 1953

Oscar Osborn Winther, *With Sherman to the Sea*, Baton Rouge, 1943

Chauncey Cook, "Letters of a Badger Boy in Blue," *Wisconsin Magazine of History*, V, 1921–22

F. B. Joyner, "With Sherman in Georgia: A Letter from the Coast," *GHQ*, XLII, 1958

Wilfred W. Black, "Marching with Sherman through Georgia and the Carolinas," *GHQ*, LII, 1968

James I. Robertson, Jr., ed., *The Diary of Dolly Lunt Burge* [1917], Athens, 1962

Kate Cumming, *A Journal of the Hospital Life in the Confederate Army*, Nashville, 1866

T. Conn Bryan, ed., "A Georgia Woman's Civil War Diary: The Journal of Minerva Leah Rowles McClatchey, 1864–65," *GHQ*, LI, 1967

Eliza Frances Andrews, *The War-Time Journal of a Georgia Girl, 1864–65* [1908], Macon, 1960

Spencer B. King, Jr., ed., "Fanny Cohen's Journal of Sherman's Occupation of Savannah," *GHQ*, XLI, 1957

B. H. Hill, *Notes on the Situation*, Augusta, 1867

Adelaide L. Fries, "The Elizabeth Sterchi Letters," *Atlanta Historical Society Bulletin*, V, 1940

Whitelaw Reid, *After the War: A Southern Tour*, New York, 1866

Willard E. Wight, "Reconstruction in Georgia: Three Letters by Edwin G. Higbee," *GHQ*, XLI, 1957

John Richard Dennett, *The South as It Is* [1866], New York, 1965

J. T. Trowbridge, *The South*, Hartford, 1866

Carl Schurz, *Condition of the South*, Washington, 1866

Joseph E. Mahaffey, ed., "Carl Schurz's Letters from the South," *GHQ*, XXXV, 1951

William A. Campbell, ed., "A Freedman's Bureau Diary by George Wagner," *GHQ*, XLVIII, 1964

Sidney Andrews, *The South since the War*, Boston, 1970

J. W. Alvord, *Letters from the South Relating to the Condition of the Freedmen*, Washington, 1870

Robert Somers, *The Southern States Since the War*, New York, 1871

Charles Stearns, *The Black Man of the South and the Rebels*, New York, 1872

Charles Nordhoff, *The Cotton States in the Spring and Summer of 1875*, New York, 1876

David C. Barrow, Jr., "A Georgia Plantation," *Scribner's Magazine*, XXI, 1881

Frances Butler Leigh, *Ten Years on a Georgia Plantation Since the War*, London, 1883

V. THE NEW SOUTH, 1872–1908

1. Studies and Articles

R. B. Nixon, *Henry W. Grady: Spokesman of the New South*, New York, 1943

Paul M. Gaston, *The New South Creed*, New York, 1970

Broadus M. Mitchell, *The Rise of Cotton Mills in the South*, Baltimore, 1921

Willard Range, "Hannibal I. Kimball," *GHQ*, XXIX, 1945

Richard W. Griffin, "Problems of the Southern Cotton Planters after the Civil War," *GHQ*, XXXIX, 1955

Collamer M. Abbott, "New England Money Goes South," *GHQ*, XLIX, 1965

John F. Stover, "Northern Financial Interests in Southern Railroads, 1865–1900," *GHQ*, XXXIX, 1955

Enoch M. Banks, *The Economics of Land Tenure in Georgia*, New York, 1905

Charles S. Johnson, Edwin R. Embree, W. W. Alexander, *The Collapse of Cotton Tenancy*, Chapel Hill, 1935

Willard Range, *A Century of Georgia Agriculture, 1850–1950*, Athens, 1954

Arthur F. Raper, *Preface to Peasantry*, Chapel Hill, 1936

Rupert P. Vance, *Human Geography in the South*, Chapel Hill, 1935

Arthur F. Raper, *Tenants of the Almighty*, New York, 1943

T. J. Woofter, Jr., *Landlord and Tenant on the Cotton Plantation*, Washington, 1936

W. T. Couch, *Culture in the South*, Chapel Hill, 1934

Clarence Heer, *Income and Wages in the South*, Chapel Hill, 1930

Arthur F. Raper and Ira DeA. Reid, *Sharecroppers All*, Chapel Hill, 1941

Howard W. Odum, *Southern Regions of the United States*, Chapel Hill, 1936

J. B. Floyd, "Rebecca Latimer Felton, Political Independent," *GHQ*, xxx, 1946

Alex M. Arnett, *The Populist Movement in Georgia*, New York, 1922

Judson C. Ward, "The New Departure Democrats in Georgia: An Interpretation," *GHQ*, XLI, 1957

John E. Talmadge, "The Death Blow to Independentism in Georgia," *GHQ*, XXXIX, 1955

John E. Talmadge, *Rebecca Latimer Felton*, Athens, 1960

A. M. Arnett, "The Populist Movement in Georgia," *GHQ*, VII, 1923

C. Vann Woodward, *Tom Watson: Agrarian Rebel* [1938], Savannah, 1973

V. O. Key, Jr., *Southern Politics in State and Nation*, New York, 1949

Clarence Cason, *Ninety Degrees in the Shade*, Chapel Hill, 1935

Allen Lumpkin Henson, *Red Galluses*, Boston, 1945

Horace Montgomery, *Cracker Parties*, Baton Rouge, 1950

2. Printed Sources

Henry W. Grady, *The New South* [1880–89], Savannah, 1972

Atticus G. Haygood, *The New South*, Oxford, 1880

Albert V. House, Jr., ed., "A Reconstruction Sharecropper Contract on a Georgia Rice Plantation," *GHQ*, XXVI, 1942

W. D. Trammell, *Ça Ira*, New York, 1874

Thomas M. Norwood, *Plutocracy or American White Slavery*, New York, 1888

Rebecca Latimer Felton, *My Memoirs of Georgia Politics*, Atlanta, 1911

Thomas E. Watson, *Life and Speeches*, Thomson, 1911

Nathaniel E. Harris, *Autobiography*, Macon, 1925

Erskine Caldwell, *Tobacco Road* [1932], Savannah, 1974

Erskine Caldwell, *God's Little Acre*, New York, 1933

Erskine Caldwell, *The Journeyman*, New York, 1964

Erskine Caldwell, *Trouble in July*, New York, 1940

VI. SOCIAL PROBLEMS AND PROGRESS, 1908–63

1. Studies and Articles

L. Moody Simms, Jr., "A Note on Sidney Lanier's Attitude toward the Negro and toward Populism," *GHQ*, LII, 1968

A. Elizabeth Taylor, "The Origins and Development of the Convict Lease System in Georgia," *GHQ*, XXVI, 1942

Derrell Roberts, "Joseph E. Brown and the Convict Lease System," *GHQ*, XLIV, 1960

A. Elizabeth Taylor, "Abolition of the Convict Lease System in Georgia," *GHQ*, XXVI, 1942

W. E. B. DuBois, "The Negro Landholder of Georgia," *Bulletin of the Department of Labor*, Washington, 1901

Horace Calvin Wingo, "Race Relations in Georgia 1872–1908," unpublished Ph.D. dissertation, University of Georgia, 1969

R. B. Brooks, "A Local Study of the Race Problems," *Political Science Quarterly*, XXVI, 1911

304

John Hammond Moore, "Jim Crow in Georgia," *South Atlantic Quarterly*, LXVI, 1967

Clarence A. Bacote, "Negro Proscriptions, Protests and Proposed Solutions in Georgia, 1880–1908," *JSH*, XXV, 1959

C. Vann Woodward, "Tom Watson and the Negro in Agrarian Politics," *JSH*, IV, 1938

Robert M. Saunders, "The Transformation of Tom Watson," *GHQ*, LIV, 1970

Dewey W. Grantham, "Georgia Politics and the Disfranchisement of the Negro," *GHQ*, XXII, 1948

Dewey W. Grantham, *Hoke Smith and the Politics of the New South*, Baton Rouge, 1958

Louis T. Rigdon II, *Georgia's County Unit System*, Decatur, 1961

James C. Bonner, "Legislative Apportionment and County Unit Voting in Georgia since 1777," *GHQ*, XLVII, 1963

Ralph Wardlaw, *Negro Suffrage in Georgia, 1867–1930*, Athens, 1932

Frank Tannenbaum, *Darker Places of the South*, New York, 1924

I. A. Newby, *Jim Crow's Defense*, Baton Rouge, 1965

Charles S. Johnson, *The Negro in American Civilization*, New York, 1930

Charles S. Johnson, *Patterns of Negro Segregation*, New York, 1943

Gunnar Myrdal, *An American Dilemma*, New York, 1944

Charlton Moseley, "Latent Klanism in Georgia, 1890–1915," *GHQ*, LVI, 1972

Clement C. Moseley, "Invisible Empire: A History of the Ku Klux Klan in Twentieth Century Georgia, 1915–65," unpublished Ph.D. dissertation, University of Georgia, 1968

Charles O. Jackson, "William J. Simmons," *GHQ*, L, 1966

John Moffatt Mecklin, *The Ku Klux Klan*, New York, 1924

David M. Chalmers, *Hooded Americanism*, New York, 1965

Richard Sterner, *The Negro's Share*, New York, 1943

Arthur F. Raper, *The Tragedy of Lynching*, Chapel Hill, 1933

John Dollard, *Caste and Class in a Southern Town*, New York, 1937

Clement C. Moseley, "The Case of Leo Frank, 1913–15," *GHQ*, LI, 1967

Twelve Southerners, *I'll Take My Stand*, New York, 1930

Hal Steed, *Georgia, Unfinished State*, New York, 1942

Sue Bailes, "Eugene Talmadge and the Board of Regents Controversy," *GHQ*, LIII, 1969

Sarah McCulloh Lemmon, "The Ideology of Eugene Talmadge," *GHQ*, XXXVIII, 1954

William L. Belvin, Jr., "The Georgia Gubernatorial Primary of 1946," *GHQ*, L, 1966

R. Ray McCain, "Reactions to the U. S. Supreme Court Segregation Decision of 1954," *GHQ*, LII, 1968

Paul Douglas Bolster, "Civil Rights Movements in Twentieth Century Georgia," unpublished Ph.D. dissertation, University of Georgia, 1972

Sarah McCulloh Lemmon, *The Public Career of Eugene Talmadge, 1926–36*, Chapel Hill, 1952

Bruce Galphin, *The Riddle of Lester Maddox*, Atlanta, 1968

2. Printed Sources

Sir George Campbell, *White and Black*, London, 1879

Ray Stannard Baker, *Following the Color Line*, New York, 1908

Ralph McGill, *South and the Southerner*, Boston, 1959

Index

310

THE CHURCH WHERE THE VETERAN
ARMIES CLASHED

The shot-holes in the little Dunker church of Antietam, and the dead in Blue and Gray as they lay after the battle-smoke had lifted, mark the center of the bloodiest single day's fighting in the Civil War. Here the grand armies of the North and South faced one another on September 17, 1862. At sunrise the action began; by 4 o'clock in the afternoon it was over, and the dead and wounded numbered twenty-three thousand five hundred. The preponderance of the army under McClellan, with his eighty-seven thousand men, was offset by the presence of three great Confederate leaders whose names had already rung round the world—Lee, Jackson, and Longstreet—with numbers less than half those opposed to them. On the 18th the armies lay exhausted; and on the 19th Lee abandoned his invasion of the North.

Semi-Centennial Memorial

The Photographic History of The Civil War

In Ten Volumes

FRANCIS TREVELYAN MILLER - Editor-in-Chief

* * *

ROBERT S. LANIER

Managing Editor

Thousands of Scenes Photographed
1861–65, with Text by many
Special Authorities

NEW YORK
THE REVIEW OF REVIEWS CO.
1911

The Photographic History
of The Civil War
In Ten Volumes

Volume Two
Two Years of Grim War

TEXT BY

HENRY W. ELSON
Professor of History, Ohio University

PHOTOGRAPH DESCRIPTIONS BY

JAMES BARNES
Author of "Naval Actions of 1812" and "David G. Farragut"

New York
The Review of Reviews Co.
1911

Printed in New York, U.S.A.

THE TROW PRESS
NEW YORK

CONTENTS

Contents

Part IV

Part V

FOREWORD TO VOLUME II

IT is the central act in the great American war drama, and the one of highest suspense, that is presented by Volume II of THE PHOTOGRAPHIC HISTORY. Volume III will be found to cover the period between the first move against Lee by Grant (May, 1864), and Appomattox—a series of battles bitterly contested, but properly described in the volume-title as "DECISIVE," since it had then become only a question of time, with skill and bravery so conspicuous on either side, before the weight of Northern resources and organization would inevitably crush the impoverished Confederacy. But prior to the unifying under Grant of the Federal military force in May, 1864, and subsequent to McClellan's Peninsula Campaign (with which Volume I closes), the actions form a veritable "tug-of-war," a giant struggle of veteran armies, the result of which no contemporary observer could determine. This is the period covered by the present volume—the combats of matched armies, while Federal and Confederate hoped alike, each praying for the triumph of the cause to which he had pledged his soul and body.

Each of the remaining seven volumes of THE PHOTOGRAPHIC HISTORY—IV to X—deals with a special side of the conflict: cavalry, soldier life, the navy, forts and artillery, prisons and hospitals, with other important phases being separately treated.

CEDAR MOUNTAIN—POPE'S ADVANCE IS CHECKED

PICKETS ON RESERVE—ACROSS THIS WHEATFIELD
THE UNION CHARGE WAS SWEPT BACK BY
"STONEWALL" JACKSON

WHERE THE COMMANDER HEARD THE CANNONADING

The Hudson farmhouse, with its mossy shingles, vines, and aged locust trees, suggests anything but the storm-center of a nation at war. Yet it was here that General John Pope set up his headquarters while his eight thousand trained soldiers under General Banks sped toward Gordonsville, to strike the first blow of what the new general had promised would be a series of victories. As this picture was taken, the New York *Herald* wagon stands plainly in view to the left of the porch; the newspaper correspondents prepared to despatch big "stories." John Pope was the leader whose swift success in capturing New Madrid and

POPE'S HEADQUARTERS DURING THE BATTLE OF CEDAR MOUNTAIN

Island Number Ten in the Mississippi campaign formed a brilliant contrast, in the popular mind, to the failure of the Eastern armies in their attempt upon Richmond. Pope himself proclaimed, "I have come to you from the West, where we have always seen the backs of our enemies." So he set out for the front with "head-quarters in the saddle." He could not know what the world later learned—that Robert E. Lee and "Stone-wall" Jackson were generals before whose genius few opponents, however brave, could make headway. And so it was too late when Pope heard the cannonading from the Hudson house on the 9th of August.

A HALT ON THE DAY OF BATTLE

The 9th of August, 1862. A sultry day in old Virginia. The brook rippling toward the Rappahannock cools the hoofs of the battery horses at halt, tired with rushing their heavy guns south from Culpeper Court House. The cannoneers lolling on horseback and caisson-seats look as if they too like to rest in the shade. Some gaze at the lucky wagoners across the creek, at ease while their horses feed. Least war-like of all seems the queer wagon to the right. They stare at it, and the civilian beside it, and at his companion wielding the

FEDERAL ARTILLERY NEARING CEDAR MOUNTAIN

clumsy apparatus for that newly discovered art—photography. Little do the actors in this quiet interlude imagine that by half-past two this afternoon the Federal batteries will plunge into range of a flaring crescent two miles long—"Stonewall" Jackson's guns; that those guns will roar destruction upon them for three hours without ceasing; and that before another sun rises, two thousand of Pope's army will lie dead and wounded beside thirteen hundred men in gray, upon the battle-ground of Cedar Mountain.

McDOWELL'S HEADQUARTERS

Manassas, July 8, 1862.   General McDowell, who had been so unfortunate in the first great battle of the war, was made commander of the Third Corps of the newly created Army of Virginia under Pope.   McDowell had his headquarters at Manassas.   He moved southward during this month with Pope's army toward Gordonville.   But Lee, by his brilliant and daring tactics, drove the Federal troops back until a three-days' battle was fought in the vicinity of the residence which the camera has preserved for us in this picture.   McDowell once more had the chagrin of seeing a beaten army falling back on Washington.

A ROUGH–HEWN CAUSEWAY (See facing page)

THE ARMY'S HANDY MEN

The Federal army, under Pope, in its advance against Lee needed much more than well drilled regiments of soldiers. Indeed, during the forward march the engineer corps was the busiest division of the army. Artillery battalions and provision trains had to have bridges to cross the numerous streams flowing into the Potomac and the Chesapeake. Three pictures on this page and the preceding show us the men at their work in that summer of long ago. The polka-dot shirt of the foreman (page 14), the roughly hewn timbers cut from the banks, the improvised derrick, the piers built in the middle of the stream around which the water is now rippling, the quiet trees on the banks—all these features stand out as clearly as they did in August of 1862, as the engineer corps was working on the north fork of the Rappahannock, near Sulphur Springs. The pictures are of the same bridge from different points of view.

CROSSING THE RAPPAHANNOCK

CEDAR MOUNTAIN

The Army of Virginia, under Pope, is now to bear the brunt of Lee's assault, while the Army of the Potomac is dismembered and sent back whence it came, to add in driblets to Pope's effective.—*Colonel Theodore A. Dodge, U.S.A., in "A Bird's-Eye View of the Civil War."*

GENERAL GEORGE B. McCLELLAN, with all his popularity at the beginning, had failed in his Peninsula campaign to fulfil the expectations of the great impatient public of the North. At the same time, while the Army of the Potomac had as yet won no great victories, the men of the West could triumphantly exhibit the trophies won at Donelson, at Pea Ridge, at Shiloh, and at Island No. 10. The North thereupon came to believe that the Western leaders were more able than those of the East. This belief was shared by the President and his Secretary of War and it led to the determination to call on the West for help.

The first to be called was General John Pope, who had won national fame by capturing New Madrid and Island No. 10 on the Mississippi River. In answer to a telegram from Secretary Stanton, Pope came to Washington in June, 1862. The secretary disclosed the plans on which he and President Lincoln had agreed, that a new army, to be known as the Army of Virginia, was to be created out of three corps, then under the respective commands of Generals McDowell, N. P. Banks, and John C. Fremont. These corps had been held from the Peninsula campaign for the purpose of protecting Washington.

Pope demurred and begged to be sent back to the West, on the ground that each of the three corps commanders was his senior in rank and that his being placed at their head would

[20]

A BREATHING SPELL

Federal Encampment at Blackburn's Ford on Bull Run, July 4, 1862. When McClellan went to the Peninsula in March of 1862 he had expected all of McDowell's Corps to be sent him as reënforcement before he made the final advance on Richmond. But the brilliant exploits of Jackson in the Shenandoah required the retention of all the troops in the vicinity of Washington. A new army, in fact, was created to make the campaign which Lincoln had originally wanted McClellan to carry out. The command was given to General John Pope, whose capture of Island No. 10 in the Mississippi had brought him into national importance. The corps of Banks, Frémont, and McDowell were consolidated to form this new army, called the "Army of Virginia." General Frémont refused to serve under his junior, and his force was given to Franz Sigel, who had won fame in 1861 in Missouri. This picture was taken about two weeks after the reorganization was completed. The soldiers are those of McDowell's Corps. They are on the old battlefield of Bull Run, enjoying the leisure of camp life, for no definite plans for the campaign have yet been formed.

WHERE JACKSON STRUCK

Cedar Mountain, Viewed from Pope's Headquarters. On the side of this mountain Jackson established the right of his battle line, when he discovered at noon of August 9th that he was in contact with a large part of Pope's army. He had started from Gordonsville, Pope's objective, to seize Culpeper Court House, but the combat took place in the valley here pictured, some five miles southwest of Culpeper, and by nightfall the fields and slopes were strewn with more than three thousand dead and wounded.

doubtless create a feeling against him. But his protests were of no avail and he assumed command of the Army of Virginia on the 26th of June. McDowell and Banks made no protest; but Fremont refused to serve under one whom he considered his junior, and resigned his position. His corps was assigned to General Franz Sigel.

The new commander, General Pope, on the 14th of July, issued an address to his army that was hardly in keeping with his modesty in desiring at first to decline the honor that was offered him. "I have come to you from the West," he proclaimed, "where we have always seen the backs of our enemies—from an army whose business it has been to seek the adversary and to beat him when found. . . . Meantime I desire you to dismiss from your minds certain phrases which I am sorry to find much in vogue among you. I hear constantly of . . . lines of retreat and bases of supplies. Let us discard such ideas. . . . Let us look before us and not behind."

The immediate object of General Pope was to make the capital secure, to make advances toward Richmond, and, if possible, to draw a portion of Lee's army away from McClellan. His first objective was Gordonsville. From this town, not far from the base of the Blue Ridge Mountains, there was a railroad connecting it with Richmond—a convenient means of furnishing men and supplies to the Confederate army. Pope decided to occupy the town and destroy the railroad. To this end he ordered Banks to Culpeper and thence to send all his cavalry to Gordonsville, capture the town and tear up ten or fifteen miles of the railroad in the direction of Richmond. But, as if a prelude to the series of defeats which General Pope was to suffer in the next six weeks, he failed in this initial movement. The sagacious Lee had divined his intention and had sent General "Stonewall" Jackson with his and General Ewell's divisions on July 13th, to occupy Gordonsville. Ewell arrived in advance of Jackson and held the town for the Confederates.

IN THE LINE OF FIRE

Where the Confederate General Winder was killed at Cedar Mountain. It was while directing the movements of four advance batteries that General Winder was struck by a shell, expiring in a few hours. Jackson reported: "It is difficult within the proper reserve of an official report to do justice to the merits of this accomplished officer. Urged by the medical director to take no part in the movements of the day because of the enfeebled state of his health, his ardent patriotism and military pride could bear no such restraint. Richly endowed with those qualities of mind and person which fit an officer for command and which attract the admiration and excite the enthusiasm of troops, he was rapidly rising to the front rank of his profession."

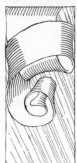

In the campaign we are describing Jackson was the most active and conspicuous figure on the Confederate side. He rested at Gordonsville for two weeks, recuperating his health and that of the army, which had been much impaired in the malarial district of the Peninsula. The fresh mountain air blowing down from the Blue Ridge soon brought back their wonted vigor. On July 27th A. P. Hill was ordered to join him, and the Confederate leader now had about twenty-five thousand men.

The movement on Gordonsville was exactly in accordance with Jackson's own ideas which he had urged upon Lee. Although believing McClellan to be in an impregnable position on the Peninsula, it was not less evident to him that the Union general would be unable to move further until his army had been reorganized and reenforced. This was the moment, he argued, to strike in another direction and carry the conflict into the Federal territory. An army of at least sixty thousand should march into Maryland and appear before the National Capital. President Davis could not be won over to the plan while McClellan was still in a position to be reenforced by sea, but Lee, seeing that McClellan remained inactive, had determined, by sending Jackson westward, to repeat the successful tactics of the previous spring in the Shenandoah valley. Such a move might result in the recall of McClellan.

And so it happened. No sooner had Halleck assumed command of all the Northern armies than the matter of McClellan's withdrawal was agitated and on August 3d the head of the Army of the Potomac, to his bitter disappointment, was ordered to join Pope on the Rappahannock. Halleck was much concerned as to how Lee would act during the Federal evacuation of the Peninsula, uncertain whether the Confederates would attempt to crush Pope before McClellan could reenforce him, or whether McClellan would be attacked as soon as he was out of his strong entrenchments at Harrison's Landing.

[24]

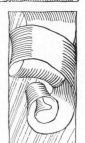

THE LEADER OF THE CHARGE

The Hero of the Federal Attack. General Samuel W. Crawford, here seen with his staff, at Cedar Mountain led a charge on the left flank of the Confederate forces that came near being disastrous for Jackson. At about six o'clock the brigade was in line. General Williams reported: "At this time this brigade occupied the interior line of a strip of woods. A field, varying from 250 to 500 yards in width, lay between it and the next strip of woods. In moving across this field the three right regiments and the six companies of the Third Wisconsin were received by a terrific fire of musketry. The Third Wisconsin especially fell under a partial flank fire under which Lieut.-Colonel Crane fell and the regiment was obliged to give way. Of the three remaining regiments which continued the charge (Twenty-eighth New York, Forty-sixth Pennsylvania, and Fifth Connecticut) every field-officer and every adjutant was killed or disabled. In the Twenty-eighth New York every company officer was killed or wounded; in the Forty-sixth Pennsylvania all but five; in the Fifth Connecticut all but eight." It was one of the most heroic combats of the war.

A Leader of Cavalry. Colonel Alfred N. Duffié was in command of the First Rhode Island Cavalry, in the Cavalry Brigade of the Second Division of McDowell's (Third) Corps in Pope's Army of Virginia. The cavalry had been used pretty well during Pope's advance. On the 8th of August, the day before the battle of Cedar Mountain, the cavalry had proceeded south to the house of Dr. Slaughter. That night Duffié was on picket in advance of General Crawford's troops, which had come up during the day and pitched camp. The whole division came to his support on the next day. When the infantry fell back to the protection of the batteries, the cavalry was ordered to charge the advancing Confederates. "Officers and men behaved admirably, and I cannot speak too highly of the good conduct of all of the brigade," reported General Bayard. After the battle the cavalry covered the retreat of the artillery and ambulances. On August 18th, when the retreat behind the Rappahannoc was ordered, the cavalry again checked the Confederate advance. During the entire campaign the regiment of Colonel Duffié did yeoman's service.

COL. ALFRED N. DUFFIÉ

The latter of the two possibilities seemed the more probable, and Pope was therefore ordered to push his whole army toward Gordonsville, in the hope that Lee, compelled to strengthen Jackson, would be too weak to fall upon the retiring Army of the Potomac.

The Union army now occupied the great triangle formed roughly by the Rappahannock and the Rapidan rivers and the range of the Blue Ridge Mountains, with Culpeper Court House as the rallying point. Pope soon found that the capturing of New Madrid and Island No. 10 was easy in comparison with measuring swords with the Confederate generals in the East.

On August 6th Pope began his general advance upon Gordonsville. Banks already had a brigade at Culpeper Court House, and this was nearest to Jackson. The small settlement was the meeting place of four roads by means of which Pope's army of forty-seven thousand men would be united. Jackson, informed of the advance, immediately set his three divisions in motion for Culpeper, hoping to crush Banks, hold the town, and prevent the uniting of the Army of Virginia. His progress was slow. The remainder of Banks's corps reached Culpeper on the 8th. On the morning of the 9th Jackson finally got his troops over the Rapidan and the Robertson rivers. Two miles beyond the latter stream there rose from the plain the slope of Slaughter Mountain, whose ominous name is more often changed into Cedar. This "mountain" is an isolated foothill of the Blue Ridge, some twenty miles from the parent range, and a little north of the Rapidan. From its summit could be seen vast stretches of quiet farmlands which had borne their annual harvests since the days of the Cavaliers. Its gentle slopes were covered with forests, which merged at length into waving grain fields and pasture lands, dotted here and there with rural homes. It was here on the slope of Cedar Mountain that one of the most severe little battles of the war took place.

THE FIRST CLASH

Battlefield of Cedar Mountain, August 9, 1862. Here the Confederate army in its second advance on Washington first felt out the strength massed against it. After Lee's brilliant tactics had turned McClellan's Peninsula Campaign into a fiasco, the Confederate Government resolved to again take the offensive. Plans were formed for a general invasion of the North, the objective points ranging from Cincinnati eastward to the Federal capital and Philadelphia. Immediately after Washington got wind of this, Lincoln (on August 4th) issued a call for three hundred thousand men; and all haste was made to rush the forces of McClellan from the Peninsula and of Cox from West Virginia to the aid of the recently consolidated army under Pope. On August 9, 1862, the vanguards of "Stonewall" Jackson's army and of Pope's intercepting forces met at Cedar Mountain. Banks, with the Second Corps of the Federal army, about eight thousand strong, attacked Jackson's forces of some sixteen thousand. The charge was so furious that Jackson's left flank was broken and rolled up, the rear of the center fired upon, and the whole line thereby thrown into confusion. Banks, however, received no reenforcements, while Jackson received strong support. The Federal troops were driven back across the ground which they had swept clear earlier in the afternoon.

The Battle of Cedar Mountain, August 9, 1862. The lower picture was taken the day after the battle that had raged for a brief two hours on the previous evening. After an artillery fire that filled half the afternoon, the advanced Federal cavalry was pressed back on the infantry supporting the batteries. Banks underestimated the strength of the Confederates. Instead of sending to Pope for reenforcements, he ordered a charge on the approaching troops. The Confederates, still feeling their way, were unprepared for this movement and were thrown into confusion. But at the moment when the Federal charge was about to end in success, three brigades of A. P. Hill in reserve were called up. They forced the Federals to retrace their steps to the point where the fighting began. Here the Federal retreat, in turn, was halted by General Pope with reenforcements. The Confederates moving up their batteries, a short-range artillery fight was kept up until midnight. At daylight it was found that Ewell and Jackson had fallen back two miles farther up the mountain. Pope advanced to the former Confederate ground and rested, after burying the dead. The following morning the Confederates had disappeared. The loss to both armies was almost three thousand in killed, wounded and missing. The battle had accomplished nothing.

On the banks of Cedar Run, seven miles south of Culpeper and but one or two north of the mountain, Banks's cavalry were waiting to oppose Jackson's advance. Learning of this the latter halted and waited for an attack. He placed Ewell's batteries on the slope about two hundred feet above the valley and sent General Winder to take a strong position on the left. So admirably was Jackson's army stationed that it would have required a much larger force, approaching it from the plains, to dislodge it. And yet, General Banks made an attempt with an army scarcely one-third as large as that of Jackson.

General Pope had made glowing promises of certain success and he well knew that the whole North was eagerly watching and waiting for him to fulfil them. He must strike somewhere and do it soon—and here was his chance at Cedar Mountain. He sent Banks with nearly eight thousand men against this brilliant Southern commander with an army three times as large, holding a strong position on a mountain side.

Banks with his infantry left Culpeper Court House on the morning of August 9th and reached the Confederate stronghold in the afternoon. He approached the mountain through open fields in full range of the Confederate cannon, which presently opened with the roar of thunder. All heedless of danger the brave men ran up the slope as if to take the foe by storm, when suddenly they met a brigade of Ewell's division face to face and a brief, deadly encounter took place. In a few minutes the Confederate right flank began to waver and would no doubt have been routed but for the timely aid of another brigade and still another that rushed down the hill and opened fire on the Federal lines which extended along the eastern bank of Cedar Run.

Meanwhile the Union batteries had been wheeled into position and their deep roar answered that of the foe on the hill. For two or three hours the battle continued with the utmost fury. The ground was strewn with dead and dying

[28]

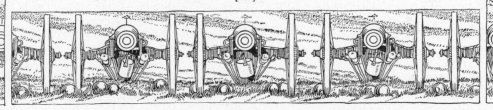

SURVIVORS OF THE FIGHTING TENTH

When Crawford's troops were driven back by A. P. Hill, he halted on the edge of a wheatfield, where he was reenforced by the Tenth Maine. For nearly half an hour it held its own, losing out of its 461 officers and men 173 in killed and wounded. A few days after the battle some survivors had a picture taken on the exact spot where they had so courageously fought. The remains of the cavalry horses can be seen in the trampled field of wheat. From left to right these men are: Lieutenant Littlefield, Lieutenant Whitney, Lieut.-Colonel Fillebrown, Captain Knowlton, and First-Sergeant Jordan, of Company C.

THE HOUSE WELL NAMED

Slaughter's house, overlooking the scene of carnage of Cedar Mountain, stood on the northern slope in the rear of the position taken by the Confederate troops under General Ewell. The brigades of Trimble and Hayes were drawn up near this house, at some distance from the brigade of Early. After the battle the whole of Jackson's army was drawn up on the slopes near it.

THE FUGITIVES

Virginia Negroes following Pope's soldiers in their retreat from Cedar mountain. From the beginning of the war Negroes had been a subject of debate. Even before Bull Run, on May 26, 1861, General B. F. Butler had declared that all fugitive slaves would be considered as contraband of war. Congress, however, decided in August that all slaves confiscated should be held subject to the decision of the United States courts. In April of 1862, General Hunter, at Hilton Head, South Carolina, declared that all slaves in his military department were "forever free," but a week later Lincoln annulled the proclamation. Hunter, however, raised a storm by organizing a regiment of fugitive slaves. It was only before Cedar Mountain—to be precise, on July 22, 1862—that "all National commanders were ordered

FOLLOWERS OF POPE'S RETREAT

to employ as many Negroes as could be used advantageously for military and naval purposes, paying them for their labor and keeping a record as to their ownership as a basis on which compensation could be made in proper cases." Ten days after the battle, Greeley published his famous letter to Lincoln, "The Prayer of Twenty Millions." On September 22, 1862, the Emancipation Proclamation was issued, and on January 1, 1863, the final proclamation was made that "Negroes would be received into the military and naval service of the United States Corps." This picture was taken about the time Greeley's letter was published-—less than two weeks after the battle of Cedar Mountain had been fought.

and human blood was poured out like water. But the odds were too great and at length, as the shades of evening were settling over the gory field, Banks began to withdraw the remnant of his troops. But he left two thousand of his brave lads—one fourth of his whole army—dead or dying along the hillside, while the Confederate losses were in excess of thirteen hundred.

The dead and wounded of both armies lay mingled in masses over the whole battle-field. While the fighting continued, neither side could send aid or relief to the maimed soldiers, who suffered terribly from thirst and lack of attention as the sultry day gave place to a close, oppressive night.

General Pope had remained at Culpeper, but, hearing the continuous cannonading and knowing that a sharp engagement was going on, hastened to the battle-field in the afternoon with a fresh body of troops under General Ricketts, arriving just before dark. He instantly ordered Banks to withdraw his right wing so as to make room for Ricketts; but the Confederates, victorious as they had been, refused to continue the contest against the reenforcements and withdrew to the woods up the mountain side. Heavy shelling was kept up by the hard-worked artillerymen of both armies until nearly midnight, while the Federal troops rested on their arms in line of battle. For two days the armies faced each other across the valley. Then both quietly withdrew. Pope's first battle as leader of an Eastern army had resulted in neither victory nor defeat.

PART I
THE RISE OF LEE

THE SECOND BATTLE AT
BULL RUN

THE UNION RETREAT—SIGEL'S CORPS RECROSSING THE
RAPPAHANNOCK, AUGUST 19, 1862

THE RAILROAD AS AN

The Federals are clearing up the railroad, the Confederate damage to which compelled Pope to fall back in order to retard Lee's advance toward Washington. "Stonewall" Jackson, who knew every foot of the Manassas region, did not despatch Ewell's forces with Stuart's cavalry to fall upon Catlett's Station and Manassas Junction for nothing. At Manassas the Confederates captured a million dollars' worth of army reserve supplies, seriously crippling Pope's movements for the remainder of the campaign. Meanwhile Jackson, pressing forward, united with Ewell and threatened Pope's exposed flank. The purpose of the advance of Jackson to give battle to Pope

ELEMENT IN WARFARE

near Manassas and Bull Run was to prevent the concentration of a heavy Federal force between his column and Longstreet's, then more than a day's march distant. The crippling of his railroad communication and the seizure of his stores were not in themselves sufficient to do this. In the pictures we see the work-trains of the Military Railroad removing the wreckage, gathering up débris to be used in repairing the road and its rolling-stock, and the tracks being relaid and guarded by the soldiers. Before Pope could reestablish his railroad communication, Lee's clever maneuvers drew the Federals into the disastrous battle of Second Bull Run.

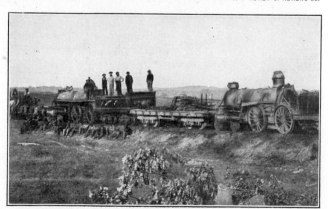

[B]

AN IMPORTANT PART OF THE WAR GAME

A problem for the practical railroad man. It takes all kinds of people to make up a world and it takes all kinds of men to make up an army. In the volunteer forces that fought in the ranks of both North and South were men of every calling, every profession, mechanics, artisans, artificers, men familiar with machine-shop practice as well as the men of field and plow, and the thinking soldier whose hand was as ready with the pen as with the sword. Was an engine-driver needed, or a farrier or carpenter, the colonel of a regiment had but to shout. But so important did the lines of communication by railway become to both armies that separate com-

REPAIRING AFTER THE CONFEDERATE RAID ON POPE'S LINE OF MARCH

mands of practical engineers, trackmen, and wreckers had to be organized and maintained. Train-wrecking seems a cruel act of deliberate vandalism, yet it is part of warfare. When penetrating the enemy's country over unpatroled and ill-guarded routes, the engine-driver might expect any time to see just ahead of him, and too late to call for brakes, the misplaced rail or the broken culvert that would hurl him and his train, laden sometimes with human freight, into river-bed or deep abyss. War leads to strenuous life and deeds of daring, and upon no force was the labor and the danger harder than the men of the track and throttle.

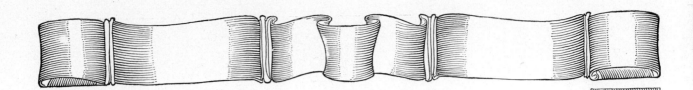

SECOND BATTLE OF BULL RUN

The battle was indeed one of which General Lee had good reason to be proud. It would be hard to find a better instance of that masterly comprehension of the actual condition of things which marks a great general than was exhibited in General Lee's allowing our formidable attack, in which more than half the Federal army was taking part, to be fully developed and to burst upon the exhausted troops of Stonewall Jackson, while Lee, relying upon the ability of that able soldier to maintain his position, was maturing and arranging for the great attack on our left flank by the powerful corps of Longstreet.—*John C. Ropes, in "The Army Under Pope."*

THE battle of Cedar Mountain was but a prelude to the far greater one that was to take place three weeks later on the banks of the little stream that had given its name, the year before, to the first important battle of the war; and here again the result to be registered was similar to that of the preceding year—a result that brought dismay to the people of the North and exultation to the adherents of the Southern cause. The three intervening weeks between the battles of Cedar Mountain and the Second Bull Run were spent in sparring, in marshaling the armed hosts, in heavy skirmishing and getting position for a final decisive struggle.

Two events of this period invite special attention. The respective heroes were J. E. B. Stuart, the daring Southern cavalry leader, and "Stonewall" Jackson. The victim in each case was General Pope. Before relating these incidents, however, we must take a general view of the field. General Pope's headquarters at this moment were at Culpeper, with a large part of his army, but he had left much of his personal baggage and many of his private papers at Catlett's, a station on the Orange and Alexandria Railroad between Culpeper and

[38]

THE UNHEEDED WARNING

Here we see Catlett's Station, on the Orange & Alexandria Railroad, which Stuart's cavalry seized in a night sortie on August 22, 1862. The damage done was not severe. Stuart was unable to burn the loaded wagon-trains surrounding the station and had to content himself with capturing horses, which he mounted with wounded Federal soldiers; he escaped at four the next morning, driven off by the approach of a superior force. Pope, at the time, was in possession of the fords of the Rappahannock, trying to check the Confederate advance toward the Shenandoah.

CATLETT'S STATION

At Manassas Junction, as it appeared in the upper picture on August 26, 1862, is one of the great neglected strategic points in the theater of the war. Twenty-five miles from Alexandria and thirty miles in a direct line from Washington, it was almost within long cannon-shot from any point in both the luckless battles of Bull Run. It was on the railway route connecting with Richmond, and at the junction of the railway running across the entrance to the Shenandoah Valley and beyond the Blue Ridge, through Manassas Gap. The Confederates knew its value,

Stuart's raid, however, so alarmed General Halleck that he immediately telegraphed Pope from Washington: "By no means expose your railroad communication with Alexandria. It is of the utmost importance in sending your supplies and reinforcements." Pope did not fall back upon his railroad communication, however, until after Jackson had seized Manassas Junction. and after the first battle of Bull Run built the fortifications which we see in the upper picture, to the left beyond the supply-cars on the railroad. Pope, after the battle of Cedar Mountain, should have covered it, extending his lines so as to protect it from Jackson's incursion through Thoroughfare Gap; instead he held the main force of his army opposing that of Lee.

Manassas Junction, while his vast store of army supplies was at the latter place.

Pope's great source of uncertainty lay in the fact that he did not know whether Lee would move against him or would follow McClellan in the latter's retreat from the Peninsula; nor did he know when the reenforcements promised from McClellan's army would reach him. Meanwhile Lee had decided to let McClellan depart in peace and to advance against Pope, with the whole Confederate army. To this end Longstreet was ordered to the scene and with his corps he reached Gordonsville on August 13th.

A few days later the two Confederate generals, Lee and Longstreet, ascended to the top of Clark's Mountain, from which, through powerful field-glasses, they obtained a good view of Culpeper, about twelve miles away. They saw that Pope's position was weak and determined to attack him without delay. Lee ordered his army to cross the Rapidan. He also sent a courier to gallop across the country with an important dispatch to General Stuart, disclosing his plans. It was now that General Pope met fortune; he captured the courier and learned of Lee's plans. Pope knew that he was not in position to meet Lee's army at Culpeper, and he withdrew from that place and took up a strong position behind the Rappahannock. Lee had strained every nerve to get at his antagonist before the latter left Culpeper and before he could be reenforced by McClellan's army. But sudden rains changed the Rappahannock from a placid stream into a rushing torrent. The Confederates were delayed and meantime the reenforcements from the Peninsula began to reach Pope's army. General Reno with a part of Burnside's corps was on the ground by August 14th. One week later came Generals Kearny and Reynolds —both splendid leaders, both destined to give their lives for their country within a year—to join the Army of Virginia with some thousands of additional fighters from the Army of the Potomac.

[40]

WHERE THE THUNDERBOLT FELL

The havoc wrought by the Confederate attack of August 26th on the Federal supply depot at Manassas Junction is here graphically preserved. When Jackson arrived at sunset of that day at Bristoe's Station, on the Orange & Alexandria Railroad, he knew that his daring movement would be reported to Pope's forces by the trains that escaped both north and south. To save themselves, the troops that had already marched twenty-five miles had to make still further exertions. Trimble volunteered to move on Manassas Junction; and, under command of Stuart, a small force moved northward through the woods. At midnight it arrived within half a mile of the Junction. The Federal force greeted it with artillery fire, but when the Confederates charged at the sound of the bugle the gunners abandoned the batteries to the assaulters. Some three hundred of the small Federal garrison were captured, with the immense stores that filled the warehouses to overflowing. The next morning Hill's and Taliaferro's divisions arrived to hold the position. The half-starved troops were now in possession of all that was needed to make them an effective force. Jackson was now in position to control the movements of the Federal army under Pope.

Lee was completely thwarted in his purpose of attacking Pope before his reenforcements arrived. But he was not idle. He sent the dauntless cavalry leader, J. E. B. Stuart, to make a raid around the Union army. Stuart did this effectively, and this was the first of the two notable events of these weeks of sparring. Crossing the Rappahannock at Waterloo Bridge with fifteen hundred mounted men as bold and dauntless as himself, Stuart dashed up the country, riding all day and all night. After the coming of night on the evening of the 22d, in the midst of a torrential rainstorm, while the darkness was so intense that every man was guided by the tread of his brother horsemen, Stuart pounced upon the Federals near Catlett's Station, overpowered the astonished guard, captured nearly two hundred prisoners, scattering the remainder of the troops stationed there far and wide in the darkness, and seized Pope's despatch-book with his plans and private papers. Stuart took also several hundred fine horses and burned a large number of wagons laden with supplies. Among his trophies was a fine uniform cloak and hat which were the personal property of General Pope. These were exchanged on the following day for General Stuart's plumed hat which a few days before had been left behind by that officer when surprised by Federal troops.

Stuart's bold raid proved a serious misfortune for the Union army. But Lee had far greater things in store. His next move was to send Jackson to Pope's rear with a large part of the Confederate army. Stealthily Jackson led his army westward, shielded by the woods, the thickets, and the low hills of the Blue Ridge. It was a quiet rural community through which he passed. The great majority of the simple country folk had never seen an army, though it is true that for many days the far-away boom of cannon had reached their ears from the valley of the Rapidan. Now here was a real army at their very doors. Nor was it a hostile army, for their sympathies were Southern. With baskets and armfuls of

[42]

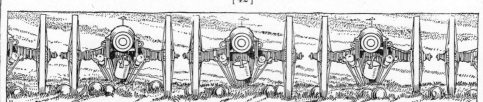

A START TOO LONG DELAYED

Where the troops of General McClellan, waiting near the round-house at Alexandria, were hurried forward to the scene of action where Pope was struggling with Jackson and Ewell. Pope had counted upon the assistance of these reënforcements in making the forward movement by which he expected to hold Lee back. The old bogey of leaving the National Capital defenseless set up a vacillation in General Halleck's mind and the troops were held overlong at Alexandria. Had they been promptly forwarded, "Stonewall" Jackson's blow at Manassas Junction could not have been struck. At the news of that disaster the troops were hurriedly despatched down the railroad toward Manassas. But Pope was already in retreat in three columns toward that point, McDowell had failed to intercept the Confederate reënforcements coming through Thoroughfare Gap, and the situation had become critical. General Taylor, with his brigade of New Jersey troops, was the first of McClellan's forces to be moved forward to the aid of Pope. At Union

BRIGADIER–GENERAL
GEORGE W. TAYLOR

Mills, Colonel Scammon, commanding the First Brigade, driven back from Manassas Junction, was further pressed by the Confederates on the morning of August 27th. Later in the day General Taylor's brigade arrived by the Fairfax road and, crossing the railroad bridge, met the Confederates drawn up and waiting near Manassas Station. A severe artillery fire greeted the Federals as they emerged from the woods. As General Taylor had no artillery, he was obliged either to retire or charge. He chose the latter. When the Confederate cavalry threatened to surround his small force, however, Taylor fell back in good order across the bridge, where two Ohio regiments assisted in holding the Confederates in check. At this point, General Taylor, who had been wounded in the retreat, was borne past in a litter. Though suffering much, he appealed to the officers to prevent another Bull Run. The brigade retired in good order to Fairfax Court House, where General Taylor died of his wounds a short time afterward.

bread and pies and cakes they cheered as best they could the tattered and hungry men on the march.

General Lee in the meantime had kept Longstreet in front of Pope's army on the Rappahannock to make daily demonstrations and feints and thus to divert Pope's attention from Jackson's movements and lead him to believe that he was to be attacked in front. The trick was eminently successful. "Stonewall" Jackson suddenly, on August 26th, emerged from the Bull Run Mountains by way of the Thoroughfare Gap and marshaled his clans on the plains of Manassas, but a few miles from the site of the famous battle of the year before.

Pope had taken alarm. He was astonished to find Jackson in his rear, and he had to decide instantly between two courses—to abandon his communications with Fredericksburg on the one hand, or with Alexandria and Washington on the other. He decided to keep in touch with Washington at all hazards. Breaking his camp on the Rappahannock, he hastened with all speed to lead his forces toward Manassas Junction, where he had stored vast quantities of provisions and munitions of war. But he was too late to save them. Jackson had been joined by Stuart and his cavalry. On the evening of the 26th they were still some miles from Manassas and Trimble was sent ahead to make sure the capture before Pope's army could arrive. Through the darkness rode these same hardy men who had a few nights before made their bold raid on Catlett's Station. Before midnight they reached Manassas. They met little opposition. The guard was overpowered. The spoils of this capture were great, including three hundred prisoners, one hundred and seventy-five horses, ten locomotives, seven long trains of provisions, and vast stores and munitions of war.

Next morning the weary and hungry foot soldiers of Jackson's army came upon the scene and whatever else they did they feasted as only hungry men can. An eye-witness wrote, "To see a starving man eating lobster-salad and

[44]

AN UNREALIZED OPPORTUNITY

Here might have been won a Federal victory that would have precluded defeat at Second Bull Run. The corps of General Heintzelman, consisting of the divisions of Hooker and Kearny, was the next detachment of McClellan's forces to arrive to the aid of Pope. On the 28th of August, Heintzelman had pushed forward to Centreville, entering it soon after "Stonewall" Jackson's rear-guard had retired. Instead of pursuing, Heintzelman drew up his forces east of Cub Run, which we see in the picture. Jackson's forces, now in a precarious position, fell back toward Thoroughfare Gap to form a junction with Longstreet's Corps, which Lee had sent forward. The battle was commenced on the west somewhat feebly by Generals McDowell and Sigel. By nightfall the Confederate left had been driven back fully a mile.

MAJOR–GENERAL SAMUEL P. HEINTZELMAN AND STAFF

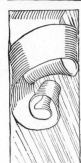

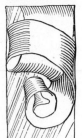

drinking Rhine wine, barefooted and in tatters, was curious; the whole thing was incredible."

The amazement at the North when the news of the capture of Manassas became known cannot be described. But the newspapers belittled it, declaring that it was merely a bold raid and that for any large force to get between Pope's army and Washington before Pope became aware of the attempt was simply impossible.

Jackson had done an astonishing thing. But his position was precarious, nevertheless. Pope was moving toward him with a far larger army, recently augmented by Heintzelman's corps from the Army of the Potomac, while Fitz John Porter with an additional force was not far off. It is true that Longstreet was hastening to the aid of Jackson, but he had to come by the same route which had brought Jackson— through Thoroughfare Gap—and Pope thought he saw a great opportunity. If he could only detain Longstreet at the gap, why should he not crush Jackson with his superior numbers? To this end he sent orders to Porter, to McDowell, and to Kearny and others whose forces were scattered about the country, to concentrate during the night of the 27th and move upon Jackson. McDowell sent Ricketts with a small force—too small—to prevent Longstreet from passing through Thoroughfare Gap, and hastened to join the main army against Jackson. But that able commander was not to be caught in a trap. He moved from Manassas Junction by three roads toward the old battle-field of Bull Run and by noon on the 28th the whole corps was once more united between Centreville and Sudley Spring. Late in the day he encountered King's division of McDowell's corps near the village of Groveton, and a sharp fight was opened and kept up till an hour after dark. The Confederates were left in possession of the field.

The following day, August 29th, was the first of the two days' battle, leaving out of account the fight of the evening

THE TWICE–WON FIELD

MAJOR–GENERAL R. S.
EWELL

MAJOR–GENERAL JAMES
LONGSTREET

Sleeping on their arms on the night of August 29th, the Federal veterans were as confident of having won a victory as were the raw troops in the beginning of the first battle of Bull Run. But the next day's fighting was to tell the tale. General Ewell had been wounded in the knee by a minie ball in the severe fight at Groveton and was unable to lead his command; but for the impetuosity of this commander was substituted that of Longstreet, nicknamed 'the War-Horse," whose arrival in the midst of the previous day's engagement had cost the Federals dear On the morning of the second day Longstreet's batteries opened the engagement. When the general advance came, as the sun shone on the parallel lines of glittering bayonets, it was Longstreet's men bringing their muskets to "the ready" who first opened fire with a long flash of flame. It was they who pressed most eagerly forward and, in the face of the Federal batteries, fell upon the troops of General McDowell at the left and drove them irresistibly back. Although the right Federal wing, in command of General Heintzelman, had not given an inch, it was this turning of the left by Longstreet which put the whole Federal army in retreat, driving them across Bull Run. The Confederates were left in possession of the field, where lay thousands of Federal dead and wounded, and Lee was free to advance his victorious troops into the North unmolested.

THE BATTLE–FIELD OF SECOND BULL RUN (MANASSAS), AUGUST 29–30, 1862

before and the desultory fighting of the preceding ten days. General Pope was still hopeful of crushing Jackson before the arrival of Longstreet, and on the morning of the 29th he ordered a general advance across Bull Run. As the noon hour approached a wild shout that arose from Jackson's men told too well of the arrival of Longstreet. Far away on the hills near Gainesville could be seen the marching columns of Longstreet, who had passed through the gap in safety and who was now rushing to the support of Jackson. The Confederate army was at last to be reunited. Jackson was greatly relieved. Pope had lost his opportunity of fighting the army of his opponent in sections.

The field was almost the same that the opposing forces had occupied a year and a month before when the first great battle of the war was fought. And many of them were the same men. Some who had engaged in that first conflict had gone home and had refused to reenlist; others had found soldiers' graves since then—but still others on both sides were here again, no longer the raw recruits that they were before, but, with their year of hard experience in the field, they were trained soldiers, equal to any in the world.

The two armies faced each other in a line nearly five miles long. There was heavy fighting here and there along the line from the early morning hours, but no general engagement until late in the afternoon. The Union right pressed hard against the Confederate left and by ten o'clock had forced it back more than a mile. But the Confederates, presently reenforced in that quarter, hurled heavy masses of infantry against the Union right and regained much that it had lost. Late in the afternoon fresh regiments under Kearny and Hooker charged the Confederate left, which was swept back and rolled in upon the center. But presently the Southern General Hood, with his famous Texan brigade, rushed forward in a wild, irresistible dash, pressed Kearny back, captured one gun, several flags and a hundred prisoners. Night then closed over

[48]

THE FIGHTING FORTY-FIRST

"C" Company of the Forty-first New York after the Second Battle of Bull Run, August 30, 1862. When the troops of Generals Milroy and Schurz were hard pressed by overpowering numbers and exhausted by fatigue, this New York regiment, being ordered forward, quickly advanced with a cheer along the Warrenton Turnpike and deployed about a mile west of the field of the conflict of July 21, 1861. The fighting men replied with answering shouts, for with the regiment that came up at the double quick galloped a battery of artillery. The charging Confederates were held and this position was assailed time and again. It became the center of the sanguinary combat of the day, and it was here that the "Bull-Dogs" earned their name. Among the first to respond to Lincoln's call, they enlisted in June, '61, and when their first service was over they stepped forward to a man, specifying no term of service but putting their names on the Honor Roll of "For the War."

BRIG.-GEN. RUFUS KING

Brigadier-General King, a division commander in this battle, was a soldier by profession, and a diplomatist and journalist by inheritance—for he was a graduate of West Point, a son of Charles King, editor of the New York *American* in 1827, and a grandson of the elder Rufus, an officer of the Revolution and Minister to the Court of St. James. He had left the army in 1836 to become Assistant Engineer of the New York & Erie Railroad, a post he gave up to become editor of the *Daily Advertiser*, and subsequently of the Milwaukee *Sentinel*. At the outbreak of the war Lincoln had appointed him Minister to Rome, but he asked permission to delay his departure, and was made a Brigadier-General of Volunteers. Later he resigned as Minister, and was assigned to McDowell's corps. At the battle of Manassas, in which the Forty-first New York earned honor, he proved an able leader. In 1867 he was again appointed as Minister of the United States to Italy.

the scene and the two armies rested on their arms until the morning.

The first day's battle is sometimes called the battle of Groveton, but usually it is considered as the first half of the second battle of Bull Run. It was a formidable conflict in itself. The Union loss was at least forty-five hundred men, the Confederate was somewhat larger. Over the gory field lay multitudes of men, the blue and the gray commingled, who would dream of battlefields no more. The living men lay down among the dead in order to snatch a little rest and strength that they might renew the strife in the morning.

It is a strange fact that Lee and Pope each believed that the other would withdraw his army during the night, and each was surprised in the morning to find his opponent still on the ground, ready, waiting, defiant. It was quite certain that on this day, August 30th, there would be a decisive action and that one of the two armies would be victor and the other defeated. The two opposing commanders had called in their outlying battalions and the armies now faced each other in almost full force, the Confederates with over fifty thousand men and the Union forces exceeding their opponents by probably fifteen thousand men. The Confederate left wing was commanded by Jackson, and the right by Longstreet. The extreme left of the Union army was under Fitz John Porter, who, owing to a misunderstanding of orders, had not reached the field the day before. The center was commanded by Heintzelman and the right by Reno.

In the early hours of the morning the hills echoed with the firing of artillery, with which the day was opened. Porter made an infantry attack in the forenoon, but was met by the enemy in vastly superior numbers and was soon pressed back in great confusion. As the hours passed one fearful attack followed another, each side in turn pressing forward and again receding. In the afternoon a large part of

THE ADVANCE THAT BECAME A RETREAT

The Stone Bridge across Bull Run.   When the Federal army silently put Bull Run between itself and Lee on the night of August 30, 1862, Pope's attempt to capture Richmond was turned into a Confederate advance upon Washington.   Lee, on discovering Pope's position at Centreville on the next day, sent "Stonewall" Jackson to turn the Federal right.   Crossing Bull Run at Sudley Ford, Jackson advanced along a country road till he reached the Little River Turnpike, on which the troops bivouacked for the night.   On September 1st he was met near Chantilly by Reno and Kearney, who had been sent by Pope to intercept him.   A fierce encounter followed in a drenching rainstorm.   The brilliant bayonet charge by Birney, in command of the division of General Philip Kearney, who had just fallen, drove back the Confederates, and Birney held the field that night.   The next morning orders came from General Halleck for the broken and demoralized army of Pope to fall back within the defenses of Washington.   Large quantities of Federal stores were left to fall into the hands of Lee, which were of great use in his advance into Maryland.

[B]

the Union army made a desperate onslaught on the Confederate left under Jackson. Here for some time the slaughter of men was fearful. It was nearing sunset. Jackson saw that his lines were wavering. He called for reenforcements which did not come and it seemed as if the Federals were about to win a signal victory. But this was not to be. Far away on a little hill at the Confederate right Longstreet placed four batteries in such a position that he could enfilade the Federal columns. Quickly he trained his cannon on the Federal lines that were hammering away at Jackson, and opened fire. Ghastly gaps were soon cut in the Federal ranks and they fell back. But they re-formed and came again and still again, each time only to be mercilessly cut down by Longstreet's artillery. At length, with the coming of darkness, the whole Union front began to waver and show signs of disorder.

General Lee, seeing this, ordered the Confederates in all parts of the field to advance. With wild, triumphant yells they did so. It was now dark and there was little more fighting; but Lee captured several thousand prisoners. Pope retreated across Bull Run with the remnant of his army and by morning was ensconced behind the field-works at Centreville.

There was no mistaking the fact that General Pope had lost the battle and the campaign. He decided to lead his army back to the entrenchments of Washington. After spending a day behind the embankments at Centreville, the retreat was begun. Lee's troops with Jackson in the advance pursued and struck a portion of the retreating army at Chantilly.

It was late in the afternoon of September 1st. The rain, accompanied by vivid lightning and terrific crashes of thunder, was falling in torrents as Stuart's horsemen, sent in advance, were driven back by the Federal infantry. Jackson now pushed two of A. P. Hill's brigades forward to ascertain the condition of the Union army. General Reno was protecting Pope's right flank, and he lost no time in proceeding against Hill. The latter was promptly checked, and both forces took

FAIRFAX COURT HOUSE, VIRGINIA

Pope's retirement from the field of Bull Run gave the famous Confederate cavalry leader, J. E. B. Stuart, a splendid opportunity for the kind of warfare he most delighted in. No sooner had the Federals started than Stuart was following them. Ascertaining that their main body was at Centreville and Fairfax Court House, he planned to make an attack on the pike between the two places. A section of the famous Washington Artillery took position just after dark on August 31st, within range of a road completely filled with a continuous stream of Federal army wagons making their way toward the Court House. A few rounds from the Confederate guns threw "everything into confusion, and such commotion, upsetting, collisions, and smash-ups were rarely ever seen." Stuart bivouacked that night near Chantilly, and after Jackson came up on September 1st, tried to force his way down the pike toward Fairfax Court House. But the Federals were too strong in number at that point. The next day (September 2d) Halleck sent word to Pope to bring his army back to Washington. Stuart then promptly took possession of Fairfax Court House, after a sharp skirmish with some of Sumner's departing troops.

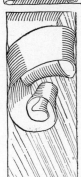

position for battle. One side and then the other fell back in turn as lines were re-formed and urged forward. Night fell and the tempest's fury increased. The ammunition of both armies was so wet that much of it could not be used. Try as they would the Confederates were unable to break the Union line and the two armies finally withdrew. The Confederates suffered a loss of five hundred men in their unsuccessful attempt to demoralize Pope in his retreat, and the Federals more than a thousand, including Generals Stevens and Kearny.

General Kearny might have been saved but for his reckless bravery. He was rounding up the retreat of his men in the darkness of the night when he chanced to come within the Confederate lines. Called on to surrender, he lay flat on his horse's back, sank his spurs into its sides, and attempted to escape. Half a dozen muskets were leveled and fired at the fleeing general. Within thirty yards he rolled from his horse's back dead.

The consternation in Washington and throughout the North when Pope's defeated army reached Arlington Heights can better be imagined than described. General Pope, who bore the brunt of public indignation, begged to be relieved of the command. The President complied with his wishes and the disorganized remnants of the Army of Virginia and the Army of the Potomac were handed to the " Little Napoleon " of Peninsula fame, George B. McClellan.

The South was overjoyed with its victory—twice it had unfurled its banner in triumph on the battlefield at Manassas by the remarkable strategy of its generals and the courage of its warriors on the firing-line. Twice it had stood literally on the road that led to the capital of the Republic, only by some strange destiny of war to fail to enter its precincts on the wave of victory.

PART I
THE RISE OF LEE

ANTIETAM—THE
INVASION OF THE NORTH

THE FIRST STAND
OF "STONEWALL'S" MEN

McCLELLAN'S LAST ADVANCE

This splendid landscape photograph of the pontoon bridge at Berlin, Maryland, was taken in October, 1862. On the 26th McClellan crossed the Potomac here for the last time in command of an army. Around this quiet and picturesque country the Army of the Potomac bivouacked during October, 1862, leaving two corps posted at Harper's Ferry to hold the outlet of the Shenandoah Valley. At Berlin (a little village of about four hundred inhabitants), McClellan had his headquarters during the reorganization of the army, which he considered necessary after Antietam. The many reverses to the Federal arms since the beginning of the war had weakened the popular hold of the Lincoln Administration, and there was constant political pressure for an aggressive move against Lee. McClellan, yielding at last to this demand, began advancing his army into Virginia. Late on the night of November 7th, through a heavy rainstorm, General Buckingham, riding post-

THE CROSSING AFTER ANTIETAM

haste from Washington, reached McClellan's tent at Rectortown, and handed him Stanton's order reliev-
ing him from command. Burnside was appointed his successor, and at the moment was with him in the
tent. Without a change of countenance, McClellan handed him the despatch, with the words: "Well, Burnside, you are to command the army." Whatever may have been McClellan's fault, the moment chosen for
his removal was most inopportune and ungracious. His last advance upon Lee was excellently planned, and
he had begun to execute it with great vigor—the van of the army having reached Warrenton on November 7th, opposed only by half of Lee's army at Culpeper, while demonstrations across the gaps of the Blue
Ridge compelled the retention of Jackson with the other half in the Shenandoah Valley. Never before had
the Federal military prospect been brighter than at that moment.

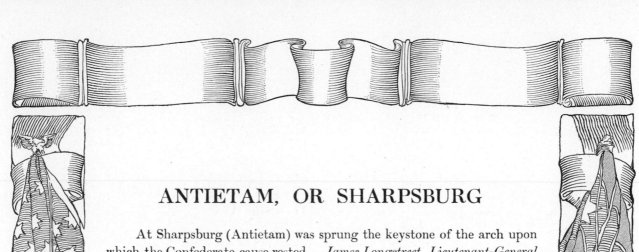

ANTIETAM, OR SHARPSBURG

At Sharpsburg (Antietam) was sprung the keystone of the arch upon which the Confederate cause rested.—*James Longstreet, Lieutenant-General C.S.A., in "Battles and Leaders of the Civil War."*

A BATTLE remarkable in its actualities but more wonderful in its possibilities was that of Antietam, with the preceding capture of Harper's Ferry and the other interesting events that marked the invasion of Maryland by General Lee. It was one of the bloodiest and the most picturesque conflicts of the Civil War, and while it was not all that the North was demanding and not all that many military critics think it might have been, it enabled President Lincoln to feel that he could with some assurance issue, as he did, his Emancipation Proclamation.

Lee's army, fifty thousand strong, had crossed the Potomac at Leesburg and had concentrated around Frederick, the scene of the Barbara Frietchie legend, only forty miles from Washington. When it became known that Lee, elated by his victory at Second Bull Run, had taken the daring step of advancing into Maryland, and now threatened the capital of the Republic, McClellan, commanding the Army of the Potomac, pushed his forces forward to encounter the invaders. Harper's Ferry, at the junction of the Potomac and the Shenandoah rivers, was a valuable defense against invasion through the Valley of Virginia, but once the Confederates had crossed it, a veritable trap. General Halleck ordered it held and General Lee sent "Stonewall" Jackson to take it, by attacking the fortress on the Virginia side.

Jackson began his march on September 10th with secret instructions from his commander to encompass and capture the

[58]

LEE LOCKS THE GATES

Sharpsburg, Maryland, September 17, 1862.   There were long minutes on that sunny day in the early fall of 1862 when Robert E. Lee, at his headquarters west of Sharpsburg, must have been in almost entire ignorance of how the battle went. Outnumbered he knew his troops were; outfought he knew they never would be. Longstreet, Hood, D. B. Hill, Evans, and D. R. Jones had turned back more than one charge in the morning; but, as the day wore on, Lee perceived that the center must be held.   Sharpsburg was the key.   He had deceived McClellan as to his numerical strength and he must continue to do so.   Lee had practically no reserves at all.   At one time General Longstreet reported from the center to General Chilton, Lee's Chief of Staff, that Cooke's North Carolina regiment— still keeping its colors at the front—had not a cartridge left.   None but veteran troops could hold a line like this, supported by only two guns of Miller's battery of the Washington Artillery.   Of this crisis in the battle General Longstreet wrote afterward: "We were already badly whipped nd were holding our ground by sheer force of desperation."   Actually in line that day on the Confederate side were only 37,000 men, and opposed to them were numbers that could be footed up to 50,000 more.   At what time in the day General Lee must have perceived that the invasion of Maryland must come to an end cannot be told.   He had lost 20,000 of his tired, footsore army by straggling on the march, according to the report of Longstreet, who adds: "Nearly one-fourth of the troops who went into the battle were killed or wounded."   At dark Lee's rearward movement had begun.

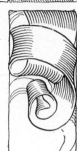

Federal garrison and the vast store of war material at this place, made famous a few years before by old John Brown. To conceal his purpose from the inhabitants he inquired along the route about the roads leading into Pennsylvania. It was from his march through Frederick that the Barbara Frietchie story took its rise. But there is every reason to believe that General Jackson never saw the good old lady, that the story is a myth, and that Mr. Whittier, who has given us the popular poem under the title of her name, was misinformed. However, Colonel H. K. Douglas, who was a member of Jackson's staff, relates, in "Battles and Leaders of the Civil War," an interesting incident where his commander on entering Middletown was greeted by two young girls waving a Union flag. The general bowed to the young women, raised his hat, and remarked to some of his officers, "We evidently have no friends in this town." Colonel Douglas concludes, "This is about the way he would have treated Barbara Frietchie."

On the day after Jackson left Frederick he crossed the Potomac by means of a ford near Williamsport and on the 13th he reached Bolivar Heights. Harper's Ferry lies in a deep basin formed by Maryland Heights on the north bank of the Potomac, Loudon Heights on the south bank, and Bolivar Heights on the west. The Shenandoah River breaks through the pass between Loudon and Bolivar Heights and the village lies between the two at the apex formed by the junction of the two rivers.

As Jackson approached the place by way of Bolivar Heights, Walker occupied Loudon Heights and McLaws invested Maryland Heights. All were unopposed except McLaws, who encountered Colonel Ford with a force to dispute his ascent. Ford, however, after some resistance, spiked his guns and retired to the Ferry, where Colonel Miles had remained with the greater portion of the Federal troops. Had Miles led his entire force to Maryland Heights he could no doubt have held his ground until McClellan came to his relief.

[60]

A REGIMENT THAT FOUGHT AT SOUTH MOUNTAIN—THE THIRTY-FIFTH NEW YORK

Here sits Colonel T. G. Morehead, who commanded the 106th Pennsylvania, of the Second Corps. At 7.20 A.M. the order came to advance, and with a cheer the Second Corps—men who for over two years had never lost a gun nor struck a color—pressed forward. But again they were halted. It was almost an hour later when Sedgwick's division, with Sumner at the head, crossed the Antietam. Arriving nearly opposite the Dunker church, it swept out over the cornfields. On it went, by Greene's right, through the West Woods; here it met the awful counter-stroke of Early's reënforced division and, stubbornly resisting, was hurled back with frightful loss.

COLONEL T. G. MOREHEAD

A HERO OF SEDGWICK'S CHARGE

Early in the morning of September 17, 1862, Knap's battery (shown below) got into the thick of the action of Antietam. General Mansfield had posted it opposite the north end of the West Woods, close to the Confederate line. The guns opened fire at seven o'clock. Practically unsupported, the battery was twice charged upon during the morning; but quickly substituting canister for shot and shell, the men held their ground and stemmed the Confederate advance. Near this spot General Mansfield was mortally wounded while deploying his troops. About noon a section of Knap's battery was detached to the assistance of General Greene, in the East Woods.

KNAP'S BATTERY, JUST AFTER THE BLOODY WORK AT ANTIETAM

But General Halleck had ordered him to hold Harper's Ferry to the last, and Miles interpreted this order to mean that he must hold the town itself. He therefore failed to occupy the heights around it in sufficient strength and thus permitted himself to be caught in a trap.

During the day of the 14th the Confederate artillery was dragged up the mountain sides, and in the afternoon a heavy fire was opened on the doomed Federal garrison. On that day McClellan received word from Miles that the latter could hold out for two days longer and the commanding general sent word: "Hold out to the last extremity. If it is possible, re-occupy the Maryland Heights with your entire force. If you can do that I will certainly be able to relieve you. . . . Hold out to the last." McClellan was approaching slowly and felt confident he could relieve the place.

On the morning of the 15th the roar of Confederate artillery again resounded from hill to hill. From Loudon to Maryland Heights the firing had begun and a little later the battle-flags of A. P. Hill rose on Bolivar Heights. Scarcely two hours had the firing continued when Colonel Miles raised the white flag at Harper's Ferry and its garrison of 12,500, with vast military stores, passed into the hands of the Confederates. Colonel Miles was struck by a stray fragment of a Confederate shell which gave him a mortal wound. The force of General Franklin, preparing to move to the garrison's relief, on the morning of the 15th noted that firing at the Ferry had ceased and suspected that the garrison had surrendered, as it had.

The Confederate Colonel Douglas, whose account of the surrender is both absorbing and authoritative, thus describes the surrender in " Battles and Leaders of the Civil War ":

" Under instructions from General Jackson, I rode up the pike and into the enemy's lines to ascertain the purpose of the white flag. Near the top of the hill I met General White and staff and told him my mission. He replied that Colonel Miles had been mortally wounded, that he was in command and

THE FIRST TO FALL

This photograph was taken back of the rail fence on the Hagerstown pike, where "Stonewall" Jackson's men attempted to rally in the face of Hooker's ferocious charge that opened the bloodiest day of the Civil War—September 17, 1862. Hooker, advancing to seize high ground nearly three-quarters of a mile distant, had not gone far before the glint of the rising sun disclosed the bayonet-points of a large Confederate force standing in a cornfield in his immediate front. This was a part of Jackson's Corps which had arrived during the morning of the 16th from the capture of Harper's Ferry and had been posted in this position to surprise Hooker in his advance. The outcome was a terrible surprise to the Confederates. All of Hooker's batteries hurried into action and opened with canister on the cornfield. The Confederates stood bravely up against this fire, and as Hooker's men advanced they made a determined resistance. Back and still farther back were Jackson's men driven across the open field, every stalk of corn in which was cut down by the battle as closely as a knife could have done it. On the ground the slain lay in rows precisely as they had stood in ranks. From the cornfield into a small patch of woods (the West Woods) the Confederates were driven, leaving the sad result of the surprise behind them. As the edge of the woods was approached by Hooker's men the resistance became stronger and more stubborn. Nearly all the units of two of Jackson's divisions were now in action, and cavalry and artillery were aiding them. "The two lines," says General Palfrey, "almost tore each other to pieces." General Starke and Colonel Douglas on the Confederate side were killed. More than half of Lawton's and Hays' brigades were either killed or wounded. On the Federal side General Ricketts lost a third of his division. The energy of both forces was entirely spent and reënforcements were necessary before the battle could be continued. Many of Jackson's men wore trousers and caps of Federal blue, as did most of the troops which had been engaged with Jackson in the affair at Harper's Ferry. A. P. Hill's men, arriving from Harper's Ferry that same afternoon, were dressed in new Federal uniforms—a part of their booty—and at first were mistaken for Federals by the friends who were anxiously awaiting them.

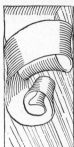 
desired to have an interview with General Jackson. . . . I conducted them to General Jackson, whom I found sitting on his horse where I had left him. . . . The contrast in appearances there presented was striking. General White, riding a handsome black horse, was carefully dressed and had on untarnished gloves, boots, and sword. His staff were equally comely in costume. On the other hand, General Jackson was the dingiest, worst-dressed and worst-mounted general that a warrior who cared for good looks and style would wish to surrender to.

"General Jackson . . . rode up to Bolivar and down into Harper's Ferry. The curiosity in the Union army to see him was so great that the soldiers lined the sides of the road. . . . One man had an echo of response all about him when he said aloud: 'Boys, he's not much for looks, but if we'd had him we wouldn't have been caught in this trap.'"

McClellan had failed to reach Harper's Ferry in time to relieve it because he was detained at South Mountain by a considerable portion of Lee's army under D. H. Hill and Longstreet. McClellan had come into possession of Lee's general order, outlining the campaign. Discovering by this order that Lee had sent Jackson to attack Harper's Ferry he made every effort to relieve it.

The affair at Harper's Ferry, as that at South Mountain, was but a prelude to the tremendous battle that was to follow two days later on the banks of the little stream called Antietam Creek, in Maryland. When it was known that Lee had led his army across the Potomac the people were filled with consternation—the people, not only of the immediate vicinity, but of Harrisburg, of Baltimore, of Philadelphia. Their fear was intensified by the memory of the Second Bull Run of a few weeks earlier, and by the fact that at this very time General Bragg was marching northward across Kentucky with a great army, menacing Louisville and Cincinnati.

As one year before, the hopes of the North had centered in George B. McClellan, so it was now with the people of the

[64]

THE THRICE–FOUGHT GROUND

The field beyond the leveled fence is covered with both Federal and Confederate dead. Over this open space swept Sedgwick's division of Sumner's Second Corps, after passing through the East and entering the West Woods. This is near where the Confederate General Ewell's division, reënforced by McLaws and Walker, fell upon Sedgwick's left flank and rear. Nearly two thousand Federal soldiers were struck down, the division losing during the day more than forty per cent. of its entire number. One regiment lost sixty per cent.—the highest regimental loss sustained. Later the right of the Confederate line crossed the turnpike at the Dunker church (about half a mile to the left of the picture) and made two assaults upon Greene, but they were repulsed with great slaughter. General D. R. Jones, of Jackson's division, had been wounded. The brave Starke who succeeded him was killed; and Lawton, who followed Starke, had fallen wounded.

A flaming mansion was the guidon for the extreme left of Greene's division when (early in the morning) he had moved forward along the ridge leading to the East Woods. This dwelling belonged to a planter by the name of Mumma. It stood in the very center of the Federal advance, and also at the extreme left of D. H. Hill's line. The house had been fired by the Confederates, who feared that its thick walls might become a vantage-point for the Federal infantry. It burned throughout the battle, the flames subsiding only in the afternoon. Before it, just across the road, a battery of the First Rhode Island Light Artillery had placed its guns. Twice were they charged, but each time they were repulsed. From Mumma's house it was less than half a mile across the open field to the Dunker church. The fence-rails in the upper picture were those of the field enclosing Mumma's land, and the heroic dead pictured lying there were in full sight from the burning mansion.

RUIN OF MUMMA'S HOUSE, ANTIETAM

East. They were ready to forget his failure to capture Richmond in the early summer and to contrast his partial successes on the Peninsula with the drastic defeat of his successor at the Second Bull Run.

When McClellan, therefore, passed through Maryland to the scene of the coming battle, many of the people received him with joy and enthusiasm. At Frederick City, he tells us in his "Own Story," he was "nearly overwhelmed and pulled to pieces," and the people invited him into their houses and gave him every demonstration of confidence.

The first encounter, a double one, took place on September 14th, at two passes of South Mountain, a continuation of the Blue Ridge, north of the Potomac. General Franklin, who had been sent to relieve Harper's Ferry, met a Confederate force at Crampton's Gap and defeated it in a sharp battle of three hours' duration. At the same time the main army under Burnside and Reno encountered a stronger force at Turner's Gap seven miles farther up. The battle here continued many hours, till late in the night, and the Union troops were victorious. General Reno was killed. Lee's loss was nearly twenty-seven hundred, of whom eight hundred were prisoners. The Federals lost twenty-one hundred men and they failed to save Harper's Ferry.

Lee now placed Longstreet and D. H. Hill in a strong position near Keedysville, but learning that McClellan was advancing rapidly, the Confederate leader decided to retire to Sharpsburg, where he could be more easily joined by Jackson.

September 16th was a day of intense anxiety and unrest in the valley of the Antietam. The people who had lived in the farmhouses that dotted the golden autumn landscape in this hitherto quiet community had now abandoned their homes and given place to the armed forces. It was a day of marshaling and maneuvering of the gathering thousands, preparatory to the mighty conflict that was clearly seen to be inevitable. Lee had taken a strong position on the west bank of Antietam

WHERE NUMBERS TOLD

Here, in the old sunken road connecting the Hagerstown and the Keedysville Turnpikes, lies the mute testimony of the stubbornness with which the Confederates stood their ground in the most heroic resistance of the day. North of this sunken road was the original position of the Confederate center under General D. H. Hill when the battle opened at dawn. As the fighting reached flood-tide, Hill sent forward the brigades of Colquitt, Ripley, and McRae to the assistance of Jackson at the left. "The men (says Hill) advanced with alacrity, secured a good position, and were fighting bravely when Captain Thompson, Fifth North Carolina, cried out: 'They're flanking us!' This cry spread like an electric shock along the ranks, bringing up vivid recollections of the flank fire at South Mountain. In a moment they broke and fell to the rear." Rallied again at the sunken road, the forces of Hill now met the combined attack of the divisions of French and Richardson of Sumner's Corps, freshly come on the field. It was resistance to the death; reënforced by the division of Anderson, Hill's men, in the face of the deadly fire poured upon them in the sunken road, bravely assumed the offensive in a determined effort to flank the Federal forces to both left and right. Seizing a vantage-point on higher ground to the left, the Federals drove them back; while on the right Barlow, changing front with his two regiments, poured in a rapid fire, capturing three hundred prisoners and two standards. Then came the direct assault; swept by the enfilading fire from both sides, the remnant of the brave men in the sunken road was driven back, leaving the "bloody lane" behind them. It was not an easy victory for the Federals. The determined fire of the Confederates had brought down a heavy harvest, among which was numbered General Richardson, mortally wounded, who had handled his division in this sanguinary contest with his usual valor and skill.

MAJOR-GENERAL I. B. RICHARDSON

[B]

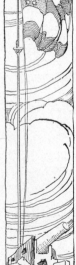

Creek a few miles from where it flows into the Potomac. He made a display of force, exposing his men to the fire of the Federal artillery, his object being to await the coming of Jackson's command from Harper's Ferry. It is true that Jackson himself had arrived, but his men were weary with marching and, moreover, a large portion of his troops under A. P. Hill and McLaws had not yet reached the field.

McClellan spent the day arranging his corps and giving directions for planting batteries. With a few companions he rode along the whole front, frequently drawing the fire of the Confederate batteries and thus revealing their location. The right wing of his army, the corps of Generals Hooker, Mansfield, and Sumner, lay to the north, near the village of Keedysville. General Porter with two divisions of the Fifth Corps occupied the center and Burnside was on the left of the Union lines. Back of McClellan's lines was a ridge on which was a signal station commanding a view of the entire field. Late on the afternoon of the 16th, Hooker crossing the Antietam, advanced against Hood's division on the Confederate left. For several hours there was heavy skirmishing, which closed with the coming of darkness.

The two great armies now lay facing each other in a grand double line three miles in length. At one point (the Union right and the Confederate left) they were so near together that the pickets could hear each other's tread. It required no prophet to foretell what would happen on the morrow.

Beautiful and clear the morning broke over the Maryland hills on the fateful 17th of September, 1862. The sunlight had not yet crowned the hilltops when artillery fire announced the opening of the battle. Hooker's infantry soon entered into the action and encountered the Confederates in an open field, from which the latter were presently pressed back across the Hagerstown pike to a line of woods where they made a determined stand. Hooker then called on General Mansfield to come to his aid, and the latter quickly did so, for he had led

THE HARVEST OF "BLOODY LANE"

Here, at "Bloody Lane" in the sunken road, was delivered the most telling blow of which the Federals could boast in the day's fighting at Antietam, September 17, 1862. In the lower picture we see the officers whose work first began to turn the tide of battle into a decisive advantage which the Army of the Potomac had every reason to expect would be gained by its superior numbers. On the Federal right Jackson, with a bare four thousand men, had taken the fight out of Hooker's eighteen thousand in the morning, giving ground at last to Sumner's fresh troops. On the Federal left, Burnside (at the lower bridge) failed to advance against Longstreet's Corps, two-thirds of which had been detached for service elsewhere. It was at the center that the forces of French and Richardson, skilfully fought by their leaders, broke through the Confederate lines and, sweeping beyond the sunken road, seized the very citadel of the center. Meagher's Irish Brigade had fought its way to a crest from which a plunging fire could be poured upon the Confederates in the sunken road. Meagher's ammunition was exhausted, and Caldwell threw his force into the position and continued the terrible combat. When the Confederates executed their flanking movement to the left, Colonel D. R. Cross, of the Fifth New Hampshire, seized a position which exposed Hill's men to an enfilading fire. (In the picture General Caldwell is seen standing to the left of the tree, and Colonel Cross leans on his sword at the extreme right. Between them stands Lieut.-Colonel George W. Scott, of the Sixty-first New York Infantry, while at the left before the tent stands Captain George W. Bulloch, A.C.S. General Caldwell's hand rests on the shoulder of Captain George H. Caldwell; to his left is seated Lieutenant C. A. Alvord.)

BRIGADIER-GENERAL CALDWELL AND STAFF

his corps across the Antietam after dark the night before. Mansfield, however, a gallant and honored veteran, fell mortally wounded while deploying his troops, and General Alpheus S. Williams, at the head of his first division, succeeded to the command.

There was a wood west of the Sharpsburg and Hagerstown turnpike which, with its outcropping ledges of rock, formed an excellent retreat for the Confederates and from this they pushed their columns into the open fields, chiefly of corn, to meet the Union attacks. For about two hours the battle raged at this point, the lines swaying to and fro, with fearful slaughter on both sides. At length, General Greene, who commanded a division of the fallen Mansfield's corps, gained possession of part of the coveted forest, near a little white church, known as the Dunker's Chapel. This was on high ground and was the key to the Confederate left wing. But Greene's troops were exposed to a galling fire from D. H. Hill's division and he called for reenforcements.

General Sumner then sent Sedgwick's division across the stream and accompanied the troops to the aid of their hard-pressed comrades. And the experience of this body of the gallant Second Corps during the next hour was probably the most thrilling episode of the whole day's battle. Sedgwick's troops advanced straight toward the conflict. They found Hooker wounded and his and Williams' troops quite exhausted. A sharp artillery fire was turned on Sedgwick before he reached the woods west of the Hagerstown pike, but once in the shelter of the thick trees he passed in safety to the western edge. Here the division found itself in an ambush. Heavy Confederate reenforcements—ten brigades, in fact—Walker's men, and McLaws', having arrived from Harper's Ferry—were hastening up, and they not only blocked the front, but worked around to the rear of Sedgwick's isolated brigades. Sedgwick was wounded in the awful slaughter that followed, but he and Sumner finally extricated their men with

THE BLUNDER AT THE BRIDGE

Burnside's Bridge, as it was called after Antietam, bears the name of a noted Federal general—not because of the brilliant maneuver which he vainly tried to execute in his efforts to cross it, but rather because of the gallant resistance offered here by the Confederates. General Toombs, with two Georgia regiments (the Second and the Twentieth) stood off a greatly superior force during the 16th and the greater part of the 17th of September. This bridge (on the road from Sharpsburg to Porterstown and Rohersville) was not forced till late in the afternoon, when Burnside, after a series of delays and ineffectual attempts, managed to throw his troops across Antietam Creek. The battle, however, was then practically decided. Toombs' forces saved the Confederate right wing—to him Lee and Longstreet gave the highest praise.

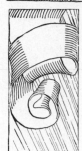

a loss of two thousand, over three hundred left dead on the ghastly field. Franklin now sent forward some fresh troops and after obstinately fighting, the Federals finally held a cornfield and most of the coveted wood over which the conflict had raged till the ground was saturated with blood.

Before the close of this bloody conflict on the Union right another, almost if not quite as deadly, was in progress near the center. General French, soon joined by General Richardson, both of Sumner's corps, crossed the stream and made a desperate assault against the Southerners of D. H. Hill's division, stationed to the south of where the battle had previously raged—French on a line of heights strongly held by the Confederates, Richardson in the direction of a sunken road, since known as "Bloody Lane." The fighting here was of a most desperate character and continued nearly four hours. French captured a few flags, several hundred prisoners, and gained some ground, but he failed to carry the heights. Richardson was mortally wounded while leading a charge and was succeeded by General Hancock; but his men finally captured Bloody Lane with the three hundred living men who had remained to defend it. The final Federal charge at this point was made by Colonel Barlow, who displayed the utmost bravery and self-possession in the thickest of the fight, where he won a brigadier-generalship. He was wounded, and later carried off the field. The Confederates had fought desperately to hold their position in Bloody Lane, and when it was captured it was filled with dead bodies. It was now about one o'clock and the infantry firing ceased for the day on the Union right, and center.

Let us now look on the other part of the field. Burnside held the Federal left wing against Lee's right, and he remained inactive for some hours after the battle had begun at the other end of the line. In front of Burnside was a triple-arched stone bridge across the Antietam, since known as "Burnside's Bridge." Opposite this bridge, on the slope which extends to a

SHERRICK'S HOUSE

In three distinct localities the battle waxed fierce from dawn to dusk on that terrible day at Antietam, September 17, 1862. First at the Federal right around the Dunker church; then at the sunken road, where the centers of both armies spent themselves in sanguinary struggle; lastly, late in the day, the struggle was renewed and ceased on the Sharpsburg road. When Burnside finally got his troops in motion, Sturgis' division of the Ninth Corps was first to cross the creek; his men advanced through an open ravine under a withering fire till they gained the opposite crest and held it until reënforced by Wilcox. To their right ran the Sharpsburg road, and an advance was begun in the direction of the Sherrick house.

The fighting along the Sharpsburg road might have resulted in a Confederate disaster had it not been for the timely arrival of the troops of General A. P. Hill. His six brigades of Confederate veterans had been the last to leave Harper's Ferry, remaining behind Jackson's main body in order to attend to the details of the surrender. Just as the Federal Ninth Corps was in the height of its advance, a cloud of dust on Harper's Ferry road cheered the Confederates to redoubled effort. Out of the dust the brigades of Hill debouched upon the field. Their fighting blood seemed to have but mounted more strongly during their march of eighteen miles. Without waiting for orders, Hill threw his men into the fight and the progress of the

Ninth Corps was stopped. Lee had counted on the arrival of Hill in time to prevent any successful attempt upon the Confederate right held by Longstreet's Corps, two-thirds of which had been detached in the thick of the fighting of the morning, when Lee's left and center suffered so severely. Burnside's delay at the bridge could not have been more fortunate for Lee if he had fixed its duration himself. Had the Confederate left been attacked at the time appointed, the outcome of Antietam could scarcely have been other than a decisive victory for the Federals. Even at the time when Burnside's tardy advance began, it must have prevailed against the weakened and wearied Confederates had not the fresh troops of A. P. Hill averted the disaster.

GENERAL A. P. HILL, C. S. A.

AFTER THE ADVANCE

In the advance along the Sharpsburg road near the Sherrick house the 79th New York "Highlanders" deployed as skirmishers. From orchards and cornfields and from behind fences and haystacks the Confederate sharpshooters opened upon them, but they swept on, driving in a part of Jones' division and capturing a battery just before A. P. Hill's troops arrived. With these reënforcements the Confederates drove back the brave Highlanders from the suburbs of Sharpsburg, which they had reached. Stubborn Scotch blood would permit only a reluctant retreat. Sharp fighting occurred around the Sherrick house with results seen in the lower picture. Night closed the battle, both sides exhausted.

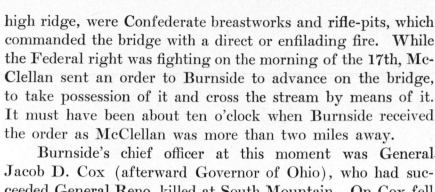

high ridge, were Confederate breastworks and rifle-pits, which commanded the bridge with a direct or enfilading fire. While the Federal right was fighting on the morning of the 17th, McClellan sent an order to Burnside to advance on the bridge, to take possession of it and cross the stream by means of it. It must have been about ten o'clock when Burnside received the order as McClellan was more than two miles away.

Burnside's chief officer at this moment was General Jacob D. Cox (afterward Governor of Ohio), who had succeeded General Reno, killed at South Mountain. On Cox fell the task of capturing the stone bridge. The defense of the bridge was in the hands of General Robert Toombs, a former United States senator and a member of Jefferson Davis' Cabinet. Perhaps the most notable single event in the life of General Toombs was his holding of the Burnside Bridge at Antietam for three hours against the assaults of the Federal troops. The Confederates had been weakened at this point by the sending of Walker to the support of Jackson, where, as we have noticed, he took part in the deadly assault upon Sedgwick's division. Toombs, therefore, with his one brigade had a heavy task before him in defending the bridge with his small force, notwithstanding his advantage of position.

McClellan sent several urgent orders to advance at all hazards. Burnside forwarded these to Cox, and in the fear that the latter would be unable to carry the bridge by a direct front attack, he sent Rodman with a division to cross the creek by a ford some distance below. This was accomplished after much difficulty. Meanwhile, in rapid succession, one assault after another was made upon the bridge and, about one o'clock, it was carried, at the cost of five hundred men. The Confederates fell back. A lull in the fighting along the whole line of battle now ensued.

Burnside, however, received another order from McClellan to push on up the heights and to the village of Sharpsburg. The great importance of this move, if successful, was

THE FLOOD–TIDE OF THE FEDERAL ADVANCE

This Lutheran church on Main Street, to the east of Sharpsburg, marked the end of the Federal assault upon Lee's position at Antietam, as the little church of the non-resistant Dunkers to the north of the town had marked its beginning in the early morning.   About three o'clock in the afternoon Burnside's skirmishers advanced to the first cross-street beyond this church, threatening the town itself.   Out on the hills beyond the town, Main Street becomes the Shepherdstown road, and along this were arriving and hurrying through the town the anxiously awaited forces of A. P. Hill.   From that moment the Federals got no nearer Sharpsburg.   Hill drove them back steadily beyond the church, recapturing the battery which they had wrested from the troops of Jones and which had done damage to the little church as well as to the Confederates. Hill's men, taking Rodman's division in flank, poured in a fire in which Rodman met his death.   Panic among his troops was averted only by Scammon, who (leading Cox's division) checked Hill for a breathing space; but Burnside's forces were steadily pushed back until at nightfall they lay discomfited, holding the bridge on the banks of Antietam creek, which he had wrested from Toombs' two Georgia regiments.

that it would cut Lee out from his line of retreat by way of Shepherdstown.

After replenishing the ammunition and adding some fresh troops, Cox advanced at three o'clock with the utmost gallantry toward Sharpsburg. The Confederates disputed the ground with great bravery. But Cox swept all before him and was at the edge of the village when he was suddenly confronted by lines in blue uniforms who instantly opened fire. The Federals were astonished to see the blue-clad battalions before them. They must be Union soldiers; but how did they get there? The matter was soon explained. They were A. P. Hill's division of Lee's army which had just arrived from Harper's Ferry, and they had dressed themselves in the uniforms that they had taken from the Federal stores.

Hill had come just in time to save Lee's headquarters from capture. He checked Cox's advance, threw a portion of the troops into great confusion, and steadily pressed them back toward the Antietam. In this, the end of the battle, General Rodman fell mortally wounded. Cox retired in good order and Sharpsburg remained in the hands of the Confederates.

Thus, with the approach of nightfall, closed the memorable battle of Antietam. For fourteen long hours more than one hundred thousand men, with five hundred pieces of artillery, had engaged in titanic combat. As the pall of battle smoke rose and cleared away, the scene presented was one to make the stoutest heart shudder. There lay upon the ground, scattered for three miles over the valleys and the hills or in the improvised hospitals, more than twenty thousand men. Horace Greeley was probably right in pronouncing this the bloodiest day in American history.

Although tactically it was a drawn battle, Antietam was decisively in favor of the North inasmuch as it ended the first Confederate attempt at a Northern invasion. General Lee realized that his ulterior plans had been thwarted by this engagement and after a consultation with his corps commanders

THE MEDIATOR

President Lincoln's Visit to the Camps at Antietam, October 8, 1862. Yearning for the speedy termination of the war, Lincoln came to view the Army of the Potomac, as he had done at Harrison's Landing. Puzzled to understand how Lee could have circumvented a superior force on the Peninsula, he was now anxious to learn why a crushing blow had not been struck. Lincoln (after Gettysburg) expressed the same thought: "Our army held the war in the hollow of their hand and they would not close it!" On Lincoln's right stands Allan Pinkerton, the famous detective and organizer of the Secret Service of the army. At the President's left is General John A. McClernand, soon to be entrusted by Lincoln with reorganizing military operations in the West.

he determined to withdraw from Maryland. On the night of the 18th the retreat began and early the next morning the Confederate army had all safely recrossed the Potomac.

The great mistake of the Maryland campaign from the standpoint of the Confederate forces, thought General Longstreet, was the division of Lee's army, and he believed that if Lee had kept his forces together he would not have been forced to abandon the campaign. At Antietam, he had less than forty thousand men, who were in poor condition for battle while McClellan had about eighty-seven thousand, most of whom were fresh and strong, though not more than sixty thousand were in action.

The moral effect of the battle of Antietam was incalculably great. It aroused the confidence of the Northern people. It emboldened President Lincoln to issue five days after its close the proclamation freeing the slaves in the seceded states. He had written the proclamation long before, but it had lain inactive in his desk at Washington. All through the struggles of the summer of 1862 he had looked forward to the time when he could announce his decision to the people. But he could not do it then. With the doubtful success of Federal arms, to make such a bold step would have been a mockery and would have defeated the very end he sought.

The South had now struck its first desperate blow at the gateways to the North. By daring, almost unparalleled in warfare, it had swung its courageous army into a strategical position where with the stroke of fortune it might have hammered down the defenses of the National capital on the south and then sweep on a march of invasion into the North. The Northern soldiers had parried the blow. They had saved themselves from disaster and had held back the tide of the Confederacy as it beat against the Mason and Dixon line, forcing it back into the State of Virginia where the two mighty fighting bodies were soon to meet again in a desperate struggle for the right-of-way at Fredericksburg.

FREDERICKSBURG
DISASTER FOR A NEW UNION LEADER

THE MILL ACROSS THE RIVER

FREDERICKSBURG

A PHOTOGRAPH TAKEN JUST AFTER THE BATTLE OF DECEMBER, 1862

Two magnificent armies faced one another here in the middle of December, 1862. Along the ground we see spread before us on the east side of the Rappahannock—the famous Stafford Heights—the men in blue were massed in a long line of camps. In the town were scattered forces of Confederate troops, and along the river front each house was a temporary citadel; even cannon frowned from the windows. The winding river, now unbridged and at high water, separated the Army of Northern Virginia under Lee from the Army of the Potomac under Burnside. Fredericksburg, deserted by women, children, the aged, and the infirm, lay helpless before the Federal guns. But along the hill against the horizon stretched Lee's army, under able generals, in an impregnable position. Between it and the town lay open ground with a few scattered houses. Stretching across the river we can see the ruins of the bridges. For a month Burnside had waited for pontoons to enable him to cross in force. On a foggy morning after their arrival, the 11th of December, a landing was effected. The fierce fire of 147 guns from Stafford Heights played havoc among the houses. The sharpshooters that had bothered the pontoniers were driven back, and soon all the Confederate forces had gathered along the ridge a mile to the west of the town. By the 12th the Federal army had crossed and deployed for battle.

THE DEATH-TRAP ON TELEGRAPH ROAD

Here Sumner's right grand division of the Army of the Potomac exemplified an implicit obedience of orders more magnificent even than that of the "Six Hundred" at Balaklava. Advancing along the Telegraph Road, seen at the right of the picture, the divisions of French and Hancock, already depleted by cruel artillery fire, charged up Marye's Heights, the eminence at the center of the picture. There a blinding flash of flame first disclosed the ambuscade in the sunken road. Ranged in ranks, first four and then six men deep, the Confederates kept up a continuous volleying against which no troops could stand. First the divisions of French and Hancock went down before it—then that of Howard. To the left the supporting divisions of Sturgis and Getty shared the efforts of their comrades with like result. Griffin's and Humphreys' divisions followed later—all to no avail. Six desperate charges were made upon Cobb's and Kershaw's troops. When darkness put an end to the slaughter, seven thousand Federal killed and wounded lay at the foot of Marye's Heights.

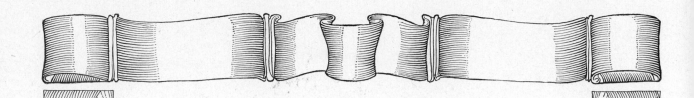

FREDERICKSBURG—DISASTER FOR A NEW UNION LEADER

The Army of the Potomac had fought gallantly; it had not lost a single cannon, all its attacks being made by masses of infantry; it had experienced neither disorder nor rout. But the defeat was complete, and its effects were felt throughout the entire country as keenly as in the ranks of the army. The little confidence that Burnside had been able to inspire in his soldiers had vanished, and the respect which everybody entertained for the noble character of the unfortunate general could not supply its place.—Comte de Paris, in "History of the Civil War in America."

THE silent city of military graves at Fredericksburg is a memorial of one of the bloodiest battles of the Civil War. The battle of Antietam had been regarded a victory by the Federals and a source of hope to the North, after a wearisome period of inaction and defeats. General George B. Mc-Clellan, in command of the Army of the Potomac, failed to follow up this advantage and strike fast and hard while the Southern army was shattered and weak. President Lincoln's impatience was brought to a climax; McClellan was relieved and succeeded by General Ambrose E. Burnside, who was looked upon with favor by the President, and who had twice declined this proffered honor. It was on November 5, 1862, nearly two months after Antietam, when this order was issued. The Army of the Potomac was in splendid form and had made plans for a vigorous campaign. On the 9th Burnside assumed command, and on the following day McClellan took leave of his beloved troops.

Burnside at once changed the whole plan of campaign, and decided to move on Fredericksburg, which lay between the Union and Confederate armies. He organized his army into

THE SECOND LEADER AGAINST RICHMOND

Major-General Ambrose Everett Burnside was a West Point graduate, inventor of a breech-loading rifle, commander of a brigade in the first battle of Bull Run, captor of Roanoke Island and Newberne (North Carolina), and commander of the Federal left at Antietam. He was appointed to the command of the Army of the Potomac and succeeded General George B. McClellan on November 8, 1862. He was a brave soldier, but was an impatient leader and inclined to be somewhat reckless. He pressed rapidly his advance against Lee and massed his entire army along Stafford Heights, on the east bank of the Rappahannock, opposite Fredericksburg. According to General B. B. Franklin (who commanded the left grand division of the army), the notion that a serious battle was necessary to Federal control of the town "was not entertained by any one." General Sumner (who led the advance of Burnside's army) held this opinion but he had not received orders to cross the river. Crossing was delayed nearly a month and this delay resulted in the Federal disaster on December 13th. This put an abrupt end to active operations by Burnside against Lee. This picture was taken at Warrenton, November 24th, on the eve of the departure of the army for its march to Fredericksburg.

three grand divisions, under Generals Sumner, Hooker, and Franklin, commanding the right, center, and left, and moved his troops from Warrenton to Falmouth. A delay of some two weeks was due to the failure of arrival of the pontoons. In a council of war held on the night of December 10th the officers under Burnside expressed themselves almost unanimously as opposed to the plan of battle, but Burnside disregarded their views and determined to carry out his original plans immediately. After some delay and desultory fighting for two days, the crossing of the army was effected by the morning of December 13th. By this time General Robert E. Lee, commanding the Confederates, had his army concentrated and entrenched on the hills surrounding the town. In their efforts to place their bridges the Federals were seriously hindered by the firing of the Confederate sharpshooters— "hornets that were stinging the Army of the Potomac into a frenzy." The Confederate fire continued until silenced by a heavy bombardment of the city from the Federal guns, when the crossing of the army into Fredericksburg was completed without further interference.

The forces of Lee were in battle array about the town. Their line stretched for five miles along the range of hills which spread in crescent shape around the lowland where the city lay, surrounding it on all sides save the east, where the river flowed. The strongest Confederate position was on the slopes of the lowest hill of the range, Marye's Heights, which rose in the rear of the town. Along the foot of this hill there was a stone wall, about four feet in height, bounding the eastern side of the Telegraph road, which at this point runs north and south, being depressed a few feet below the surface of the stone wall, thus forming a breastwork for the Confederate troops. Behind it a strong force was concealed, while higher up, in several ranks, the main army was massed, stretching along the line of hills. The right wing, consisting of thirty thousand troops on an elevation near Hamilton's Cross-

THE BUSY BASE OF THE ARMY OF THE POTOMAC

Aquia Creek Landing, Virginia, February, 1863. In the movements of Burnside and Hooker along the Rappahannock in the winter of 1862–3 this point became the base of supplies for the Army of the Potomac. Transports and supply-ships from Alexandria were bringing down troops, food, clothing, arms, ammunition, and artillery, and unloading them at the pontoon piers, such as shown in this picture, whence they were forwarded along the line of the Richmond, Fredericksburg & Potomac Railroad to general headquarters at Falmouth Station. The position at Aquia Creek had been occupied alternately by the Federal and Confederate forces from the beginning of the war. Federal troops landed here in August, 1862, before the second battle of Bull Run. After Lee's brilliant victory at Chancellorsville, which drove Hooker in defeat north of the Rappahannock, the great Confederate leader pressed boldly forward. The Federal base of supplies remained at Aquia Creek until Hooker's army marched toward the upper Potomac in pursuit.

ing of the Fredericksburg and Potomac Railroad, was commanded by "Stonewall" Jackson. The left, on Marye's Heights and Marye's Hill, was commanded by the redoubtable Longstreet. The Southern forces numbered about seventy-eight thousand.

Into the little city below and the adjoining valleys, the Federal troops had been marching for two days. Franklin's Left Grand Division of forty thousand was strengthened by two divisions from Hooker's Center Grand Division, and was ordered to make the first attack on the Confederate right under Jackson. Sumner's Right Grand Division, also reenforced from Hooker's forces, was formed for assault against the Confederate's strongest point at Marye's Hill.

All this magnificent and portentous battle formation had been effected under cover of a dense fog, and when it lifted on that fateful Saturday there was revealed a scene of truly military grandeur. Concealed by the somber curtain of nature the Southern hosts had fixed their batteries and entrenched themselves most advantageously upon the hills, and the Union legions, massed in menacing strength below, now lay within easy cannon-shot of their foe. The Union army totaled one hundred and thirteen thousand men. After skirmishing and gathering of strength, it was at length ready for the final spring and the death-grapple.

When the sun's rays broke through the fog during the forenoon of December 13th, Franklin's Grand Division was revealed in full strength in front of the Confederate right, marching and countermarching in preparation for the coming conflict. Officers in new, bright uniforms, thousands of bayonets gleaming in the sunshine, champing steeds, rattling gun-carriages whisking artillery into proper range of the foe, infantry, cavalry, batteries, with officers and men, formed a scene of magnificent grandeur which excited the admiration even of the Confederates. This maneuver has been called the grandest military scene of the war.

THE DETAINED GUNS

Fredericksburg, February, 1863.   In the foreground, looking from what is approximately the same position as the opening picture, are three guns of Tyler's Connecticut battery.   It was from all along this ridge that the town had suffered its bombardment in December of the previous year.   Again the armies were separated by the Rappahannock River.   There was a new commander at the head of the Army of the Potomac—General Hooker.   The plundered and deserted town now held by the Confederates was to be made the objective of another attack.   The heights beyond were once more to be assaulted; bridges were to be rebuilt. But all to no purpose.   This ground of much contention was deserted some time before Lee advanced to his invasion of Pennsylvania.   Very slowly the inhabitants of Fredericksburg had returned to their ruined homes.   The town was a vast Federal cemetery, the dead being buried in gardens and backyards, for during its occupancy almost every dwelling had been turned into a temporary hospital.   After the close of the war these bodies were gathered and a National Cemetery was established on Willis' Hill, on Marye's Heights, the point successfully defended by Lee's veterans.

Heavy pontoon-boats, each on its separate wagon, were sometimes as necessary as food or ammunition.   At every important crossing of the many rivers that had to be passed in the Peninsula Campaign the bridges had been destroyed. There were few places where these streams were fordable. Pontoons, therefore, made a most important adjunct to the Army of the Potomac.

PONTOON-BOATS IN TRANSIT

Yet with all this brave show, we have seen that Burnside's subordinate officers were unanimous in their belief in the rashness of the undertaking. Enthusiasm was sadly lacking. The English military writer, Colonel Henderson, has explained why this was so:

And yet that vast array, so formidable of aspect, lacked that moral force without which physical power, even in its most terrible form, is but an idle show. Not only were the strength of the Confederate position, the want of energy of preliminary movements, the insecurity of their own situation, but too apparent to the intelligence of the regimental officers and men, but they mistrusted their commander. Northern writers have recorded that the Army of the Potomac never went down to battle with less alacrity than on this day at Fredericksburg.

The first advance began at 8:30 in the morning, while the fog was still dense, upon Jackson's right. Reynolds ordered Meade with a division, supported by two other divisions under Doubleday and Gibbon, to attack Jackson at his weakest point, the extreme right of the Confederate lines, and endeavor to seize one of the opposing heights. The advance was made in three lines of battle, which were guarded in front and on each flank by artillery which swept the field in front as the army advanced. The Confederates were placed to have an enfilading sweep from both flanks along the entire front line of march. When Reynolds' divisions had approached within range, Jackson's small arms on the left poured in a deadly fire, mowing down the brave men in the Union lines in swaths, leaving broad gaps where men had stood.

This fire was repeated again and again, as the Federals pressed on, only to be repulsed. Once only was the Confederate line broken, when Meade carried the crest, capturing flags and prisoners. The ground lost by the Confederates was soon recovered, and the Federals were forced to retire. Some of the charges made by the Federals during this engagement were heroic in the extreme, only equaled by the opposition met

THE FLAMING HEIGHTS

This photograph from the Fredericksburg river-bank recalls a terrible scene. On those memorable days of December 11 and 12, 1862, from these very trenches shown in the foreground, the ragged gray riflemen saw on that hillside across the river the blue of the uniforms of the massed Federal troops. The lines of tents made great white spaces, but the ground could hardly be seen for the host of men who were waiting, alas! to die by thousands on this coveted shore. From these hills, too, burst an incessant flaming and roaring cannon fire. Siege-guns and field artillery poured shot and shell into the town of Fredericksburg. Every house became a target, though deserted except for a few hardy and venturesome riflemen. There was scarcely a dwelling that escaped. Ruined and battered and bloody, Fredericksburg three times was a Federal hospital, and its backyards became little cemeteries.

A TARGET AT FREDERICKSBURG FOR THE FEDERAL GUNS

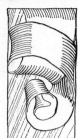

from the foe. In one advance, knapsacks were unslung and bayonets fixed; a brigade marched across a plowed field, and passed through broken lines of other brigades, which were retiring to the rear in confusion from the leaden storm.

The fire became incessant and destructive; many fell, killed or wounded; the front line slackened its pace, and without orders commenced firing. A halt seemed imminent, and a halt in the face of the terrific fire to which the men were exposed meant death; but, urged on by regimental commanders in person, the charge was renewed, when with a shout they leaped the ditches, charged across the railroad, and upon the foe, killing many with the bayonet and capturing several hundred prisoners. But this was only a temporary gain. In every instance the Federals were shattered and driven back. Men were lying dead in heaps, the wounded and dying were groaning in agony. Soldiers were fleeing; officers were galloping to and fro urging their lines forward, and begging their superior officers for assistance and reenforcement.

A dispatch to Burnside from Franklin, dated 2:45, was as follows: " My left has been very badly handled; what hope is there of getting reenforcements across the river?" Another dispatch, dated 3:45, read: " Our troops have gained no ground in the last half hour."

In their retreat the fire was almost as destructive as during the assault. Most of the wounded were brought from the field after this engagement, but the dead were left where they fell. It was during this engagement that General George D. Bayard was mortally wounded by a shot which had severed the sword belt of Captain Gibson, leaving him uninjured. The knapsack of a soldier who was in a stooping posture was struck by a ball, and a deck of cards was sent flying twenty feet in the air. Those witnessing the ludicrous scene called to him, " Oh, deal me a hand!" thus indicating the spirit of levity among soldiers even amid such surroundings. Another soldier sitting on the ground suddenly leaped high above the

[90]

THE BRIDGES THAT A BAND OF MUSIC THREATENED

At Franklin Crossing, on the Rappahannock, occurred an incident that proves how little things may change the whole trend of the best-laid plans. The left Union wing under the command of General Franklin, composed of the First Army Corps under General Reynolds, and the Sixth under General W. S. Smith, was crossing to engage in the battle of Fredericksburg. For two days they poured across these yielding planks between the swaying boats to the farther shore. Now, in the crossing of bridges, moving bodies of men must break step or even well-built structures might be threatened. The colonel of one of the regiments in General Devens' division that led the van ordered his field music to strike up just as the head of the column swept on to the flimsy planking; before the regiment was half-way across, unconsciously the men had fallen into step and the whole fabric was swaying to the cadenced feet. Vibrating like a great fiddlestring, the bridge would have sunk and parted, but a keen eye had seen the danger. "Stop that music!" was the order, and a staff officer spurred his horse through the men, shouting at top voice. The lone charge was made through the marching column: some jumped into the pontoons to avoid the hoofs; a few went overboard; but the head of the column was reached at last, and the music stopped. A greater blunder than this, however took place on the plains beyond. Owing to a misunderstanding of orders, 37,000 troops were never brought into action; 17,000 men on their front bore the brunt of a long day's fighting.

heads of his comrades as a shell struck the spot, scooping a wheelbarrowful of earth, but the man was untouched.

Entirely independent of the action in which the Left Grand Division under Franklin was engaged against the right wing of the Confederate line, Sumner's Right Grand Division was engaged in a terrific assault upon the works on Marye's Heights, the stronghold of the Confederate forces. Their position was almost impregnable, consisting of earthworks, wood, and stone barricades running along the sunken road near the foot of Marye's Hill. The Federals were not aware of the sunken road, nor of the force of twenty-five hundred under General Cobb concealed behind the stone wall, this wall not being new work as a part of the entrenchments, but of earlier construction. When the advance up the road was made they were harassed by shot and shell and rifle-balls at every step, but the men came dashing into line undismayed by the terrific fire which poured down upon them.

The Irish Brigade, the second of Hancock's division, under General Meagher, made a wonderful charge. When they returned from the assault but two hundred and fifty out of twelve hundred men reported under arms from the field, and all these were needed to care for their wounded comrades. The One Hundred and Sixteenth Pennsylvania regiment was new on the field of battle, but did fearless and heroic service. The approach was completely commanded by the Confederate guns. Repeatedly the advance was repulsed by well-directed fire from the batteries.

Once again Sumner's gallant men charged across a railroad cut, running down one side and up the other, and still again attempted to escape in the same manner, but each time they were forced to retire precipitately by a murderous fire from the Confederate batteries. Not only was the Confederate fire disastrous upon the approach and the successive repulses by the foe, but it also inflicted great damage upon the masses of the Federal army in front of Marye's Hill.

MEN WHO CHARGED ON MARYE'S HEIGHTS

Officers of the famous "Irish Brigade," which lost more than 41 per cent. of its strength in the first assault at Marye's Heights. The "Irish Brigade" (consisting of the Twenty-eighth Massachusetts, the Sixty-third, Sixty-ninth, and Eighty-eighth New York, and the One Hundred and Sixteenth Pennsylvania) was commanded by General Thomas F. Meagher and advanced in Hancock's division to the first assault on December 13, 1862. At Antietam this brigade had spent its ammunition at the sunken road and then retired in splendid order. Again, in the charge at Marye's, the lines of the Irish soldiers were "beautifully and rapidly formed," and they moved steadily up the ridge until within a few yards of another and more deadly sunken road, the unexpected fire from which mowed them down. Of the 1,315 men which Meagher led into battle, 545 fell in that charge. Hancock's entire command sustained that day a loss of 40.2 per cent., the second highest percentage of any division in any one engagement in the war. After the charge on Marye's Heights it numbered only 2,800 men. This group was photographed at Harrison's Landing, on the James River, in July, 1862.

The Confederates' effective and successful work on Marye's Hill in this battle was not alone due to the natural strength of their position, but also to the skill and generalship of the leaders, and to the gallantry, courage, and well-directed aim of their cannoneers and infantry.

Six times the heroic Union troops dashed against the invulnerable position, each time to be repulsed with terrific loss. General Couch, who had command of the Second Corps, viewing the scene of battle from the steeple of the court-house with General Howard, says: "The whole plain was covered with men, prostrate and dropping, the live men running here and there, and in front closing upon each other, and the wounded coming back. I had never before seen fighting like that, nothing approaching it in terrible uproar and destruction."

General Howard reports that Couch exclaimed: "Oh, great God! see how our men, our poor fellows, are falling!" At half-past one Couch signaled Burnside: "I am losing. Send two rifle batteries."

The point and method of attack made by Sumner was anticipated by the Confederates, careful preparation having been made to meet it. The fire from the Confederate batteries harassed the Union lines, and as they advanced steadily, heroically, without hurrah or battle-cry, the ranks were cut to pieces by canister and shell and musket-balls. Heavy artillery fire was poured into the Union ranks from front, right, and left with frightful results. Quickly filling up the decimated ranks they approached the stone wall masking the death-trap where General Cobb lay with a strong force awaiting the approach. Torrents of lead poured into the bodies of the defenseless men, slaying, crushing, destroying the proud army of a few hours before. As though in pity, a cloud of smoke momentarily shut out the wretched scene but brought no balm to the helpless victims of this awful carnage. The ground was so thickly strewn with dead bodies as seriously to impede the movements of a renewed attack. These repeated assaults in such good

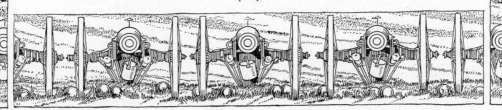

THE SUMMIT OF SLAUGHTER

Marye's House marked the center of the Confederate position on the Heights, before which the Federals fell three deep in one of the bravest and bloodiest assaults of the war. The eastern boundary of the Marye estate was a retaining wall, along which ran a sunken road; on the other side of this was a stone wall, shoulder high, forming a perfect infantry parapet. Here two brigades of Confederates were posted and on the crest above them were the supporting batteries, while the slope between was honeycombed with the rifle-pits of the sharpshooters, one of which is seen in the picture. Six times did the Federals, raked by the deadly fire of the Washington Artillery, advance to within a hundred yards of the sunken road, only to be driven back by the rapid volleys of the Confederate infantry concealed there. Less than three of every five men in Hancock's division came back from their charge on these death-dealing heights. The complete repulse of the day and the terrific slaughter were the barren results of an heroic effort to obey orders.

order caused some apprehension on the part of General Lee, who said to Longstreet after the third attack, "General, they are massing very heavily and will break your line, I am afraid." But the great general's fears proved groundless.

General Cobb was borne from the field mortally wounded, and Kershaw took his place in the desperate struggle. The storm of shot and shell which met the assaults was terrific. Men fell almost in battalions; the dead and wounded lay in heaps. Late in the day the dead bodies, which had become frozen from the extreme cold, were stood up in front of the soldiers as a protection against the awful fire to shield the living, and at night were set up as dummy sentinels.

The steadiness of the Union troops, and the silent, determined heroism of the rank and file in these repeated, but hopeless, assaults upon the Confederate works, were marvelous, and amazed even their officers. The real greatness in a battle is the fearless courage, the brave and heroic conduct, of the men under withering fire. It was the enlisted men who were the glory of the army. It was they, the rank and file, who stood in the front, closed the gaps, and were mowed down in swaths like grass by cannon and musket-balls.

After the sixth disastrous attempt to carry the works of the Confederate left it was night; the Federal army was repulsed and had retired; hope was abandoned, and it was seen that the day was lost to the Union side. Then the shattered Army of the Potomac sought to gather the stragglers and care for the wounded. Fredericksburg, the beautiful Virginia town, was a pitiable scene in contrast to its appearance a few days before. Ancestral homes were turned into barracks and hospitals. The charming drives and stately groves, the wonted pleasure grounds of Colonial dames and Southern cavaliers, were not filled with grand carriages and gay parties, but with war horses, soldiers, and military accouterments. Aside from desultory firing by squads and skirmishers at intervals there was no renewal of the conflict.

THE FATEFUL CROSSING

From this, the Lacy House, which Sumner had made his headquarters, he directed the advance of his right grand division of the Army of the Potomac on December 11, 1862. Little did he dream that his men of the Second Corps were to bear the brunt of the fighting and the most crushing blow of the defeat on the 13th. Soon after three o'clock on the morning of the 11th the columns moved out with alacrity to the river bank and before daybreak, hidden at first by the fog, the pontoniers began building the bridges. Confederate sharpshooters drove off the working party from the bridge below the Lacy House and also from the middle bridge farther down. As the mist cleared, volunteers ferried themselves over in the boats and drove off the riflemen. At last, at daybreak of the 12th, the town of Fredericksburg was occupied, but the whole of another foggy day was consumed in getting the army concentrated on the western shore. Nineteen batteries (one hundred and four guns) accompanied Sumner's troops, but all save seven of these were ordered back or left in the streets of Fredericksburg. Late on the morning of the 13th the confused and belated orders began to arrive from Burnside's headquarters across the river; one was for Sumner to assault the Confederate batteries on Marye's Heights. At nightfall Sumner's men retired into Fredericksburg, leaving 5,444 dead or dying on the field. "Oh, those men, those men over there! I cannot get them out of my mind!" wailed Burnside in an agony of failure. Yet he was planning almost in the same breath to lead in person his old command, the Ninth Corps, in another futile charge in the morning. On the night of the 14th, better judgment prevailed and the order came to retire across the Rappahannock.

Here, on the heights behind Fredericksburg, Lee's veterans who had fought at Antietam opposed the Army of the Potomac under its new commander. Had Lee been given his choice he could not have selected a more advantageous position. Burnside's futile attempts to wrest these heights from the Confederates cost him 12,653 men in killed, wounded, and missing. On the heights behind Fredericksburg, Lee's soldiers, working night and day, had thrown up a double line of strong entrenchments and constructed a road to facilitate the transfer of troops behind the defenses. Everything that the engineering talent of the Confederacy could suggest had been done. By the time Burnside moved his 113,000 troops against the 78,000 of Lee, Jackson, and Longstreet on December 13, 1862, Marye's Heights had been made impregnable. Four months later, in the Chancellorsville campaign (May 3, 1863), Sedgwick's men fought over this same ground and carried the position. But then the main body of Lee's army was hotly engaged with Hooker and the Heights were not strongly defended. This photograph of Willis's Hill (just south of Marye's) was taken after Sedgwick occupied the position in 1863. Willis's Hill was, with great appropriateness, made a National Cemetery at Fredericksburg after the war.

WILLIS'S HILL,

NEAR MARYE'S HEIGHTS

[B]

THE PLANS THAT FAILED

From his headquarters at the Phillips house, Burnside directed the disastrous maneuvers of his army during the battle of December 13th.   On December 9th Burnside called his generals together and persisted in his plan for a direct assault upon Lee, who was strongly entrenched in a position of his own choosing.   The slaughter at Marye's Heights on the 13th proved him in the wrong.   Nevertheless, Burnside on the field that night gave orders to renew the attack the next morning.   Returning to the Phillips house about 1 A.M., he found among the others Colonel Rush C. Hawkins, who had come at the request of Generals Willcox, Humphreys, Meade, and Getty, who had all faced that terrible fire on Telegraph Road.   A conference ensued in the presence of Sumner, Hooker, and Franklin, and Burnside was at last dissuaded.

THE UNLUCKY HEADQUARTERS

The ruins of the Phillips house stand as an aftermath of Burnside's unfortunate career at the head of the Army of the Potomac.   The wisest decision that he made in that house was in the early morning of December 14th—not to renew the attack.   In the old mansion he had formed the fatal plan of direct assault. Here also he issued his order for the famous "mud march" by which, in the dead of winter, he sought to retrieve failure by putting his army in motion to flank Lee, January 21, 1863.   All his efforts had come to naught, and not one of his generals longer agreed with him.   His resignation from the command followed on January 26th.   In February the Phillips house was set on fire; and in the picture on the preceding page the photographer has caught the Federals (now commanded by Hooker) trying to extinguish the flames.

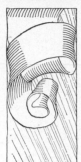

The bloody carnage was over, the plan of Burnside had ended in failure, and thousands of patriotic and brave men, blindly obedient to their country's command, were the toll exacted from the Union army. Burnside, wild with anguish at what he had done, walking the floor of his tent, exclaimed, "Oh, those men—those men over there," pointing to the battlefield, "I am thinking of them all the time." In his report of the battle to Washington, Burnside gave reasons for the issue, and in a manly way took the responsibility upon himself, and most highly commended his officers and men. He said, "For the failure in the attack I am responsible, as the extreme gallantry, courage, and endurance shown by them [officers and men] were never excelled."

President Lincoln's verdict in regard to this battle is adverse to the almost unanimous opinion of the historians. In his reply, December 22d, to General Burnside's report of the battle, he says, "Although you were not successful, the attempt was not an error, nor the failure other than an accident." Burnside, at his own request, was relieved of the command of the Army of the Potomac, however, on January 25, 1863, and was succeeded by General Hooker. The Union loss in killed, wounded, and missing was 12,653, and the Confederates lost 5,377.

After the battle the wounded lay on the field in their agony exposed to the freezing cold for forty-eight hours before arrangements were effected to care for them. Many were burned to death by the long, dead grass becoming ignited by cannon fire. The scene witnessed by the army of those screaming, agonizing, dying comrades was dreadful and heartrending. Burnside's plan had been to renew the battle, but the overwhelming opinion of the other officers prevailed. The order was withdrawn and the defeated Union army slipped away under the cover of darkness on December 15th, and encamped in safety across the river. The battle of Fredericksburg had passed into history.

PART I
THE RISE OF LEE

CHANCELLORSVILLE AND JACKSON'S FLANKING MARCH

READY TO COVER THE RAPPAHANNOCK—THE 150TH PENNSYLVANIA,
THREE WEEKS BEFORE THE BATTLE OF CHANCELLORSVILLE

WAR'S HEAVIEST LABOR

Here a construction corps is rebuilding the railroad bridge across Bull Run. The men are armed with crowbars and axes, and in the constant wielding of such peaceful implements throughout the war many who never fired a musket became expert in the occupations of peace. This photograph was taken in March, 1863, while Hooker was reëstablishing railway communications to make possible his contemplated advance toward Gordonsville, Virginia, with the expectation of driving Lee back upon Richmond. During the previous year, in the disastrous campaign of Pope, most of the bridges along the Orange & Alexandria Railroad had been destroyed and much of the line torn up. In order to flank Lee's position at Fredericksburg, it was imperative for the Army of the Potomac to abandon its base at Aquia Creek and draw supplies overland from Alexandria. In the spring Hooker was pushing the railroad repairs.

RAPID REPAIRS

This picture of the almost completed bridge across Bull Run shows how thoroughly the work was done—and how quickly, for the photograph was taken in March, 1863, only a short time after that on the opposite page. The hopes of Hooker and his army ran high; rested and heavily reënforced, it again outnumbered Lee's Army of Northern Virginia. It seemed certain that such a superior force must at last wrest a decisive victory from the Confederates. Hooker's plan of campaign was excellent. Demonstrating strongly against Lee's right, he intended to cross the fords of the Rappahannock and Rapidan with his main body and, flanking Lee by the left, draw him from his fastness at Fredericksburg to battle on the open plain. Cavalry was to be sent two weeks in advance of the infantry to sweep around in Lee's rear toward Gordonsville and cut his communications, to compel a retreat upon Richmond. But it was not Lee who retreated after Chancellorsville!

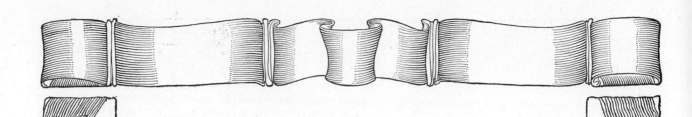

CHANCELLORSVILLE AND JACKSON'S FLANKING MARCH

The interval of two months between the battles of Chancellorsville and Gettysburg was for the South—notwithstanding the irreparable loss it sustained in the death of Jackson—the brightest period of the Civil War. But its brightness was that of a false and treacherous light. The over-confidence born of the victory of Chancellorsville carried the Army of Northern Virginia against the impregnable front of the Federal lines at Gettysburg; and it was the victory of Gettysburg that sustained the Army of the Potomac in its desperate wrestling in the Wilderness, and in gaining the point of vantage from which it finally started on the arduous, decisive, and fateful race to Appomattox.—*Major John Bigelow, Jr., U.S.A., in "The Campaign of Chancellorsville."*

THE Rappahannock River flows out of the hills at the foot of the Blue Ridge Mountains in a southeasterly course. Falmouth is on the north bank, about a mile from Fredericks-burg, which lies on the opposite shore. Along the banks of this peaceful river were fought some of the most important battles of the Civil War. This region was the scene of the conflict of Fredericksburg, December 12–13, 1862, and the later battle of May 1–5, 1863. Chancellorsville is a little over two miles south of the river and about ten miles west of Fredericksburg.

After the Fredericksburg campaign the Union forces encamped at Falmouth for the winter, while Lee remained with the Southern army on the site of his successful contest at Fredericksburg. Thus the two armies lay facing each other within hailing distance, across the historic river, waiting for the coming of spring. Major-General Joseph Hooker, popu-larly known as "Fighting Joe" Hooker, who had succeeded Burnside in command of the Army of the Potomac, soon had

A MAN OF WHOM MUCH WAS EXPECTED

General Joseph Hooker.   A daring and experienced veteran of the Mexican War, Hooker had risen in the Civil War from brigade commander to be the commander of a grand division of the Army of the Potomac, and had never been found wanting.   His advancement to the head of the Army of the Potomac, on January 26, 1863, was a tragic episode in his own career and in that of the Federal arms. Gloom hung heavy over the North after Fredericksburg.   Upon Hooker fell the difficult task of redeeming the unfulfilled political pledges for a speedy lifting of that gloom.   It was his fortune only to deepen it.

the troops on a splendid campaign footing by a positive and vigorous method of reorganization, and aroused them to enthusiastic loyalty.

It was the month of April, and field and woodland had begun to put on the bright colors of spring. There was activity about the Federal army headquarters that indicated a renewal of hostilities. The hospitals had been well cleared, the forces had been recruited, ammunition and arms replenished and put in order, horses groomed and well fed, uniforms renewed, and the Army of the Potomac was in excellent condition to advance against its foe. President Lincoln had visited the camp, and reviewed the army, thrilling the men with his inspiring presence and personality. It was well known that he had a very deep concern in the welfare of the soldiers. After the review he asked, " What will become of all these men when the war is over? " His parting admonition to Hooker was this wise advice, " In your next battle, put in all your men." By a strange fatality that is just what Hooker failed to do, and a great misfortune overtook his army.

Hooker abandoned Burnside's method of organization. Under " Fighting Joe," instead of three grand divisions, there were seven army corps, each under a major-general, and a cavalry corps. At this time the Union forces aggregated between one hundred and twenty-five and one hundred and thirty thousand men; Lee's forces were estimated at about sixty thousand. Hooker's corps commanders were: Reynolds, in command of the First; Couch, the Second; Sickles, the Third; Meade, the Fifth; Sedgwick, the Sixth; Howard, the Eleventh; Slocum, the Twelfth, and Stoneman, who was in command of the cavalry corps.

Hooker conceived a plan of campaign which was ingenious and masterful, and had he carried it out there would have been a different story to tell about Chancellorsville. The plan was to deploy a portion of the army to serve as a decoy to Lee, while the remainder of the host at the same time

NEW LEADERS AND NEW PLANS

General Joseph Hooker and his Staff.   These were the men whose work it was, during the winter after Fredericksburg, to restore the *esprit du corps* of the Army of the Potomac.   The tireless energy and magnetic personality of Hooker soon won officers from their disaffection and put an end to desertions—which had been going on at the rate of two hundred per day before he took command.   By spring everything seemed propitious for an aggressive campaign, the plans for which were brilliantly drawn and at first vigorously carried out, giving truth to Lincoln's expressed belief that Hooker was "a trained and skilful soldier."   In that remarkable letter of admonition to Hooker upon assuming command, Lincoln added: "But beware of rashness, beware of rashness; with energy and with sleepless vigilance go forward and give us victories."   By some strange fate it was not rashness but quite the contrary which compassed the failure of "Fighting Joe" Hooker at Chancellorsville.   His first forward advance was executed with his usual bold initiative.   Before Lee could fully divine his purpose, Hooker with thirty-six thousand men was across his left flank in a favorable position, with the main body of his army at hand ready to give battle.   Then came Hooker's inexplicable order to fall back upon Chancellorsville.   That very night, consulting in the abandoned Federal position, Lee and Jackson formed the plan which drove Hooker back across the Rappahannock in ignominious defeat.

occupied the vicinity of Chancellorsville, a country mansion, in the center of the wilderness that stretched along the Rappahannock.

The movement of the army began on the 27th of April when Sedgwick was sent east of Fredericksburg with a large force to attract the attention of the Confederates. Another force was left in camp to give the appearance that the main army was still there, while in fact it was secretly being moved to Chancellorsville. The strategy was carried out successfully. On April 30th the army, except a force under Sedgwick composing the First, Third, and Sixth Corps, was concentrated on Lee's left flank, the entire field and its approaches being commanded by the Fifth, Eleventh, and Twelfth Corps, part of the Second Corps, and Stoneman's cavalry of the Army of the Potomac. Victory seemed assured. Hooker, in an order issued on that day, said, " Now the enemy must flee shamefully or come out of his defenses to accept battle on our own ground, to his certain destruction." The contemplated field of battle was high ground about half way between this plateau and the Chancellor house. The Federal army was not yet in position on this open and favorably located field. At eleven o'clock in the morning Hooker started the movement of the army to the point where he intended it to be in line of battle at two o'clock on the afternoon of May 1st.

Lee was a great general and a master in strategy. He had learned of Hooker's plan and, paying but little attention to Sedgwick, had collected his forces and turned to face Hooker. By a rapid night march he met the Union army before it had reached its destination. He was pushed back, however, by Sykes, of Meade's corps, who occupied the position assigned to him. Meade was on the left, and Slocum on the right, with adequate support in the rear. All was in readiness and most favorable for the " certain destruction " of the Confederates predicted by " Fighting Joe " when, to the amazement and consternation of all his officers, Hooker

LEADERS OF THE FRUITLESS RAID

Major-General George Stoneman and Staff; photographed in April, 1863, a month before it fell to the lot of these gallant cavalry officers to lead ten thousand sabers on a daring but futile expedition. Sweeping around in the rear of the Confederate army, it was their intention to cut Lee's railroad communication with Richmond. According to Hooker's plan, this advance movement was to begin April 13th, two weeks before that of his main army, but heavy rains delayed the expedition until the 27th and Hooker's whole force set out simultaneously with the cavalry. Thus Stoneman's work was wasted, for the Army of the Potomac was defeated and in full retreat before the cavalry could strike. On the 5th of May Stoneman recalled his detachments and, leaving his headquarters at Louisa Court House, rejoined the army at Falmouth on the 8th. The most daring raid of the expedition was performed by Colonel Kilpatrick, with his Second New York Cavalry. Dashing across the country, he passed within two and a half miles of Richmond, creating great consternation. Turning down the peninsula, he ended his long ride at Gloucester Point, which was garrisoned by the Federals. With great boldness the regiment rode forth from this refuge. Eluding the Confederates and repulsing a strong force, it rebuilt a bridge and returned safely to Falmouth on June 3d, bringing two hundred prisoners, forty wagons, and a thousand contraband slaves. Hooker, dissatisfied with what the cavalry had accomplished, removed Stoneman from his command.

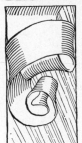

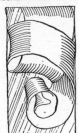

ordered the whole army to retire to the position it had occupied the day before, leaving the advantage to his opponents.

Lee quickly moved his army into the position thus relinquished, and began feeling the Federal lines with skirmishers and some cannonading during the evening of May 1st. By the next morning the two armies were in line of battle.

The danger in which the Confederate army now found itself was extreme. One large Federal army was on its front, while another was at its rear, below Fredericksburg. But Lee threw the hopes of success into one great and decisive blow at Hooker's host. Dividing an army in the face of the foe is extremely dangerous and contrary to all accepted theories of military strategy; but there comes a time when such a course proves the salvation of the legions in peril. Such was the case at Chancellorsville on May 2, 1863.

At 7 A.M. the cannonading began its death-song and was soon followed by infantry demonstrations, but without serious results. The action was continued. Early in the afternoon, Hooker by a ruse was beguiled into the belief that Lee's army was in full retreat. What Hooker had seen and believed to be a retreat was the marching of Jackson's forces, about twenty-six thousand strong, from the battlefield. What he did not see, however, was that, after a few miles, Jackson turned abruptly and made for the right flank of the Federal host, the Eleventh Corps, under Howard. It was after half-past five when Jackson broke from the woods into which he had marched in a paralyzing charge upon the unprepared troops of Howard.

The approach of this Confederate force was first intimated to the Federals by the bending of shrubbery, the stampede of rabbits and squirrels, and the flocks of birds in wild flight, as before a storm. Then appeared a few skirmishers, then a musket volley, and then the storm broke in all its fury —the war scream, the rattling musketry, the incessant roar of cannon. The Confederates fought heroically. The knowledge

THE CORPS THAT STOOD ALONE

Major-General John Sedgwick and Staff. Sedgwick's Sixth Corps alone and unaided executed the most successful maneuver during the Chancellorsville battles of May 1–4, 1863. For two days Sedgwick had been keeping up a strong demonstration against Lee's extreme right below Fredericksburg. On the night of May 2d, after Jackson had routed the entire Eleventh Corps, came the order from Hooker for Sedgwick to move forward toward Chancellorsville, "attack and destroy any forces met with on the march," then fall upon Lee's rear. By midnight the Sixth Corps was in motion and at dawn advanced against Marye's Heights. Only after a fierce uphill fight was that bloody field won from Early's 9,000 Confederates. At night, forced back by Lee, he established communication with Hooker, but could get no definite orders. Next morning word came not to attack unless Hooker did likewise. But Hooker's inactivity encouraged Lee to send heavy forces to crush the Sixth Corps. All the afternoon, cut off from help, the corps fought off assault after assault till nightfall of May 4th. Then, upon the receipt of orders, Sedgwick retired north of the Rappahannock.

SICKLES REVIEWS HIS EIGHTEEN THOUSAND TROOPS, UNAWARE OF JACKSON'S FLANKING MARCH

The photograph, presented one-half above and one-half below, is a reflection of history in the very making. It was at midnight on May 1, 1863, that Lee and Jackson sat on two cracker-boxes before their fire in the abandoned Union camp, and conceived the audacious idea of flanking the Federals. It was 5.30 the next morning that Jackson formed his devoted veterans in column, then bade his last farewell to his chief, and rode into the tangled forest. And it was the same morning that a Union photographer made this picture of Major-General Daniel E. Sickles reviewing his Third Corps of the Army of the Potomac, 18,000 horse, foot, and artillery—all unsuspecting that a couple of miles distant 31,000 in gray were pushing across their front and around to the unprotected rear of the Union encampment. The confidence of the Federals was only natural. Who would have suspected that Lee, with less than 45,000 men, all told, would deliberately have detached more than two-thirds of them in the face of Hooker's encamped 70,000? But Lee was a military genius, and genius knows when to dare—especially with a leader in the field like "Stonewall" Jackson, no less secret than swift. And so it befell that when the Confederate column was spied passing over a bare hill about a mile and a half from the left of Sickles's line, General Hooker supposed that such a movement could mean only a retreat. He ordered a pursuit. This drew a division away from a point where soon it was sorely needed. For Jackson's Corps, having passed around the Federal right, formed in battle-line, burst through the woods in the rear of the unsuspecting Federals, and drove them in utter rout. It was a piece of strategy as daring as it was masterly.

"STONEWALL" JACKSON—TWO WEEKS BEFORE HIS MORTAL WOUND

The austere, determined features of the victor of Chancellorsville, just as they appeared two weeks before the tragic shot that cost the Confederacy its greatest Lieutenant-General—and, in the opinion of sound historians, its chief hope for independence.   Only once had a war photograph of Jackson been taken up to April, 1863, when, just before the movement toward Chancellorsville, he was persuaded to enter a photographer's tent at Hamilton's Crossing, some three miles below Fredericksburg, and to sit for his last portrait.   At a glance one can feel the self-expression and power in this stern worshiper of the God of Battles; one can understand the eulogy written by the British military historian, Henderson: "The fame of 'Stonewall' Jackson is no longer the exclusive property of Virginia and the South: it has become the birthright of every man privileged to call himself an American."

[B]

that "Old Jack" was on the field was inspiration enough for them. The charge was so precipitous, so unexpected and terrific that it was impossible for the Federals to hold their lines and stand against the impact of that awful onslaught which carried everything before it. The regiments in Jackson's path, resisting his advance, were cut to pieces and swept along as by a tidal wave, rolled up like a scroll, multitudes of men, horses, mules, and cattle being piled in an inextricable mass. Characteristic of Jackson's brilliant and unexpected movements, it was like an electric flash, knocking the Eleventh Corps into impotence, as Jackson expected it would. This crowning and final stroke of Jackson's military genius was not impromptu, but the result of his own carefully worked-out plan, which had been approved by Lee.

General Hooker was spending the late afternoon hours in his headquarters at the Chancellor house. To the eastward there was considerable firing, where his men were carrying out the plan of striking Lee in flank. Jackson was retreating, of that he was sure, and Sickles, with Pleasanton's cavalry and other reenforcements, was in pursuit. Everything seemed to be going well. About half-past six the sounds of battle grew suddenly louder and seemed to come from another direction. A staff-officer went to the front of the house and turned his field-glass toward the west.

"My God, here they come!"

At the startled cry Hooker sprang upon his horse and dashed down the road. He encountered portions of the Eleventh Corps pouring out of the forest—a badly mixed crowd of men, wagons, and ambulances. They brought the news that the right wing was overwhelmed. Hurriedly Hooker sought his old command, Berry's division of the Third Corps, stationed in support of the Eleventh. "Forward, with the bayonet!" he commanded.

An officer who witnessed the scene says the division advanced with a firm and steady step, cleaving the multitude

WILDERNESS CHURCH—THE SCENE OF JACKSON'S SECOND RUSH

The shots that riddled the roof of this humble meeting-house were fired on an evening of triumph and panic. Beyond the church, as the sun sank low on May 2d, stretched the main Union line, Howard's Eleventh Corps. The troops had stacked their arms and lay at ease. Supper was cooking. Suddenly bugle-calls came from the west. Then a roar of human voices swept the forest. A double battle-line in gray burst from the woods, ran over the gunners, and shattered the divisions into fragments. Gallant Federal officers did their best to re-form their lines. With the little church at about the center, a stand was made by five thousand men of Schurz's division, with some of Devens'—but without respite Jackson gave the call to advance. After twenty minutes of furious fighting, the Confederate battle-flag flew in the clearing. It was then that the fugitives from the Eleventh Corps came in sight.

of disbanded Federals as the bow of a vessel cleaves the waves of the sea. It struck the advance of the Confederates obliquely and checked it, with the aid of the Twelfth Corps artillery.

A dramatic, though tragic, feature of the rout was the charge of the Eighth Pennsylvania cavalry, under Major Keenan, in the face of almost certain death, to save the artillery of the Third Corps from capture. The guns rested upon low ground and within reach of the Confederates. The Federals had an equal opportunity to seize the artillery, but required a few minutes to prepare themselves for action. The Confederate advance must be checked for these few moments, and for this purpose Keenan gallantly led his five hundred cavalrymen into the woods, while his comrades brought the guns to bear upon the columns in gray. He gained the necessary time, but lost his life at the head of his regiment, together with Captain Arrowsmith and Adjutant Haddock, who fell by his side.

The light of day had faded from the gruesome scene. The mighty turmoil was silenced as darkness gathered, but the day's carnage was not ended. No camp-fires were lighted in the woods or on the plain. The two hostile forces were concealed in the darkness, watching through the shadows, waiting for—they knew not what. Finally at midnight the order " Forward " was repeated in subdued tones along the lines of Sickles' corps. Out over the open and into the deep, dark thicket the men in blue pursued their stealthy advance upon the Confederate position. Then the tragedies of the night were like that of the day, and the moon shed her peaceful rays down upon those shadowy figures as they struggled forward through the woods, in the ravines, over the hillocks. The Federals, at heavy loss, gained the position, and the engagement assumed the importance of a victory.

It was on this day that death robbed the South of one of her most beloved warriors. After darkness had

Within an hour after Jackson's sudden and deadly charge, his men captured Dowdall's Tavern. Here Howard, commander of the Eleventh Corps, now fleeing before the Confederate rush, was holding his headquarters when the blow fell. The trenches in the picture below were the goal in a race between Jackson's men and the men of Williams's Federal division. This had been sent to support Sickles and tried too late to recover the position that it had left, unaware of the Confederate flanking movement. Jackson captured two hundred men of the One Hundred and Twenty-eighth Pennsylvania as they tried to get to their places. Williams after falling back finally checked the Confederates, aided by Barry of the Third Corps and fresh artillery. As night fell, Jackson with his staff ventured on his last reconnaissance. The picture on the

DOWDALL'S TAVERN

right shows the tangled wood through which he passed and the fury of the fire that lopped off the stunted trees. Through a fatal mischance, some Confederates stationed along the road to the north of this spot fired upon what they thought to be a Federal scouting party—and there mortally wounded their own general. Jackson had turned back along the road itself, and his men had orders to fire upon any advance from the Federal position. The next day, with a cry of "Remember Jackson!" the line in gray again swept forward, and by nine in the morning had carried the rude breastworks in the left-hand picture. Hooker withdrew his entire army. Yet the Confederate victory lacked the completeness that would have been expected with Jackson in the saddle; and the Confederacy had lost one of its greatest captains.

WHERE THE FEDERALS MADE A STAND
SOUTH OF THE "PLANK ROAD"

TREES SHATTERED BY THE FIRING NEAR
THE SPOT WHERE JACKSON FELL

overspread the land, Jackson, accompanied by members of his staff, undertook a reconnaissance of the Federal lines. He was planning a night attack. He came upon a line of Union infantry lying on its arms and was forced to turn back along the plank road, on both sides of which he had stationed his own men with orders to fire upon any body of men approaching from the direction of the Federal battle-lines. The little cavalcade of Confederate officers galloped along the highway, directly toward the ambuscade, and apparently forgetful of the strict orders left with the skirmishers. A sudden flash of flame lighted the scene for an instant, and within that space of time the Confederacy was deprived of one of its greatest captains—Jackson was severely wounded, and by his own men and through his own orders. When the news spread through Jackson's corps and through the Confederate army the grief of the Southern soldiers was heartbreaking to witness. The sorrow spread even into the ranks of the Federal army, which, while opposed to the wounded general on many hard-fought battle-grounds, had learned to respect and admire " Stonewall " Jackson.

The loss of Jackson to the South was incalculable. Lee had pronounced him the right arm of the whole army. Next to Lee, Jackson was considered the ablest general in the Confederate army. His shrewdness of judgment, his skill in strategy, his lightning-like strokes, marked him as a unique and brilliant leader. Devoutly religious, gentle and noble in character, the nation that was not to be disunited lost a great citizen, as the Confederate army lost a great captain, when a few days later General Jackson died.

That night orders passed from the Federal headquarters to Sedgwick, below Fredericksburg, eleven miles away. Between him and Hooker stood the Confederate army, flushed with its victories of the day. Immediately in his front was Fredericksburg, with a strong guard of Southern warriors. Beyond loomed Marye's Heights, the battle-ground on which

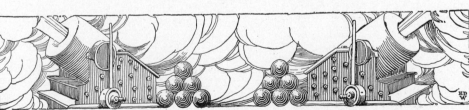

THE DEMOLISHED HEADQUARTERS

From this mansion, Hooker's headquarters during the battle of Chancellorsville, he rode away after the injury he received there on May 3d, never to return. The general, dazed after Jackson's swoop upon the right, was besides in deep anxiety as to Sedgwick. The latter's forty thousand men had not yet come up. Hooker was unwilling to suffer further loss without the certainty of his coöperation. So he decided to withdraw his army. The movement was the signal for increased artillery fire from the Confederate batteries, marking the doom of the old Chancellor house. Its end was accompanied by some heart-rending scenes. Major Bigelow thus describes them: "Missiles pierced the walls or struck in the brickwork; shells exploded in the upper rooms, setting the building on fire; the chimneys were demolished and their fragments rained down upon the wounded about the building. All this time the women and children (including some slaves) of the Chancellor family, nineteen persons in all, were in the cellar. The wounded were removed from in and around the building, men of both armies nobly assisting one another in the work."

Burnside had in the preceding winter left so many of his brave men in the vain endeavor to drive the Confederate defenders from the crest.

The courageous Sedgwick, notwithstanding the formidable obstacles that lay on the road to Chancellorsville, responded immediately to Hooker's order. He was already on the south side of the river, but he was farther away than Hooker supposed. Shortly after midnight he began a march that was fraught with peril and death. Strong resistance was offered the advancing blue columns as they came to the threshold of Fredericksburg, but they swept on and over the defenders, and at dawn were at the base of the heights. On the crest waved the standards of the Confederate Washington Artillery. At the foot of the slope was the stone wall before which the Federals had fought and died but a few months before, in the battle of Fredericksburg. Reenforcements were arriving in the Confederate trenches constantly. The crest and slopes bristled with cannon and muskets. The pathways around the heights were barricaded. The route to the front seemed blocked; still, the cry for help from Hooker was resounding in the ears of Sedgwick

Gathering his troops, he attacked directly upon the stone wall and on up the hillside, in the face of a terrific storm of artillery and musketry. The first assault failed; a flank movement met with no better success; and the morning was nearly gone when the Confederates finally gave way at the point of the bayonet before the irresistible onset of men in blue. The way to Chancellorsville was open; but the cost to the Federals was appalling. Hundreds of the soldiers in blue lay wrapped in death upon the bloody slopes of Marye's Heights.

It was the middle of the afternoon, and not at daybreak, as Hooker had directed, when Sedgwick appeared in the rear of Lee's legions. A strong force of Confederates under Early prevented his further advance toward a juncture with Hooker's army at Chancellorsville. Since five o'clock in the

[122]

THE STONE WALL AT FREDERICKSBURG

Behind the deadly stone wall of Marye's Heights after Sedgwick's men had swept across it in the gallant charge of May 3, 1863. This was one of the strongest natural positions stormed during the war. In front of this wall the previous year, nearly 6,000 of Burnside's men had fallen, and it was not carried. Again in the Chancellorsville campaign Sedgwick's Sixth Corps was ordered to assault it. It was defended the second time with the same death-dealing stubbornness but with less than a fourth of the former numbers—9,000 Confederates against 20,000 Federals. At eleven o'clock in the morning the line of battle, under Colonel Hiram Burnham, moved out over the awful field of the year before, supported to right and left by flanking columns. Up to within twenty-five yards of the wall they pressed, when again the flame of musketry fire belched forth, laying low in six minutes 36.5 per cent. of the Fifth Wisconsin and the Sixth Maine. The assailants wavered and rallied, and then with one impulse both columns and line of battle hurled themselves upon the wall in a fierce hand-to-hand combat. A soldier of the Seventh Massachusetts happened to peer through a crack in a board fence and saw that it covered the flank of the double line of Confederates in the road. Up and over the fence poured the Federals and drove the Confederates from the heights.

morning the battle had been raging at the latter place, and
Jackson's men, now commanded by Stuart, though being
mowed down in great numbers, vigorously pressed the attack
of the day while crying out to one another " Remember Jackson," as they thought of their wounded leader.

While this engagement was at its height General Hooker,
leaning against a pillar of the Chancellor house, was felled
to the ground, and for a moment it was thought he was
killed. The pillar had been shattered by a cannon-ball.
Hooker soon revived under the doctor's care and with great
force of will he mounted his horse and showed himself to
his anxious troops. He then withdrew his army to a stronger
position, well guarded with artillery. The Confederates did
not attempt to assail it. The third day's struggle at Chancellorsville was finished by noon, except in Lee's rear, where
Sedgwick fought all day, without success, to reach the main
body of Hooker's army. The Federals suffered very serious
losses during this day's contest. Even then it was believed
that the advantage rested with the larger Army of the Potomac and that the Federals had an opportunity to win. Thirty-
seven thousand Union troops, the First, and three-quarters
of the Fifth Corps, had been entirely out of the fight on that
day. Five thousand men of the Eleventh Corps, who were
eager to retrieve their misfortune, were also inactive.

When night came, and the shades of darkness hid the
sights of suffering on the battlefield, the Federal army was
resting in a huge curve, the left wing on the Rappahannock
and the right on the Rapidan. In this way the fords across
the rivers which led to safety were in control of the Army of
the Potomac. Lee moved his corps close to the bivouacs of the
army in blue. But, behind the Confederate battle-line, there was
a new factor in the struggle in the person of Sedgwick, with
the remnants of his gallant corps, which had numbered nearly
twenty-two thousand when they started for the front, but now
were depleted by their terrific charge upon Marye's Heights

THE WORK OF ONE SHELL

Part of the Havoc Wrought on Marye's Heights by the Assault of Sedgwick on May 3, 1863.   No sooner had they seized the stone wall than the victorious Federals swarmed up and over the ridge above, driving the Confederates from the rifle-pits, capturing the guns of the famous Washington Artillery which had so long guarded the Heights, and inflicting slaughter upon the assaulting columns.   If Sedgwick had had cavalry he could have crushed the divided forces of Early and cleared the way for a rapid advance to attack Lee's rear.   In the picture we see Confederate caisson wagons and horses destroyed by a lucky shot from the Second Massachusetts' siege-gun battery planted across the river at Falmouth to support Sedgwick's assault.   Surveying the scene stands General Herman Haupt, Chief of the Bureau of Military Railways, the man leaning against the stump.   By him is W. W. Wright, Superintendent of the Military Railroad.   The photograph was taken on May 3d, after the battle.   The Federals held Marye's Heights until driven off by fresh forces which Lee had detached from his main army at Chancellorsville and sent against Sedgwick on the afternoon of the 4th.

OVER THE RUINED TOWN

Here stand the Federal cannoneers at their posts on the last morning of the Chancellorsville struggle, ready to open fire with their 32-pounders against the fateful Marye's Heights across the river—where Sedgwick and his gallant Sixth Corps were to pluck the only shred of victory that remained to the beaten Army of the Potomac at the close of Hooker's futile and costly campaign. On the night of May 2d came the order to advance. The men of the Sixth Corps, already drawn up in battle, slept on their arms till dawn, ready to push forward and play their part in the conflict, the distant heavy booming of which had shaken the air as they had stood all day impatiently waiting. The troops of the Sixth Corps marched out across the plain from the river at four o'clock in the morning; and as they reached the eastern part of Fredericksburg the Confederate batteries opened upon them from above, while the skirmishers rose in swarms before them and poured volley after volley into their ranks, the conflict being hottest around a large mansion

FEDERAL BATTERY BEFORE FREDERICKSBURG, MAY 3, 1863

in the town, where both sides dodged behind the garden-fence of the outhouses and fought furiously. For a brief interval the Federals were held in check, but the rifled guns on Stafford Heights were already hurling their huge shells across the river and the wide valley, to burst in the Confederate works on the ridge before which Sedgwick's men waited for the order to charge. Field batteries were unlimbered and these added their iron hail to the hammering that was being inflicted on Marye's Heights, where so many brave Federals had lost their lives the previous December. At half-past ten Sedgwick, seeing that the Heights could be taken only by direct assault, ordered General Newton to command the charge, and the two commanders anxiously watched for the outcome of another hurling of flesh and blood up the slope against the sunken road which held such bitter memories. The columns went forward as coolly as did Pickett's men at Gettysburg, closing up ranks as men fell, till they swept over the hilltop, and Marye's Heights was won.

and the subsequent hard and desperate struggle with Early in the afternoon.

Lee was between two fires—Hooker in front and Sedgwick in the rear, both of whose forces were too strong to be attacked simultaneously. Again the daring leader of the Confederate legions did the unexpected, and divided his army in the presence of the foe, though he was without the aid of his great lieutenant, " Stonewall " Jackson.

During the night Lee made his preparations, and when dawn appeared in the eastern skies the movement began. Sedgwick, weak and battered by his contact with Early on the preceding afternoon, resisted bravely, but to no avail, and the Confederates closed in upon him on three sides, leaving the way to Banks's Ford on the Rappahannock open to escape. Slowly the Federals retreated and, as night descended, rested upon the river bank. After dark the return to the northern side was begun by Sedgwick's men, and the Chancellorsville campaign was practically ended.

The long, deep trenches full of Federal and Confederate dead told the awful story of Chancellorsville. If we gaze into these trenches, which by human impulse we are led to do, after the roar and din of the carnage is still, the scene greeting the eye will never be forgotten. Side by side, the heroes in torn and bloody uniforms, their only shrouds, were gently laid.

The Union loss in killed and wounded was a little over seventeen thousand, and it cost the South thirteen thousand men to gain this victory on the banks of the Rappahannock. The loss to both armies in officers was very heavy.

The two armies were weary and more than decimated. It appeared that both were glad at the prospect of a cessation of hostilities. On the night of May 5th, in a severe storm, Hooker conveyed his corps safely across the river and settled the men again in their cantonments of the preceding winter at Falmouth. The Confederates returned to their old encampment at Fredericksburg.

PART II
OPENING THE MISSISSPPI

BATON ROUGE—AN ARSENAL RECAPTURED

HOMES DESTROYED TO CLEAR THE WAY FOR
FORTS—BATON ROUGE, 1862

ON THE MISSISSIPPI

As the Federal forces gradually recovered the Mississippi for the Union, many troops were necessary to hold its banks. Whole regiments were detached from the main army for this purpose. The Thirteenth Connecticut was organized in November, 1861, and belonged to Grover's division of the Nineteenth Army Corps. Here a portion of the regiment is seen drawn up on the banks of the Mississippi, in Louisiana. From their neat appearance and white gloves they have evidently been on headquarters duty, and possibly have been in recent touch with the quartermaster's stores; their uniforms are in fine condition and their caps brand new. After its service in the vicinity of the Mississippi, where the regiment had taken part in the operations against Port Hudson and the capture of Donaldsonville and the constant fighting and skirmishing in western Louisiana, the Thirteenth Connecticut went on the ill-fated Red River expedition and bore itself bravely at Monett's Bluff and Cane River Crossing. The men from Connecticut assisted the Michigan and Wisconsin woodsmen in building the famous dam at Alexandria that released the imprisoned gunboats. During July and August the seasoned veterans enjoyed a well-earned furlough after their arduous campaign, and upon its expiration they returned to duty and were attached to Sheridan's Army of the Shenandoah, for service in the East.

PATROLLING THE RIVER

To split the Confederacy apart was the Federal aim in the fall of 1862. It was necessary to the possession and command of the great waterway of the Mississippi that a constant patrol should be established after it was opened, and for this purpose, aside from the heavily armored gunboats, there was maintained a fleet of light-draught stern- and side-wheel vessels. This vessel (pictured by the Southern photographer Lytle) is No. 8 of the lightly armored "tin-clads." It was by means of these vessels of light draught that the shallow tributaries could be used as highways for the transportation of troops and supplies. The fleet or flotilla was at first really a division of the army. The crews were a miscellaneous lot of artillery-men and drafts made up from regi-ments in the service along the river. The early organization caused great confusion. In numerous cases naval officers in command of vessels were given military rank. Captain Foote found that he ranked only as a colonel, and that every brigadier could inter-fere with him. In November, 1861, he received the appointment of flag-officer that gave him the same rank as a major-general, and put him above the orders of any except the comman-der of the department; still he com-manded soldiers, and it was not until late in the year of 1861 that any trained naval men of the rank and file were placed on the river gunboats.

THE CAMP THAT BECAME A BATTLE-FIELD

The Federal Camp at Baton Rouge, Photographed Before the Battle of August 5, 1862. When the operations in the vicinity of Vicksburg had come to an end the Second Brigade (under the command of General Thomas Williams) of the Department of the Gulf once more went into camp at Baton Rouge, pitching tents within the limits of the city. On the 5th the Confederates under General J. C. Breckinridge attacked in two divisions in the early morning, their movements being hidden by a very dense fog. At first the Confederates were most successful and they seized a camp that lay in front of the Union battle-line. But the Federals soon advanced; the Confederates made three charges upon them but were finally driven back in much disorder. General Williams was killed. Baton Rouge was evacuated shortly after. The town was not burned on account of its many public institutions.

WHERE THE HOSPITALS FURNISHED REËNFORCEMENTS

The Federal Camp Banks, at Baton Rouge, near the Penitentiary, taken in late July, 1862. This is another view of what was soon to become a battle-field. We are looking down at the camp of the Seventh Vermont and the Twenty-first Indiana; on the extreme right is the camp of Nims' battery. This point was attacked fiercely, as it was supposed to be held by regiments much depleted by sickness, but at the first alarm the men in the hospitals picked up their rifles and fell into line. After General Williams' death the command devolved upon Colonel Cahill, of the Ninth Connecticut, an Irish regiment. By evening the Confederates had abandoned the ground that they had won in the fight.

THE BREAD–LINE AT BATON ROUGE

This picture was taken just at the close of the war in 1865. It is a remarkable and interesting picture. The Verandah House, the building shown on the left, is where General W. T. Sherman stopped in 1859, when he was Superintendent of the Louisiana Seminary of Learning and Military Academy. The group of colored people lining the sidewalk are waiting for their issue of rations. The skill of Lytle, the photographer, is shown by the fact that the man walking is hardly blurred and the mule's ears in the foreground might have been taken by an instantaneous shutter. The view below shows the home of the Union soldiers who remained in Baton Rouge from its occupation on May 12, 1862. Brigadier-General Thomas Williams had been assigned from Butler's force at New Orleans to assist Farragut to clear the Mississippi. Williams' headquarters was Baton Rouge, but during most of May, June, and July he was in the vicinity of Vicksburg operating in conjunction with Farragut's fleet. When he arrived at Baton Rouge at the end of July the barracks was almost a hospital, for half the men were on the sick-list.

THE COURT HOUSE AT BATON ROUGE

The Parade of a Part of a Regiment of Federal Troops at Baton Rouge. It would take a long search to find a finer body of men than these trained and seasoned veterans here drawn up in line. The campaign on the lower Mississippi was a survival of the fittest in more ways than one. Sickness was rife, and only those in the best condition and the hardiest kept in trim for active service. In many cases regiments could muster only 120 men. Camp fevers and the threat of the yellow scourge were always present. The returns of the regiments employed in the vicinity of New Orleans show a startling mortality. The Thirteenth Connecticut lost by disease 160 men. The Twenty-first Indiana, whose casualty list in the battle of Baton Rouge was 126, lost twice that number from sickness. A larger proportion of sick to killed and wounded prevailed in the Fourteenth Maine and the Seventh Vermont—the former losing 332 and the latter 407.

DRESS–PARADE OF FEDERAL TROOPS AT BATON ROUGE

BY ORDER OF THE COMMANDING OFFICER

Buildings in Line of Fire Condemned and Destroyed at Baton Rouge by Order of Colonel Halbert E. Paine.   This view was photographed by Mr. Lytle after the drawn battle of the 5th of August, 1862, when the Federals had retreated from their outer camps and had concentrated on the Arsenal grounds between the cemetery and the river bank, at the northwestern end of the town.   In order that the houses should not afford protection to any attacking party, those in the immediate vicinity (on the southeastern flank of the fortified Arsenal) were set on fire and razed to the ground.   In this picture the heavy stockade that surrounded the garrison is plainly visible, as is also the roof of one of the barracks.   Nevertheless, although the Federal troops were never attacked in their stronghold, General Butler determined to concentrate his forces in New Orleans, and Baton Rouge was abandoned.

PART II
OPENING THE MISSISSIPPI

THE ASSAULT
ON CORINTH

PUSHING THROUGH TENNESSEE, 1862
UNION BRIDGE OVER THE ELK RIVER AT PULASKI

THE RUSE OF THE WHISTLES

The Tishomingo Hotel was an old hostelry forming practically the railway station at Corinth, Miss., and here was played a little comedy by way of prelude to the tragic spectacle that was to happen on this very scene. After the battle of Shiloh, General Beauregard retreated to Corinth, where soon the Confederate army numbered about eighty thousand men. Halleck, who had assumed command in person, after a little delay started in pursuit at the head of the largest army ever assembled west of the Alleghanies, numbering more than 135,000 effective men. But the great forces did not come to decisive blows; Halleck, as usual, did not act with energy. For more than a month he went on gathering still more reenforcements, planning and organizing, all the time closing in slowly on Corinth. It was expected that a conclusive battle would soon take place, but Beauregard did not risk the test of arms. Keeping his intentions absolutely secret, he decided to evacuate. This plan was carried out with great cleverness; his army with its stores and munitions

THE GUARDED TRACK, CORINTH, MISSISSIPPI, 1862

boarded the assembled railway trains on the night of May 29, 1862, and the roads to the southward were filled with wagons and marching troops. But along the Confederate front the watch-fires burned brightly; and Halleck's army, waiting within earshot, heard sounds of commotion—the tooting of locomotive whistles and, with every fresh clear blast, loud cheers. It was rumored through the Federal camp that strong Confederate reenforcements were arriving. Into the gray of the morning this continued. The troops awoke with the nervous expectancy of battle, but before them lay a deserted town. The whistling and the cheering had covered Beauregard's retreat. The "movement of artillery" that had been reported had been some old wagons driven round in a circle. General Pope was sent in pursuit of the wily Confederate leader, but failed to force him to a stand. The evacuation had opened the Tennessee River, and finally resulted in giving the Federals the control of the Mississippi from Cairo to Memphis.

WHERE TRAGEDY FOLLOWED COMEDY AT CORINTH

Across the road, at the extreme right, against Battery Robinett, frowning above the camp, the Confederates charged on October 4th with terrible results, some of which are shown in the picture following. Only a short distance down the track from the old hotel and railway station shown in the preceding picture, the photographer had aimed his camera to take this view. Months had passed since over this very ground had swept two charges memorable in the annals of the Civil War. On the left of the picture is Battery Williams. Over this foreground the Confederates bravely advanced in the attempt to take two positions. By firmly holding his ground, General Rosecrans leaped at once into national fame.

THE DAY AFTER THE MAGNIFICENT ASSAULT THAT FAILED

As the camera snapped, October 5, 1862, every object in this picture was a tragedy. Directly in the foreground lies a Confederate soldier who had swept along in the grand and terrible charge against the ramparts of Battery Robinett, to fall within fifty yards of the goal. Even nearer the battery lies the battle-charger of the colonel of the Texas Brigade. And to the left has been reverently laid the body of Colonel Rogers himself—the brave leader who leaped from his dying horse, seized the colors, and on foot dashed up the parapet straight into the last charge of grape-shot. "Then," writes one of the Federal defenders (General John Crane, the adjutant of the Seventeenth Wisconsin), "we learned who it was—Colonel William P. Rogers, of the Second Texas. General Rosecrans asked us to uncover his face; he said, 'He was one of the bravest men that ever led a charge. Bury him with military honors and mark his grave so that his friends may claim him.'" Colonel Rogers is said to have been the fifth standard-bearer to fall in that last desperate charge of the Texas Brigade.

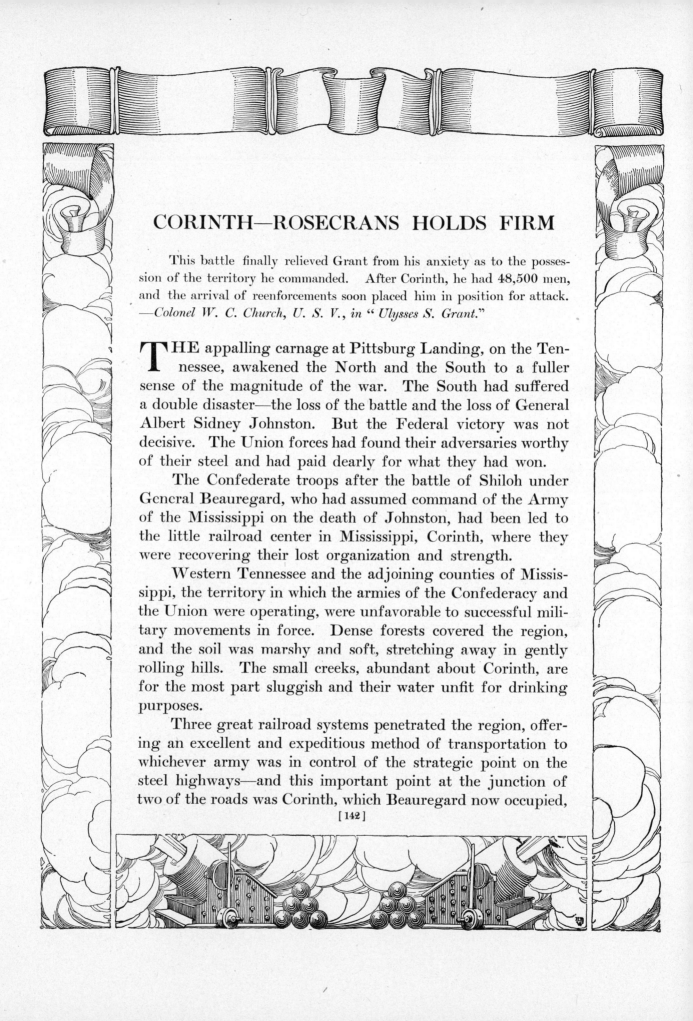

CORINTH—ROSECRANS HOLDS FIRM

This battle finally relieved Grant from his anxiety as to the possession of the territory he commanded. After Corinth, he had 48,500 men, and the arrival of reenforcements soon placed him in position for attack. —*Colonel W. C. Church, U. S. V., in " Ulysses S. Grant."*

THE appalling carnage at Pittsburg Landing, on the Tennessee, awakened the North and the South to a fuller sense of the magnitude of the war. The South had suffered a double disaster—the loss of the battle and the loss of General Albert Sidney Johnston. But the Federal victory was not decisive. The Union forces had found their adversaries worthy of their steel and had paid dearly for what they had won.

The Confederate troops after the battle of Shiloh under General Beauregard, who had assumed command of the Army of the Mississippi on the death of Johnston, had been led to the little railroad center in Mississippi, Corinth, where they were recovering their lost organization and strength.

Western Tennessee and the adjoining counties of Mississippi, the territory in which the armies of the Confederacy and the Union were operating, were unfavorable to successful military movements in force. Dense forests covered the region, and the soil was marshy and soft, stretching away in gently rolling hills. The small creeks, abundant about Corinth, are for the most part sluggish and their water unfit for drinking purposes.

Three great railroad systems penetrated the region, offering an excellent and expeditious method of transportation to whichever army was in control of the strategic point on the steel highways—and this important point at the junction of two of the roads was Corinth, which Beauregard now occupied,

GENERAL EARL VAN DORN, C.S.A.

THE CONFEDERATE COMMANDER AT CORINTH

General Earl Van Dorn was born in Mississippi in 1821; he was graduated from West Point in 1842, and was killed in a personal quarrel in 1863. Early in the war General Van Dorn had distinguished himself by capturing the steamer "Star of the West" at Indianola, Texas. He was of a tempestuous nature and had natural fighting qualities. During the month of August he commanded all the Confederate troops in Mississippi except those under General Price, and it was his idea to form a combined movement with the latter's forces and expel the invading Federals from the northern portion of his native State and from eastern Tennessee. The concentration was made and the Confederate army, about 22,000 men, was brought into the disastrous battle of Corinth. Brave were the charges made on the entrenched positions, but without avail.

THE CONFEDERATE SECOND IN COMMAND

General Sterling Price was a civilian who by natural inclination turned to soldiering. He had been made a brigadier-general during the Mexican War, but early allied himself with the cause of the Confederacy. At Pea Ridge, only seven months before the battle of Corinth, he had been wounded. Of the behavior of his men, though they were defeated and turned back on the 4th, he wrote that it was with pride that sisters and daughters of the South could say of the officers and men, "My brother, father, fought at Corinth." And nobly they fought indeed. General Van Dorn, in referring to the end of that bloody battle, wrote these pathetic words: "Exhausted from loss of sleep, wearied from hard marching and fighting, companies and regiments without officers, our troops—let no one censure them—gave way. The day was lost."

GENERAL STERLING PRICE, C.S.A.

and upon which the Federal authorities cast longing glances as soon as the present campaign had begun.

However, it became clear to Beauregard that although his opponent did not immediately pursue, it would be impossible to hold Corinth. Soon after Shiloh the Union army was re-enforced to more than double the strength it had been before. Four days after the battle, General H. W. Halleck arrived at the Landing and took command in person; ten days later General John Pope, who had captured Island No. 10, on April 7th, joined his army to that at the Landing, and this, with other reenforcements, raised the number to a hundred thousand.

Beauregard had been joined by Van Dorn and Sterling Price from beyond the Mississippi, but, although the rolls showed now a force of over one hundred and twelve thousand he could not muster much more than fifty thousand men at any time and he prepared to give up Corinth whenever the great Northern force should move against it. About the 1st of May the movement of the Federal hosts, reorganized and now consisting of the Army of the Tennessee under General Thomas, the Army of the Ohio under Buell, and the Army of the Mississippi under Pope, began. Grant was second in command of the whole force, under Halleck. Slowly and cautiously, entrenching at every night halt, Halleck moved upon Corinth, guarding always against attack. He arrived before the town on May 25th. He met with but slight resistance. But Beauregard, although he had thrown up entrenchments and was maintaining a bold front, stealthily prepared to evacuate the town and save his army. Troops, provided with three days' cooked rations, manned the trenches confronting the Federal line, waiting for the order to advance. The Confederate soldiers had no inkling of the intentions of their leader. As the days passed and the command to attack was not given, the men behind the breastworks became restless.

Meanwhile, the patients in the hospitals within the town were being hurried away, and with great trainloads of stores

BEFORE THE SOD HID THEM

The Gathered Confederate Dead Before Battery Robinett—taken the morning after their desperate attempt to carry the works by assault. No man can look at this awful picture and wish to go to war. These men, a few hours before, were full of life and hope and courage. Without the two last qualities they would not be lying as they are pictured here. In the very foreground, on the left, lies their leader, Colonel Rogers, and almost resting on his shoulder is the body of the gallant Colonel Ross. We are looking from the bottom of the parapet of Battery Robinett. Let an eye-witness tell of what the men saw who looked toward the houses on that bright October day, and then glanced along their musket-barrels and pulled the triggers: "Suddenly we saw a magnificent brigade emerge in our front; they came forward in perfect order, a grand but terrible sight. At their head rode the commander, a man of fine physique, in the prime of life—quiet and cool as though on a drill. The artillery opened, the infantry followed; notwithstanding the slaughter they were closer and closer. Their commander [Colonel Rogers] seemed to bear a charmed life. He jumped his horse across the ditch in front of the guns, and then on foot came on. When he fell, the battle in our front was over."

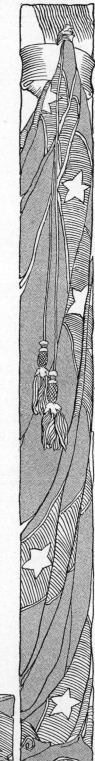

were sent south over the Mobile and Ohio Railroad. On the night of the 29th, the preparations for the evacuation of the town by the Confederates were completed. Most of the troops were withdrawn from the trenches to the railroad, and there instructed concerning the part they were to play in the strategy to deceive the Federals.

Late that night a train rolled into the station, and the Federal pickets heard a lusty cheer arise from the Confederate ranks. Other trains followed, and the sounds of exuberation increased. Word quickly spread through the Federal camps that heavy reenforcements had come to the Confederates. The Northerners spent the early morning hours preparing to resist the attack they expected would be made with the coming of dawn.

At break of day the Federals, waiting in battle-line, could see no signs of life in the pits confronting them. The pickets crept forward to investigate. A thunderous explosion shook the town. It was the destruction of the last of the Confederate stores. The Southerners had evacuated the village, and Corinth, with all its strategic advantage, with its command of the great railroads connecting the Mississippi valley with the Atlantic coast and with the Gulf of Mexico, fell into the hands of the North. Both of the great armies were quickly broken up. Halleck, in possession of Corinth, looked to Chattanooga as the next objective, and Buell led the Army of the Ohio back to middle Tennessee as a preliminary move in that direction.

In the midsummer, Halleck was made general-in-chief of all the Northern armies and went to Washington. He left Grant in control of the West. Meantime, Beauregard was relieved of the command of the Confederate Army of the Mississippi and it was handed over to General Bragg. Leaving a portion of his army in Mississippi with Van Dorn and Price, Bragg began, late in August, his famous expedition into Kentucky, pursued by Buell with the Army of the Ohio. A part of the Federal Army of the Mississippi remained at Corinth,

THE BATTERY THAT CONTROLLED THE RIGHT OF WAY

Battery Williams, that can just be seen at the left of the picture, controlled the cutting through which the Memphis & Charleston Road ran on its way between Corinth and the Mississippi. It faced the right flank of Fort Robinett, distant about half a mile. During the action of October 4th, when the gallant Texans bravely assailed Battery Robinett, Battery Williams with all its guns was playing steadily upon the Confederate left flank, and so closely did they follow that brave and brilliant charge that two shells from the battery landed inside the Federal earthworks and burst there. Most of the houses seen in the mid-distance are barracks erected by the Fifty-seventh and Fifty-second Illinois Infantry. It was directly from this ground, in front of the railway station, that the Confederate advance took place. A short distance to the left of the freight-house stood a small cottage. General Rosecrans, as he rode along the Federal line, noticed that the porch and windows were filled with Confederates, who were firing at long range at the batteries. Immediately he ordered two field-pieces to open upon the dwelling with grape and canister. Hardly a man escaped alive. The town suffered severely from the fire of both Confederate and Federal artillery, but most of the inhabitants had retreated to their cellars and no casualties were reported. Note the bales of precious cotton gathered from some storehouse, worth almost their weight in gold before the war was over.

[B]

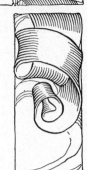

where there were immense military stores, under the command of General William S. Rosecrans. After inflicting a defeat on Sterling Price, September 19th, in a severe combat at Iuka, Mississippi, Rosecrans was settled snugly at Corinth with two divisions and cavalry of his army, and two divisions of the Federal Army of West Tennessee, in all about twenty-three thousand men. Van Dorn then joined his Army of West Tennessee with Price's Corps, or Army of the West, and decided to make a desperate attempt to capture Corinth. It was a daring venture, for Corinth was well fortified and Rosecrans' army was slightly larger than his own.

The battle of Corinth, October 3–4, 1862, does not compare in magnitude with the greatest battles of the war; but for ferocity of fighting, it was not surpassed by any. Rosecrans did not believe that Van Dorn would attack him, and when the latter appeared in force in the neighborhood on October 3rd he supposed that it was only a feint and that the real object of the Confederate attack was to be Jackson, about sixty miles north, in Tennessee, where Grant's headquarters were, or Bolivar, Tennessee, about forty miles northwest, where Hurlbut's division of Grant's Army of West Tennessee was at that time located.

However, Rosecrans was prepared for any emergency. He sent Colonel Oliver with three regiments to take an advanced position on a hill, near the Chewalla road, to watch the movements of the Confederates. A desultory cannonade was begun and soon Rosecrans sent General McArthur to the front with his brigade. In a short time a sharp battle was raging. Then came a sudden determined Confederate charge by which the Union forces were driven from the hill and two of their heavy guns captured. The Union commander was now convinced that the attack was no feint, but that the purpose of the Southern general was to make a grand assault on Corinth with a view of defeating its defenders and capturing the great stores within its fortifications.

WINTER QUARTERS AT CORINTH

A Photograph Taken During the Federal Occupation, Winter of 1862. These little cottages—bungalows we should call them—resemble much the summer residences erected by the holiday-makers on the sea-coast at some wintering resort. Many were built by soldier-carpenters who found time to turn their hands to carpentering, and even to architectural decoration. All trades were represented in the army, and during a lull in the fighting the men plied their avocations. Besides the artisans that were of use to the commanding generals—such as mechanics, locomotive engineers, machinists, and farriers—there were tailors and shoemakers, watchmakers and barbers, and all the little trades by which men with time on their hands could turn an honest penny. Some regiments became renowned for the neatness of their quarters. It was a matter of prideful boastings. In this picture a soldier has fashioned a well-cut overcoat out of a gaudy blanket. These are officers' quarters. The man smoking the long cigar as he sits on the veranda railing is a captain. A bearded lieutenant stands on the steps of the second house, and another young officer has apparently adopted for the time a tow-headed child of a Corinth family.

The hours of the afternoon were given to disposing the various divisions of the army to the best advantage for the defense of the town; but it was no easy task because of the annoying Confederate fire from the surrounding hills. Before either side opened a general engagement it was night, and both armies slept on their arms, confident that a fierce battle was in store for the coming day.

The early hours of the night were spent by Rosecrans in rearranging his battle-lines, and before he went to sleep about 3 A.M., his forces had drawn closer to the town. The Federal left, under McKean, rested near Corona College; next in line was Stanley, in support of Battery Robinett, a small fortification mounting three guns; in the center of the battle-line, was Davies, and Hamilton was assigned to the right wing. Thus stood the weary warriors in blue, who had struggled desperately in the terrific heat of the preceding day and were now exhausted. The line was crescent shaped, and covered the northern and western approaches to Corinth, extended a mile in length and rested on the edge of the town. The Confederate divisions, commanded by Lovell, Maury, and Hébert stood arrayed in another great crescent, conforming to the curve of Rosecrans' battle-line. About four o'clock on the morning of the 4th the sleeping village was awakened by the shells that shrieked over the housetops and fell bursting in the streets.

During the night a Confederate battery had been planted a few hundred yards from the Union lines, opposite Stanley's position, and now opened with several Parrott guns. Little damage was done, except that the teamsters, sutlers, and other non-combatants were kept in a ferment of excitement. No reply was made till near daylight, when a Union battery opened on the Confederate guns, and the latter were silenced and disabled in a few minutes. Indian summer had descended over the land, bringing its enervating heat from which the soldiers of both armies suffered. The sun peeped over the eastern hills, and its rays were soon beating down upon the bivouacs.

PHOTOGRAPHERS OF THE WESTERN ARMIES

The Civil War was the first great war to be photographed. The art had just arisen. The daguerreotype had been superseded by the tintype, and the wet-plate method (still in vogue in the best portrait galleries) was then in the height of its excellence. It is a fortunate thing in recording the history of the time that the camera was in existence. In Corinth there was a firm of photographers occupying a little wooden shack in the outskirts of the town. They did a thriving business during the occupancy by the Confederates and by the Federals. George Armstead was a wonderful photographer—rivaling Brady at his best. In the picture he is standing back to the left, near where some of his negatives are printing in the sun; in front of the shop a drummer-boy stands with folded arms near the civilians who loll against the post. What would we not give for a nearer glimpse of the samples of Armstead's work on the right of the doorway! The little frame of portrait tintypes on the other side would also give us to-day a thrill of interest. They are the only relics, perhaps, of men who lie in far-off graves—duplicates of the only mementoes that their people, who are now old, possess. In turning the pages of this volume many will exclaim, "Look, there he is!"

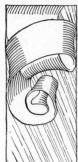
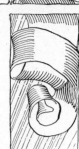

During the day the temperature rose to ninety-four degrees in the shade.

Soon after daybreak the skirmishers of both sides began with scattering shots, which presently came thicker and faster; the batteries came into play, and shells were falling and bursting all around. So it continued until half-past nine. Then came a sudden and amazing change in the whole aspect of the battle. A vast column of gleaming bayonets was seen to flash from the woods east of the Memphis and Charleston Railroad; long lines of determined, gray-clad troops of Price's divisions quickly formed and began to march swiftly and steadily along the Purdy road, toward Davies and Hamilton, behind whom lay the town of Corinth. Presently the great column took the shape of a wedge as it moved impetuously forward.

General Rosecrans was prepared for the charge. He had skilfully planned to entice the Confederates to attack at a point where his carefully placed batteries and infantry could sweep the road with direct, cross, and enfilading fires. There was an outburst from the Federal guns. Gaps were torn in the moving gray column, but they were instantly filled and the lines moved on with great steadiness. A gently sloping hill led up to the Federal position. As Price's troops began the ascent, volley after volley of grape, canister, and shell were poured into their ranks, but still they marched on with a valor not surpassed by Leonidas and his Spartans at Thermopylæ.

Colonel Sweeny, who commanded a brigade of Davies' division on that memorable 4th of October, gives a vivid picture of this remarkable charge:

An ominous silence took place for a few moments, when a sharp rattling of musketry was heard, accompanied by heavy volleys, and the enemy's columns burst from the woods in front and to the right, driving the sharpshooters before them and following close upon their heels. Colonel Burke's regiment fought like heroes and disputed every inch of ground as they fell back on my position. I cautioned my men, who were lying on the ground, to reserve their fire until the enemy got within

OHIO TROOPS ON THE BATTLE-FIELD OF CORINTH

The Eighty-first Ohio, pictured here drawn up at "parade rest," enlisted in August, 1861; when its term expired in 1864, it reënlisted and served to the end of the war. The youth of these men is very evident; yet when this picture was taken they were already tried and proved veterans. Attached to Sweeney's division of the Sixteenth Army Corps, they fought through most of the actions in Tennessee and Mississippi, but were not present at the time of the Confederate attack on the fortifications we see behind them—Battery Williams to the left, and Battery Robinett to the right. The Eightieth Ohio was present at this action and was attached to the second brigade of the second division of the Army of the Mississippi under Rosecrans. Its commander, Major Lanning, was killed. Well can Ohio be proud of her record in the war; nearly twenty-one thousand men remained in the field and served after their three-years' enlistment had expired, and most of these reënlistments embraced a very large proportion of the original volunteers of '61.

point-blank range, and then fire low and keep perfectly cool. It was a terribly beautiful sight to see the columns advance, in despite of a perfect storm of grape and canister, shell, and rifle-ball; still on they marched and fired, though their ranks were perceptibly thinned at every step. The brigade stood firm as a rock, and the men loaded and fired with the coolness and precision of veterans, when all of a sudden the troops on the right of the redan (a brigade of Hamilton's division) gave way and broke. The First Missouri Artillery, in the redan, and the two pieces on the left of the Fifty-second Illinois limbered up and galloped off in wild confusion through our reserves, killing several of our men and scattering the rest. My line remained still unbroken, pouring deadly volleys into the enemy's ranks, who, taking advantage of the panic on the right, moved their columns obliquely in that direction and charged up to the redan. . . .

I now ordered the line to charge on the enemy, who had by this time gained the crest of the hill in our front. With a shout that was heard through our whole lines the men of the First Brigade rushed upon them. Those who had given way a short time before, being evidently ashamed of the momentary panic that had seized them, seemed determined to wipe out the stain upon their courage by their reckless daring. The foe, reluctant to abandon the advantage they had gained, fought stubbornly for a while, but was finally compelled to give way, retreating in great confusion through the swamps and abatis to the woods, hotly pursued by our men.

In spite of the desperate resistance, the center of the Federal line was penetrated, and Price's troops drove the regiments back into the town, scattering the Union soldiers among the houses. The storming Confederates advanced to the north side of the square and posted themselves around a house close to where General Halleck had maintained his headquarters the summer before. Two field-pieces opened upon them, and the daring Southerners were whirled back, leaving seven of their number dead in the dooryard, after one round of grape and canister. Union troops stationed in the town hurried up and General Sullivan immediately supported the shattered center. His men retook Battery Powell while General Hamilton

A CAMP MEETING WITH A PURPOSE

There was something of extreme interest taking place when this photograph was taken at Corinth. With arms stacked, the soldiers are gathered about an improvised stand sheltered with canvas, listening to a speech upon a burning question of the hour—the employment of colored troops in the field. A question upon which there were many different and most decided opinions prevailing in the North, and but one nearly universal opinion holding south of Mason and Dixon's line. General Thomas, at the moment this photograph was taken, was addressing the assembled troops on this subject. Some prominent Southerners, among them General Patrick Cleburne, favored the enrollment of Negroes in the Confederate army.

collected his scattered division and charged upon the Confederate left, driving it across an open field over which the recaptured Union artillery hurled a pitiless fire. It was now one o'clock in the afternoon and the battle on the Federal right was over.

The Confederate commanders had planned a general assault, Price and Van Dorn acting in concert, but on different points of Rosecrans' line. Van Dorn delayed in reaching his position, and Price's majestic and thrilling charge had been in progress half an hour or more when the standards of the Army of West Tennessee emerged from the woods, in front of Stanley's division and batteries Robinett and Williams. The Federal troops were eagerly watching affairs on their right, when their attention was called to the gray wave plunging over fallen trees and through growths of underbrush in front of Battery Robinett. A sheet of flame burst from the fort, and the advance line of Confederates was enveloped in smoke, many of its numbers falling dead and wounded. A second storming column appeared, and again the Federal guns smote the daring Confederates. Again and again the courageous Southerners charged until they finally won the ditch surrounding the battery, and after a desperate hand-to-hand fight gained the interior of the fort, the defenders falling back to another position. At the head of the attacking regiments stood Colonel W. P. Rogers of the Second Texas regiment of Maury's division.

The Southerners had almost gained this important point in the Federal line, when a burst of flame appeared in Battery Williams, and two shells hurtled across the intervening space and fell into the Confederate ranks. Simultaneously, Fuller's Ohio brigade of Stanley's division and the Eleventh Missouri appeared in the rear of the fort where they had been concealed, and delivered six successive volleys into the gray ranks at the front of the battery. When the smoke cleared the front of the fort was clear of living Confederates. They could not stand the terrific storm of lead and iron. Many of them fell to rise

PROVOST MARSHAL'S HEADQUARTERS AT CORINTH

During the occupation of a town where soldiers were in predominance, there was one man who was responsible for the conduct of the troops, and also for the practical government and policing of the streets, and the control of the inhabitants' actions. Such was the provost marshal. He was head constable, police-court judge, health department, and general almoner. Negroes from the outlying districts had flocked, as usual, into Corinth in nondescript wagons drawn by oxen and mules, and sometimes both, as we see here pictured.

FOOD FOR POWDER

Give a glance at these seventeen men, who, for some reason that we cannot tell, have chosen to stand before the camera and be "taken." Note one thing first—there is not one smiling face nor one look of the holiday soldier about this little group. Able, grim, stern-hearted veterans—their faces show it. Among them all there is not a single merry-maker. These men have faced death often, they have seen their comrades die. They have looked across the sights of their muskets at the ragged men in gray, and peered through the enveloping smoke to see if their shots have told. These are not the machine-made soldiers of the European armies. They are the development of the time and hour. The influence of emigration is plainly shown. Here is a Scotchman—

FEDERAL TROOPS AT CORINTH

An old soldier of the Queen, perhaps, who knew the Mutiny and the Crimea. Here are Swedes and Germans, Irish and French; but, predominating, is the American type—the Yankee, and the man of many blends from the mid-West and the North woods. There are two or three regulars standing in the center—artillerymen with bell buttons. On the extreme right are two men of the saber, with short jackets. Beyond them is the battle-field of October. It is now winter, but these men saw that field shrouded in battle smoke. They saw Price and Van Dorn's brave troops come yelling and charging across the railway track and the road beyond up to the very guns of Battery Robinett, which we see rising like a mound or hillock beyond the line of the railway shed.

no more. The others began to waver. Then came a panic. They broke and fled in great disorder. Volley after volley was fired at the fleeing men. They were now pursued by the victors, across ravines, over hills, and among the fallen trees. Many threw away their guns and surrendered, others escaped, and still others gave their lives for the cause in which they believed. Fifty-six bodies of brave Confederates were found in a space of a few rods about Battery Robinett and were buried in one pit. Among them was Colonel Rogers, who had fallen while planting his battle-flag on the parapet. The wild shouts of the victorious Federals rang through the streets of Corinth, above the moaning of the wounded and dying. By two o'clock Rosecrans was convinced that the Confederate generals did not intend to make another attack and were retreating in force, but his troops were too weary to follow after on that day.

Later in the afternoon McPherson arrived with four regiments sent by Grant, and these were ordered to begin the pursuit at daylight the next morning. Meanwhile, Hurlbut with his division was hastening from Bolivar to the Confederate rear. On the night of the 4th he bivouacked on the west bank of the Hatchie River near Davis' Bridge, right in the path of Van Dorn. The following morning General Ord arrived and took command of the Federal forces.

Owing to a number of mishaps and delays Rosecrans never overtook the Confederate army, but when Van Dorn's advance guard attempted to seize the Hatchie bridge on the morning of the 5th, it was most spiritedly attacked and driven off by Ord, who was severely wounded. Although the Confederates greatly outnumbered their opponents, Van Dorn, fearful of Rosecrans in his rear, moved down the east bank of the Hatchie, crossed six miles below, and made his way to Holly Springs. On these three October days the Federals lost over twenty-five hundred and the Confederates forty-eight hundred. Of these over two thousand had been captured by Rosecrans and Ord.

PART II

OPENING THE MISSISSIPPI

THE MIDWINTER COMBAT
AT STONE'S RIVER

THE MURFREESBORO COURTHOUSE UNDER GUARD—1863

THE SINEWS OF WAR

This busy scene along the Nashville wharf on December 18, 1862, gives a clear idea of the magnitude of the preparations at the Federal army base thirteen days before the battle opened around Murfreesboro, at which point Bragg was threatening Nashville. Rosecrans could not move forward to attack him without supplies, and the river steamers which played so important a part in all the military operations in the West were hurrying up the Cumberland heavily loaded with the munitions and sustenance that made possible the coming battles. The first boat completely visible in the picture at the right is the "Mercury," a famous Ohio River packet at the time. Next to her lies the "Lizzie Martin," and then the "Palestine," another Ohio racer. She has a hole stove in her prow just above the water-line, and the ship's carpenter in his yawl is busily repairing it. Confederate batteries constantly menaced the Federal transports as they plied up and down the rivers. The renowned Tom Napier sometimes scared and captured a vessel with his dummy wooden guns.

SUPPLY STEAMERS AT NASHVILLE, DECEMBER, 1862

Beyond the "Palestine" lie the "Reveillie," the "Irene," the "Belle Peoria" (a famous Mississippi boat from St. Louis), and last the "Rob Roy"—all discharging their tons of freight, paid for by the Government at war-time prices. On the snow-covered wharf are piled barrels of whiskey (the standard brand familiarly known as "Cincinnati rot-gut," distilled for the Government's own use), while the roustabouts are rolling ashore barrels of sugar and hogsheads of molasses to be mixed with the coffee which weary soldiers are to brew for themselves in the field. There are thousands of barrels of flour still to be unloaded. In symmetrical piles lie myriad boxes each stencilled "Pilot bread from U. S. Government Bakery, Evansville, Ind." Many an old Confederate knew the taste of this hard-tack and had to depend upon capturing a supply of it to stay his hunger. Confederate prisoners in their confinement watched many such scenes as this, wondering what newcomers would be added to their numbers during the ensuing campaign.

[B]

CONFEDERATES WHO FOUGHT THE GUNS AT STONE'S RIVER

The Washington Artillery, mustered in at New Orleans, was one of the crack military organizations of the Confederacy. In this rare picture a Confederate photographer has caught a jolly group of them, confident and care-free, whiling away the hours in camp. The photograph was taken the year before the battle of Stone's River. Ere that conflict the youngsters had received their baptism of fire at Shiloh and had acquitted themselves like men. Their gallant force was attached to Anderson's First Brigade and then to General Samuel Jones's Corps, of Bragg's army. At the battle of Stone's River they fought in Breckinridge's division of Hardee's Corps. It was they who made the daring rush to plant their batteries on the hill, and suffered so severely from the galling fire of

MEN OF THE FAMOUS WASHINGTON ARTILLERY

Mendenhall's Federal guns across the river.   On that hard-fought battlefield they were differently occupied than in the picture.   Their deeds in the swift moments of the conflict were not acted out to the accompaniment of a merry tune; each man played his part amid the roar of cannon and the clash of arms, and many paid the piper with his life for that awful music.   Even in the confident poses and smiling faces of the picture are apparent all the dash and spirit which they displayed later at Stone's River.   This brave Confederate organization distinguished itself on all the fields where it fought.   Not till Chancellorsville did it ever lose a gun; in that engagement five pieces were captured from it, when Sedgwick's 20,000 wrested Marye's Heights from the 9,000 Lee had left there.

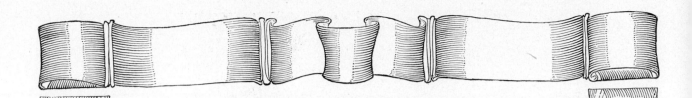

STONE'S RIVER, OR MURFREESBORO

As it is, the battle of Stone's River seems less clearly a Federal victory than the battle of Shiloh. The latter decided the fall of Corinth; the former did not decide the fall of Chattanooga. Offensively it was a drawn battle, as looked at from either side. As a defensive battle, however, it was clearly a Union victory.—*John Fiske in "The Mississippi Valley in the Civil War."*

THE battle of Corinth developed a man—William S. Rosecrans—whose singular skill in planning the battle, and whose dauntless courage in riding between the firing-lines at the opportune moment, drew the country's attention almost as fully as Grant had done at Fort Donelson. And at this particular moment the West needed, or thought it needed, a man. The autumn months of 1862 had been spent by Generals Bragg and Buell in an exciting race across Kentucky, each at the head of a great army. Buell had saved Louisville from the legions of Bragg, and he had driven the Confederate Army of the Mississippi from the State; but he had not prevented his opponent from carrying away a vast amount of plunder, nor had he won decisive results at the battle of Perryville, which took place October 8, 1862, four days after the battle of Corinth. Thereupon the Federal authorities decided to relieve Buell of the Army of the Ohio and to give it to General Rosecrans.

On October 30, 1862, Rosecrans assumed command at Nashville of this force, which was now designated as the Army of the Cumberland. Bragg had concentrated his army at Murfreesboro, in central Tennessee, about thirty miles southeast of Nashville and a mile east of a little tributary of the Cumberland River called Stone's River. Here occurred, two months later, the bloodiest single day's battle in the West,

THE GUARDED DEPOT—STEVENSON IN 1862

This little Alabama town first became the subject of a war photograph during General Buell's campaign. It sprang into strategic importance as a base of supplies, and in order to hold it Buell sent forward Colonel A. S. Barker, who began the construction of extensive defenses, pressing into service some five hundred Negroes. Barker succeeded in completing two large redoubts and seven lockhouses; so defensible was the position made that during Hood's invasion of Tennessee it was not attacked by the Confederates.

THE STRENGTHENED FORTS

This picture of Fort Barker, at Stevenson, shows the care with which the Federals defended this advance base. In this fort, which was about 150 feet square, there were barbette platforms for seven guns and an extensive magazine, and bomb-proof. Fort Mitchell, south of the station on the other side of the railroad, was equally strong. The two forts guarded the approach from the north.

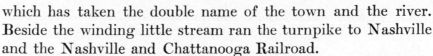

which has taken the double name of the town and the river. Beside the winding little stream ran the turnpike to Nashville and the Nashville and Chattanooga Railroad.

Bragg had the advantage in cavalry. In addition to Wheeler's command there were the troops of Forrest and Morgan, who acted independently of the Army of the Mississippi, now known as the Army of Tennessee. These men, with several hundred horsemen, raided through the country, regardless of mud, snow, or ice, and at one time threatened Nashville, the Federal supply-depot. They tore up railroads, burned bridges, and left a trail of destruction in their wake. One night, early in December, Morgan pounced upon the town of Hartsville, overpowered the guard of several hundred Federal troops, captured and carried them to Murfreesboro.

Christmas day, in 1862, was passed by Bragg's army in whatever festivities the little town of Murfreesboro could afford. The fratricidal strife that was draining both the North and the South was forgotten for the moment. A general belief had circulated in the Confederate camps that the Federal commander, harassed on every side by the raiders, would have enough to do to keep his army intact, and would not make a general advance on Bragg. But soon there was a different story to tell. On the day after Christmas, the news reached the little town that the Federal army had emerged from Nashville, that it was headed directly for Murfreesboro, and that a great battle was imminent.

The battle-ground toward which the Federal army was marching was broken and heavily wooded, with an occasional open field, and gentle rises on which artillery and infantry could be posted. But cavalry was practically useless in this rough country. Stone's River, which ran through the battle-ground, was tortuous in its channel and shallow; its banks were fringed with clumps of cedar brakes. Numerous turnpikes converged at the little town of Murfreesboro from the surrounding towns; the principal highway being the Nashville

LEADERS OF A GALLANT STAND AT STONE'S RIVER

General William P. Carlin and Staff. Early in the war Carlin made a name for himself as colonel of the Thirty-eighth Illinois Infantry, which was stationed at Pilot Knob, Mossouri, and was kept constantly alert by the raids of Price and Jeff Thompson. Carlin rose rapidly to be the commander of a brigade, and joined the forces in Tennessee in 1862. He distinguished himself at Perryville and in the advance to Murfreesboro. At Stone's River his brigade, almost surrounded, repulsed an overwhelming force of Confederates. This picture was taken a year after that battle, while the brigade was in winter quarters at Ringgold, Georgia. The band-stand was built by the General's old regiment.

turnpike, which, after crossing the river, took the general direction of its course for some distance.

General Bragg did not lose a moment in marshaling his army into well-drawn battle-lines. His army was in two corps with a cavalry division under General Wheeler, Forrest and Morgan being on detached service. The left wing, under General Hardee, and the center, under Polk, were sent across Stone's River, the right wing, a division under John C. Breckinridge, remaining on the eastern side of the stream to guard the town. The line was three miles in length, and on December 30th the Federal host that had come from Nashville stood opposite, in a parallel line. It was also in three sections. The left wing, opposite Breckinridge, was commanded by Thomas L. Crittenden, whose brother was a commander in the Confederacy. They were sons of the famous United States senator from Kentucky, John J. Crittenden. The Federal center, opposite Polk, was commanded by George H. Thomas, and the right wing, opposing the Confederate left, was led by Alexander McD. McCook, one of the well-known " Fighting McCook " brothers. The effective Federal force was about forty-three thousand men; the Confederate army numbered about thirty-eight thousand. That night they bivouacked within musket range of each other and the camp-fires of each were clearly seen by the other as they shone through the cedar groves that interposed. Thus lay the two great armies, ready to spring upon each other in deadly combat with the coming of the morning.

Rosecrans had permitted McCook to thin out his lines over too much space, while on that very part of the field Bragg had concentrated his forces for the heaviest attack. The plans of battle made by the two opposing commanders were strikingly similar. Rosecrans' plan was to throw his left wing, under Crittenden, across the river upon the Confederate right under Breckinridge, to crush it in one impetuous dash, and to swing around through Murfreesboro to the Franklin road and

MEN WHO LEARNED WAR WITH SHERMAN

The Twenty-first Michigan Infantry. In the Murfreesboro campaign, the regiment, detached from its old command, fought in the division of Brigadier-General "Phil" Sheridan, a leader who became scarcely less renowned in the West than Sherman and gave a good account of himself and his men at Stone's River. Most of the faces in the picture are those of boys, yet severe military service has already given them the unmistakable carriage of the soldier. The terrible field of Chickamauga lay before them, but a few months in the future; and after that, rejoining their beloved "Old Tecumseh," they were to march with him to the sea and witness some of the closing scenes in the struggle.

cut off the Confederate line of retreat. Bragg, on the other hand, intended to make a similar dash upon the Union right, pivot upon his center, press back McCook upon that center, crumpling the Federals and seizing the Nashville turnpike to cut off Rosecrans' retreat toward Nashville. Neither, of course, knew of the other's plan, and much would depend on who would strike first.

At the early light of the last day of the year the Confederate left wing moved upon the Union right in a magnificent battle-line, three-quarters of a mile in length and two columns deep. At the same time the Confederate artillery opened with their cannon. McCook was astonished at so fierce and sudden a charge. The gallant Patrick Cleburne, one of the ablest commanders in the Southern armies, led his division, which had been brought from the Confederate right, in the charge. The Federal lines were ill prepared for this sudden onslaught, and before McCook could arrange them several batteries were overpowered and eleven of the heavy guns were in the hands of the Confederates.

Slowly the Union troops fell back, firing as they went; but they had no power to check the impetuous, overwhelming charge of the onrushing foe. McCook's two right divisions, under Johnson and Jeff. C. Davis, were driven back, but his third division, which was commanded by a young officer who had attracted unusual attention at the battle of Perryville—Philip H. Sheridan—held its ground. At the first Confederate advance, Sill's brigade of Sheridan's division drove the troops in front of it back into their entrenchments, and in the charge the brave Sill lost his life.

While the battle raged with tremendous fury on the Union right, Rosecrans was three miles away, throwing his left across the river. Hearing the terrific roar of battle at the other end of the line, Rosecrans hastened to begin his attack on Breckinridge hoping to draw a portion of the Confederate force away from McCook. But as the hours of the forenoon

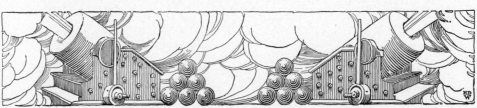

FIGHTERS IN THE WEST

This picture of Company B of the Twenty-first Michigan shows impressively the type of men that the rough campaigning west of the Alleghanies had molded into veterans. These were Sherman's men, and under the watchful eye and in the inspiring presence of that general thousands of stalwart lads from the sparsely settled States were becoming the very bone and sinew of the Federal fighting force. The men of Sherman, like their leader, were forging steadily to the front. They had become proficient in the fighting which knows no fear, in many hard-won combats in the early part of the war. Greater and more magnificent conflicts awaited those who did not find a hero's grave.

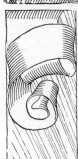

passed he was dismayed as he noted that the sound of battle was coming nearer, and he rightly divined that his right wing was receding before the dashing soldiers of the South. He ordered McCook to dispute every inch of the ground; but McCook's command was soon torn to pieces and disorganized, except the division of Sheridan.

The latter stood firm against the overwhelming numbers, a stand that attracted the attention of the country and brought him military fame. He checked the onrushing Confederates at the point of the bayonet; he formed a new line under fire. In his first position Sheridan held his ground for two hours. The Confederate attack had also fallen heavily on Negley, who was stationed on Sheridan's left, and on Palmer, both of Thomas' center. Rousseau commanding the reserves, and Van Cleve of Crittenden's forces were ordered to the support of the Union center and right. Here, for two hours longer the battle raged with unabated fury, and the slaughter of brave men on both sides was appalling. Three times the whole Confederate left and center were thrown against the Union divisions, but failed to break the lines. At length when their cartridge boxes were empty Sheridan's men could do nothing but retire for more ammunition, and they did this in good order to a rolling plain near the Nashville road. But Rousseau of Thomas' center was there to check the Confederate advance.

It was now past noon, and still the battle roar resounded unceasingly through the woods and hills about Murfreesboro. Though both hosts had struggled and suffered since early morning, they still held to their guns, pouring withering volleys into each other's ranks. The Federal right and center had been forced back at right angles to the position they had held when day dawned; and the Confederate left was swung around at right angles to its position of the morning. The Federal left rested on Stone's River, while Bragg's right was on the same stream and close to the line in blue. Meantime, Rosecrans had massed his artillery on a little hill over-

AN UNCEASING WORK OF WAR

In the picture the contraband laborers often pressed into service by Federals are repairing the "stringer" track near Murfreesboro after the battle of Stone's River. The long lines of single-track road, often involving a change from broad-gauge to narrow-gauge, were entirely inadequate for the movement of troops in that great area. In these isolated regions the railroads often became the supreme objective of both sides. When disinclined to offer battle, each struck in wild raids against the other's line of communication. Sections of track were tipped over embankments; rails were torn up, heated red-hot in bonfires, and twisted so that they could never be used again. The wrecking of a railroad might postpone a maneuver for months, or might terminate a campaign suddenly in defeat. Each side in retreat burned its bridges and destroyed the railroad behind it. Again advancing, each had to pause for the weary work of repair.

looking the field of action. He had also re-formed the broken lines of the right and center and called in twelve thousand fresh troops. Then, after a brief lull, the battle opened again and the ranks of both sides were torn with grape and canister and bursting shells.

In answer to Bragg's call for reenforcements came Breckinridge with all but one brigade of his division, a host of about seven thousand fresh troops. The new Confederate attack began slowly, but increased its speed at every step. Suddenly, a thundering volley burst from the line in blue, and the front ranks of the attacking column disappeared. Again, a volley tore through the ranks in gray, and the assault was abandoned.

The battle had raged for nearly eleven hours, when night enveloped the scene, and the firing abated slowly and died away. It had been a bloody day—this first day's fight at Stone's River—and except at Antietam it had not thus far been surpassed in the war. The advantage was clearly with the Confederates. They had pressed back the Federals for two miles, had routed their right wing and captured many prisoners and twenty-eight heavy guns. But Rosecrans determined to hold his ground and try again.

The next day was New Year's and but for a stray fusillade, here and there, both armies remained inactive, except that each quietly prepared to renew the contest on the morrow. The renewal of the battle on January 2nd was fully expected on both sides, but there was little fighting till four in the afternoon. Rosecrans had sent General Van Cleve's division on January 1st across the river to seize an elevation from which he could shell the town of Murfreesboro. Bragg now sent Breckinridge to dislodge the division, and he did so with splendid effect. But Breckinridge's men came into such a position as to be exposed to the raking fire of fifty-two pieces of Federal artillery on the west side of the river. Returning the deadly and constant fire as best they could, they stood the storm of shot and shell for half an hour when they retreated to a place

ALONG THE HAZARDOUS ADVANCE FROM MURFREESBORO

Portion of the Bridgeport Bridge from Long Island to the East Bank of the Tennessee. The island, 1,232 feet at this point, divides the stream opposite Bridgeport, Alabama. The Union troops crossed at four points (at all of which the river was very wide), the division of Reynolds to the north of Bridgeport by means of captured boats, while that of Brannan crossed on rafts. The main crossing of McCook's Corps was at Caperton's Ferry, where the one complete pontoon-bridge had been laid. The army was all across by September 10th, but even greater difficulties now confronted it. The greatest of these obstacles were the steeps of Raccoon Mountain—the towering heights of Lookout Mountain rising before them, almost impassable to wagons and destitute of water. Beyond these, Missionary Ridge and a succession of lesser ranges must be crossed before Bragg's railroad connections with Atlanta could be struck at Dalton. Yet the trains which had already been brought across the Cumberland Mountains into Tennessee must ever be carried forward, loaded with twenty-five days' supplies and ammunition enough for the two great battles that were to follow.

of safety, leaving seventeen hundred of their number dead or wounded on the field. That night the two armies again lay within musket shot of each other. The next day brought no further conflict and during that night General Bragg moved away to winter quarters at Shelbyville, on the Elk River.

Murfreesboro, or Stone's River, was one of the great battles of the war. The losses were about thirteen thousand to the Federals and over ten thousand to the Confederates. Both sides claimed victory—the South because of Bragg's signal success on the first day; the North because of Breckinridge's fearful repulse at the final onset and of Bragg's retreating in the night and refusing to fight again. A portion of the Confederate army occupied Shelbyville, Tennessee, and the larger part entrenched at Tullahoma, eighteen miles to the southeast.

Six months after the battle of Stone's River, the Federal army suddenly awoke from its somnolent condition—a winter and spring spent in raids and unimportant skirmishes—and became very busy preparing for a long and hasty march. Rosecrans' plan of campaign was brilliant and proved most effective. He realized that Tullahoma was the barrier to Chattanooga, and determined to drive the Confederates from it.

On June 23, 1863, the advance began. The cavalry, under General Stanley, had received orders to advance upon Shelbyville on the 24th, and during that night to build immense and numerous camp-fires before the Confederate stronghold at Shelbyville, to create the impression that Rosecrans' entire army was massing at that point. But the wily leader of the Federals had other plans, and when Stanley, supported by General Granger, had built his fires, the larger force was closing in upon Tullahoma.

The stratagem dawned upon Bragg too late to check Rosecrans' plans. Stanley and Granger made a brilliant capture of Shelbyville, and Bragg retired to Tullahoma; but finding here that every disposition had been made to fall upon his rear, he continued his southward retreat toward Chattanooga.

PART II
OPENING THE MISSISSIPPI

THE SIEGES OF VICKSBURG AND PORT HUDSON

CONFEDERATE FORTS THAT HELD THE STEEP RIVER-BANKS
AT PORT HUDSON, 1863

FEDERAL GUNS AND A CONFEDERATE CAMERA

The Second, Fourth, and Sixth Massachusetts Light Artillery at Baton Rouge, in May, 1862, photographed by Lytle, of the Confederate Secret Service. When Farragut's fleet, after the capture of New Orleans, moved up the Mississippi on May 2d, General Williams, with fourteen hundred men, including two sections of Everett's (Sixth) battery, accompanied it. The ambitious plan was the opening of the Mississippi and the establishment of communication with the Federal forces to the north. Occupying Baton Rouge, the expedition pushed on to Vicksburg. Here Farragut's guns could not be sufficiently elevated to silence the batteries on the bluff,

THE FIRST BATTERIES SENT AGAINST VICKSBURG

in the face of which Williams could not land. After three weeks on the crowded transports, the men were returned to Baton Rouge and went into camp. On the 20th of June, General Williams again set out for Vicksburg with four regiments and Nims's (Second) and Everett's (Sixth) Massachusetts batteries. At Ellis's Bluff, and again at Grand Gulf, the troops drove off the Confederate field-batteries that opened on the gunboats. But at Vicksburg no effective land attack could be made and the troops, whose numbers had been reduced by overwork, malaria, and scurvy from thirty-two hundred to but eight hundred fit for duty, returned to Baton Rouge.

FORWARDING THE RAW RECRUITS—CAIRO

In the fall of 1862 all the available river-steamers were busy transporting newly organized regiments from Cairo to Memphis to take part in the independent expedition against Vicksburg, which had been proposed by Major-General John A. McClernand and in command of which he had been placed by secret orders from Lincoln and Stanton. Not even Grant was informed of this division of authority. McClernand, who was influential in the West, raised in Indiana, Illinois, and Iowa some thirty regiments of volunteers, two-thirds of which had been forwarded to Cairo and Memphis by November 10th, and at the latter place were being drilled into shape by Sherman. Both Sherman and Grant supposed that they were the promised reënforcements for the expedition which they had planned together. On December 12th Sherman was ready to move, and on the 19th transports arrived at Memphis and the embarkation of the troops began. Next day they moved down the river, convoyed by Porter's fleet. On the 26th Sherman landed thirteen miles up the Yazoo River and advanced to Chickasaw Bluffs, where on the 29th he assaulted the defenses of Vicksburg to the north. The news of the failure of Grant's land expedition at Oxford had reached McClernand instead of Sherman, and as the latter general emerged from the swamps with his defeated divisions, McClernand, on New Year's Day, met him at the mouth of the Yazoo and superseded him in command.

FEDERAL TRANSPORTS ON THE MISSISSIPPI
ONE SMOKESTACK DAMAGED BY CONFEDERATE FIRE FROM THE RIVER BANK

WHERE GRANT'S CAMPAIGN WAS HALTED

The Courthouse at Oxford, Mississippi. The second attempt to capture Vicksburg originated with Grant. Since he had sprung into fame at Fort Donelson early in 1862, he had done little to strengthen his reputation; but to all urgings of his removal Lincoln replied: "I can't spare this man; he fights." He proposed to push southward through Mississippi to seize Jackson, the capital. If this could be accomplished, Vicksburg (fifty miles to the west) would become untenable. At Washington his plan was overruled to the extent of dividing his forces. Sherman, with a separate expedition, was to move from Memphis down the Mississippi directly against Vicksburg. It was Grant's hope that by marching on he could unite with Sherman in an assault upon this key to the Mississippi. Pushing forward from Grand Junction, sixty miles, Grant reached Oxford December 5, 1862, but his supplies were still drawn from Columbus, Kentucky, over a single-track road to Holly Springs, and thence by wagon over roads which were rapidly becoming impassable. Delay ensued in which Van Dorn destroyed Federal stores at Holly Springs worth $1,500,000. This put an end to Grant's advance. In the picture we see an Illinois regiment guarding some of the 1200 Confederate prisoners taken during the advance and here confined in the Courthouse.

VICKSBURG PROVES IMPREGNABLE

Chickasaw Bayou.   Here rested Sherman's extreme left, December 28, 1862, after a day's advance over bottom-lands of extreme difficulty.   From this point, after sharp skirmishing which discomforted the advancing Federals, at nightfall the Confederates retired to their works on the bluff beyond, confident of being able to repel the assault that was to come. That confidence was not misplaced.   Sherman had miscalculated in two particulars— chiefly in supposing that Grant was close at hand to support him.   Furthermore, he did not know that his movements had been daily reported and that Johnston and Pemberton were fully aware of his strength.   On the very day that Sherman landed on the Yazoo, Pemberton arrived in Vicksburg with reënforcements, bringing the garrison up to twelve thousand, while Sherman supposed that he was to contend with but half that number. Fully prepared for uncompromising defense, the Confederates were bound to win.

WHERE SHERMAN FAILED

Chickasaw Bluffs. Stretching northeast from Vicksburg, Walnut Hill forms a perfect natural fortress overlooking the bottom-lands toward the Yazoo, rising to a height of two hundred feet, as seen in the picture. In the whole twelve miles between Haynes' Bluff (where Sherman landed) and Vicksburg, there were but five points where troops could pass from the Yazoo through the network of bayous and swamps to attack this bluff, and all these points were commanded by Confederate batteries. Sherman had considerable difficulty in properly posting his troops during the determined skirmishing kept up by the Confederates on the 28th. On the 29th, at noon, he gave the signal for the assault. The two brigades of De Courcy and Blair, together with the Fourth Iowa—six thousand men in all—bore the brunt of the fighting and charged gallantly up to the Confederate works. There, unsupported, they were cut to pieces by the cross-fire that was poured upon them. Sherman, who had lost nearly two thousand, decided that the position was impregnable. A thousand men could have held it against ten times their number.

THE LEADER AT HAYNES' BLUFF

U. S. S. *Choctaw*, resting peacefully at Vicksburg after the surrender. She had led the other gunboats in the attack upon Haynes' Bluff on the Yazoo, simultaneous with Sherman's second demonstration against the defenses northeast of Vicksburg. Grant distracted Pemberton long enough to enable the Federals to concentrate to the south of the city for its final investment. Since the end of January, Grant (again in supreme command) had been working hard with tentative operations, first for the completion of the canal begun by General Williams the previous year, then for the cutting of the levee at Yazoo Pass to flood the bottom-lands and enable gunboats to engage in amphibious warfare.

"WHISTLING DICK"—THE PET OF THE CONFEDERATE GUNNERS

This 18-pounder rifle, made at the Tredegar Iron Works at Richmond, was mounted in the Vicksburg water-batteries overlooking the Mississippi. Porter's fleet was exposed to its fire when it passed down the river on the night of April 16, 1863. From the peculiar sound of its missiles speeding through the air it earned the nickname "Whistling Dick." It was a monster of its time; its fire sunk the Federal gunboat *Cincinnati* on May 28th. Finally it was disabled and silenced by the Federal batteries from across the river.

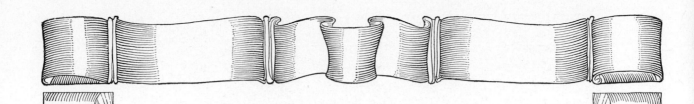

VICKSBURG AND PORT HUDSON

On the banks of this, the greatest river in the world, the most decisive and far-reaching battle of the war was fought. Here at Vicksburg over one hundred thousand gallant soldiers and a powerful fleet of gunboats and ironclads in terrible earnestness for forty days and nights fought to decide whether the new Confederate States should be cut in twain; whether the great river should flow free to the Gulf, or should have its commerce hindered. We all know the result—the Union army under General Grant, and the Union navy under Admiral Porter were victorious. The Confederate army, under General Pemberton, numbering thirty thousand men, was captured and General Grant's army set free for operating in other fields. It was a staggering blow from which the Confederacy never rallied.—*Lieutenant-General Stephen D. Lee, C.S.A., at the dedication of the Massachusetts Volunteers' statue at the Vicksburg National Military Park, Vicksburg, Mississippi, November 14, 1903.*

THE Mississippi River, in its lower course, winds like a mighty serpent from side to side along a vast alluvial bottom, which in places is more than forty miles in width. On the eastern bank, these great coils here and there sweep up to the bluffs of the highlands of Tennessee and Mississippi. On these cliffs are situated Memphis, Port Hudson, Grand Gulf, and Vicksburg. The most important of these from a military point of view was Vicksburg, often called the " Gibraltar of the West." Situated two hundred feet above the current, on a great bend of the river, its cannon could command the waterway for miles in either direction, while the obstacles in the way of a land approach were almost equally insurmountable.

The Union arms had captured New Orleans, in the spring of 1862, and Memphis in June of that year; but the Confederates still held Vicksburg and Port Hudson and the two hundred and fifty miles of river that lies between them. The military

WHERE VICKSBURG'S FATE WAS SEALED

The Battle-field of Champion's Hill. Here on May 16, 1863, Grant crowned his daring maneuver against Vicksburg from the south with complete success. Once across the river below Grand Gulf, after an easy victory at Port Gibson, he was joined by Sherman. The army struck out across the strange country south of the Big Black River and soon had driven Pemberton's southern outposts across that stream. Grant was now on solid ground; he had successfully turned the flank of the Confederates and he grasped the opportunity to strike a telling blow. Pressing forward to Raymond and Jackson, he captured both, and swept westward to meet the astounded Pemberton, still vacillating between attempting a junction with Johnston or attacking Grant in the rear. But Grant, moving with wonderful precision, prevented either movement. On May 16th a battle ensued which was most decisive around Champion's Hill. Pemberton was routed and put to flight, and on the next day the Federals seized the crossings of the Big Black River. Spiking their guns at Haynes' Bluff, the Confederates retired into Vicksburg, never to come out again except as prisoners. In eighteen days from the time he crossed the Mississippi, Grant had gained the advantage for which the Federals had striven for more than a year at Vicksburg.

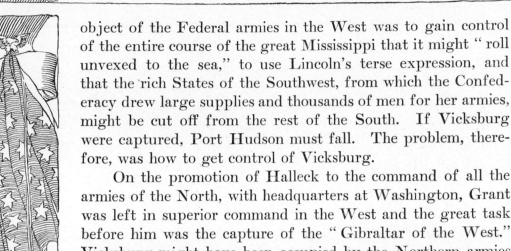

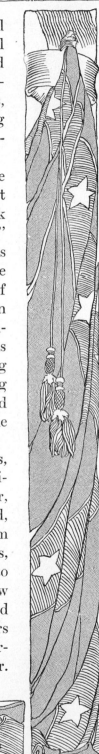

object of the Federal armies in the West was to gain control of the entire course of the great Mississippi that it might "roll unvexed to the sea," to use Lincoln's terse expression, and that the rich States of the Southwest, from which the Confederacy drew large supplies and thousands of men for her armies, might be cut off from the rest of the South. If Vicksburg were captured, Port Hudson must fall. The problem, therefore, was how to get control of Vicksburg.

On the promotion of Halleck to the command of all the armies of the North, with headquarters at Washington, Grant was left in superior command in the West and the great task before him was the capture of the "Gibraltar of the West." Vicksburg might have been occupied by the Northern armies at any time during the first half of the year 1862, but in June of that year General Bragg sent Van Dorn with a force of fifteen thousand to occupy and fortify the heights. Van Dorn was a man of prodigious energy. In a short time he had hundreds of men at work planting batteries, digging rifle-pits above the water front and in the rear of the town, mounting heavy guns and building bomb-proof magazines in tiers along the hillsides. All through the summer, the work progressed under the direction of Engineer S. H. Lockett, and by the coming of winter the city was a veritable Gibraltar.

From the uncompleted batteries on the Vicksburg bluffs, the citizens and the garrison soldiers viewed the advance division of Farragut's fleet, under Commander Lee, in the river, on May 18, 1863. Fifteen hundred infantry were on board, under command of General Thomas Williams, and with them was a battery of artillery. Williams reconnoitered the works, and finding them too strong for his small force he returned to occupy Baton Rouge. The authorities at Washington now sent Farragut peremptory orders to clear the Mississippi and accordingly about the middle of June, a flotilla of steamers and seventeen mortar schooners, under Commander D. D. Porter, departed from New Orleans and steamed up the river.

[190]

THE BRIDGE THE CONFEDERATES BURNED AT BIG BLACK RIVER

THE FIRST FEDERAL CROSSING—SHERMAN'S PONTOONS

The pursuit of Pemberton's army brought McClernand's Corps to the defenses of the Big Black River Bridge early on May 17, 1863. McPherson was close behind. McClernand's division carried the defenses and Bowen and Vaughn's men fled with precipitate haste over the dreary swamp to the river and crossed over and burned the railroad and other bridges just in time to prevent McClernand from following. The necessary delay was aggravating to Grant's forces. The rest of the day and night was consumed in building bridges. Sherman had the only pontoon-train with the army and his bridge was the first ready at Bridgeport, early in the evening.

Simultaneously Farragut headed a fleet of three war vessels and seven gunboats, carrying one hundred and six guns, toward Vicksburg from Baton Rouge. Many transports accompanied the ships from Baton Rouge, on which there were three thousand of Williams' troops.

The last days of June witnessed the arrival of the combined naval forces of Farragut and Porter below the Confederate stronghold. Williams immediately disembarked his men on the Louisiana shore, opposite Vicksburg, and they were burdened with implements required in digging trenches and building levees.

The mighty Mississippi, at this point and in those days, swept in a majestic bend and formed a peninsula of the western, or Louisiana shore. Vicksburg was situated on the eastern, or Mississippi shore, below the top of the bend. Its batteries of cannon commanded the river approach for miles in either direction. Federal engineers quickly recognized the strategic position of the citadel on the bluff; and also as quickly saw a method by which the passage up and down the river could be made comparatively safe for their vessels, and at the same time place Vicksburg " high and dry " by cutting a channel for the Mississippi through the neck of land that now held it in its sinuous course.

While Farragut stormed the Confederate batteries at Vicksburg, Williams began the tremendous task of diverting the mighty current across the peninsula. Farragut's bombardment by his entire fleet failed to silence Vicksburg's cannon-guards, although the defenders likewise failed to stop the progress of the fleet. The Federal naval commander then determined to dash past the fortifications, trusting to the speed of his vessels and the stoutness of their armor to survive the tremendous cannonade that would fall upon his flotilla. Early in the morning of June 28th the thrilling race against death began, and after two hours of terrific bombardment aided by the mortar boats stationed on both banks, Farragut's fleet with

[192]

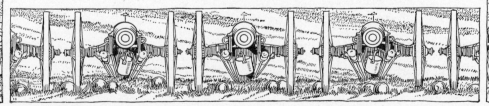

Vicksburg, taken under fire.

THE GATE TO THE MISSISSIPPI

The handwriting is that of Surgeon Bixby, of the Union hospital ship "Red Rover." In his album he pasted this unique photograph from the western shore of the river where the Federal guns and mortars threw a thousand shells into Vicksburg during the siege. The prominent building is the courthouse, the chief landmark during the investment. Here at Vicksburg the Confederates were making their last brave stand for the possession of the Mississippi River, that great artery of traffic. If it were wre ted from them the main source of their supplies would be cut off. Pemberton, a brave and capable officer and a Pennsylvanian by birth, worked unremittingly for the cause he had espoused. Warned by the early attacks of General Williams and Admiral Farragut, he had left no stone unturned to render Vicksburg strongly defended. It had proved impregnable to attack on the north and east, and the powerful batteries planted on the river-front could not be silenced by the fleet nor by the guns of the Federals on the opposite shore. But Grant's masterful maneuver of cutting loose from his base and advancing from the south had at last out-generaled both Pemberton and Johnston. Nevertheless, Pemberton stoutly held his defenses. His high river-battery is photographed below, as it frowned upon the Federals opposite.

the exception of three vessels passed through the raging inferno to the waters above Vicksburg, with a loss of fifteen killed and thirty wounded. On the 1st of July Flag-Officer Davis with his river gunboats arrived from Memphis and joined Farragut.

Williams and his men, including one thousand negroes, labored like Titans to complete their canal, but a sudden rise of the river swept away the barriers with a terrific roar, and the days of herculean labor went for naught. Again Williams' attempt to subdue the stronghold was abandoned, and he returned with his men when Farragut did, on July 24th, to Baton Rouge to meet death there on August 5th when General Breckinridge made a desperate but unsuccessful attempt to drive the Union forces from the Louisiana capital.

Farragut urged upon General Halleck the importance of occupying the city on the bluff with a portion of his army; but that general gave no heed; and while even then it was too late to secure the prize without a contest, it would have been easy in comparison to that which it required a year later.

In the mean time, the river steamers took an important part in the preliminary operations against the city. Davis remained at Memphis with his fleet for about three weeks after the occupation of that city on the 6th of June, meanwhile sending four gunboats and a transport up the White River, with the Forty-sixth Indiana regiment, under Colonel Fitch. The object of the expedition, undertaken at Halleck's command, was to destroy Confederate batteries and to open communication with General Curtis, who was approaching from the west. It failed in the latter purpose but did some effective work with the Southern batteries along the way.

The one extraordinary incident of the expedition was the disabling of the *Mound City,* one of the ironclad gunboats, and the great loss of life that it occasioned. When near St. Charles the troops under Fitch were landed, and the *Mound City* moving up the river, was fired on by concealed batteries

THE WELL-DEFENDED CITADEL

Behind these fortifications Pemberton, driven from the Big Black River, gathered his twenty-one thousand troops to make the last stand for the saving of the Mississippi to the Confederacy.   In the upper picture we see Fort Castle, one of the strongest defenses of the Confederacy.   It had full sweep of the river; here "Whistling Dick" (one of the most powerful guns in possession of the South) did deadly work.   In the lower picture we see the fortifications to the east of the town, before which Grant's army was now entrenching.   When Vicksburg had first been threatened in 1862, the Confederate fortifications had been laid out and work begun on them in haste with but five hundred spades, many of the soldiers delving with their bayonets.   The sites were so well chosen and the work so well done that they had withstood attacks for a year.   They were to hold out still longer.   By May 18th the Federals had completely invested Vicksburg, and Grant and Sherman rode out to Haynes' Bluff to view the open river to the north, down which abundant supplies were now coming for the army.   Sherman, who had not believed that the plan could succeed, frankly acknowledged his mistake.   But the Mississippi was not yet theirs.   Sherman, assaulting the fortifications of Vicksburg, the next day, was repulsed.   A second attack, on the 22d, failed and on the 25th Grant settled down to starve Pemberton out.

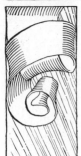
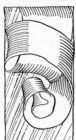

under the direction of Lieutenant Dunnington. A 32-pound shot struck the vessel, crashed through the side and passed through the steam-drum. The steam filled the vessel in an instant. Many of the men were so quickly enveloped in the scalding vapor that they had no chance to escape. Others leaped overboard, some being drowned and some rescued through the efforts of the *Conestoga* which was lying near. While straining every nerve to save their lives, the men had to endure a shower of bullets from Confederate sharpshooters on the river banks. Of the one hundred and seventy-five officers and men of the *Mound City* only twenty-five escaped death or injury in that fearful catastrophe. Meanwhile, Colonel Fitch with his land forces rushed upon the Confederate batteries and captured them. The unfortunate vessel was at length repaired and returned to service.

For some time it had been known in Federal military and naval circles that a powerful ironclad similar to the famous *Monitor* of Eastern waters was being rushed to completion up the Yazoo. The new vessel was the *Arkansas*. She and a sister ship were building at Memphis when the capture of that city was anticipated by the destruction of one of them. The work on the *Arkansas* was far enough advanced for her to be taken to Yazoo City for the finishing touches. The Union fleet was not unduly terrified by tales of the monster, but nevertheless Farragut and Davis determined to find out what they could about her. Three vessels were chosen for the reconnaissance— the ironclad *Carondelet,* the wooden *Tyler,* and the Ellet ram *Queen of the West.* Bravely they steamed up the Yazoo on the morning of July 15th, but before they had gone more than six miles they encountered the *Arkansas,* under the command of Captain Isaac N. Brown, coming down the river.

The *Carondelet,* though supported at a distance by the *Tyler,* fled before her stronger antagonist, being raked from stem to stern, struck several times with solid shot, and saved from destruction only by running into shallow water where

THE WORK OF THE BESIEGERS

Battery Sherman, on the Jackson Road, before Vicksburg. Settling down to a siege did not mean idleness for Grant's army. Fortifications had to be opposed to the formidable one of the Confederates and a constant bombardment kept up to silence their guns, one by one. It was to be a drawn-out duel in which Pemberton, hoping for the long-delayed relief from Johnston, held out bravely against starvation and even mutiny. For twelve miles the Federal lines stretched around Vicksburg, investing it to the river bank, north and south. More than eighty-nine battery positions were constructed by the Federals. Battery Sherman was exceptionally well built—not merely revetted with rails or cotton-bales and floored with rough timber, as lack of proper material often made necessary. Gradually the lines were drawn closer and closer as the Federals moved up their guns to silence the works that they had failed to take in May. At the time of the surrender Grant had more than 220 guns in position, mostly of heavy caliber. By the 1st of July besieged and besiegers faced each other at a distance of half-pistol shot. Starving and ravaged by disease, the Confederates had repelled repeated attacks which depleted their forces, while Grant, reenforced to three times their number, was showered with supplies and ammunition that he might bring about the long-delayed victory which the North had been eagerly awaiting since Chancellorsville.

the *Arkansas* could not follow her. The *Arkansas* was injured also and her brave captain was twice wounded; but, not being disabled, she steamed on and out into the Mississippi, driving the *Tyler* and the *Queen* before her. A few miles above Vicksburg the *Arkansas* ran into the midst of the Federal fleet. She steamed slowly through the maze of hostile vessels, and the tempest of broadsides, returning them with the utmost steadiness, until she was safely lodged under the guns of Vicksburg.

But the day's events were not ended. In the dusk of evening, all of Farragut's fleet accompanied by the ram *Sumter* stole down the river to finish the plucky *Arkansas*. But she changed her position as soon as it was dark and the Union vessels had difficulty in finding her. They came down the river amid the roar of cannon, but only one 11-inch shot struck her as the fleet went by, and down the river, and the broadsides from the *Arkansas* killed five and wounded sixteen of the Union crews. None of Farragut's fleet was ever seen above Vicksburg again. It returned to New Orleans, July 24th.

The *Arkansas* had another fight for her life on July 22d. Commander William D. Porter with the *Essex*, aided by the *Queen of the West,* made the attack. The crew of the *Arkansas* had been reduced by half, but the remainder fought savagely and saved their vessel from destruction.

The month of July had not been favorable to the Federal hopes. Farragut had returned to New Orleans. General Williams had gone with him as far as Baton Rouge. Davis now went with his fleet back to Helena. Halleck was succeeded by Grant. Vicksburg entered upon a period of quiet.

But this condition was temporary. The city's experience of blood and fire had only begun. During the summer and autumn of 1862, the one thought uppermost in the mind of General Grant was how to gain possession of the stronghold. He was already becoming known for his bull-dog tenacity. In the autumn, two important changes took place, but one day apart. On October 14th, General John C. Pemberton

A GOOD POLITICIAN WHO BECAME A GREAT SOLDIER

MAJOR–GENERAL JOHN ALEXANDER LOGAN AND STAFF IN VICKSBURG, JULY, 1863

John A. Logan, a War Democrat who left Congress to fight as a private in a Michigan regiment at Bull Run, was one of the mainstays of the Federal cause in the West. A successful lawyer and brilliant orator, he proved to be one of the most successful civilian generals of the war. In Grant's Vicksburg campaign, Logan's soldierly qualities came particularly into prominence. His division of McPherson's Corps distinguished itself in the battle of Raymond, Mississippi, and again at that of Champion's Hill, which sounded the knell of Vicksburg. It was Logan's division that marched in on the Jackson road to take possession of the fallen city, July 4, 1863. For his services in the campaign Logan was made a major-general.

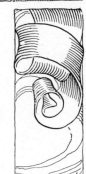

succeeded Van Dorn in command of the defenses of Vicksburg, and on the next day David D. Porter succeeded Davis as commander of the Federal fleet on the upper Mississippi.

So arduous was the task of taking Vicksburg that the wits of General Grant, and those of his chief adviser, General W. T. Sherman, were put to the test in the last degree to accomplish the end. Grant knew that the capture of this fortified city was of great importance to the Federal cause, and that it would ever be looked upon as one of the chief acts in the drama of the Civil War.

The first plan attempted was to divide the army, Sherman taking part of it from Memphis and down the Mississippi on transports, while Grant should move southward along the line of the Mississippi Central Railroad to cooperate with Sherman, his movements to be governed by the efforts of the scattered Confederate forces in Mississippi to block him. But the whole plan was destined to failure, through the energies of General Van Dorn and others of the Confederate army near Grant's line of communication.

The authorities at Washington preferred the river move upon Vicksburg, as the navy could keep the line of communication open. The stronghold now stood within a strong line of defense extending from Haynes' Bluff on the Yazoo to Grand Gulf on the Mississippi, thirty miles below Vicksburg. To prepare for Sherman's attack across the swamps of the Yazoo, Admiral Porter made several expeditions up that tortuous stream to silence batteries and remove torpedoes. In one of these he lost one of the Eads ironclads, the *Cairo*, blown up by a torpedo, and in another the brave Commander Gwin, one of the heroes of Shiloh, was mortally wounded.

Sherman, with an army of thirty-two thousand men, left Memphis on December 20th, and landed a few days later some miles north of Vicksburg on the banks of the Yazoo. On the 29th he made a daring attack in three columns on the Confederate lines of defense at Chickasaw Bayou and suffered a

INVESTING BY INCHES

Logan's Division undermining the most formidable redoubt in the defenses of Vicksburg. The position was immediately in front of this honeycombed slope on the Jackson road. Upon these troops fell most of the labor of sapping and mining, which finally resulted in the wrecking of the fort so gallantly defended by the veterans of the Third Louisiana. As the Federal lines crept up, the men working night and day were forced to live in burrows. They became proficient in such gopher work as the picture shows. Up to the "White House" (Shirley's) the troops could be marched in comparative safety, but a short distance beyond they were exposed to the Confederate sharpshooters, who had only rifles and muskets to depend on; their artillery had long since been silenced. Near this house was constructed "Coonskin's" Tower; it was built of railway iron and cross-ties under the direction of Second Lieutenant Henry C. Foster, of Company B, Twenty-third Indiana. A backwoodsman and dead-shot, he was particularly active in paying the Confederate sharpshooters in their own coin. He habitually wore a cap of raccoon fur, which gave him his nickname and christened the tower, from which the interior of the Confederate works could be seen.

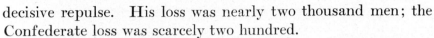

decisive repulse. His loss was nearly two thousand men; the Confederate loss was scarcely two hundred.

Two hundred feet above the bayou, beyond where the Federals were approaching, towered the Chickasaw Bluffs, to which Pemberton hastened troops from Vicksburg as soon as he learned Sherman's object. At the base of the bluff, and stretching away to the north and west were swamps and forests intersected by deep sloughs, overhung with dense tangles of vines and cane-brakes. Federal valor vied with Confederate pluck in this fight among the marshes and fever-infested jungle-land.

One of Sherman's storming parties, under General G. W. Morgan, came upon a broad and deep enlargement of the bayou, McNutt Lake, which interposed between it and the Confederates in the rifle-pits on the slopes and crest of the bluff. In the darkness of the night of December 28th, the Federal pontoniers labored to construct a passage-way across the lake. When morning dawned the weary pontoniers were chagrined to discover their well-built structure spanning a slough leading in another direction than toward the base of the bluff. The bridge was quickly taken up, and the Federals recommenced their labors, this time in daylight and within sight and range of the Southern regiments on the hill. The men in blue worked desperately to complete the span before driven away by the foe's cannon; but the fire increased with every minute, and the Federals finally withdrew.

Another storming party attempted to assail the Confederates from across a sandbar of the bayou, but was halted at the sight and prospect of overcoming a fifteen-foot bank on the farther side. The crumbling bank was surmounted with a levee three feet high; the steep sides of the barrier had crumbled away, leaving an overhanging shelf, two feet wide. Two companies of the Sixth Missouri regiment volunteered to cross the two hundred yards of exposed passage, and to cut a roadway through the rotten bank to allow their comrades a free

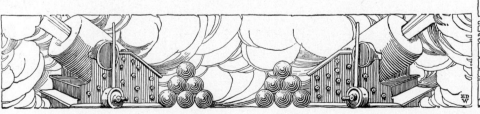

THE FIRST MONUMENT AT THE MEETING PLACE

Independence Day, 1863, was a memorable anniversary of the nation's birth; it brought to the anxious North the momentous news that Meade had won at Gettysburg and that Vicksburg had fallen in the West. The marble shaft in the picture was erected to mark the spot where Grant and Pemberton met on July 3d to confer about the surrender. Under a tree, within a few hundred feet of the Confederate lines, Grant greeted his adversary as an old acquaintance. They had fought in the same division for a time in the Mexican War. Each spoke but two sentences as to the surrender, for Grant lived up to the nickname he gained at Donelson, and Pemberton's pride was hurt. The former comrades walked and talked awhile on other things, and then returned to their lines. Next day the final terms were arranged by correspondence, and the Confederates marched out with colors flying; they stacked their arms and, laying their colors upon them, marched back into the city to be paroled. Those who signed the papers not to fight until exchanged numbered 29,391. The tree where the commanders met was soon carried away, root and branch, by relic-hunters. Subsequently the monument which replaced it was chipped gradually into bits, and in 1866 a 64-pounder cannon took its place as a permanent memorial.

VICKSBURG IN POSSESSION OF THE FEDERALS

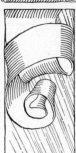

path to the bluff beyond. To add to the peril of the crossing, the sandbar was strewn with tangles of undergrowth and fallen trees, and the Confederate shells and bullets were raining upon the ground. Still, the gallant troops began their dash. From the very start, a line of wounded and dead Missourians marked the passage of the volunteers. The survivors reached the bank and desperately sought to dig the roadway. From the shrubbery on the bank suddenly appeared Confederate sharpshooters who poured their fire into the laboring soldiers; the flame of the discharging muskets burned the clothing of the Federals because the hostile forces were so close. Human endurance could not stand before this carnage, and the brave Missourians fled from the inferno. Sherman now found the northern pathway to Vicksburg impassable, and withdrew his men to the broad Mississippi.

Earlier in the same month had occurred two other events which, with the defeat of Chickasaw, go to make up the triple disaster to the Federals. On the 11th, General Nathan Forrest, one of the most brilliant cavalry leaders on either side, began one of those destructive raids which characterize the Civil War. With twenty-five hundred horsemen, Forrest dashed unopposed through the country north of Grant's army, tore up sixty miles of railroad and destroyed all telegraph lines.

Meantime, on December 20th, the day on which Sherman left Memphis, General Van Dorn pounced upon Holly Springs, in Mississippi, like an eagle on its prey, capturing the guard of fifteen hundred men and burning the great store of supplies, worth $1,500,000, which Grant had left there. Through the raids of Forrest and Van Dorn, Grant was left without supplies and for eleven days without communication with the outside world. He marched northward to Grand Junction, in Tennessee, a distance of eighty miles, living off the country. It was not until January 8, 1863, that he heard, through Washington, of the defeat of Sherman in his assault on Chickasaw Bluffs.

SHIRLEY'S RESIDENCE, "THE WHITE HOUSE"

Illinois sent into the war Grant, Logan, McClernand, Grierson, and other prominent leaders in the Vicksburg campaign. It was one of the few States which furnished troops in excess of their quota. The Seventy-second Illinois Infantry, whose synonym was "First Board of Trade," together with other Illinois regiments, saw severe active service along the Mississippi and at Vicksburg; it served in General McArthur's division of the Seventeenth Corps, and distinguished itself on November 30th of the following year in the battle of Franklin, Tenn.

BARRACKS OF FIFTH U. S. COLORED HEAVY ARTILLERY

VICKSBURG IN FEDERAL HANDS

Shirley's "White House," on the Jackson road, stood between the opposing lines; although a target for both sides, it remained practically uninjured. General Lieb's colored regiment was recruited in Louisiana and Mississippi and organized at Vicksburg in August, 1863. It suffered a heavy loss in deaths from fever, being stationed along the river. In the assault on Port Hudson colored troops were first used by the Federals in a general engagement — the First Louisiana Native Guard of the "Corps d'Afrique," organized by General Butler.

HEADQUARTERS 72ND ILLINOIS VOLUNTEERS

Grant and Sherman had no thought of abandoning Vicksburg because of this failure. But a month of unfortunate military dissension over rank in the command of Sherman's army resulted in General John A. McClernand, armed with authority from Washington, coming down from Illinois and superseding Sherman. On January 11, 1864, he captured Arkansas Post, a stronghold on the Arkansas River. But Grant, having authority to supersede McClernand in the general proceedings against Vicksburg, did so, on January 30th, and arguments on military precedence were forgotten.

Grant was determined to lead his Army of the Tennessee below Vicksburg and approach the city from the south, without breaking with his base of supplies up the river. Two projects, both of which were destined to fail, were under way during the winter and spring months of 1863. One of these was to open a way for the river craft through Lake Providence, west of the Mississippi, through various bayous and rivers into the Red River, a detour of four hundred miles.

Another plan was to cut a channel through the peninsula of the great bend of the Mississippi, opposite Vicksburg. For six weeks, thousands of men worked like marmots digging this ditch; but, meantime, the river was rising and, on March 8th, it broke over the embankment and the men had to run for their lives. Many horses were drowned and a great number of implements submerged. The "Father of Waters" had put a decisive veto on the project and it had to be given up. Still another plan that failed was to cut through the Yazoo Pass and approach from the north by way of the Coldwater, the Tallahatchie, and the Yazoo rivers.

Failure with Grant only increased his grim determination. He *would* take Vicksburg. His next plan was destined to bring success. It was to transfer his army by land down the west bank of the Mississippi to a point below the city and approach it from the south and west. This necessitated the running of the batteries by Porter's fleet—an extremely

THE CONFEDERACY CUT IN TWAIN

The Levee at Vicksburg, February, 1864. For seven months the Federals had been in possession of the city, and the Mississippi— now open through its entire course—cut off the struggling Confederacy in the East from the South and Southwest, the storehouses of their resources and their main dependence in continuing the struggle. But even such a blow as this, coming on top of Gettysburg, did not force the brave people of the South to give up the struggle. In the picture the only remaining warlike signs are the tents on the opposite shore. But on both sides of the river the Confederates were still desperately striving to reunite their territory. In the East another year and more of the hardest kind of fighting was ahead; another severing in twain of the South was inevitable before peace could come, and before the muskets could be used to shoot the crows, and before their horses could plough the neglected fields.

GUNS THAT HELPED TO REDUCE PORT HUDSON

This picture is another example of the accuracy and completeness with which Lytle, the Confederate Secret Service photographer at Baton Rouge, recorded the numbers and equipment of the Federal forces operating in Louisiana. This body of artillery first enlisted as the Twenty-first Volunteers in 1861, and sustained the heavy loss of one hundred and twenty-six men while acting as infantry in the battle of Baton Rouge, August 5, 1862. It served with distinction throughout the war, its number of veteran reënlistments being five hundred and three—the largest in any body of Indiana troops. In March, 1863, the regiment was changed to artillery; and in Augur's division of the Nineteenth Corps it accompanied General Banks in his first expedition against Port Hudson, as well as in the final investment of that place. Banks, who had been sent with between fifteen thousand and twenty thousand troops to suc-

FIRST INDIANA HEAVY ARTILLERY, 1863

ceed General Butler in command of the Department of the Gulf, arrived at New Orleans in the middle of December, 1862, with orders from Halleck to advance up the Mississippi, and (in coöperation with Grant) to hold an unbroken line of communication by land from New Orleans to Vicksburg. When this was accomplished he was to occupy the Red River country as a basis for future operations against Texas. During the winter, Banks confined his attention to operations west of the Mississippi, with varying success. Early in March, at the request of Farragut, who had determined to run past the Port Hudson batteries with his fleet, Banks moved forward with about seventeen thousand men to make a demonstration against that place with his artillery. He did not get near enough to do this, however, and was still building bridges when near midnight of March 14th Farragut's guns began to boom from the river.

THE LAST STRONGHOLD ON THE MISSISSIPPI

Confederate Fortifications on the bluff overlooking the Mississippi at Port Hudson, Louisiana.   At Port Hudson the east bank of the river rises steeply in a bluff eighty feet high, forming a perfect natural fortress. When Breckinridge failed in his attempt to recapture Baton Rouge in 1862, he retired to Port Hudson, thirty miles farther up the river, and by the middle of August the fortifying of that place was well advanced, the object being to hold the Mississippi between this point and Vicksburg, so that supplies coming from Arkansas by way of the Red River would not be cut off from the Confederacy.   Within the heavy parapets, twenty feet thick, the Confederates mounted twenty siege-guns along the bluff, completely commanding the river.   It was therefore no light task that Farragut took upon himself when on the night of March 14th he attempted to run by these batteries with his fleet.   Five of his seven vessels were disabled, the *Mississippi* running aground and being abandoned and burned by her commander.   Farragut, in the famous *Hartford*, with the *Albatross* lashed to her side, barely escaped running aground under the guns of the batteries in the darkness.   Finally he got safely by, and the object of the gallant fight was accomplished.

THE WELL–PLANTED BATTERIES

Confederate Siege-gun Mounted in the River Fortifications at Port Hudson.   Twenty of these great pieces thundered at Farragut's fleet till long after midnight on March 14, 1863.   Although the objective was not so important to the Federals as in the famous fight at New Orleans, the engagement at Port Hudson was scarcely less brilliant, and its outcome was more costly to the navy, which lost the valuable steam corvette *Mississippi*, mounting nineteen guns.   The fleet lost 113 men in action.   Farragut had the superiority in number and weight of metal, but this was more than offset by the advantageous position of the Confederates.   A successful shot from the ship could do little more than tear up the earth in the fortifications on the bluff, while every shot from the shore that told might mean the piercing of a boiler or the disabling of a rudder, rendering a ship helpless.   To add to the disadvantages, Farragut's intention was discovered at the outset.   A river steamer approached with flaring lights and tooting whistles and ran through the fleet, up to the *Hartford*, merely bringing the word that Banks was within five miles of Port Hudson.   Thus the fleet was discovered and the Confederates, illuminating the river with piles of blazing pine-knots, trained their guns with deadly precision on the advancing vessels.

[B]

perilous enterprise. The army was divided into four corps, commanded respectively by Sherman, McClernand, McPherson, and Hurlbut. The latter was stationed at Memphis. On March 29th, the movement of McClernand from Milliken's Bend to a point opposite Grand Gulf was begun. He was soon followed by McPherson and a few weeks later by Sherman. It required a month for the army, with its heavy artillery, to journey through the swamps and bogs of Louisiana.

While this march was in progress, something far more exciting was taking place on the river. Porter ran the batteries of Vicksburg with his fleet. After days of preparation the fleet of vessels, protected by cotton bales and hay about the vital parts of the boats, with heavy logs slung near the water-line—seven gunboats, the ram *General Price,* three transports, and various barges were ready for the dangerous journey on the night of April 16th. Silently in the darkness, they left their station near the mouth of the Yazoo, at a quarter past nine. For an hour and a half all was silence and expectancy. The bluffs on the east loomed black against the night sky. Suddenly, the flash of musketry fire pierced the darkness.

In a few minutes every battery overlooking the river was a center of spurting flame. A storm of shot and shell was rained upon the passing vessels. Not one escaped being struck many times. The water of the river was lashed into foam by the shots and shell from the batteries. The gunboats answered with their cannon. The air was filled with flying missiles. Several houses on the Louisiana shore burst into flame and the whole river from shore to shore was lighted with vivid distinctness. A little later, a giant flame leaped from the bosom of the river. A vessel had caught fire. It was the transport *Henry Clay.* It burned to the water's edge, nearly all its crew escaping to other vessels. Grant described the scene as " magnificent, but terrible "; Sherman pronounced it " truly sublime."

By three in the morning, the fleet was below the city and ready to cooperate with the army. One vessel had been

WITHIN THE PARAPET AT PORT HUDSON IN THE SUMMER OF 1863

These fortifications withstood every attack of Banks' powerful army from May 24 to July 9, 1863. Like Vicksburg, Port Hudson could be reduced only by a weary siege. These pictures, taken within the fortifications, show in the distance the ground over which the investing army approached to the two unsuccessful grand assaults they made upon the Confederate defenders. The strength of the works is apparent. A continuous line of parapet, equally strong, had been thrown up for the defense of Port Hudson, surrounding the town for a distance of three miles and more, each end terminating on the riverbank. Four powerful forts were located at the salients, and the line throughout was defended by thirty pieces of field artillery. Brigadier-General Beall, who commanded the post in 1862, constructed these works. Major-General Frank Gardner succeeded him in command at the close of the year.

THE WELL-DEFENDED WORKS

CONFEDERATE FORTIFICATIONS BEFORE PORT HUDSON

Gardner was behind these defenses with a garrison of about seven thousand when Banks approached Port Hudson for the second time on May 24th. Gardner was under orders to evacuate the place and join his force to that of Johnston at Jackson, Mississippi, but the courier who brought the order arrived at the very hour when Banks began to bottle up the Confederates. On the morning of May 25th Banks drove in the Confederate skirmishers and outposts and, with an army of thirty thousand, invested the fortifications from the eastward. At 10 A.M., after an artillery duel of more than four hours, the Federals advanced to the assault of the works. Fighting in a dense forest of magnolias, amid thick undergrowth and among ravines choked with felled timber, the progress of the troops was too slow for a telling attack. The battle has been described as "a gigantic bushwhack." The Federals at the center reached the ditch in front of the Confederate works but were driven off. At nightfall the attempt was abandoned. It had cost Banks nearly two thousand men.

destroyed, several others were crippled; thirteen men had been wounded, but Grant had the assistance he needed. About a week later, six more transports performed the same feat and ran the batteries; each had two barges laden with forage and rations in tow.

Grant's next move was to transfer the army across the river and to secure a base of supplies. There, on the bluff, was Grand Gulf, a tempting spot. But the Confederate guns showed menacingly over the brow of the hill. After a fruit-less bombardment by the fleet on April 29th, it was decided that a more practical place to cross the river must be sought below.

Meanwhile, Sherman was ordered by his chief to advance upon the formidable Haynes' Bluff, on the Yazoo River, some miles above the scene of his repulse in the preceding December. The message had said, "Make a demonstration on Haynes' Bluff, and make all the *show* possible." Sherman's transports, and three of Porter's gungoats, were closely followed by the Confederate soldiers who had been stationed at the series of de-fenses on the range of hills, and when they arrived at Snyder's Mill, just below Haynes' Bluff, on April 30th, General Hébert and several Louisiana regiments were awaiting them. On that day and the next the Confederates fiercely engaged the Union fleet and troops, and on May 2d Sherman withdrew his forces to the western bank of the Mississippi and hastened to Grant. The feint had been most successful. The Confederates had been prevented from sending reenforcements to Grand Gulf, and Grant's crossing was greatly facilitated.

The fleet passed the batteries of Grand Gulf and stopped at Bruinsburg, six miles below. A landing was soon made, the army taken across on April 30th, and a march to Port Gibson, twelve miles inland, was begun. General Bowen, Con-federate commander at Grand Gulf, came out and offered battle. He was greatly outnumbered, but his troops fought gallantly throughout most of the day, May 1st, before yielding

THE GUN THAT FOOLED THE FEDERALS

A "Quaker gun" that was mounted by the Confederates in the fortifications on the bluff at the river-front before Port Hudson. This gun was hewn out of a pine log and mounted on a carriage, and a black ring was painted around the end facing the river. Throughout the siege it was mistaken by the Federals for a piece of real ordnance. To such devices as this the beleaguered garrison was compelled constantly to resort in order to impress the superior forces investing Port Hudson with the idea that the position they sought to capture was formidably defended. The ruse was effective. Port Hudson was not again attacked from the river after the passing of Farragut's two ships.

WITHIN "THE CITADEL"

This bastion fort, near the left of the Confederate line of defenses at Port Hudson, was the strongest of their works, and here Weitzel and Grover's divisions of the Federals followed up the attack (begun at daylight of June 14th) that Banks had ordered all along the line in his second effort to capture the position. The only result was simply to advance the Federal lines from fifty to two hundred yards nearer. In front of the "citadel" an advance position was gained from which a mine was subsequently run to within a few yards of the fort.

the field. Port Gibson was then occupied by the Union army, and Grand Gulf, no longer tenable, was abandoned by the Confederates.

Grant now prepared for a campaign into the interior of Mississippi. His first intention was to cooperate with General Banks in the capture of Port Hudson, after which they would move together upon Vicksburg. But hearing that Banks would not arrive for ten days, Grant decided that he would proceed to the task before him without delay. His army at that time numbered about forty-three thousand. That under Pemberton probably forty thousand, while there were fifteen thousand Confederate troops at Jackson, Mississippi, soon to be commanded by General Joseph E. Johnston, who was hastening to that capital.

The Federal leader now determined on the bold plan of making a dash into the interior of Mississippi, beating Johnston and turning on Pemberton before their forces could be joined. This campaign is pronounced the most brilliant in the Civil War. It was truly Napoleonic in conception and execution. Grant knew that his base of supplies at Grand Gulf would be cut off by Pemberton as soon as he moved away from it. He decided, therefore, against the advice of his generals, to abandon his base altogether.

A more daring undertaking could scarcely be imagined. With a few days' rations in their haversacks the troops were to make a dash that would possibly take several weeks into the heart of a hostile country. This was certainly defying fate. When General Halleck heard of Grant's daring scheme he wired the latter from Washington, ordering him to move his army down the river and cooperate with Banks. Fortunately, this order was received too late to interfere with Grant's plans.

As soon as Sherman's divisions joined the main army the march was begun, on May 7th. An advance of this character must be made with the greatest celerity and Grant's army showed amazing speed. McPherson, who commanded the right

FIFTY-ONE PIECES OF ARTILLERY FELL INTO THE HANDS OF THE FEDERALS AT THE SURRENDER OF PORT HUDSON, MANY OF THEM BATTERED INTO SILENCE BY THE LONG BOMBARDMENT KEPT UP BY THREE FEDERAL FIELD-BATTERIES AND AN ENTIRE REGIMENT OF HEAVY ARTILLERY (THE FIRST IN-DIANA) ON THE FEDERAL SIDE.

THE CONFEDERATES HAD ONLY FIELD-PIECES WITH WHICH TO DEFEND THEIR WORKS AGAINST THE INVESTING ARMY. THE BATTERED GUNS SHOWN IN THE PICTURES WERE MOUNTED IN THE CAMP OF DURYEA'S AND BAINBRIDGE'S BAT-TERIES. THESE WORKS WERE GAR-RISONED BY THE FIFTEENTH ARKANSAS CONFEDERATE INFANTRY

wing, proceeded toward Jackson by way of Raymond and at the latter place encountered five thousand Confederates, on May 12th, who blocked his way and were prepared for fight. The battle of Raymond lasted two hours. McPherson was completely successful and the Confederates hastened to join their comrades in Jackson.

McPherson lost no time. He moved on toward Jackson, and as the last of his command left Raymond the advance of Sherman's corps reached it. That night, May 13th, Grant ordered McPherson and Sherman to march upon Jackson next morning by different roads, while McClernand was held in the rear near enough to reenforce either in case of need. The rain fell in torrents that night and, as Grant reported, in places the water was a foot deep in the road. But nothing could daunt his determined army. At eleven o'clock in the morning of the 14th, a concerted attack was made on the capital of Mississippi. A few hours' brisk fighting concluded this act of the drama, and the Stars and Stripes were unfurled on the State capitol. Among the spoils were seventeen heavy guns. That night, Grant slept in the house which Johnston had occupied the night before.

Meantime, Johnston had ordered Pemberton to detain Grant by attacking him in the rear. But Pemberton considered it more advisable to move toward Grand Gulf to separate Grant from his base of supplies, not knowing that Grant had abandoned his base. And now, with Johnston's army scattered, Grant left Sherman to burn bridges and military factories, and to tear up the railroads about Jackson while he turned fiercely on Pemberton. McPherson's corps took the lead. Grant called on McClernand to follow without delay. Then, hearing that Pemberton was marching toward him, he called on Sherman to hasten from Jackson. At Champion's Hill (Baker's Creek) Pemberton stood in the way, with eighteen thousand men.

The battle was soon in progress—the heaviest of the

THE NAVY HELPS ON LAND

A View within Federal Battery No. 10. One of the investing works before Port Hudson. Farragut's fleet of gunboats and mortar-boats assisted materially from the river above and below Port Hudson. Guns were also taken ashore from the gunboats and placed in position to assist in the bombardment which quickly laid the little hamlet of Port Hudson in ruins. This battery was situated on a wooded height about a mile to the east of the town; its 9-inch Dahlgren guns were kept warm hurling shells at the Confederate forti-fications throughout the siege. Lieutenant Terry, of the "Richmond," was in command of this battery with a detachment from his vessel, which in the effort to run past Port Hudson in March had received a shot in her safety-valves, rendering her engines useless and forcing her to turn back. The "Richmond" mounted twenty such guns as are seen in the picture, besides two heavy rifles.

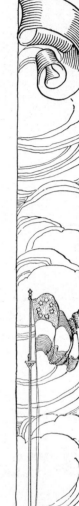

campaign. It continued for seven or eight hours. The Confederates were defeated with a loss of nearly all their artillery and about half their force, including four thousand men who were cut off from the main army and failed to rejoin it. On the banks of the Big Black River, a few miles westward, the Confederates made another stand, and here the fifth battle of the investment of Vicksburg took place. It was short, sharp, decisive. The Confederates suffered heavy losses and the remainder hastened to the defenses of Vicksburg. They had set fire to the bridge across the Big Black, and Grant's army was detained for a day—until the Confederates were safely lodged in the city.

The Federal army now invested Vicksburg, occupying the surrounding hills. It was May 18th when the remarkable campaign to reach Vicksburg came to an end. In eighteen days, the army had marched one hundred and eighty miles through a hostile country, fought and won five battles, captured a State capital, had taken twenty-seven heavy cannon and sixty field-pieces, and had slain or wounded six thousand men and captured as many more. As Grant and Sherman rode out on the hill north of the city, the latter broke into enthusiastic admiration of his chief, declaring that up to that moment he had felt no assurance of success, and pronouncing the campaign one of the greatest in history.

The great problem of investing Vicksburg was solved at last. Around the doomed city gleamed the thousands of bayonets of the Union army. The inhabitants and the army that had fled to it as a city of refuge were penned in. But the Confederacy was not to yield without a stubborn resistance. On May 19th, an advance was made on the works and the besieging lines drew nearer and tightened their coils. Three days later, on May 22nd, Grant ordered a grand assault by his whole army. The troops, flushed with their victories of the past three weeks, were eager for the attack. All the corps commanders set their watches by Grant's in order to begin

THE GUNS THAT WORKED AT CLOSE RANGE

In advance of Lieutenant Terry's naval battery, at the edge of another wooded height, stood Federal Battery No. 9 (Cox's), within about 300 yards of the Confederate fortifications, its two 12-pounder rifles doing telling work against the Confederate forts in their front.   The Federals pushed their entrenchments nearest to the works of the defenders at this part of the line—so near that a duplicate of Grant's message to Banks announcing the surrender of Vicksburg was thrown within the Confederate lines on July 7th.   This picture shows the method of constructing field fortifications, the parapet here being revetted with cotton-bales.

the assault at all points at the same moment—ten o'clock in the morning. At the appointed time, the cannon from the encircling lines burst forth in a deafening roar. Then came the answering thunders from the mortar-boats on the Louisiana shore and from the gunboats anchored beneath the bluff. The gunboats' fire was answered from within the bastions protecting the city. The opening of the heavy guns on the land side was followed by the sharper crackle of musketry—thousands of shots, indistinguishable in a continuous roll.

The men in the Federal lines leaped from their hiding places and ran to the parapets in the face of a murderous fire from the defenders of the city, only to be mowed down by hundreds. Others came, crawling over the bodies of their fallen comrades now and then they planted their colors on the battlements of the besieged city, to be cut down by the galling Confederate fire. Thus it continued hour after hour, until the coming of darkness. The assault had failed. The Union loss was about three thousand brave men; the Confederate loss was probably not much over five hundred.

Grant had made a fearful sacrifice; he was paying a high price but he had a reason for so doing—Johnston with a reenforcing army was threatening him in the rear; by taking Vicksburg at this time he could have turned on Johnston, and could have saved the Government sending any more Federal troops; and, to use his own words, it was needed because the men " would not have worked in the trenches with the same zeal, believing it unnecessary, as they did after their failure, to carry the enemy's works."

On the north side of the city overlooking the river, were the powerful batteries on Fort Hill, a deadly menace to the Federal troops, and Grant and Sherman believed that if enfiladed by the gunboats this position could be carried. At their request Admiral Porter sent the *Cincinnati* on May 27th to engage the Confederate guns, while four vessels below the town did the same to the lower defenses. In half an hour five

WHERE MEN WORKED LIKE MOLES

In burrows such as these the Federal soldiers worked incessantly from June 14th until the surrender of Port Hudson in an effort to undermine "the citadel," the strongest fortification in the Confederate lines near the Jackson road. Cotton-bales roped about were used as sap-rollers to protect the men from sharpshooters. The heat under the semi-tropical sun was terrible, drying up the brooks and distilling miasma from the pestilential swamp near by. The illness and mortality among the Federals were enormous, and yet the men worked on the saps uncomplainingly, and by July 7th the central one had been carried within seventeen feet of the ditch of the fort, and a storming party of a thousand volunteers had been organized to assault the works as soon as the two heavily charged mines should be sprung. That very day came the word that Vicksburg had fallen, and the work of the sappers and miners was useless.

THE SAP AGAINST "THE CITADEL"

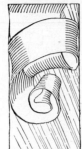

of the *Cincinnati's* guns were disabled; and she was in a sinking condition. She was run toward the shore and sank in three fathoms of water.

The army now settled down to a wearisome siege. For six weeks, they encircled the city with trenches, approaching nearer and nearer to the defending walls; they exploded mines; they shot at every head that appeared above the parapets. One by one the defending batteries were silenced. The sappers slowly worked their way toward the Confederate ramparts. Miners were busy on both sides burrowing beneath the fortifications. At three o'clock on the afternoon of June 25th a redoubt in the Confederate works was blown into the air, breaking into millions of fragments and disclosing guns, men, and timber. With the mine explosion, the Federal soldiers before the redoubt began to dash into the opening, only to meet with a withering fire from an interior parapet which the Confederates had constructed in anticipation of this event. The carnage was appalling to behold; and when the soldiers of the Union finally retired they had learned a costly lesson which withheld them from attack when another mine was exploded on July 1st.

Meantime, let us take a view of the river below and the life of the people within the doomed city. Far down the river, two hundred and fifty miles from Vicksburg, was Port Hudson. The place was fortified and held by a Confederate force under General Gardner. Like Vicksburg, it was besieged by a Federal army, under Nathaniel P. Banks, of Cedar Mountain fame. On May 27th, he made a desperate attack on the works and was powerfully aided by Farragut with his fleet in the river. But aside from dismounting a few guns and weakening the foe at a still heavier cost to their own ranks, the Federals were unsuccessful. Again, on June 10th, and still again on the 14th, Banks made fruitless attempts to carry Port Hudson by storm. He then, like Grant at Vicksburg, settled down to a siege. The defenders of Port Hudson proved their courage by enduring every hardship.

THE USES OF ADVERSITY

War brings out more strongly than anything else the truth of the trite old adage that necessity is the mother of invention. In the operations on the James River a locomotive mounted on a flat-boat was used as an extemporized stationary engine for working a pile-driver. The Confederates at Port Hudson put one to as strange a use. Lifted free from the rails and with a belt attached to the driving-wheels, it was used to operate a grist-mill that ground the corn into rough meal, which was their substitute for flour. It did the work in a very satisfactory manner. There were large quantities of grain and corn that had been brought into Port Hudson before it was invested, and the Red River country, as long as it was kept open and accessible, provided the garrison with supplies. But at the time of the investment the Confederate quartermaster was hard put to it to answer the demands made upon him to feed the overworked and hungry men that night and day toiled and slept at the guns. Powder and shell were also running short. Despite the privations suffered by the garrison, they, being used to the climate, suffered less from sickness than did the Federal troops, many detachments of which were encamped along the low-lying and swampy ground that lay at the bend of the river to the north.

THE CHURCH USED AS A GRANARY

At Vicksburg, during the whole six weeks of the siege, the men in the trenches worked steadily, advancing the coils about the city. Grant received reenforcement and before the end of the siege his army numbered over seventy thousand. Day and night, the roar of artillery continued. From the mortars across the river and from Porter's fleet the shrieking shells rose in grand parabolic curves, bursting in midair or in the streets of the city, spreading havoc in all directions. The people of the city burrowed into the ground for safety. Many whole families lived in these dismal abodes, their walls of clay being shaken by the roaring battles that raged above the ground. In one of these dens, sixty-five people found a home. The food supply ran low, and day by day it became scarcer. At last, by the end of June, there was nothing to eat except mule meat and a kind of bread made of beans and corn meal.

It was ten o'clock in the morning of July 3d. White flags were seen above the parapet. The firing ceased. A strange quietness rested over the scene of the long bombardment. On the afternoon of that day, the one, too, on which was heard the last shot on the battlefield of Gettysburg, Grant and Pemberton stood beneath an oak tree, in front of McPherson's corps, and opened negotiations for the capitulation. On the following morning, the Nation's birthday, about thirty thousand soldiers laid down their arms as prisoners of war and were released on parole. The losses from May 1st to the surrender were about ten thousand on each side.

Three days later, at Port Hudson, a tremendous cheer arose from the besieging army. The Confederates within the defenses were at a loss to know the cause. Then some one shouted the news, "Vicksburg has surrendered!"

The end had come. Port Hudson could not hope to stand alone; the greater fortress had fallen. Two days later, July 9th, the gallant garrison, worn and weary with the long siege, surrendered to General Banks. The whole course of the mighty Mississippi was now under the Stars and Stripes.

PART III
THE CRISIS

GETTYSBURG

AFTER THE BATTLE—A SHARPSHOOTER

FEELING FOR LEE'S ARMY

Battery D, Second United States Artillery, Going into Action, June 5, 1863. This was part of the reconnaisance in force under Sedgwick, whom Hooker ordered to cross three miles below Fredericksburg on June 3d and find out if Lee's army still held its old position. The cavalry had brought in reports of some new movement by the Army of Northern Virginia, and Hooker believed that another invasion of the North was impending. It was imperative that this should be checked at once. Every effort was made to discover the real position of the Confederates in order to give battle. Lee, on his side, was equally anxious for a decisive engagement. The

THE NORTH AGAIN THREATENED

It was this Virginia village (seventy-five miles from Washington, on the Orange & Alexandria Railroad) that Lee chose as the point of concentration for his forces preparatory to his last daring invasion of the North, which ended at Gettysburg. Culpeper was no stranger to war's alarms. Two brigades of Pleasonton's cavalry were sent off by Hooker on June 7th to definitely determine Lee's position. Riding in the direction of Culpeper, they ran into a similar force of the Confederates under Stuart, which proved too strong for the

SPARRING BEFORE GETTYSBURG

victory at Chancellorsville had elated the Confederacy with hopes of early recognition by Europe. Exaggerated reports of disaffection at the North led the Government at Richmond to urge an immediate advance. Lee promptly complied. His strongest hope was that he might draw Hooker into a position where the Federals could be advantageously attacked and a blow struck that would end the war. So cleverly was Lee's movement masked by the resistance of Hill's Corps to Howe's division of the Sixth Corps on June 5th that Sedgwick was deceived into reporting that the greater portion of Lee's force still held their old positions.

CULPEPER COURT HOUSE

Federals. The encounter left no doubt in Hooker's mind that Lee was preparing for an aggressive movement either against Washington or into Maryland. On June 13th it was clear that Lee was massing his forces in the direction of Culpeper. Hooker at once began throwing his lines out toward Culpeper, with the purpose of keeping abreast of Lee by advancing south of the Blue Ridge—and the race for the Potomac was on. This picture was taken in November, 1863, when Culpeper was occupied by the Federals.

THE HIGH–WATER MARK OF THE CONFEDERACY

Just as we see it here, the Confederates first saw Gettysburg. Down these roads and past these houses they marched to the high-water mark of their invasion of the North. It was quite by accident that the little town became the theater of the crucial contest of the Civil War. On the morning of June 30th Heth's division of General D. H. Hill's Corps was marching upon the town from the west. It came on confidently, expecting no resistance, meaning only to seize a supply of shoes much needed by the footsore Army of Northern Virginia, which had marched triumphantly from Culpeper to the heart of Pennsylvania. Between Heth's men and their goal lay two brigades of Federal cavalry under Buford. Riding into the town from the opposite direction came Major Kress, sent by General Wadsworth to get these same shoes for his division of the Federals. Before the tavern Kress found Buford and explained his errand. "You

THE LITTLE TOWN OF GETTYSBURG, PENNSYLVANIA

had better return immediately to your command," said Buford. "Why, what is the matter, General?" asked Kress. At that instant a single gun boomed in the distance, and Buford, mounting, replied as he spurred his horse to the gallop, "That's the matter." The world had never seen a finer body of fighting men than Lee's Army of Northern Virginia, then massing rapidly toward Gettysburg. More than seventy-three thousand five hundred strong they came, every man a veteran, contemptuous of adversaries whose superior numbers had never yet been made to count completely against them. In the center of the panorama rises Cemetery Ridge, where the defeated First and Eleventh Federal Corps slept on their arms on the night of July 1st, after having been driven back through the town by the superior forces of Hill and Ewell. The lower eminence to the right of it is Culp's Hill. At the extreme right of the picture stands Round Top.

THE CRISIS BRINGS FORTH THE MAN

Major-General George Gordon Meade and Staff. Not men, but a man is what counts in war, said Napoleon; and Lee had proved it true in many a bitter lesson administered to the Army of the Potomac. At the end of June, 1863, for the third time in ten months, that army had a new commander. Promptness and caution were equally imperative in that hour. Meade's fitness for the post was as yet undemonstrated; he had been advanced from the command of the Fifth Corps three days before the army was to engage in its greatest battle. Lee must be turned back from Harrisburg and Philadelphia and kept from striking at Baltmore and Washington, and the somewhat scattered Army of the Potomac must be concentrated. In the very first flush of his advancement, Meade exemplified the qualities of sound generalship that placed his name high on the list of Federal commanders.

GETTYSBURG—WHERE STIRRING DEEDS BROUGHT FORTH IMMORTAL WORDS

This is Gettysburg, the sleepy little Pennsylvania town that leaped into the focus of the world's eye on those scorching death-ridden days of July, 1863, and down the street comes swaying in cadenced steps a marching regiment. We are looking at them just as the inhabitants, gathered here in their quaint old costumes, saw them. Here are the defenders returned again to the place whose name spells victory and glorious memories on their tattered battle-flags. It is the 19th of November, 1863. Lincoln is here to speak those glowing words that every schoolboy knows, and dedicate the National Cemetery, where lie the Blue and Gray, and where their children's children make yearly pilgrimages.

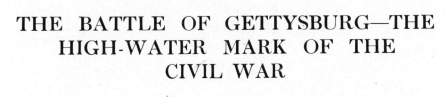

THE BATTLE OF GETTYSBURG—THE HIGH-WATER MARK OF THE CIVIL WAR

We cannot dedicate—we cannot consecrate—we cannot hallow this ground. The brave men, living and dead, who struggled here have consecrated it, far above our poor power to add or detract. The world will little note, nor long remember what we say here, but it can never forget what they did here. It is for us, the living, rather, to be dedicated here to the unfinished work which they who fought here have thus far so nobly advanced. It is rather for us to be here dedicated to the great task remaining before us—that from these honored dead we take increased devotion to that cause for which they gave the last full measure of devotion—that we here highly resolve that these dead shall not have died in vain—that this nation, under God, shall have a new birth of freedom—and that government of the people, by the people, for the people, shall not perish from the earth.—*Abraham Lincoln, on November 19, 1863, four months after this battle, in his "Gettysburg Address."*

THE military operations of the American Civil War were carried on for the most part south of the Mason and Dixon line; but the greatest and most famous of the battles was fought on the soil of the old Keystone State, which had given birth to the Declaration of Independence and to the Constitution of the United States.

Gettysburg is a quiet hamlet, nestling among the hills of Adams County, and in 1863 contained about fifteen hundred inhabitants. It had been founded in 1780 by James Gettys, who probably never dreamed that his name thus given to the village would, through apparently accidental circumstances, become famous in history for all time.

The hills immediately around Gettysburg are not rugged

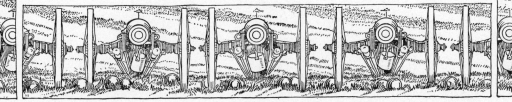

ROBERT E. LEE IN 1863

It was with the gravest misgivings that Lee began his invasion of the North in 1863. He was too wise a general not to realize that a crushing defeat was possible. Yet, with Vicksburg already doomed, the effort to win a decisive victory in the East was imperative in its importance. Magnificent was the courage and fortitude of Lee's maneuvering during that long march which was to end in failure. Hitherto he had made every one of his veterans count for two of their antagonists, but at Gettysburg the odds had fallen heavily against him. Jackson, his resourceful ally, was no more. Longstreet advised strongly against giving battle, but Lee unwaveringly made the tragic effort which sacrificed more than a third of his splendid army.

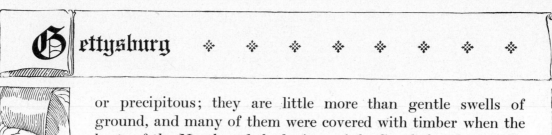
or precipitous; they are little more than gentle swells of ground, and many of them were covered with timber when the hosts of the North and the legions of the South fought out the destiny of the American republic on those memorable July days in 1863.

The village is the radiating point of several important roads, known by the names of the respective towns to which they lead. The one leading directly into the town from the north is known as the Carlisle road. It passes through the village and deflects to the southeast, becoming the Baltimore turnpike. East of the Carlisle road is the Harrisburg road, and west of it the Mummasburg road. This latter crosses a wooded ridge known as Oak Hill, and this hill became the center of operations on the first day of the battle. West of the village about half a mile a Lutheran theological seminary is situated on a ridge which extends north and south and is called Seminary Ridge. Directly south of Gettysburg, almost parallel with Seminary Ridge and about a mile from it, lies Cemetery Ridge. Three miles from the town, Cemetery Ridge culminates in a bold, rocky peak, with steep, rugged slopes several hundred feet in height, which is called Round Top. North of Round Top, and quite near it, is a similar peak about half as high, called Little Round Top. About five hundred yards west of Little Round Top another rugged peak, known as the Devil's Den, rises from the lowland marshes at the junction of a small creek which runs along the western base of Cemetery Ridge, and is known as Plum Run, with a smaller tributary. The Devil's Den is about one hundred feet lower than Little Round Top, and its slopes are covered with huge boulders and seamed with crevasses. The largest of these pits, and the one from which the hill took its name, is on the slope facing toward Little Round Top, and formed a natural breastwork of solid rock.

The valley between Cemetery Ridge and Seminary Ridge was rolling farm-land, with cultivated fields and orchards

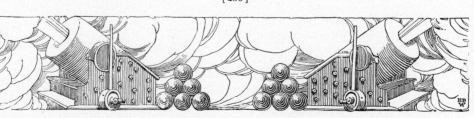

HANCOCK, "THE SUPERB"

Every man in this picture was wounded at Gettysburg. Seated, is Winfield Scott Hancock; the boy-general, Francis C. Barlow (who was struck almost mortally), leans against the tree. The other two are General John Gibbon and General David B. Birney. About four o'clock on the afternoon of July 1st a foam-flecked charger dashed up Cemetery Hill bearing General Hancock. He had galloped thirteen miles to take command. Apprised of the loss of Reynolds, his main dependence, Meade knew that only a man of vigor and judgment could save the situation. He chose wisely, for Hancock was one of the best all-round soldiers that the Army of the Potomac had developed. It was he who re-formed the shattered corps and chose the position to be held for the decisive struggle.

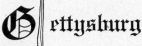

spreading across the landscape. At the southern end of the valley to the west of Round Top the lowland was covered with heavy timber, and the ground was strewn with huge rocks. Near the northwestern base of the Devil's Den there was a broad wheat-field, with the grain ripening in the summer sun. A short distance to the north of the wheat-field, on a slight elevation, stood the farmhouse and barns of the Trostle farm. To the west and slightly to the south of the Trostle farm the land rises gradually to a low hill which stands midway between the Trostle farm and the crest of Seminary Ridge. On the eastern slope of this hill, and reaching to its crest, there was an extensive peach orchard. The western side of the orchard bordered on the broad Emmitsburg road, which stretched away from Gettysburg to the southwest to Emmitsburg, a short distance over the Maryland line. A mile and a half west of Gettysburg flows Willoughby Run, while at about the same distance on the east and nearly parallel to the run flows a somewhat larger stream called Rock Creek. Between Rock Creek and the northern extremity of Cemetery Ridge is situated Culp's Hill, on whose sides the armies in blue and gray struggled heroically during the three days' fight. The area of the entire battle-ground is something over twenty-five square miles, all of which may be seen at a glance from any one of the five observatories which have since been erected on the ground by the Government.

Lee's army was flushed with victory after Chancellorsville and was strengthened by the memory of Fredericksburg. Southern hopes were high after Hooker's defeat on the Rappahannock, in May, 1863, and public opinion was unanimous in demanding an invasion of Northern soil. On the other hand, the Army of the Potomac, under its several leaders, had met with continual discouragement, and, with all its patriotism and valor, its two years' warfare showed but few bright pages to cheer the heart of the war-broken soldier, and to inspire the hopes of the anxious public in the North.

[238]

MUTE PLEADERS IN THE CAUSE OF PEACE

There was little time that could be employed by either side in caring for those who fell upon the fields of the almost uninterrupted fighting at Gettysburg. On the morning of the 4th, when Lee began to abandon his position on Seminary Ridge, opposite the Federal right, both sides sent forth ambulance and burial details to remove the wounded and bury the dead in the torrential rain then falling. Under cover of the hazy atmosphere, Lee was getting his whole army in motion to retreat. Many an unfinished shallow grave, like the one above, had to be left by the Confederates. In this lower picture some men of the Twenty-fourth Michigan infantry are lying dead on the field of battle. This regiment—one of the units of the Iron Brigade—left seven distinct rows of dead as it fell back from battle-line to battle-line, on the first day. Three-fourths of its members were struck down.

MEN OF THE IRON BRIGADE

Leaving General Stuart with ten thousand cavalry and a part of Hill's corps to prevent Hooker from pursuing, Lee crossed the Potomac early in June, 1863, concentrated his army at Hagerstown, Maryland, and prepared for a campaign in Pennsylvania, with Harrisburg as the objective. His army was organized in three corps, under the respective commands of Longstreet, Ewell, and A. P. Hill. Lee had divided his army so as to approach Harrisburg by different routes and to assess the towns along the way for large sums of money. Late in June, he was startled by the intelligence that Stuart had failed to detain Hooker, and that the Federals had crossed the Potomac and were in hot pursuit.

Lee was quick to see that his plans must be changed. He knew that to continue his march he must keep his army together to watch his pursuing antagonist, and that such a course in this hostile country would mean starvation, while the willing hands of the surrounding populace would minister to the wants of his foe. Again, if he should scatter his forces that they might secure the necessary supplies, the parts would be attacked singly and destroyed. Lee saw, therefore, that he must abandon his invasion of the North or turn upon his pursuing foe and disable him in order to continue his march. But that foe was a giant of strength and courage, more than equal to his own; and the coming together of two such forces in a mighty death-struggle meant that a great battle must be fought, a greater battle than this Western world had hitherto known.

The Army of the Potomac had again changed leaders, and George Gordon Meade was now its commander. Hooker, after a dispute with Halleck, resigned his leadership, and Meade, the strongest of the corps commanders, was appointed in his place, succeeding him on June 28th. The two great armies—Union and Confederate—were scattered over portions of Maryland and southern Pennsylvania. Both were marching northward, along almost parallel lines. The Confederates

THE FIRST DAY'S TOLL

The lives laid down by the blue-clad soldiers in the first day's fighting made possible the ultimate victory at Gettysburg. The stubborn resistance of Buford's cavalry and of the First and Eleventh Corps checked the Confederate advance for an entire day. The delay was priceless; it enabled Meade to concentrate his army upon the heights to the south of Gettysburg, a position which proved impregnable. To a Pennsylvanian, General John F. Reynolds, falls the credit of the determined stand that was made that day. Commanding the advance of the army, he promptly went to Buford's support, bringing up his infantry and artillery to hold back the Confederates.

McPHERSON'S WOODS

At the edge of these woods General Reynolds was killed by a Confederate sharpshooter in the first vigorous contest of the day. The woods lay between the two roads upon which the Confederates were advancing from the west, and General Doubleday (in command of the First Corps) was ordered to take the position so that the columns of the foe could be enfiladed by the infantry, while contending with the artillery posted on both roads. The Iron Brigade under General Meredith was ordered to hold the ground at all hazards. As they charged, the troops shouted: "If we can't hold it, where will you find the men who can?" On they swept, capturing General Archer and many of his Confederate brigade that had entered the woods from the other side. As Archer passed to the rear, Doubleday, who had been his classmate at West Point, greeted him with "Good morning! I'm glad to see you!"

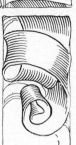
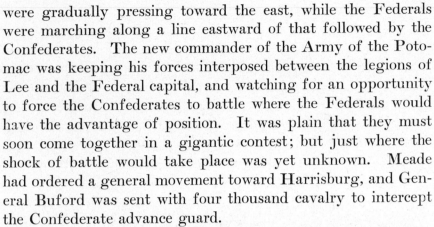

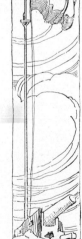

were gradually pressing toward the east, while the Federals were marching along a line eastward of that followed by the Confederates. The new commander of the Army of the Potomac was keeping his forces interposed between the legions of Lee and the Federal capital, and watching for an opportunity to force the Confederates to battle where the Federals would have the advantage of position. It was plain that they must soon come together in a gigantic contest; but just where the shock of battle would take place was yet unknown. Meade had ordered a general movement toward Harrisburg, and General Buford was sent with four thousand cavalry to intercept the Confederate advance guard.

On the night of June 30th Buford encamped on a low hill, a mile west of Gettysburg, and here on the following morning the famous battle had its beginning.

On the morning of July 1st the two armies were still scattered, the extremes being forty miles apart. But General Reynolds, with two corps of the Union army, was but a few miles away, and was hastening to Gettysburg, while Longstreet and Hill were approaching from the west. Buford opened the battle against Heth's division of Hill's corps. Reynolds soon joined Buford, and three hours before noon the battle was in progress on Seminary Ridge. Reynolds rode out to his fighting-lines on the ridge, and while placing his troops, a little after ten o'clock in the morning, he received a sharpshooter's bullet in the brain. The gallant Federal leader fell dead. John F. Reynolds, who had been promoted for gallantry at Buena Vista in the Mexican War, was one of the bravest and ablest generals of the Union army. No casualty of the war brought more widespread mourning to the North than the death of Reynolds.

But even this calamity could not stay the fury of the battle. By one o'clock both sides had been greatly reenforced, and the battle-line extended north of the town from Seminary Ridge to the bank of Rock Creek. Here for hours the roar

FEDERAL DEAD AT GETTYSBURG, JULY 1, 1863

All the way from McPherson's Woods back to Cemetery Hill lay the Federal soldiers, who had contested every foot of that retreat until nightfall. The Confederates were massing so rapidly from the west and north that there was scant time to bring off the wounded and none for attention to the dead. There on the field lay the shoes so much needed by the Confederates, and the grim task of gathering them began. The dead were stripped of arms, ammunition, caps, and accoutrements as well—in fact, of everything that would be of the slightest use in enabling Lee's poorly equipped army to continue the internecine strife. It was one of war's awful expedients.

SEMINARY RIDGE, BEYOND GETTYSBURG

Along this road the Federals retreated toward Cemetery Hill in the late afternoon of July 1st. The success of McPherson's Woods was but temporary, for the Confederates under Hill were coming up in overpowering numbers, and now Ewell's forces appeared from the north. The First Corps, under Doubleday, "broken and defeated but not dismayed," fell back, pausing now and again to fire a volley at  the pursuing Confederates. It finally joined the Eleventh Corps, which had also been driven back to Cemetery Hill. Lee was on the field in time to watch the retreat of the Federals, and advised Ewell to follow them up, but Ewell (who had lost 3,000 men) decided upon discretion. Night fell with the beaten Federals, reënforced by the Twelfth Corps and part of the Third, facing nearly the whole of Lee's army.

[B]

THE PRICE OF VICTORY

Such scenes as these marked every one of the detached battle-fields at Gettysburg. The lower picture is a result of the first day's fighting near McPherson's Woods, through which the Iron Brigade swept with the cry, "We've come to stay!" The picture above was taken near the spot where the First Minnesota was sacrificed to stem the advance of the Confederates after their victory at the Peach Orchard. Hancock, while patching up a second line to protect Sickles' retreating troops, saw a heavy column of Confederates emerge from a clump of trees and advance toward a weak point in his line. Dashing up to Colonel Colvill, Hancock shouted: "Do

THE MEN WHO "CAME TO STAY"

WHERE A SHELL DROPPED

you see those colors? Take them!" And the First Minnesota, in five minutes, captured the colors and stemmed the advance. Of the 262 officers and men who obeyed that order, half a hundred lay dead on the field and 174 others were wounded. The regiment's total mortality from that charge was 75, more than 28 per cent. of the number engaged—the highest known short of an Indian massacre. The Federals lost at Gettysburg 3,063 killed, 14,492 wounded, and 5,435 missing (Fox's figures). The Confederate loss was 3,903 killed, 18,735 wounded, and 5,425 missing (Livermore's figures). Total loss on both sides, 51,053.

NEAR THE BLOODY ANGLE

of the battle was unceasing. About the middle of the after-noon a breeze lifted the smoke that had enveloped the whole battle-line in darkness, and revealed the fact that the Federals were being pressed back toward Gettysburg. General Carl Schurz, who after Reynolds' death directed the extreme right near Rock Creek, leaving nearly half of his men dead or wounded on the field, retreated toward Cemetery Hill, and in passing through the town the Confederates pursued and cap-tured a large number of the remainder. The left wing, now unable to hold its position owing to the retreat of the right, was also forced back, and it, too, took refuge on Cemetery Hill, which had been selected by General O. O. Howard; and the first day's fight was over. It was several hours be-fore night, and had the Southerners known of the disorganized condition of the Union troops, they might have pursued and captured a large part of the army. Meade, who was still some miles from the field, hearing of the death of Reynolds, had sent Hancock to take general command until he himself should arrive.

Hancock had ridden at full speed and arrived on the field between three and four o'clock in the afternoon. His presence soon brought order out of chaos. His superb bearing, his air of confidence, his promise of heavy reenforcements during the night, all tended to inspire confidence and to renew hope in the ranks of the discouraged army. Had this day ended the affair at Gettysburg, the usual story of the defeat of the Army of the Potomac would have gone forth to the world. Only the advance portions of both armies had been engaged; and yet the battle had been a formidable one. The Union loss was severe. A great commander had fallen, and the rank and file had suffered the fearful loss of ten thousand men.

Meade reached the scene late in the night, and chose to make this field, on which the advance of both armies had acci-dentally met, the place of a general engagement. Lee had come to the same decision, and both called on their outlying

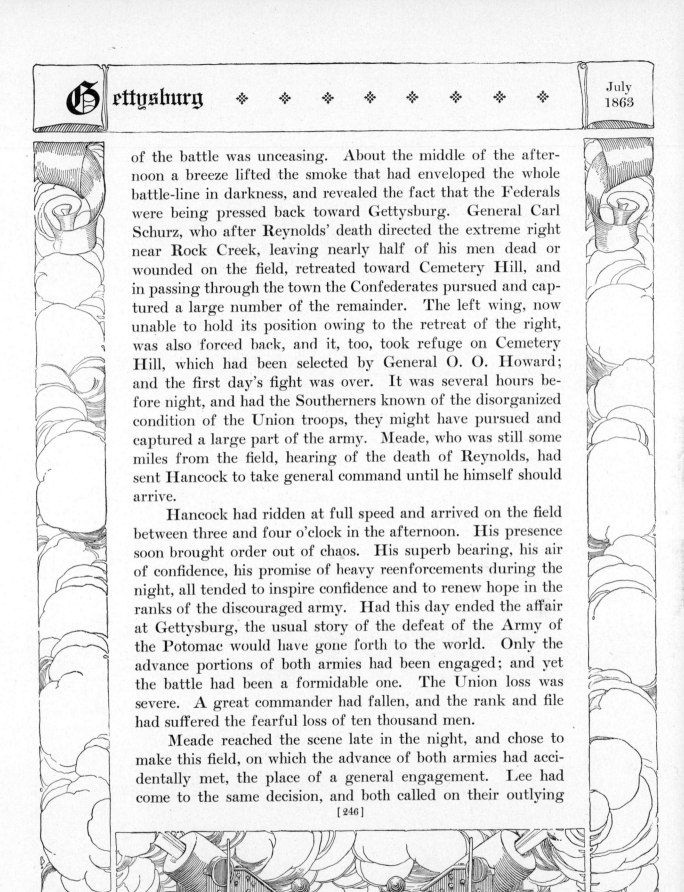

THE CARNAGE OF BLOODY ANGLE

Trostle's House, Sickles' headquarters at the beginning of the second day. The house stood some distance back from the Emmitsburg road, overlooking the Peach Orchard, from which the Confederates finally drove the sturdy men of the Third Corps. Whether or not it was a tactical error for Sickles to post his command along the road so far in advance of the line is a subject of discussion. The result cost many lives, and nearly lost to the Federals the key to their position. Back from the Peach Orchard Sickles' men were driven, past Trostle's House, where Bigelow's Ninth Massachusetts battery made its glorious stand, and near which Sickles himself lost his leg. All the way back to Round Top the ground was strewn with dead.

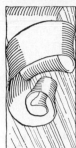
legions to make all possible speed to Gettysburg. Before morning, nearly all the troops of both armies had reached the field. The Union army rested with its center on Cemetery Ridge, with its right thrown around to Culp's Hill and its left extended southward toward the rocky peak called Round Top. The Confederate army, with its center on Seminary Ridge, its wings extending from beyond Rock Creek on the north to a point opposite Round Top on the south, lay in a great semi-circle, half surrounding the Army of the Potomac. But Lee was at a disadvantage. First, "Stonewall" Jackson was gone, and second, Stuart was absent with his ten thousand cavalry. Furthermore, Meade was on the defensive, and had the advantage of occupying the inner ring of the huge half circle. Thus lay the two mighty hosts, awaiting the morning, and the carnage that the day was to bring. It seemed that the fate of the Republic was here to be decided, and the people of the North and the South watched with breathless eagerness for the decision about to be made at Gettysburg.

The dawn of July 2d betokened a beautiful summer day in southern Pennsylvania. The hours of the night had been spent by the two armies in marshaling of battalions and maneuvering of corps and divisions, getting into position for the mighty combat of the coming day. But, when morning dawned, both armies hesitated, as if unwilling to begin the task of bloodshed. They remained inactive, except for a stray shot here and there, until nearly four o'clock in the afternoon.

The fighting on this second day was chiefly confined to the two extremes, the centers remaining comparatively inactive. Longstreet commanded the Confederate right, and opposite him on the Union left was General Daniel E. Sickles. The Confederate left wing, under Ewell, was opposite Slocum and the Union right stationed on Culp's Hill.

The plan of General Meade had been to have the corps commanded by General Sickles connect with that of Hancock and extend southward near the base of the Round Tops.

IN THE DEVIL'S DEN

Upon this wide, steep hill, about five hundred yards due west of Little Round Top and one hundred feet lower, was a chasm named by the country folk "the Devil's Den." When the position fell into the hands of the Confederates at the end of the second day's fighting, it became the stronghold of their sharpshooters, and well did it fulfill its name. It was a most dangerous post to occupy, since the Federal batteries on the Round Top were constantly shelling it in an effort to dislodge the hardy riflemen, many of whom met the fate of the one in the picture. Their deadly work continued, however, and many a gallant officer of the Federals was picked off during the fighting on the afternoon of the second day. General Vincent was one of the first victims; General Weed fell likewise; and as Lieutenant Hazlett bent over him to catch his last words, a bullet through the head prostrated that officer lifeless on the body of his chief.

Sickles found this ground low and disadvantageous as a fighting-place. In his front he saw the high ground along the ridge on the side of which the peach orchard was situated, and advanced his men to this position, placing them along the Emmitsburg road, and back toward the Trostle farm and the wheat-field, thus forming an angle at the peach orchard. The left flank of Hancock's line now rested far behind the right flank of Sickles' forces. The Third Corps was alone in its position in advance of the Federal line. The Confederate troops later marched along Sickles' front so that Longstreet's corps overlapped the left wing of the Union army. The Northerners grimly watched the bristling cannon and the files of men that faced them across the valley, as they waited for the battle to commence.

The boom of cannon from Longstreet's batteries announced the beginning of the second day's battle. Lee had ordered Longstreet to attack Sickles in full force. The fire was quickly answered by the Union troops, and before long the fight extended from the peach orchard through the wheat-field and along the whole line to the base of Little Round Top. The musketry commenced with stray volleys here and there—then more and faster, until there was one continuous roar, and no ear could distinguish one shot from another. Longstreet swept forward in a magnificent line of battle, a mile and a half long. He pressed back the Union infantry, and was seriously threatening the artillery.

At the extreme left, close to the Trostle house, Captain John Bigelow commanded the Ninth Battery, Massachusetts Light Artillery. He was ordered to hold his position at all hazards until reenforced. With double charges of grape and canister, again and again he tore great gaps in the advancing line, but it re-formed and pressed onward until the men in gray reached the muzzles of the Federal guns. Again Bigelow fired, but the heroic band had at last to give way to the increased numbers of the attack, which finally resulted in a hand-

THE UNGUARDED LINK

Little Round Top, the key to the Federal left at Gettysburg, which they all but lost on the second day —was the scene of hand-to-hand fighting rarely equaled since long-range weapons were invented. Twice the Confederates in fierce conflict fought their way near to this summit, but were repulsed. Had they gained it, they could have planted artillery which would have enfiladed the left of Meade's line, and Gettysburg might have been turned into an overwhelming defeat. Beginning at the right, the Federal line stretched in the form of a fish-hook, with the barb resting on Culp's Hill, the center at the bend in the hook on Cemetery Hill, and the left (consisting of General Sickles' Third Corps) forming the shank to the southward as far as Round Top. On his own responsibility Sickles had advanced a portion of his line, leaving Little Round Top unprotected. Upon this advanced line of Sickles, at the Peach Orchard on the Emmitsburg road, the Confederates fell in an effort to turn what they supposed to be Meade's left flank. Only the promptness of General Warren, who discovered the gap and remedied it in time, saved the key.

to-hand struggle with a Mississippi regiment. Bigelow was wounded, and twenty-eight of his hundred and four men were left on the bloody field, while he lost sixty-five out of eighty-eight horses, and four of six guns. Such was one of many deeds of heroism enacted at Gettysburg.

But the most desperate struggle of the day was the fight for the possession of Little Round Top. Just before the action began General Meade sent his chief engineer, General G. K. Warren, to examine conditions on the Union left. The battle was raging in the peach orchard when he came to Little Round Top. It was unoccupied at the time, and Warren quickly saw the great importance of preventing its occupation by the Confederates, for the hill was the key to the whole battle-ground west and south of Cemetery Ridge. Before long, the engineer saw Hood's division of Longstreet's corps moving steadily toward the hill, evidently determined to occupy it. Had Hood succeeded, the result would have been most disastrous to the Union army, for the Confederates could then have subjected the entire Union lines on the western edge of Cemetery Ridge to an enfilading fire. Warren and a signal officer seized flags and waved them, to deceive the Confederates as to the occupation of the height. Sykes' corps, marching to the support of the left, soon came along, and Warren, dashing down the side of the hill to meet it, caused the brigade under Colonel Vincent and a part of that under General Weed to be detached, and these occupied the coveted position. Hazlett's battery was dragged by hand up the rugged slope and planted on the summit.

Meantime Hood's forces had come up the hill, and were striving at the very summit; and now occurred one of the most desperate hand-to-hand conflicts of the war—in which men forgot that they were human and tore at each other like wild beasts. The opposing forces, not having time to reload, charged each other with bayonets—men assaulted each other with clubbed muskets—the Blue and the Gray grappled in

THE SECOND DAY'S FIGHT

The battle of Gettysburg was a crescendo of carnage—each day marked by a special climax more dramatic and deadly than the preceding one. That of the second day was the struggle for Little Round Top. It began with the thrilling charge by Longstreet's men of Hood's division. Turning Ward's flank, on they swept from Devil's Den up the ravine between the Round Tops, confident that Little Round Top was undefended. Near the crest Vincent's brigade, posted in the nick of time by General Warren, burst upon them with the bayonet. Up and down the slope the struggling lines undulated, broken rapidly by the trees and boulders into single-handed combats; men and muskets in a moment were scattered all about. Just as Vincent's right was about to be overwhelmed, the 140th New York came upon the crest, led by the gallant young Colonel O'Rorke, who fell dead at the first volley. The regiment, rallied by Vincent, held their ground, but there Vincent, too, was killed. Meanwhile Hazlett's regular battery had

THE BATTLE–FIELD AMID THE TREES

THE WOODED SLOPE OF LITTLE ROUND TOP

dragged its guns with great difficulty to the crest, where Generals Weed and Hazlett soon fell together. Colonel Rice, of the Forty-fourth New York (now in command in place of Vincent), had repulsed the assaults on his right and center. There was a lull, during which the Confederates stole around from the woods and fell with fury on the left of the line. Here Chamberlain's regiment, the Twentieth Maine, rapidly swinging around the rear of the mountain to meet the attack, was forced over the crest. Rallying, they drove back the Confederates in their turn. Twice more the struggling men fought back and forth over the summit, strewing the slopes with the fallen. Then a brigade of the Pennsylvania reserves and one from the Fifth Corps dashed over the hill. Chamberlain's brave men who were left greeted the reënforcements with a shout, dashed forward in a final charge, and drove the Confederates through the valley between the Round Tops. The Twentieth Maine had lost a third of its men and spent its last round of ammunition.

mortal combat and fell dead, side by side. The privates in the front ranks fought their way onward until they fell, the officers sprang forward, seized the muskets from the hands of the dying and the dead, and continued the combat. The furious struggle continued for half an hour, when Hood's forces gave way and were pressed down the hillside. But they rallied and advanced again by way of a ravine on the left, and finally, after a most valiant charge, were driven back at the point of the bayonet.

Little Round Top was saved to the Union army, but the cost was appalling. The hill was covered with hundreds of the slain. Scores of the Confederate sharpshooters had taken position among the crevasses in the Devil's Den, where they could overlook the position on Little Round Top, and their unerring aim spread death among the Federal officers and gunners. Colonel O'Rourke and General Vincent were dead. General Weed was dying; and, as Hazlett was stooping to receive Weed's last message, a sharpshooter's bullet laid him—dead—across the body of his chief.

During this attack, and for some hours thereafter, the battle continued in the valley below on a grander scale and with demon-like fury. Here many thousands were engaged. Sickles' whole line was pressed back to the base of the hill from which it had advanced in the morning. Sickles' leg was shattered by a shell, necessitating amputation, while scores of his brave officers, and thousands of his men, lay on the field of battle when the struggle ceased at nightfall. This valley has been appropriately named the " Valley of Death."

Before the close of this main part of the second day's battle, there was another clash of arms, fierce but of short duration, at the other extreme of the line. Lee had ordered Ewell to attack Cemetery Hill and Culp's Hill on the north, held by Slocum, who had been weakened by the sending of a large portion of the Twelfth Corps to the assistance of the left wing. Ewell had three divisions, two of which were commanded by

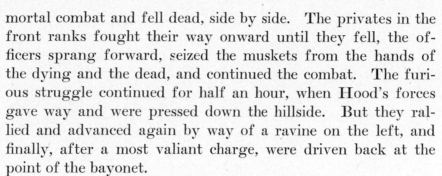

MEN WHO HELD LITTLE ROUND TOP

When General Warren discovered the defenseless condition of Little Round Top, he spied the division of Brigadier-General James Barnes marching to the relief of their comrades fighting along the Emmitsburg road. Warren, on his own responsibility, rode over to General Barnes and detached Vincent's brigade, hurrying it back to guard Little Round Top. It was not long before the men of the Forty-fourth New York were engaged in a fierce hand-to-hand combat with the determined Confederates of Hood, worming their way from tree to tree and boulder to boulder, in a running fight up the slope. The men of the Forty-fourth New York were among the finest in the service; they were enlisted from every county in their native State, and were selected in accordance with strict requirements as to fitness. The average age of the regiment was twenty-two; its heaviest battle loss (one hundred and eleven), occurred in the defense of Little Round Top at Gettysburg. The ground seemed impregnable, but the Southerners, rushing on from their victory at "the bloody angle," climbed the slopes in such a desperate onslaught that the Federals, not having time to load, advanced to repel the attack with the bayonet. The hillside after the battle was literally strewn with the dead and wounded. To the prompt and brave work of Vincent's brigade, in which fought the Forty-fourth New York, was due, in part, the fact that Little Round Top was not taken in that first assault. The repulse of the Confederates gave the Federals time to bring up a battery and strengthen the position against the repeated charges of the afternoon.

WHERE THE SECOND DAY'S ATTACK ENDED

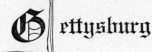
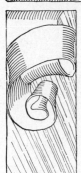

Generals Early and Johnson. It was nearly sunset when he sent Early to attack Cemetery Hill. Early was repulsed after an hour's bloody and desperate hand-to-hand fight, in which muskets and bayonets, rammers, clubs, and stones were used. Johnson's attack on Culp's Hill was more successful. After a severe struggle of two or three hours General Greene, who alone of the Twelfth Corps remained on the right, succeeded, after reenforcement, in driving the right of Johnson's division away from its entrenchments, but the left had no difficulty in taking possession of the abandoned works of Geary and Ruger, now gone to Round Top and Rock Creek to assist the left wing.

Thus closed the second day's battle at Gettysburg. The harvest of death had been frightful. The Union loss during the two days had exceeded twenty thousand men; the Confederate loss was nearly equal. The Confederate army had gained an apparent advantage in penetrating the Union breastworks on Culp's Hill. But the Union lines, except on Culp's Hill, were unbroken. On the night of July 2d, Lee and his generals held a council of war and decided to make a grand final assault on Meade's center the following day. Against this decision Longstreet protested in vain. His counsel was that Lee withdraw to the mountains, compel Meade to follow, and then turn and attack him. But Lee was encouraged by the arrival of Pickett's division and of Stuart's cavalry, and Longstreet's objections were overruled. Meade and his corps commanders had met and made a like decision—that there should be a fight to the death at Gettysburg.

That night a brilliant July moon shed its luster upon the ghastly field on which thousands of men lay, unable to rise. Many of them no longer needed help. Their last battle was over, and their spirits had fled to the great Beyond. But there were great numbers, torn and gashed with shot and shell, who were still alive and calling for water or for the kindly touch of a helping hand. Nor did they call wholly in vain. Here and

THE GROUND THAT WAS REGAINED

The indomitable photographer, Brady, in his famous duster, is sitting amid the battered trees on Culp's Hill, whose scars mark the scene of the recent crucial contest. The possession of the hill at nightfall of July 2d encouraged Lee to renew the general assault next day. This was the extreme right of the Federal position. Hancock, arriving on the afternoon of the first day, had seen its importance and sent a shattered brigade of Doubleday's First Corps to hold it. The marvelous fighting of Longstreet's men on the 2d had laid low 6,000 Federals before the Round Tops at the Federal left, and by nightfall Johnson's division of Ewell's Corps drove the defenders of Culp's Hill from their entrenchments. But Ewell, owing to the darkness, did not perceive the value of his new position. A short musket-shot beyond Culp's Hill, the artillery reserves and the supply trains of the Union army lay almost unprotected. At daylight of the 3d, Johnson's lines were attacked by the Second Massachusetts and the Twentieth Indiana, but these regiments were almost annihilated. But after seven hours of fighting the Confederates retreated.

there in the moonlight little rescuing parties were seeking out whom they might succor. They carried many to the improvised hospitals, where the surgeons worked unceasingly and heroically, and many lives were saved.

All through the night the Confederates were massing artillery along the crest of Seminary Ridge. The sound horses were carefully fed and watered, while those killed or disabled were replaced by others. The ammunition was replenished and the guns were placed in favorable positions and made ready for their work of destruction.

On the other side, the Federals were diligently laboring in the moonlight, and ere the coming of the day they had planted batteries on the brow of the hill above the town as far as Little Round Top. The coming of the morning revealed the two parallel lines of cannon, a mile apart, which signified only too well the story of what the day would bring forth.

The people of Gettysburg, which lay almost between the armies, were awakened on that fateful morning—July 3, 1863 —by the roar of artillery from Culp's Hill, around the bend toward Rock Creek. This knoll in the woods had, as we have seen, been taken by Johnson's men the night before. When Geary and Ruger returned and found their entrenchments occupied by the Confederates they determined to recapture them in the morning, and began firing their guns at daybreak. Seven hours of fierce bombardment and daring charges were required to regain them. Every rod of space was disputed at the cost of many a brave man's life. At eleven o'clock this portion of the Twelfth Corps was again in its old position.

But the most desperate onset of the three days' battle was yet to come—Pickett's charge on Cemetery Ridge—preceded by the heaviest cannonading ever heard on the American continent.

With the exception of the contest at Culp's Hill and a cavalry fight east of Rock Creek, the forenoon of July 3d

THE HEIGHT OF THE BATTLE–TIDE

Near this gate to the local cemetery of Gettysburg there stood during the battle this sign: "All persons found using firearms in these grounds will be prosecuted with the utmost rigor of the law." Many a soldier must have smiled grimly at these words, for this gateway became the key of the Federal line, the very center of the cruelest use of firearms yet seen on this continent. On the first day Reynolds saw the value of Cemetery Hill in case of a retreat. Howard posted his reserves here, and Hancock greatly strengthened the position. One hundred and twenty Confederate guns were turned against it that last afternoon. In five minutes every man of the Federals had been forced to cover; for an hour and a half the shells fell fast, dealing death and laying waste the summer verdure in the little graveyard. Up to the very guns of the Federals on Cemetery Hill, Pickett led his devoted troops. At night of the 3d it was one vast slaughter-field. On this eminence, where thousands were buried, was dedicated the soldiers' National Cemetery.

[B]

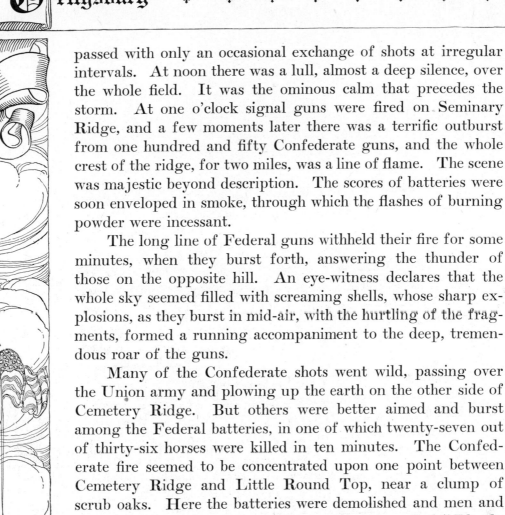

passed with only an occasional exchange of shots at irregular intervals. At noon there was a lull, almost a deep silence, over the whole field. It was the ominous calm that precedes the storm. At one o'clock signal guns were fired on Seminary Ridge, and a few moments later there was a terrific outburst from one hundred and fifty Confederate guns, and the whole crest of the ridge, for two miles, was a line of flame. The scene was majestic beyond description. The scores of batteries were soon enveloped in smoke, through which the flashes of burning powder were incessant.

The long line of Federal guns withheld their fire for some minutes, when they burst forth, answering the thunder of those on the opposite hill. An eye-witness declares that the whole sky seemed filled with screaming shells, whose sharp explosions, as they burst in mid-air, with the hurtling of the fragments, formed a running accompaniment to the deep, tremendous roar of the guns.

Many of the Confederate shots went wild, passing over the Union army and plowing up the earth on the other side of Cemetery Ridge. But others were better aimed and burst among the Federal batteries, in one of which twenty-seven out of thirty-six horses were killed in ten minutes. The Confederate fire seemed to be concentrated upon one point between Cemetery Ridge and Little Round Top, near a clump of scrub oaks. Here the batteries were demolished and men and horses were slain by scores. The spot has been called " Bloody Angle."

The Federal fire proved equally accurate and the destruction on Seminary Ridge was appalling. For nearly two hours the hills shook with the tremendous cannonading, when it gradually slackened and ceased. The Union army now prepared for the more deadly charge of infantry which it felt was sure to follow.

They had not long to wait. As the cannon smoke drifted away from between the lines fifteen thousand of Longstreet's

The Now-or-never Charge of Pickett's Men. When the Confederate artillery opened at one o'clock on the afternoon of July 3d, Meade and his staff were driven from their headquarters on Cemetery Ridge. Nothing could live exposed on that hillside, swept by cannon that were being worked as fast as human hands could work them. It was the beginning of Lee's last effort to wrest victory from the odds that were against him. Longstreet, on the morning of the 3d, had earnestly advised against renewing the battle against the Gettysburg heights. But Lee saw that in this moment the fate of the South hung in the balance; that if the Army of Northern Virginia did not win, it would never again become the aggressor. Pickett's division, as yet not engaged, was the force Lee designated for the assault; every man was a Virginian, forming a veritable Tenth Legion in valor. Auxiliary divisions swelled the charging column to 15,000. In the middle of the afternoon the Federal guns ceased firing. The time for the charge had come. Twice Pickett

PICKETT—THE MARSHALL NEY OF GETTYSBURG

asked of Longstreet if he should go forward. Longstreet merely bowed in answer. "Sir, I shall lead my division forward," said Pickett at last, and the heavy-hearted Longstreet bowed his head. As the splendid column swept out of the woods and across the plain the Federal guns reopened with redoubled fury. For a mile Pickett and his men kept on, facing a deadly greeting of round shot, canister, and the bullets of Hancock's resolute infantry. It was magnificent—but every one of Pickett's brigade commanders went down and their men fell by scores and hundreds around them. A hundred led by Armistead, waving his cap on his sword-point, actually broke through and captured a battery, Armistead falling beside a gun. It was but for a moment. Longstreet had been right when he said: "There never was a body of fifteen thousand men who could make that attack successfully." Before the converging Federals the thinned ranks of Confederates drifted wearily back toward Seminary Ridge. Victory for the South was not to be.

MEADE'S HEADQUARTERS ON CEMETERY RIDGE

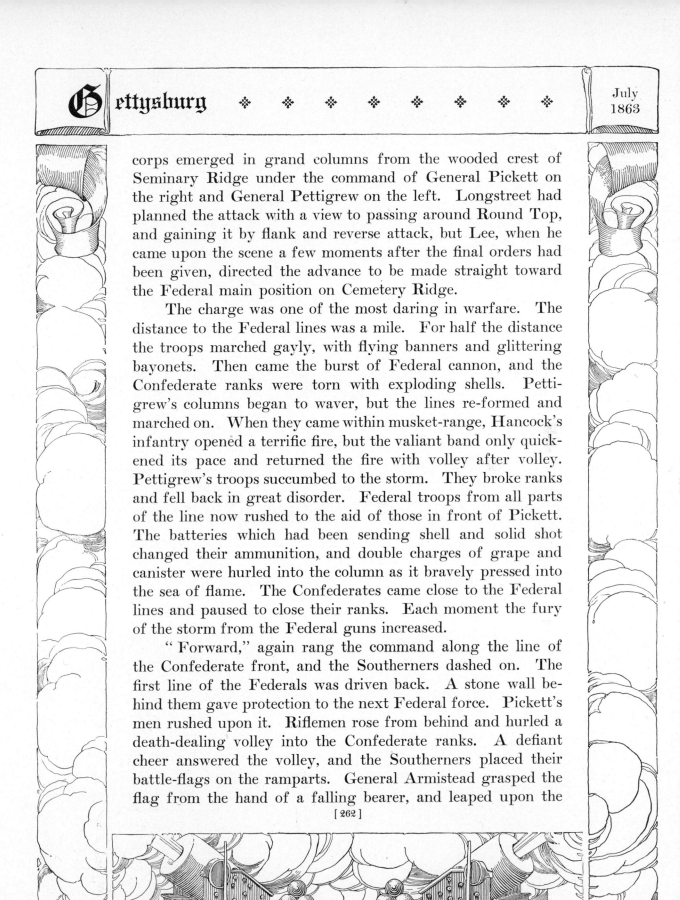

corps emerged in grand columns from the wooded crest of
Seminary Ridge under the command of General Pickett on
the right and General Pettigrew on the left. Longstreet had
planned the attack with a view to passing around Round Top,
and gaining it by flank and reverse attack, but Lee, when he
came upon the scene a few moments after the final orders had
been given, directed the advance to be made straight toward
the Federal main position on Cemetery Ridge.

The charge was one of the most daring in warfare. The
distance to the Federal lines was a mile. For half the distance
the troops marched gayly, with flying banners and glittering
bayonets. Then came the burst of Federal cannon, and the
Confederate ranks were torn with exploding shells. Pettigrew's columns began to waver, but the lines re-formed and
marched on. When they came within musket-range, Hancock's
infantry opened a terrific fire, but the valiant band only quick-
ened its pace and returned the fire with volley after volley.
Pettigrew's troops succumbed to the storm. They broke ranks
and fell back in great disorder. Federal troops from all parts
of the line now rushed to the aid of those in front of Pickett.
The batteries which had been sending shell and solid shot
changed their ammunition, and double charges of grape and
canister were hurled into the column as it bravely pressed into
the sea of flame. The Confederates came close to the Federal
lines and paused to close their ranks. Each moment the fury
of the storm from the Federal guns increased.

" Forward," again rang the command along the line of
the Confederate front, and the Southerners dashed on. The
first line of the Federals was driven back. A stone wall behind them gave protection to the next Federal force. Pickett's
men rushed upon it. Riflemen rose from behind and hurled a
death-dealing volley into the Confederate ranks. A defiant
cheer answered the volley, and the Southerners placed their
battle-flags on the ramparts. General Armistead grasped the
flag from the hand of a falling bearer, and leaped upon the

The prelude to Pickett's magnificent charge was a sudden deluge of shells from 159 long-range Confederate guns trained upon Cemetery Ridge. General Meade and his staff were instantly driven from their headquarters (already illustrated) and within five minutes the concentrated artillery fire had swept every unsheltered position on Cemetery Ridge clear of men. In the woods, a mile and a half distant, Pickett and his men watched the effect of the bombardment, expecting the order to "Go Forward" up the slope (shown in the picture). The Federals had instantly opened with their eighty available guns, and for three hours the most terrific artillery duel of the war was kept up. Then the Federal fire slackened, as though the batteries were silenced. The Confederates' artillery ammunition also was now low. "For God's sake, come on!" was the word to Pickett. And at Longstreet's reluctant nod the commander led his 14,000 Virginians across the plain in their tragic charge up Cemetery Ridge.

WHERE PICKETT CHARGED

In that historic charge was Armistead, who achieved a momentary victory and met a hero's death. On across the Emmitsburg road came Pickett's dauntless brigades, coolly closing up the fearful chasms torn in their ranks by the canister. Up to the fence held by Hays' brigade dashed the first gray line, only to be swept into confusion by a cruel enfilading fire. Then the brigades of Armistead and Garnett moved forward, driving Hays' brigade back through the batteries on the crest. Despite the death-dealing bolts on all sides, Pickett determined to capture the guns; and, at the order, Armistead, leaping the fence and waving his cap on his sword-point, rushed forward, followed by about a hundred of his men. Up to the very crest they fought the Federals back, and Armistead, shouting, "Give them the cold steel, boys!" seized one of the guns. For a moment the Confederate flag waved triumphantly over the Federal battery. For a brief interval the fight raged fiercely at close quarters. Armistead was shot down beside the gun he had taken, and his men were driven back. Pickett, as he looked around the top of the ridge he had gained, could see his men fighting all about with clubbed muskets and even flag-staffs against the troops that were rushing in upon them from all sides. Flesh and blood could not hold the heights against such terrible odds, and with a heart full of anguish Pickett ordered a retreat. The despairing Longstreet, watching from Seminary Ridge, saw through the smoke the shattered remnants drift sullenly down the slope and knew that Pickett's glorious but costly charge was ended.

GENERAL L. A. ARMISTEAD, C.S.A.

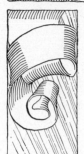

wall, waving it in triumph. Almost instantly he fell among the Federal troops, mortally wounded. General Garnett, leading his brigade, fell dead close to the Federal line. General Kemper sank, wounded, into the arms of one of his men.

Pickett had entered a death-trap. Troops from all directions rushed upon him. Clubbed muskets and barrel-staves now became weapons of warfare. The Confederates began surrendering in masses and Pickett ordered a retreat. Yet the energy of the indomitable Confederates was not spent. Several supporting brigades moved forward, and only succumbed when they encountered two regiments of Stannard's Vermont brigade, and the fire of fresh batteries.

As the remnant of the gallant division returned to the works on Seminary Ridge General Lee rode out to meet them. His demeanor was calm. His features gave no evidence of his disappointment. With hat in hand he greeted the men sympathetically. "It was all my fault," he said. "Now help me to save that which remains."

The battle of Gettysburg was over. The cost in men was frightful. The losses of the two armies reached fifty thousand, about half on either side. More than seven thousand men had fallen dead on the field of battle.

The tide could rise no higher; from this point the ebb must begin. Not only here, but in the West the Southern cause took a downward turn; for at this very hour of Pickett's charge, Grant and Pemberton, a thousand miles away, stood under an oak tree on the heights above the Mississippi and arranged for the surrender of Vicksburg.

Lee could do nothing but lead his army back to Virginia. The Federals pursued but feebly. The Union victory was not a very decisive one, but, supported as it was by the fall of Vicksburg, the moral effect on the nation and on the world was great. The period of uncertainty was ended. It required but little prophetic vision to foresee that the Republic would survive the dreadful shock of arms.

THE MAN WHO HELD THE CENTER

Headquarters of Brigadier-General Alexander S. Webb. It devolved upon the man pictured here (booted and in full uniform, before his headquarters tent to the left of the picture) to meet the shock of Pickett's great charge. In command of three Pennsylvania regiments (the Seventy-First, Seventy-Second, and One Hundred and Sixth) of Hancock's Second Corps, Webb was equal to the emergency. Stirred to great deeds by the example of a patriotic ancestry, he felt that upon his holding his position depended the outcome of the day. His front had been the focus of the Confederate artillery fire. Batteries to right and left of his line were practically silenced. Young Lieutenant Cushing, mortally wounded, fired the last serviceable gun and fell dead as Pickett's men came on. Wheeler's First New York Battery dashed up to take Cushing's place and was captured by the men of Armistead. Webb at the head of the Seventy-second Pennsylvania fought back the on-rush, posting a line of slightly wounded in his rear. Webb himself fell wounded but his command checked the assault till Hall's brilliant charge turned the tide at this point.

THE GOLDEN OPPORTUNITY

The Potomac from Berlin Heights, July, 1863. Instead of a wall of steel in his rear, as might have happened, Lee met only open roads in his retreat after Gettysburg. After the failure of Pickett's charge, Lee and his generals began rallying their troops behind the guns as a protection against the counter-charge which all felt sure was bound to come. Hancock, lying in an ambulance, severely wounded, argued that as he had been struck by a ten-penny nail the Confederate ammunition must be exhausted. His deduction was correct, but although he summoned his waning strength to dictate an approval of the charge, should it be ordered, no advance was made. Meade could have sent forward an entire corps (Sedgwick's) which had not been engaged. By the afternoon of July 4th, Lee's shattered forces were in full retreat toward the Potomac, beyond which lay safety.

THE LEISURELY PURSUIT

Meade's army crossing the Potomac at Berlin, eighteen days after the battle of Gettysburg. Lincoln never ceased to regret that he had not gone in person to Gettysburg to push the pursuit of Lee. Not till July 5th did Meade put his army in motion to follow the Confederates, who had marched all afternoon and all night in the pouring rain, impeded with heavy trains of ammunition which might easily have been captured. Lee found the pontoon bridges which he had left at Falling Waters destroyed by a Federal raiding party sent by General French from Frederick, and drew up his army for the battle that he anticipated must be fought before recrossing the Potomac. Not till the night of July 13th did Meade determine upon an attack. Meanwhile Lee had gained the time necessary to repair his bridges and retreat into Virginia. Meade could not follow directly. Only after a long march through the neighborhood of Harper's Ferry did he get his army across. Before he could strike the Confederates again, Lee was strongly posted along the line of the Rapidan.

CHAPTER ONE

PART IV
ALONG THE TENNESSEE

CHICKAMAUGA—A CONFEDERATE VICTORY

1864
UNION STOREHOUSES AT BRIDGEPORT, TENNESSEE RIVER

LEE & GORDON'S MILLS ON THE CHICKAMAUGA, SEPTEMBER, 1863

Dozing in the autumn sunlight of 1863, this obscure building, bearing by chance the patronymics of two great Southern generals, was suddenly to mark a strategic point in the most sanguinary of the battles of the West. It stood on the west branch of Chickamauga Creek, which flowed through the fertile valley between Missionary Ridge and Pigeon Mountain. Through the passes of the one the Federals under Rosecrans were advancing on September 12th, while the Confederates under Bragg held the approaches at the other. Between them flowed the little stream, undoubtedly the scene of some prehistoric conflict, for the Indians had named it Chickamauga, "River of Death." In 1863 the word was about to be written into American history to designate a two-days' battle in which the South lost more in killed and wounded than at Gettysburg and the North almost the same number as at Chancellorsville. The storm center

THE BLOODIEST BATTLE–FIELD OF THE WAR

of the mighty conflict had shifted to the West.   After Gettysburg the Army of Northern Virginia and the Army of the Potomac lay warily watching each other, each disinclined to become the aggressor.   Lincoln had been urging Rosecrans to move his Army of the Cumberland on from Murfreesboro and attack Bragg's entrenched position in south central Tennessee so as to prevent Bragg from detaching troops to raise the siege of Vicksburg.   At last, on June 24, 1863, he took the initiative, and then, with what is considered by some military writers the war's masterpiece of strategy, he drove Bragg out of Tennessee into Georgia.   Rosecrans' advance was in Bragg's abandoned works around Tullahoma on July 3d and in Chattanooga on September 9th, all without a battle.   Burnside, with the Army of the Ohio, captured Knoxville on September 3d.   But Tennessee was not to be abandoned by the Confederates without a fight.

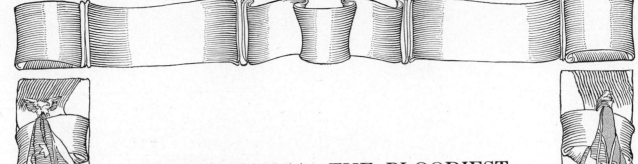

CHICKAMAUGA—THE BLOODIEST CONFLICT IN THE WEST

In its dimensions and its murderousness the battle of Chickamauga was the greatest battle fought by our Western armies, and one of the greatest of modern times. In our Civil War it was exceeded only by Gettysburg and the Wilderness; in European history we may compare with it such battles as Neerwinden, or Malplaquet, or Waterloo.—*John Fiske in "The Mississippi Valley in the Civil War."*

THE town of Chattanooga, Tennessee, lies in a great bend of the Tennessee River and within a vast amphitheater of mountains, ranging in a general southwesterly direction, and traversed at intervals by great depressions or valleys. These passes form a natural gateway from the mid-Mississippi valley to the seaboard States. To dislodge the Confederate army under General Bragg from this natural fortress would remove the last barrier to the invading Federals, and permit an easy entry upon the plains of Georgia. The importance of this position was readily apparent to the Confederate Government, and any approach by the Federal forces toward this point was almost certain to be met by stubborn resistance.

Rosecrans' forward movement from Murfreesboro, in the early summer of 1863, forced Bragg over the Cumberland Mountains and across the Tennessee. The Confederate leader destroyed the railroad bridge at Bridgeport and entrenched himself in and around Chattanooga. The advanced portion of the Federal army had made its way as far as Stevenson, Alabama, when circumstances compelled a halt. It was found impossible to transport needed forage and supplies over the terrible roads of eastern Tennessee. Rosecrans could go no

ON THE WAY TO CHICKAMAUGA

To the Elk River Bridge (near Decherd, Tennessee) the enterprising army photographer who was recording Rosecrans' advance had followed the Army of the Cumberland in July, 1863. The two distinct maneuvers that led to Chickamauga fully sustained the reputation of Rosecrans as one of the greatest strategic generals of the war. The first movement was executed in nine days, during which time the troops struggled with their heavy trains along roads little better than bogs. Torrential rains, such as Tennessee had rarely known before, fell incessantly; the artillery had to be dragged through the mire by hand. Despite such difficulties, Rosecrans succeeded in flanking Bragg, compelling him to retreat from his strong position at Tullahoma. South of that place, on the Nashville & Chattanooga Railroad, this bridge was made the objective of Wilder's mounted infantry, which swept around in Bragg's rear, striking the railroad at Decherd, destroying the commissary depot and cutting the rail connection with Chattanooga. A detachment pushed forward to the bridge, but it was too strongly guarded to be destroyed. The Confederates burnt it in their retreat to Chattanooga, but was rebuilt by Rosecrans; it was completed by the Federal engineers on July 13th.

further until the Nashville and Chattanooga Railroad was repaired as far as Stevenson and Bridgeport, and storage depots established at these and neighboring places. Consequently it was not until August 16th that the movement over the Cumberland Mountains began. Rosecrans had the choice of approaching Chattanooga from the north side of the river, a seventy-mile march through a rough, mountainous country, ill supplied with water and forage, or of crossing the Tennessee on the southwest and moving on the town over Sand and Lookout mountains. He chose the latter for all but a small portion of his force, although it was the more hazardous.

Between August 29th and September 4th Crittenden, Thomas, and McCook got their corps over at various places between Shellmound and Caperton's Ferry. General Granger, with the reserve corps, took charge of the rear. When Crittenden received orders for crossing the river he was commanded to leave the brigades of Hazen and Wagner behind to threaten Chattanooga from the north. For some days Wagner had been shelling the town, and Bragg, fully expecting the early approach of the Army of the Cumberland from this direction, had concentrated his forces at and above Chattanooga. Rosecrans, consequently, was able to accomplish the difficult crossing of the Tennessee without interference.

He found the Confederates in possession of the north end of Lookout Mountain and decided to dislodge his adversary by endangering his line of communication from the south and east. McCook on the Federal right was sent across Lookout Mountain at Winston's Gap, forty-six miles south of Chattanooga to occupy Alpine, east of the mountains. Thomas went to McLemore's Cove, east of Missionary Ridge, while Crittenden, on the left, was stationed in Lookout Valley to keep his eye on Chattanooga. The cavalry was sent forward to destroy the Western and Atlantic Railroad near Dalton, Georgia. On September 8th, before all these moves had been accomplished, Bragg abandoned his stronghold.

WHERE THE PONTOONS RAN SHORT

The Railroad Bridge over the Tennessee River at Bridgeport, Alabama, August, 1863. In the movement against Chattanooga, Rosecrans chose the Tennessee River for his line. Feinting strongly with Crittenden's command to the north of Bragg's position, he crossed the main body of his army to the south. There was much impatience in Washington that the movement was not more promptly executed, but serious difficulties delayed it. It took three weeks to repair the railroad, and on August 25th the first supply-train was pushed through Stevenson, Alabama, where the new commissary base was established. Meanwhile the Tennessee, greatly swollen by recent rains, presented a formidable barrier. There were not enough pontoons, and at Bridgeport Sheridan had to piece out the bridge with trestle-work.

[B]

Crittenden the next day marched around the north end of
Lookout and entered the town, while Hazen and Wagner
crossed over from the opposite bank of the Tennessee.

Rosecrans believed that Bragg was in full retreat toward
Rome, Georgia, and Crittenden, leaving one brigade in Chattanooga, was ordered to pursue. Bragg encouraged his adversary in the belief that he was avoiding an engagement
and sent spies as deserters into the Federal ranks to narrate
the details of his flight. Meanwhile, he was concentrating at
Lafayette, about twenty-five miles south of Chattanooga.
Hither General S. B. Buckner, entirely too weak to cope
with Burnside's heavy column approaching from Kentucky,
brought his troops from Knoxville. Breckinridge and two
brigades arrived from Mississippi, while twelve thousand of
Lee's veterans, under Lee's most trusted and illustrious lieutenant, Longstreet, were hastening from Virginia to add their
numbers to Bragg's Army of Tennessee.

The three corps of the Union army, as we have seen, were
now separated over a wide extent of territory by intervening
ridges, so intent was Rosecrans on intercepting the vanished
Bragg. But the latter, by no means vanished, and with his
face toward Chattanooga, considered the position of his antagonist and discovered his own army almost opposite the
Federal center. Crittenden was advancing toward Ringgold,
and the remoteness of Thomas' corps on his right precluded
any immediate union of the Federal forces.

Bragg was quick to grasp the opportunity made by Rosecrans' division of the army in the face of his opponent. He
at once perceived the possibilities of a master-stroke; to crush
Thomas' advanced divisions with an overwhelming force.

The attempt failed, owing to a delay in the attack, which
permitted the endangered Baird and Negley to fall back.
Bragg then resolved to throw himself upon Crittenden, who
had divided his corps. Polk was ordered to advance upon that
portion of it at Lee and Gordon's Mills, but when Bragg came

THE FIRST TO REACH THE BATTLE-FIELD

General James S. Negley and Staff.   General Negley (standing uncovered in this picture) formed with his division the advance-guard in the forward movement from the Tennessee against Bragg.   This picture (taken at Cove Spring, near Stevenson, Alabama, before the advance) shows the arduous character of the country through which the march was made.   Crossing the Tennessee at Caperton's Ferry, Negley's division pressed forward, and on September 9th held the passes of Lookout Mountain.   Next day, crossing Missionary Ridge, he took up position in McLemore's Cove.   This was destined to become the battle-field of Chickamauga, and here Negley's advance was checked.   Bragg, instead of being in retreat, was concentrating in his front, eager to crush the corps of Thomas, which he knew had come up too confidently, unsupported by the rest of Rosecrans' army. On the 11th Negley's position became precarious; Bragg was sending against him such a superior force that he was in great danger of losing his train.   With great energy and skill, supported by Baird's division, he succeeded in falling back to a strong position in front of Stevens' Gap without the loss of a single wagon.   Negley, who was made a major-general for his bravery at Stone's River, was censured by the irascible Rosecrans for his supposed disobedience of orders at Chickamauga.   Subsequent investigation completely exonerated him.   With only a handful of his men he had saved fifty guns in the rout of the 20th.

to the front early on the 13th, expecting to witness the annihilation of the Twenty-first Corps, he found to his bitter disappointment that the bishop-general had made no move and that Crittenden had reunited his divisions and was safe on the west bank of the Chickamauga. Thus his splendid chances of breaking up the Army of the Cumberland were ruined.

When Bragg's position became known to Rosecrans, great was his haste to effect the concentration of his army. Couriers dashed toward Alpine with orders for McCook to join Thomas with the utmost celerity. The former started at once, shortly after midnight on the 13th, in response to Thomas's urgent call. It was a real race of life and death, attended by the greatest hardships. Ignorant of the roads, McCook submitted his troops to a most exhausting march, twice up and down the mountain, fifty-seven miles of the most arduous toil, often dragging artillery up by hand and letting it down steep declines by means of ropes. But he closed up with Thomas on the 17th, and the Army of the Cumberland was saved from its desperate peril.

Crittenden's corps now took position at Lee and Gordon's Mills on the left bank of Chickamauga Creek, and the Federal troops were all within supporting distance. In the Indian tongue Chickamauga means "The River of Death," a name strangely prophetic of that gigantic conflict soon to be waged by these hostile forces throughout this beautiful and heretofore peaceful valley.

The Confederate army, its corps under Generals Polk, D. H. Hill, and Buckner, was stationed on the east side of the stream, its right wing below Lee and Gordon's Mills, and the left extending up the creek toward Lafayette. On the Federal side Thomas was moved to the left, with Crittenden in the center and McCook on the right. The strength of the army was about fifty-seven thousand men. On the 18th of September, Longstreet's troops were arriving from Virginia, and by the morning of the 19th the greater part of the Confederate army

[278]

THE LEADER OF THE RIGHT WING

General Alexander McD. McCook at Chickamauga.   While Thomas, preceded by Negley, was pressing forward to McLemore's Cove, McCook advanced the right wing of the army to the southward within twenty miles of Lafayette, where Bragg had his headquarters.   Crittenden, meanwhile, with the left wing, was advancing from Chattanooga on the north.   It was the opportunity to strike one of these widely separated corps that Bragg missed.   At midnight on September 13th McCook received the order to hurry back and make junction with Thomas.   Then began a race of life and death over fifty-seven miles of excruciating marching, back across Lookout Mountain and northward through Lookout Valley to Stevens' Gap, where he arrived on the 17th.   After a brief rest the right wing marched through half the night to its designated position on the battle-field, and by the morning of the 18th Rosecrans' army was at last concentrated.   General McCook (of a family that sent a father and five sons into the war) had distinguished himself at Shiloh and Corinth, and with the First Corps of the Army of the Ohio had borne the brunt of the battle at Perryville.   At Stone's River he commanded the right wing of the army, which suffered such severe disaster.   Again at Chickamauga the right wing, after sending reënforcements to Thomas at the left, was driven back in rout.

had crossed the Chickamauga. The two mighty armies were now face to face, and none could doubt that the impending struggle would be attended by frightful loss to both sides.

It was Bragg's intention to send Polk, commanding the right wing, in a flanking movement against the Federal left under Thomas, and thus intervene between it and Chattanooga. The first encounter, at 10 o'clock in the morning of the 19th, resulted in a Confederate repulse, but fresh divisions were constantly pushed forward under the deadly fire of the Federal artillery. The Federals were gradually forced back by the incessant charge of the Confederates; but assailed and assailant fought with such great courage and determination that any decided advantage was withheld from either. Meanwhile, the Federal right was hard pressed by Hood, commanding Longstreet's corps, and a desperate battle ensued along the entire line. It seemed, however, more like a struggle between separate divisions than the clash of two great armies. When night descended the Federals had been forced back from the creek, but the result had been indecisive.

Disaster to the Union army had been averted by the use of powerful artillery when the infantry seemed unable to withstand the onslaught. Rosecrans had assumed the defensive, and his troops had so far receded as to enable the Confederates to form their lines on all the territory fought over on that day. During the night preparations were made in both camps for a renewal of the battle on the following morning, which was Sunday. A fresh disposition of the troops was made by both leaders. Near midnight General Longstreet arrived on the field, and was at once placed in command of the Confederate left, Polk retaining the right. Not all of Longstreet's troops arrived in time for the battle, but Bragg's whole force now amounted to seventy thousand.

Thomas was given command of the Union left, with McCook at his right, while Crittenden's forces occupied the center, but to the rear of both Thomas and McCook. Thomas had

THE CONFEDERATE LEADER AT CHICKAMAUGA

Major-General Braxton Bragg, C.S.A.   Born, 1815; West Point, 1837; Died, 1876.   Bragg's name before 1861 was perhaps better known in military annals than that of any other Southern leader because of his brilliant record in the Mexican War.   In the Civil War he distinguished himself first at Shiloh and by meritorious services thereafter.   But his delays rendered him scarcely a match for Rosecrans, to say nothing of Grant and Sherman.   Flanked out of two strong positions, he missed the opportunity presented by Rosecrans' widely separated forces and failed to crush the Army of the Cumberland in detail, as it advanced to the battle of Chickamauga.   The error cost the Confederates the loss of Tennessee, eventually.

spent the night in throwing up breastworks on the brow of Snodgrass Hill, as it was anticipated that the Confederates would concentrate their attack upon his position.

Hostilities began with a general movement of the Confederate right wing in an attempt to flank the Union left. General Bragg had ordered Polk to begin the attack at daybreak, but it was nearly ten o'clock in the morning before Breckinridge's division, supported by General Cleburne, advanced upon Thomas' entrenchments. Fighting desperately, the Confederates did not falter under the heavy fire of the Federals, and it seemed as if the latter must be driven from their position. Rosecrans, in response to urgent requests for reenforcements, despatched troops again and again to the aid of Thomas, and the assault was finally repulsed. Cleburne's division was driven back with heavy loss, and Breckinridge, unable to retain any advantage, was forced to defend his right, which was being seriously menaced. The battle at this point had been desperately waged, both sides exhibiting marked courage and determination. As on the previous day, the Confederates had been the aggressors, but the Federal troops had resisted all attempts to invade their breastworks.

However, the fortunes of battle were soon to incline to the side of the Southern army. Bragg sent Stewart's division forward, and it pressed Reynolds' and Brannan's men back to their entrenchments. Rosecrans sent Wood word to close up on Reynolds. Through some misunderstanding in giving or interpreting this order, General Wood withdrew his division from its position on the right of Brannan. By this movement a large opening was left almost in the center of the battle-line. Johnson's, Hindman's, and Kershaw's divisions rushed into the gap and fell upon the Union right and center with an impetus that was irresistible. The Confederate general, Bushrod Johnson, has given us an unforgetable picture of the thrilling event: "The resolute and impetuous charge, the rush of our heavy columns sweeping out from the shadow and gloom of the forest

THE TOO–ADVANCED POSITION

Crawfish Spring, to the South of the Chickamauga Battle-field. Rosecrans, in concentrating his troops on the 18th of September, was still possessed of the idea that Bragg was covering his retreat upon his railroad connections at Dalton. Instead, the Confederate commander had massed his forces on the other side of Chickamauga and was only awaiting the arrival of Longstreet to assume the aggressive. On the morning of the 19th, McCook's right wing at Crawfish Spring was strongly threatened by the Confederates, while the real attack was made against the left in an effort to turn it and cut Rosecrans off from a retreat upon Chattanooga. All day long, brigade after brigade was marched from the right of the Federal line in order to extend the left under Thomas and withstand this flanking movement. Even after nightfall, Thomas, trying to re-form his lines and carry them still farther to the left for the work of the morrow, brought on a sharp conflict in the darkness. The Confederates had been held back, but at heavy cost. That night, at the Widow Glenn's house, Rosecrans consulted his generals. The exhausted Thomas, when roused from sleep for his opinion, invariably answered, "I would strengthen the left." There seemed as yet to be no crisis at hand, and the council closed with a song by the debonair McCook.

into the open fields flooded with sunlight, the glitter of arms, the onward dash of artillery and mounted men, the retreat of the foe, the shouts of the hosts of our army, the dust, the smoke, the noise of fire-arms—of whistling balls, and grape-shot, and of bursting shell—made up a battle-scene of unsurpassed grandeur. Here, General Hood gave me the last order I received from him on the field, 'Go ahead and keep ahead of everything.'" A moment later, and Hood fell, severely wounded, with a minie ball in his thigh.

Wood's right brigade was shattered even before it had cleared the opening. Sheridan's entire division, and part of Davis' and Van Cleve's, were driven from the field. Longstreet now gave a fine exhibition of his military genius. The orders of battle were to separate the two wings of the opposing army. But with the right wing of his opponents in hopeless ruin, he wheeled to the right and compelled the further withdrawal of Federal troops in order to escape being surrounded. The brave soldier-poet, William H. Lytle, fell at the head of his brigade as he strove to re-form his line. McCook and Crittenden were unable, in spite of several gallant efforts, to rally their troops and keep back the onrushing heroes of Stone's River and Bull Run. The broken mass fled in confusion toward Chattanooga, carrying with it McCook, Crittenden, and Rosecrans. The latter telegraphed to Washington that his army had been beaten. In this famous charge the Confederates took several thousand prisoners and forty pieces of artillery.

Flushed with victory, the Confederates now concentrated their attack upon Thomas, who thus far, on Horseshoe Ridge and its spurs, had repelled all attempts to dislodge him. The Confederates, with victory within their grasp, and led by the indomitable Longstreet, swarmed up the slopes in great numbers, but they were hurled back with fearful slaughter. Thomas was looking anxiously for Sheridan, whom, as he knew, Rosecrans had ordered with two brigades to his support.

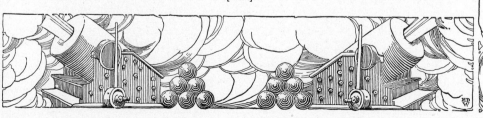

WHERE THE LINES WERE SWEPT BACK

Lee & Gordon's mill, seen in the picture, marked the extreme right of the Federal line on the second day at Chickamauga. From it, northward, were posted the commands of McCook and Crittenden, depleted by the detachments of troops the day before to strengthen the left. All might have gone well if the main attack of the Confederates had continued to the left, as Rosecrans expected. But hidden in the woods, almost within a stone's throw of the Federal right on that misty morning, was the entire corps of Longstreet, drawn up in columns of brigades at half distance—"a masterpiece of tactics," giving space for each column to swing right or left. Seizing a momentous opportunity which would have lasted but thirty minutes at the most, Longstreet hurled them through a gap which, owing to a misunderstanding, had been left open, and the entire Federal right was swept from the field.

But in Longstreet's rout of the right wing Sheridan, with the rest, had been carried on toward Chattanooga, and he found himself completely cut off from Thomas, as the Confederates were moving parallel to him. Yet the indomitable Sheridan, in spite of his terrible experience of the morning, did not give up the attempt. Foiled in his efforts to get through McFarland's Gap, he moved quickly on Rossville and came down the Lafayette road toward Thomas' left flank.

Meanwhile, advised by the incessant roar of musketry, General Gordon Granger, in command of the reserve corps near Rossville, advanced rapidly with his fresh troops. Acting with promptness and alacrity under orders, Granger sent Steedman to Thomas' right.

Directly across the line of Thomas' right was a ridge, on which Longstreet stationed Hindman with a large command, ready for an attack on Thomas' flank—a further and terrible menace to the nearly exhausted general, but it was not all. In the ridge was a small gap, and through this Kershaw was pouring his division, intent on getting to Thomas' rear. Steedman, with two brigades, drove Kershaw back and swept Hindman from the ridge. This was done in twenty minutes of terrific conflict and frightful slaughter.

The fighting grew fiercer, and at intervals was almost hand to hand. The casualties among the officers, who frequently led their troops in person, were mounting higher and higher as the moments passed. For six long hours the assaults continued, but the Union forces stood their ground. Ammunition ran dangerously low, but Steedman had brought a small supply, and when this was distributed each man had about ten rounds. Finally, as the sun was setting in the west, the Confederate troops advanced in a mighty concourse. The combined forces of Kershaw, Law, Preston, and Hindman once more rushed forward, gained possession of their lost ridge at several points, but were unable to hold their ground. The Union lines stood firm, and the Confederates retired to their

THE HOUSE WHENCE HELP CAME

Here, at his headquarters, holding the Federal line of retreat at Rossville Gap (the Confederate objective in the battle), General Gordon Granger heard with increasing anxiety the sounds of the conflict, three miles away, growing more and more ominous. Finally, in disobedience of orders, he set in motion his three brigades to the relief of Thomas, pushing forward two of them under Steedman. These arrived upon the field early in the afternoon, the most critical period of the battle, as Longstreet charged afresh on Thomas' right and rear. Seizing a battle-flag, Steedman (at the order of General Granger) led his command in a counter-charge which saved the Army of the Cumberland. This old house at Rossville was built by John Ross, a chief of the Cherokee Indians, and he lived in it till 1832, giving his name to the hamlet. Half-breed descendants of the Cherokees who had intermarried with both whites and Negroes were numerous in the vicinity of Chickamauga, and many of them fought with their white neighbors on the Confederate side.

original position at the foot of the slope. Thomas was saved. The onslaught on the Federal left of the battlefield was one of the heaviest attacks made on a single point during the war.

History records no grander spectacle than Thomas' stand at Chickamauga. He was ever afterwards known as "The Rock of Chickamauga." Under the cover of darkness, Thomas, having received word from Rosecrans to withdraw, retired his army in good order to Rossville, and on the following day rejoined Rosecrans in Chattanooga. The battle of Chickamauga, considering the forces engaged, was one of the most destructive of the Civil War. The Union army lost approximately sixteen thousand men, and while the loss to the Confederate army is not definitely known, it was probably nearly eighteen thousand. The personal daring and tenacious courage displayed in the ranks of both armies have never been excelled on any battlefield. The Confederate generals, Helm, Deshler, and Preston Smith were killed; Adams, Hood, Brown, Gregg, Clayton, Hindman, and McNair were wounded. The Federal side lost Lytle. The battle is generally considered a Confederate victory, and yet, aside from the terrible loss of human life, no distinct advantage accrued to either side. The Federal army retained possession of Chattanooga, but the Confederates had for the time checked the Army of the Cumberland from a further occupation of Southern soil.

It is a singular coincidence that the generals-in-chief of both armies exercised but little supervision over the movements of their respective troops. The brunt of the battle fell, for the most part, upon the commanders of the wings. To the subordinate generals on each side were awarded the highest honors. Longstreet, because of his eventful charge, which swept the right wing of the Union army from the field, was proclaimed the victor of Chickamauga; and to General Thomas, who by his firmness and courage withstood the combined attack of the Confederate forces when disaster threatened on every side, is due the brightest laurels from the adherents of the North.

PART IV

ALONG THE TENNESSEE

———

THE BATTLES
AT CHATTANOOGA

———

ON LOOKOUT MOUNTAIN—1864

IN THE BELEAGUERED CITY

In the parlor of this little dwelling sat Ulysses S. Grant on the evening of October 23, 1863. Muddy and rain-soaked from his long ride, he was gravely consulting with General Thomas and his officers. The Army of the Cumberland was in a serious predicament, summed up by Thomas' reply to Grant's first order from Nashville: "We will hold the town till we starve." Grant had starved a Confederate army out of Vicksburg; and now Bragg's army, reënforced by troops from Johnston, had settled down before Chattanooga to starve out, in turn, what was then the most important Federal force in the West. Strongly posted on Missionary Ridge and Lookout Mountain and in Chattanooga Valley to the south and southeast of the town, Bragg controlled the railroad, making it impossible for supplies to come over it from Bridgeport, Ala. Everything had to be brought into Chattanooga by wagon-trains over a roundabout route of nearly

HEADQUARTERS OF GENERAL THOMAS AT CHATTANOOGA

thirty miles.   The passage of wagons over the roads was difficult even in good weather, and they were rapidly becoming impassable from the autumn rains.   Bragg's forces had fallen upon and burned some three hundred Federal wagons, and with those that were left it was impossible to bring in more than the scantiest supplies.   The men had been for weeks on half-rations; all the artillery horses had starved to death; an occasional herd of beef cattle was driven down from Nashville through the denuded country and upon arrival would be aptly characterized by the soldiers as "beef dried on the hoof."   This and hard bread were their only sustenance.   Grant, now in command of all the Federal forces from the Alleghanies to the Mississippi, was first confronted by the necessity of hastening the delivery of supplies.   Either the Army of the Cumberland must be fed or Bragg would regain the ground that had been lost in Tennessee.

[B]

THE ATTACK THAT HAD TO WAIT

Near this spot General Sherman crossed his advance column in boats on the night of November 23d and captured all the Confederate pickets along the river except one. Grant, after seizing Brown's Ferry and thus opening a new route for his supplies, ordered Sherman to join him by forced marches. Immediately upon arrival the wearied soldiers of the Army of the Tennessee were assigned the task of opening the main attack upon Bragg's line to the southeast of Chattanooga on Missionary Ridge. Grant did not consider the Army of the Cumberland strong enough to attack Bragg alone, and consequently had postponed such a movement until Sherman could come up. By the 23d of November Sherman's divisions lay in camp, concealed behind the hills near the river bank, at the right of this structure, all ready to cross on a pontoon-bridge which had already been laid higher up the stream.

THE UNEXPECTED VICTORY

The Northeast Slope of Lookout Mountain. This photograph was taken from the hill to the north, where Hooker directed his troops in their "battle above the clouds" on the morning of November 24, 1863. Up this mountain-side Hooker's men fought their way to Pulpit Rock, a height of 2,400 feet. Grant's plan was for nothing more than a demonstration by Hooker to drive the Confederates back from reinforcing their right, where Sherman was to do the heavy work. Hooker's divisions had never before fought together, but with fine ardor they drove Stevenson's six brigades up this slope, and, fighting in the mist, swept them from their entrenchments on the mountain-top. Thus victory first came at the farther end of the line.

THE BATTLES ON LOOKOUT MOUNTAIN AND MISSIONARY RIDGE

AFTER CHATTANOOGA: "The Confederate lines . . . could not be rebuilt. The material for reconstructing them was exhausted. The blue-crested flood which had broken these lines was not disappearing. The fountains which supplied it were exhaustless. It was still coming with an ever increasing current, swelling higher and growing more resistless. This triune disaster [Vicksburg, Gettysburg, Missionary Ridge] was especially depressing to the people because it came like a blight upon their hopes which had been awakened by recent Confederate victories."—*General John B. Gordon, C. S. A., in "Reminiscences of the Civil War."*

FOLLOWING the defeat of Rosecrans' army at Chickamauga, in September, 1863, Bragg at once took strong positions on Missionary Ridge and Lookout Mountain. From these heights he was able to besiege the entire Army of the Cumberland in Chattanooga and obstruct the main arteries of supply to the Federal troops. Rosecrans was forced to abandon the route along the south bank of the Tennessee River, which led from Bridgeport, in Alabama, and to depend exclusively upon a long and mountainous wagon road on the north side of the river for the transportation of supplies. The Confederate cavalry, crossing the Tennessee above Chattanooga, fell upon the trains entangled in the mud of the Sequatchie valley, destroying in one day three hundred wagons, and killing or capturing about eighteen hundred mules. Within a short time the wisdom of Bragg's plan became apparent; famine threatened the Union army and several thousand horses and mules had already died from starvation. By his relentless vigil, the Confederate leader seemed destined to achieve a greater victory over his opponent than had hitherto attended his efforts in actual conflict.

THE BESIEGED

At this point, where Citico Creek joins the Tennessee, the left of the Eleventh Corps of the Army of the Cumberland rested on the river bank, the limit of the Federal line of defense, east of Chattanooga. Here, on high ground overlooking the stream, was posted Battery McAloon to keep the Confederates back from the river, so that timber and firewood could be rafted down to the besieged army. In the chill of autumn, with scanty rations, the soldiers had a hard time keeping warm, as all fuel within the lines had been consumed. The Army of the Cumberland was almost conquered by hardship. Grant feared that the soldiers "could not be got out of their trenches to assume the offensive." But it was these very men who achieved the most signal victory in the battle of Chattanooga.

Meanwhile, a complete reorganization of the Federal forces in the West was effected. Under the title of the Military Division of the Mississippi, the Departments of the Ohio, the Cumberland, and the Tennessee were united with Grant as general commanding, and Rosecrans was replaced by Thomas at the head of the Army of the Cumberland.

A hurried concentration of the Federal forces was now ordered by General Halleck. Hooker with fifteen thousand men of the Army of the Potomac came rapidly by rail to Bridgeport. Sherman, with a portion of his army, about twenty thousand strong, was summoned from Vicksburg and at once embarked in steamers for Memphis. General Grant decided to assume personal charge of the Federal forces; but before he reached his new command, Thomas, ably assisted by his chief engineer, General W. F. Smith, had begun to act on a plan which Rosecrans had conceived, and which proved in the end to be a brilliant conception. This was to seize a low range of hills known as Raccoon Mountain on the peninsula made by a bend of the river, on its south side and west of Chattanooga, and establish a wagon road to Kelly's Ferry, a point farther down the river to which supplies could be brought by boat from Bridgeport, and at the same time communication effected with Hooker.

A direct line was not only secured to Bridgeport, but Hooker advanced with a portion of his troops into Lookout Valley and after a short but decisive skirmish drove the Confederates across Lookout Creek, leaving his forces in possession of the hills he had gained. The route was now opened between Bridgeport and Brown's Ferry; abundant supplies were at once available and the Army of the Cumberland relieved of its perilous position.

Unlike the condition which had prevailed at Chickamauga, reenforcements from all sides were hastening to the aid of Thomas' army; Hooker was already on the ground; Sherman was advancing rapidly from Memphis, and he arrived in

OPENING "THE CRACKER LINE"

The U. S. S. *Chattanooga* was the first steamboat built by the Federals on the upper Tennessee River. Had the gunboats on the Ohio been able to come up the Tennessee River nearly three hundred miles, to the assistance of Rosecrans, Bragg could never have bottled him up in Chattanooga. But between Florence and Decatur, Alabama, Muscle Shoals lay in the stream, making the river impassable. While Bragg's pickets invested the railroad and river, supplies could not be brought up from Bridgeport; and besides, with the exception of one small steamboat (the *Dunbar*), the Federals had no boats on the river. General W. F. Smith, Chief Engineer of the Army of the Cumberland, had established a saw-mill with an old engine at Bridgeport for the purpose of getting out lumber from logs rafted down the river, with which to construct pontoons. Here Captain Arthur Edwards, Assistant Quartermaster, had been endeavoring since the siege began to build a steamboat consisting of a flat-bottom scow, with engine, boiler, and stern-wheel mounted upon it. On October 24th, after many difficulties and discouragements had been overcome, the vessel was launched successfully and christened the *Chattanooga*. On the 29th she made her trial trip. That very night, Hooker, in the battle of Wauhatchie, definitely established control of the new twelve-mile "Cracker Line" from Kelley's Ferry, which Grant had ordered for the relief of the starving army. The next day the little *Chattanooga*, with steam up, was ready to start from Bridgeport with a heavy load of the much-needed supplies, and her arrival was anxiously awaited at Kelley's Ferry, where the wagon-trains were all ready to rush forward the rations and forage to Chattanooga. The mechanics were still at work upon the little vessel's unfinished pilot-house and boiler-deck while she and the two barges she was to tow were being loaded, and at 4 A.M. on November 30th she set out to make the 45-mile journey against unfavorable head-winds.

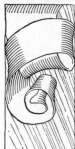
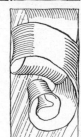

person on November 15th, while Burnside's forces at Knoxville offered protection to the left flank of the Federal army.

The disposition of the Confederate troops at this time was a formidable one; the left flank rested on the northern end of Lookout Mountain and the line extended a distance of twelve miles across Chattanooga Valley to Missionary Ridge. This position was further strengthened by entrenchments throughout the lowlands. Despite the danger which threatened his army from the converging Union forces, General Bragg determined to attack Burnside and despatched Longstreet with twenty thousand of his best troops to Knoxville. His army materially weakened, the Confederate general continued to hold the same extended position, although his combined force was smaller than had opposed Rosecrans alone at Chickamauga.

On the 23d of November, after a long and fatiguing march over roads almost impassable by reason of continuous rains, Sherman crossed the Tennessee by the pontoon bridge at Brown's Ferry, recrossed it above Chattanooga, and was assigned a position to the left of the main army near the mouth of Chickamauga Creek. Grant had now some eighty thousand men, of whom sixty thousand were on the scene of the coming battle, and, though fearful lest Burnside should be dislodged from his position at Knoxville, he would not be diverted from his purpose of sweeping the Confederates from the front of Chattanooga. It had been Grant's plan to attack on the 24th, but information reached him that Bragg was preparing a retreat. He, therefore, on the 23d, ordered Thomas to advance upon Bragg's center.

Preparations for the movement were made in full view of the Confederates; from the appearance of the troops, clad in their best uniforms, the advance line of the Southern army was content to watch this display, in the belief that the maneuvering army was parading in review. Suddenly, the peaceful pageant turned into a furious charge, before which the

THE WELCOME NEWCOMER

The home-made little steamboat *Chattanooga* was beset with difficulties and dangers on her memorable voyage of November 30th. She made but slow progress against the wind and the rapid current of the tortuous Tennessee. Fearful of breaking a steam pipe or starting a leak, she crawled along all day, and then was enveloped in one of the darkest of nights, out of which a blinding rain stung the faces of her anxious crew. Assistant Quartermaster William G. Le Duc, in command of the expedition, helped the pilot to feel his way through the darkness. At last the camp-fires of the Federals became guiding beacons from the shore and soon the *Chattanooga* tied up safely at Kelley's Ferry. The "Cracker Line" was at last opened—in the nick of time, for there were but four boxes of hard bread left in the commissary at Chattanooga, where four cakes of hard bread and one-quarter of a pound of pork were being issued as a three-days' ration.

Confederate pickets, taken by surprise, retreated from the first line of earthworks, and Thomas, with little loss to either side, captured Orchard Knob, between Chattanooga and Missionary Ridge. From this point, which was almost a mile in advance of the position occupied during the morning, Grant directed the movements of his army on the following day.

The Federal position was of less extent than that occupied by the Confederates. Sherman was in command of the left wing, while Thomas held the center, and "Fighting Joe" Hooker, with the Union right in Lookout Valley, threatened Lookout Mountain. The plan of battle was for Sherman to engage the Confederate right and sever communications between Bragg and Longstreet; Hooker was to carry out an assault on the Southern left flank, and at the same time maintain connection with Bridgeport. With both wings assailed by a superior force, it was believed that Bragg must reenforce these positions and permit Thomas, with overwhelming numbers, to concentrate upon the center.

On the 24th, two distinct movements were in progress. Sherman met with but little opposition in his initial attack upon the Confederate right and promptly seized and occupied the north end of Missionary Ridge. The Confederates, late in the afternoon, fought desperately to regain the hill but were finally repulsed, and Sherman fortified the position he had gained. In the mean time, Hooker, early in the day, had begun his operations against Lookout Mountain. Standing like a lone sentinel above the surrounding valleys, its steep, rocky, and deeply furrowed slopes, rising into a high, palisaded crest, frowned defiance upon the advancing troops, while a well-constructed line of defenses completed the imposing barrier.

Hooker had in addition to his own troops a division of Sherman's army (Osterhaus') which, owing to damage to the pontoon bridge at Brown's Ferry, had been prevented from joining its own leader. As ordered by Hooker, General Geary took his division up the valley to Wauhatchie, crossed the creek

WHERE AN ARMY GAVE ITS OWN ORDERS

At Missionary Ridge (seen in the distance in the lower picture) the Army of the Cumberland removed forever from Grant's mind any doubt of its fighting qualities.   Grant, anxious to develop Bragg's strength, ordered Thomas, on November 23d, to demonstrate against the forces on his front.   Moving out as if on parade, the troops under Gordon Granger drove back the Confederates and captured Orchard Knob (or Indian Hill) a day before it had been planned to do so.   Still another surprise awaited Grant on the 25th, when from this eminence he watched the magnificent spectacle of the battle of Chattanooga.   Thomas' men again pressed forward in what was ordered as a demonstration against Missionary Ridge.   Up and over it they drove the Confederates from one entrenchment after another, capturing the guns parked in the lower picture.   "By whose orders are those troops going up the hill?"   "Old Pap" Thomas, who knew his men better than did Grant, replied that it was probably by their own orders.   It was the most signal victory of the day.

THE CAPTURED CONFEDERATE GUNS

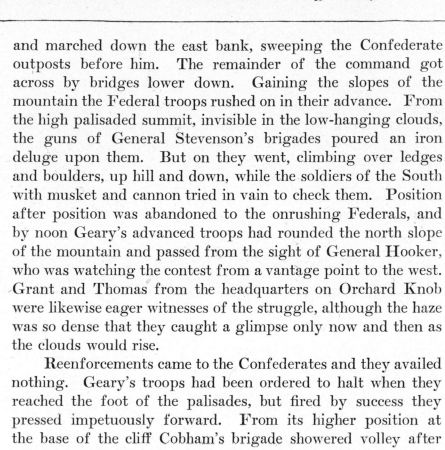

and marched down the east bank, sweeping the Confederate outposts before him. The remainder of the command got across by bridges lower down. Gaining the slopes of the mountain the Federal troops rushed on in their advance. From the high palisaded summit, invisible in the low-hanging clouds, the guns of General Stevenson's brigades poured an iron deluge upon them. But on they went, climbing over ledges and boulders, up hill and down, while the soldiers of the South with musket and cannon tried in vain to check them. Position after position was abandoned to the onrushing Federals, and by noon Geary's advanced troops had rounded the north slope of the mountain and passed from the sight of General Hooker, who was watching the contest from a vantage point to the west. Grant and Thomas from the headquarters on Orchard Knob were likewise eager witnesses of the struggle, although the haze was so dense that they caught a glimpse only now and then as the clouds would rise.

Reenforcements came to the Confederates and they availed nothing. Geary's troops had been ordered to halt when they reached the foot of the palisades, but fired by success they pressed impetuously forward. From its higher position at the base of the cliff Cobham's brigade showered volley after volley upon the Confederate main line of defense, while that of Ireland gradually rolled up the flank. The Federal batteries on Moccasin Point across the river were doing what they could to clear the mountain. The Southerners made a last stand in their walls and pits around the Craven house, but were finally driven in force over rocks and precipices into Chattanooga Valley.

Such was the "battle in the clouds," a wonderful spectacle denied the remainder of Hooker's troops holding Lookout Valley. That general says, "From the moment we had rounded the peak of the mountain it was only from the roar of battle and the occasional glimpses our comrades in the valley could catch of our lines and standards that they knew of the

THE MEN WHO COMPLETED THE VICTORY

General Hooker and Staff at Lookout Mountain. Hooker's forces of about 9,700 men had been sent from the East to reënforce Rose-crans, but until the arrival of Grant they were simply so many more mouths to feed in the besieged city. In the battle of Wauhatchie, on the night of October 20th, they drove back the Confederates and established the new line of communication. On November 24th they, too, had a surprise in store for Grant. Their part in the triple conflict was also ordered merely as a "demonstration," but they astounded the eyes and ears of their comrades with the spectacular fight by which they made their way up Lookout Mountain. The next day, pushing on to Rossville, the daring Hooker attacked one of Bragg's divisions and forced it into precipitate retreat.

HOOKER'S CAMP AT THE BASE OF LOOKOUT MOUNTAIN

strife or its progress, and when from these evidences our true condition was revealed to them their painful anxiety yielded to transports of joy which only soldiers can feel in the earliest moments of dawning victory."

By two in the afternoon the clouds had settled completely into the valley and the ensuing darkness put an end to further operations. Hooker established and strengthened a new position and waited for reenforcements, which General Carlin brought from Chattanooga at five o'clock. Until after midnight an irregular fire was kept up, but the Confederates could not break the new line. Before dawn General Stevenson abandoned the summit, leaving behind twenty thousand rations and the camp equipage of his three brigades. Hooker, anticipating this move, sent several detachments to scale the palisades. A party of six men from the Eighth Kentucky regiment, by means of ladders, was the first to reach the summit, and the waving Stars and Stripes greeted the rising sun of November 25th on Lookout Mountain, amid the wild and prolonged cheers of " Fighting Joe's " valiant troops.

The fighting of Sherman and Hooker on the 24th secured to Grant's army a distinct advantage in position. From the north end of Lookout Mountain across Chattanooga Valley to the north end of Missionary Ridge the Union forces maintained an unbroken front.

The morning of the 25th dawned cold, and an impenetrable mist which lay deep in the valleys was soon driven away. From Orchard Knob, a point almost in the center of the united Federal host, General Grant watched the preparations for the battle. At sunrise, Sherman's command was in motion. In his front, an open space intervened between his position and a ridge held by the Confederates, while just beyond rose a much higher hill. Toward the first ridge the attacking column, under General Corse, advanced rapidly and in full view of the foe. For a time it seemed as if the Confederates must recede before the terrific onslaught, but the advance was abruptly

[304]

THE BATTLE–FIELD ABOVE THE CLOUDS

Entrenchments on Lookout Mountain.   Up such rugged heights as these, heavily timbered and full of chasms, Hooker's men fought their way on the afternoon of November 24th.   Bridging Lookout Creek, the troops crossed, hidden by the friendly mist, and began ascending the mountain-sides, driving the Confederates from one line of rifle-pits and then from another.   The heavy musketry fire and the boom of the Confederate battery on the top of the mountain apprised the waiting Federals before Chattanooga that the battle had begun.   Now and again the fitful lifting of the mist disclosed to Grant and Thomas, watching from Orchard Knob, the men of Hooker fighting upon the heights.   Then all would be curtained once more.   At two o'clock in the afternoon the mist became so heavy that Hooker and his men could not see what they were doing, and paused to entrench.   By four o'clock, however, he had pushed on to the summit and reported to Grant that his position was impregnable.   Direct communication was then established and reënforcements sent.

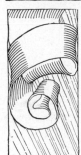

checked after a very close and stubborn struggle, when within a short distance of the entrenchment.

Unmindful of the numbers which opposed him, General Hardee not only succeeded in repulsing the attack, but, assuming the offensive, drove back the forces under General John E. Smith, who had sought to turn his left, and captured several hundred prisoners. The Federals, quickly re-forming their lines, renewed the assault and for several hours the fighting was desperate on both sides. A general advance of the Northern forces had been withheld, awaiting the arrival of Hooker who, under orders from Grant, was sweeping down Chickamauga Valley, and was to operate against the Confederate left and rear, in the expectation that Bragg would further weaken his line by massing at those points. But Hooker's army had been delayed several hours by repairs to the bridge crossing Chattanooga Creek. Although Sherman had failed in his attempt to turn the Confederate right he had forced Bragg to draw heavily upon his center for reenforcements. Grant, satisfied that Hooker was not far off, ordered the signal—six guns fired in rapid succession from the battery on Orchard Knob—for a general advance of Thomas' army upon the Confederate center.

It was now three o'clock in the afternoon. The four division commanders of the Army of the Cumberland, Sheridan, Wood, Baird, and Johnson, gave the word to advance. Between Orchard Knob and the base of Missionary Ridge, a mile away, is a broad valley covered for the most part with heavy timber. This had to be crossed before the entrenchments at the foot of the hill could be assaulted. Scarcely were the Cumberland troops in motion when fifty pieces of artillery on the crest of Missionary Ridge opened a terrific fire upon them. But the onward rush of the Federals was not checked in the slightest degree. The line of entrenchments at the base was carried with little opposition. Most of Breckinridge's men abandoned the ditches as the Federal skirmishers approached

THE PEAK OF VICTORY—THE MORNING AFTER THE BATTLE

Pulpit Rock, the Summit of Lookout Mountain.   Before dawn of November 25th, Hooker, anticipating the withdrawal of the Confederates, sent detachments to seize the very summit of the mountain, here 2,400 feet high.
Six volunteers from the Eighth Kentucky Regiment scaled the palisades by means of the ladders seen in this
picture, and made their way to the top.   The rest of the regiment quickly followed; then came the Ninety-sixth
Illinois.   The rays of the rising sun disclosed the Stars and Stripes floating in triumph from the lofty peak
"amid the wild and prolonged cheers of the men whose dauntless valor had borne them to that point."

[B]

and sought refuge up the hill, breaking and throwing into confusion other troops as they passed through.

At the foot of Missionary Ridge Thomas' army had reached its goal. Its orders carried it no further. But, as General Wood has related, " the enthusiasm and impetuosity of the troops were such that those who first reached the entrenchments at the base of the ridge bounded over them and pressed on up the ascent. . . . Moreover the entrenchments were no protection against the artillery on the ridge. To remain would be destruction—to return would be both expensive in life, and disgraceful. Officers and men, all seemed impressed with this truth. . . . Without waiting for an order the vast mass pressed forward in the race for glory, each man anxious to be the first on the summit. . . . Artillery and musketry could not check the impetuous assault. The troops did not halt to fire. To have done so would have been ruinous. Little was left to the commanders of the troops than to cheer on the foremost—to encourage the weaker of limb and to sustain the very few who seemed to be faint-hearted."

Midway up the slope was a small line of rifle-pits, but these proved of no use in stemming the Federal tide. In the immediate front, however, Major Weaver of the Sixtieth North Carolina rallied a sufficient number of the demoralized Confederates to send a well-directed and effective fire upon the advancing troops. At this point the first line of oncoming Federals was vigorously repulsed, and thrown back to the vacated Confederate trenches. General Bragg, noticing this, rode along the ridge to spread his good news among the troops, but he had not gone far when word was brought that the right flank was broken and that the Federal standard had been seen on the summit. A second and a third flag appeared in quick succession. Bragg sent General Bate to drive the foe back, but the disaster was so great that the latter was unable to repair it. Even the artillery had abandoned the infantry. The Confederate flank had gone, and within an hour of the start from

THE FLANKING PASS

The Gap in Missionary Ridge at Rossville. Through this Georgia mountain-pass runs the road to Ringgold. Rosecrans took advantage of it when he turned Bragg's flank before the battle of Chickamauga; and on November 25, 1863, Thomas ordered Hooker to advance from Lookout Mountain to this point and strike the Confederates on their left flank, while in their front he (Thomas) stood ready to attack. The movement was entirely successful, and in a brilliant battle, begun by Hooker, Bragg's army was swept from Missionary Ridge and pursued in retreat to Georgia.

THE SKIRMISH LINE

Multiply the number of these men by ten, strike out the tents, and we see vividly how the advancing line of Thomas' Army of the Cumberland appeared to the Confederates as they swept up the slope at Missionary Ridge to win the brilliant victory of November 25th. This view of drilling Federal troops in Chattanooga preserves the exact appearance of the line of battle only a couple of months before the picture was taken. The skirmishers, thrown out in advance of the line, are "firing" from such positions as the character of the ground makes most effective. The main line is waiting for the order to charge.

CONQUERING THE CURRENT

The "Suck" in the Tennessee River below Chattanooga. Through this narrow gorge in Raccoon Mountain the water rushes with such force that vessels cannot stem the current under their own steam. The little *Chattanooga* could not be rendered the customary assistance of windlass and shore-lines while Bragg's forces invested the river, consequently she could ascend it only so far as Kelly's Ferry. In the picture one of the river steamers acquired after the occupation is being warped through this difficult part of the stream.

COPYRIGHT, 1911, REVIEW OF REVIEWS CO.

THE RIVER OPENED

The success of the little *Chattanooga* spurred the Federal saw-mill at Bridgeport to renewed activity. Captain Edwards' shipyard was greatly enlarged after the defeat of Bragg, and in a remarkably short time thirteen staunch transports and four light-draft gunboats were built. Their trial trips during the spring and summer of 1864 were watched with interest because of the difficulties of navigation at "the Suck," where the current of the Tennessee River prevented the small craft from ascending under their own steam.

THE READY RIVER ROUTE

Here, waiting to get through the "Suck," below Chattanooga, are some of the light-draft river steamers which enabled Grant to establish communications almost immediately after his successful encounter with Bragg. The smoke of the Chattanooga battles had scarely cleared away when the two little steamboats then at the disposal of the Federals were loaded with supplies for Burnside, besieged in Knoxville. They were to steam up the Tennessee, abreast of the troops, as far as the mouth of the Holston River, so that their freight might reach Burnside's famished troops as soon as the reënforcements drove off Longstreet. When this was done the river steamers plying between Knoxville and Chattanooga were kept busy and the former became a secondary base. Preparations for the Spring campaign were now set afoot. There were two objectives in Grant's mind. General Joseph E. Johnston had succeeded Bragg in

FEDERAL TRANSPORTS IN THE TENNESSEE, WINTER OF 1863–4

command of the Confederate forces, and to vanquish his army and obtain possession of Atlanta were the important things. But Grant looked further into the future. An expedition against Mobile was seriously considered, and from Nashville, to which place Grant had returned, the telegraph wires were kept busy. Every effort was made to strengthen the Federal positions and prepare for the important movements that were to follow. Early in January, 1864, the Commander-in-Chief, with his staff, returned to Chattanooga, and, boarding one the little river steamers, proceeded up the Tennessee as far as its junction with the Clinch River, up to which point the tedious repairs of the railroad from Knoxville to Chattanooga had progressed. From Knoxville Grant and his staff rode out over the frozen and difficult road to inspect the line of communication from Cumberland Gap that it was necessary to abandon or improve.

PREPARING FOR PERMANENT OCCUPATION

Bragg was now definitely driven from Tennessee, and his beaten army lay in winter quarters at Dalton, Georgia, holding the railroad to Atlanta. Longstreet had failed at Knoxville, and after a winter of hardship in the unfriendly mountain regions was to make his way back to Lee for the final struggle. This bridge was the last link in the connection by rail between Nashville and Chattanooga, and the Federal engineers at once set about rebuilding it so that trains might be run into the latter city, which was now made

MILITARY RAILROAD BRIDGE OVER CHATTANOOGA CREEK, DECEMBER, 1863

a military post.   The original structure was destroyed by Bragg September 7, 1863, when he withdrew from Chattanooga, outflanked by Rosecrans.   Grant had saved the Army of the Cumberland and Chattanooga, and Sherman had pressed forward to the relief of Burnside at Knoxville, driving off Longstreet.   Chattanooga and Knoxville, now occupied by the Federals, were to become new bases for still greater and more aggressive operations by Sherman against the Confederate army in Georgia the following year.

COUNTRY HARD TO HOLD

Whiteside Valley, Tennessee. Over such difficult ground as this the Army of the Cumberland had to make its way in the Chattanooga campaign. Therein lay one valid reason why the Confederates were not sooner swept from eastern Tennessee, as President Lincoln and the War Department at Washington impatiently expected. Only the men who marched over the mountain roads knew to the full the hardships that the task involved. Railroad communications were constantly threatened and interrupted and, when this happened, the daily bread of the soldiers must be hauled in groaning wagon-trains by long, roundabout routes over the almost impassable mountain roads. On these roads points open to attack had to be properly guarded. Even the crude bridges shown in the picture must be commanded by protecting blockhouses or the army might be without food for days.

COMMUNICATION COMPLETED

Railroad Bridge Across the Ravine of Running Water at Whiteside, Tennessee. In this picture stands one of the most notable of the almost incredible achievements of army engineers in the Civil War. Between Whiteside and Wauhatchie the railroad on its way in Chattanooga curves southward almost along the boundary of Alabama, and the destroyed bridge at Whiteside had to be replaced before trains could be run into Chattanooga, which was to be held as a Federal military post and base for future operations in Georgia. Here, fourteen miles from Chattanooga, the engineers built this four-tier trestle-bridge, 780 feet long and 116 feet high in the center, completing the work in a remarkably short time toward the close of 1863. Plans for Sherman's Atlanta campaign were already formulating and it was necessary that this bridge in its isolated position should be strongly held. The camp of the Federal detachment constantly on guard here is seen in the picture, and two of the four double-cased blockhouses, which served as refuges from any attack.

Orchard Knob the crest of Missionary Ridge was occupied by Federal troops. Sheridan did not stop here. He went down the eastern slope, driving all in front of him toward Chickamauga Creek. On a more easterly ridge he rested until midnight, when he advanced to the creek and took many prisoners and stores.

While the Army of the Cumberland accomplished these things, Hooker was advancing his divisions at charging pace from the south. Cruft was on the crest, Osterhaus in the eastern valley, and Geary in the western—all within easy supporting distance. Before Cruft's onrush the left wing of Bragg's army was scattered in all directions from the ridge. Many ran down the eastern slope into Osterhaus' column and the very few who chose a way of flight to the west, were captured by Geary. The bulk of them, however, fell back from trench to trench upon the crest until finally, as the sun was sinking, they found themselves surrounded by Johnson's division of the Army of the Cumberland. Such was the fate of Stewart's division; only a small portion of it got away.

On the Confederate right Hardee held his own against Sherman, but with the left and center routed and in rapid flight Bragg realized the day was lost. He could do nothing but cover Breckinridge's retreat as best he might and order Hardee to retire across Chickamauga Creek.

Thus ended the battle of Chattanooga. Bragg's army had been wholly defeated, and, after being pursued for some days, it found a resting place at Dalton among the mountains of Georgia. The Federal victory was the result of a campaign carefully planned by Generals Halleck and Grant and ably carried out by the efforts of the subordinate generals.

The losses in killed and wounded sustained by Grant were over fifty-eight hundred and those of Bragg about sixty-six hundred, four thousand being prisoners. But the advantage of the great position had been forever wrested from the Southern army.

PART V

ENGAGEMENTS
OF THE CIVIL WAR

THE SIEGE OF CHARLESTON, JULY–SEPTEMBER, 1863.
A BREACHING BATTERY IN THE MARSHES. BELOW
ARE FEDERAL MORTARS ON MORRIS ISLAND,
TURNED AGAINST SUMTER

ENGAGEMENTS OF THE CIVIL WAR

WITH LOSSES ON BOTH SIDES

AUGUST, 1862—APRIL, 1864

CHRONOLOGICAL summary and record of historical events, and of important engagements between the Union and the Confederate armies, in the Civil War in the United States, showing troops participating, losses and casualties, collated and compiled by George L. Kilmer from the official records of the Union and Confederate armies filed in the United States War Department. Minor engagements are omitted; also some concerning which statistics, especially Confederate, are not available.

AUGUST, 1862.

3.—Jonesboro', L'Anguille Ferry, Ark. *Union*, 1st Wis. Cav.; *Confed.*, Parsons' Texas Rangers. Losses: *Union*, 11 killed, 33 wounded, 21 missing; *Confed.**

5.—Baton Rouge, La. *Union*, 14th Me., 6th Mich., 7th Vt., 21st Ind., 30th Mass., 9th Conn., 4th Wis., 2d, 4th, and 6th Mass. Batteries; *Confed.*, Four brigades under command of Gen. John C. Breckinridge, Semmes' Battery and Pond's Partisan Rangers. Losses: *Union*, 82 killed, 255 wounded, 34 missing; *Confed.*, 84 killed, 316 wounded, 78 missing; *Union*, Brig.-Gen. Thomas Williams killed.

—Malvern Hill, Va. *Union*, Portion of Hooker's Div., Third Corps, and Richardson's Div., Second Corps and Cavalry, Army of the Potomac; *Confed.*, Divisions of Longstreet, McLaws, Jones, and Ripley, Army of Northern Virginia, Gen. R. E. Lee commanding. Losses: *Union*, 3 killed, 11 wounded; *Confed.*, 100 captured.

6.—Kirksville, Mo. *Union*, Detachments commanded by Col. John McNeil, 2d Mo. Cav.; *Opponents*, Porter's independent forces. Losses: *Union*, 28 killed, 60 wounded (estimated); Porter's loss, 128 killed, 200 wounded (estimated).

—Matapony or Thornburg, Va. *Union*, Gen. John Gibbons' Brigade; *Confed.*, Stuart's Cav. Losses: *Union*, 1 killed, 12 wounded, 72 missing; *Confed.**

9.—Cedar Mountain, Va., also called Slaughter Mountain, Southwest Mountain, Cedar Run, and Mitchell's Station. *Union*, Second Corps, Maj.-Gen. Banks; Third Corps, Maj.-Gen. McDowell; Army of Virginia, under command of Maj.-Gen. Pope; *Confed.*, Army commanded by Gen. T. J. ("Stonewall") Jackson as follows: Gen. C. S. Winder's Division; Gen. R. S. Ewell's Division; Gen. A. P. Hill's Division. Losses: *Union*, 450 killed, 660 wounded, 290 missing; *Confed.*, 229 killed, 1,047 wounded, 31 missing; *Union*, Brig.-Gens. Augur, Carroll, and Geary wounded; *Confed.*, Brig.-Gen. C. S. Winder killed.

10 to 13.—Grand River, Lee's Ford, Chariton River, Walnut Creek, Compton Ferry, Switzler's Mills, and Yellow Creek, Mo. *Union*, 9th Mo. Cav.; *Opponents*, Poindexter's Independent forces. Losses: *Union*, 5 wounded. Poindexter lost 150 men killed and wounded, 100 captured [estimated].

11.—Independence, Mo. *Union*, 7th Mo. Cav.; *Confed.*, Col. J. T. Hughes' command. Losses: *Union*, 26 killed, 30 wounded, 256 missing; *Confed.**

12.—Gallatin, Tenn. *Union*, 28th Ky. (4 co's) surrendered to Morgan's Cavalry.

16.—Lone Jack, Mo. *Union*, 7th Mo. Cav.; *Confed.*, Col. Cockrell's Cav. Losses: *Union*, 43 killed, 54 wounded, 73 missing; *Confed.*, 118 killed and wounded.

* No record found.

THE GENERAL–IN–CHIEF IN 1862

Major-General Henry Wager Halleck; born 1814; West Point 1839; died 1872. Sherman credits Halleck with having first discovered that Forts Henry and Donelson, where the Tennessee and the Cumberland Rivers so closely approach each other, were the keypoints to the defensive line of the Confederates in the West.   Succeeding Fremont in November, 1861, Halleck, importuned by both Grant and Foote, authorized the joint expedition into Tennessee, and after its successful outcome he telegraphed to Washington: "Make Buell, Grant, and Pope major-generals of volunteers and give me command in the West.   I ask this in return for Donelson and Henry." He was chosen to be General-in-Chief of the Federal Armies at the crisis created by the failure of McClellan's Peninsula Campaign.   Halleck held this position from July 11, 1862, until Grant, who had succeeded him in the West, finally superseded him at Washington.

19.—Clarksville, Tenn. *Union,* 71st Ohio (5 co's) surrendered to Confederates commanded by Col. A. R. Johnson. Losses: *Union,* 350 captured.

23.—Big Hill, Madison Co., Ky. *Union,* 3d Tenn. (Houk's Battalion), 7th Ky. Cav.; *Confed.,* 1st La. Cav. Losses: *Union,* 120 killed, wounded, and missing (estimate); *Confed.,* 4 killed, 12 wounded.

23 to 25.—Skirmishes on the Rappahannock at Waterloo Bridge, Lee Springs, Freeman's Ford and Sulphur Springs, Va. *Union,* Milroy's Brigade, Army of Virginia; *Confed.,* Gen. Longstreet's command. Losses: *Confed.,* 27 killed, 94 wounded; *Union,* Brig.-Gen. Bohlen captured.

23 to Sept. 1.—Pope's Campaign in Virginia. *Union,* Army of Virginia, commanded by Gen. John Pope; *Confed.,* Army of Northern Virginia, commanded by Gen. R. E. Lee. Losses: *Union,* 1747 killed, 8452 wounded, and 4623 missing; *Confed.,* 1090 killed, 6154 wounded.

25 and 26.—Fort Donelson and Cumberland Iron Works, Tenn. *Union,* 71st Ohio (4 co's), 5th Ia. Cav.; *Confed.,* Col. Woodward's command. Losses: *Union,* 31 killed and wounded; *Confed.,* 30 killed and wounded.

27.—Bull Run Bridge, Va. *Union,* 11th and 12th Ohio, 1st, 2d, 3d, and 4th N. J.; *Confed.,* Part of Gen. "Stonewall" Jackson's command. Losses: * *Union,* Brig.-Gen. G. W. Taylor mortally wounded.

—Kettle Run, Va. *Union,* Maj.-Gen. Hooker's Div. of Third Corps; *Confed.,* Ewell's Division of Jackson's Corps. Losses: *Union,* 300 killed and wounded; *Confed.,* 300 killed and wounded.

28 and 29.—Groveton and Gainesville, Va. *Union,* First Corps, Maj.-Gen. Sigel, Third Corps, Maj.-Gen. McDowell, Army of Virginia, Hooker's and Kearny's Divisions of Third Corps and Reynolds' Division of First Corps, Army of Potomac, Ninth Corps, Maj.-Gen. Reno, Buford's cavalry brigade (Second Corps); *Confed.,* Army of Northern Virginia commanded by Gen. Robert E. Lee, as follows: Right Wing, Gen. James Longstreet's Corps; Left Wing, Gen. T. J. Jackson's Corps; Cavalry Division, Gen. J. E. B. Stuart. Casualties included in those given for the campaign, Aug. 23 to Sept. 1.

—McMinnville, Tenn. *Union,* 18th Ohio (2 co's) 9th Mich. (1 co); *Confed.,* Forrest's Cav. Losses: *Union,* 9 wounded; *Confed.,* 12 killed, 41 wounded.

30.—Second Battle of Bull Run or Manassas, Va. Same troops as engaged at Groveton and Gainesville on the 28th and 29th, with the addition of Porter's Fifth Corps (*Union*). Casualties included as above.

—Bolivar, Tenn. *Union,* 20th, 78th Ohio, 2d Ill. Cav. (4 co's), 11th Ill. Cav. (2 co's) 9th Ind. Battery; *Confed.,* Armstrong's Cavalry. Losses: *Union,* 5 killed, 18 wounded, 64 missing. *Confed.,* 100 killed and wounded (estimate).

—Richmond, Ky. *Union,* 12th, 16th, 55th, 66th, 69th and 71st Ind., 95th Ohio, 18th Ky., 6th and 7th Ky. Cav., Batteries D and G Mich. Art.; *Confed.,* Four brigades under Generals Kirby Smith and Patrick Cleburne. Losses: *Union,* 200 killed, 700 wounded, 4000 missing; *Confed.,* 250 killed, 500 wounded.

SEPTEMBER, 1862

1.—Britton's Lane, Tenn. *Union,* 20th and 30th Ill., 4th Ill. Cav., Foster's (Ohio) Cav., Battery A 2d Ill. Art. *Confed.,* Gen. F. C. Armstrong's command. Losses: *Union,* 5 killed, 51 wounded, 52 missing; *Confed.,* 179 killed, 100 wounded. (Union Report.)

—Chantilly, Va. *Union,* McDowell's Corps, Army of Virginia. Hooker's and Kearny's Divisions of Third Corps, Army of Potomac, Reno's Ninth Corps; *Confed.,* "Stonewall" Jackson's Corps. Losses: *Union,* 1300 killed, wounded, and missing; *Confed.,* 800 *killed,* wounded, and missing; *Union,* Maj.-Gen. Kearny and Brig.-Gen. Stevens killed.

6.—Washington, N. C. *Union,* 24th Mass., 1st N. C., 3d N. Y. Cav.; *Confed.,* Gen. J. G. Martin's command. Losses: *Union,* 7 killed, 47 wounded; *Confed.,* 30 killed, 100 wounded.

10.—Fayetteville, W. Va. *Union,* 34th, 37th Ohio, 4th W. Va.; *Confed.,* Gen. W. W. Loring's command. Losses: *Union,* 13 killed, 80 wounded.

* No record found.

A DARING MOVE OF SEPTEMBER, 1862

Ruins of the Bridge at Harper's Ferry, Virginia. Lee had invaded Maryland. Boldly dividing his army, which was but two-thirds as strong as that of McClellan, who was confronting him with seventy-five thousand men, he sent the swift and silent Jackson to capture Harper's Ferry, renowned as the place where John Brown was captured. Europe, watching with keen interest the progress of the war, was dazzled by the splendid coöperation of the two great Confederate leaders. By the stroke at Harper's Ferry Lee removed an element of danger from his rear, while his advance into Maryland was causing consternation throughout the North. The Federal garrison of twelve thousand five hundred men at Harper's Ferry, out-numbered and out-maneuvered by Jackson, surrendered on September 15th, after a two-days' defense, and Jackson rejoined Lee in Maryland just in time to stem the tide at Antietam.

[B]

12 to 15.—Harper's Ferry, Va. *Union,* 39th, 111th, 115th, 125th, and 126th N. Y., 12th N. Y. Militia, 32d, 60th, and 87th Ohio, 9th Vt., 65th Ill., 15th Ind., 1st and 3d Md. Home Brigade, 8th N. Y. Cav., 12th Ill. Cav., 7th Squadron R. I. Cav., five batteries of Artil.; *Confed.,* Gen. T. J. Jackson's Corps; Gen. R. H. Anderson's Division; Gen. J. G. Walker's Division; Gen. Lafayette McLaws' Division. Losses: *Union,* 44 killed, 173 wounded, 12520 missing and captured; *Confed.,* 500 killed and wounded.

14.—Turner's and Crampton's Gap, South Mountain, Md. *Union,* First Corps, Maj.-Gen. Hooker; Sixth Corps, Maj.-Gen. Franklin; Ninth Corps, Maj.-Gen. Reno; *Confed.,* Gen. D. H. Hill's Division; Gen. Lafayette McLaws' Division. Losses: *Union,* 443 killed, 1806 wounded. *Confed.,* 500 killed, 2343 wounded, 1500 captured; *Union,* Maj.-Gen. Reno killed; *Confed.,* Brig.-Gen. Garland killed.

14 to 16.—Mumfordsville, Ky. *Union,* 18th U. S. Inft., 28th and 33d Ky., 17th, 50th, 60th, 67th, 68th, 74th, 78th, and 89th Ind., Conkle's Battery, 13th Ind. Artil., and Louisville Provost Guard; *Confed.,* Army of the Tennessee, commanded by Gen. Braxton Bragg. Losses: *Union,* 50 killed, 3566 captured and missing; *Confed.,* 714 killed and wounded.

17.—Antietam or Sharpsburg, Md. *Union,* Army of the Potomac, commanded by Maj.-Gen. Geo. B. McClellan, as follows: First Corps, Maj.-Gen. Joseph Hooker; Second Corps, Maj.-Gen. E. V. Sumner; Fifth Corps, Maj.-Gen. Fitz-John Porter; Sixth Corps, Maj.-Gen. W. B. Franklin; Ninth Corps, Maj.-Gen. A. E. Burnside; Twelfth Corps, Maj.-Gen. J. K. F. Mansfield, Brig.-Gen. Alpheus Williams; Couch's Div., Fourth Corps; Pleasonton's Cavalry; *Confed.,* Army of Northern Virginia, commanded by Gen. Robert E. Lee, as follows: Maj.-Gen. James Longstreet's Corps; Maj.-Gen. T. J. Jackson's Corps; Reserve Artillery, Gen. W. N. Pendleton, Gen. J. E. B. Stuart's Cavalry. Losses: *Union,* 2010 killed, 9416 wounded, 1043 missing; *Confed.,* total in the campaign, 1890 killed, 9770 wounded, 2304 missing; *Union,* Maj.-Gen. Mansfield killed, Maj.-Gens. Hooker and Richardson, and

Brig.-Gens. Rodman, Weber, Sedgwick, Hartsuff, Dana, and Meagher wounded; *Confed.,* Brig.-Gens. Branch, Anderson, and Starke killed, Maj.-Gen. Anderson, Brig.-Gens. Toombs, Lawton, Ripley, Rodes, Gregg, Armistead, and Ransom wounded.

19 and 20.—Iuka, Miss. *Union,* Stanley's and Hamilton's Divisions, Army of the Mississippi, under Maj.-Gen. Rosecrans; *Confed.,* Gen. Sterling Price, Army of the West; Gen. Henry Little's Division, Gen. Frank C. Armstrong's Cavalry. Losses: *Union,* 144 killed, 598 wounded; *Confed.,* 263 killed, 692 wounded, 561 captured; *Confed.,* Brig.-Gens. Little killed and Whitfield wounded.

20.—Blackford's Ford, Shepherdstown, Va. *Union,* Fifth Corps, Griffin's and Barnes' Brigades; *Confed.,* Gen. A. P. Hill's Division. Losses: *Union,* 92 killed, 131 wounded, 103 missing; *Confed.,* 33 killed, 231 wounded.

30.—Newtonia, Mo. *Union,* 1st Brigade Army of Kansas, 4th Brigade Mo. Militia Cav.; *Confed.,* 3000 Indians under Col. D. H. Cooper, Gen. Shelby's Cav. Losses: *Union,* 50 killed, 80 wounded, 115 missing; *Confed.,* 220 killed, 280 wounded.

OCTOBER, 1862.

1.—Shepherdstown, Va. *Union,* 8th Ill., 8th Penna., 3d Ind. Cav., Pennington's Battery; *Confed.,* Stuart's Cav. Losses: *Union,* 12 wounded; *Confed.,* 60 killed.

3 and 4.—Corinth, Miss. *Union,* McKean's, Davies', Hamilton's, and Stanley's Divisions, Army of the Miss.; *Confed.,* Army of West Tennessee, commanded by Gen. Earl Van Dorn, Gen. Price's Corps, and Gen. Mansfield Lovell's Division of Mississippians. Losses: *Union,* 315 killed, 1812 wounded, 232 missing; *Confed.,* 1423 killed, 5692 wounded, 2248 missing. *Union,* Brig.-Gens. Hackleman killed and Oglesby wounded.

5.—Metamora, on Big Hatchie River, Miss. *Union,* Hurlburt's and Ord's Divisions; *Confed.,* Rear-Guard of Van Dorn's Army. Losses: *Union,* 500 killed and wounded; *Confed.,* 400 killed and wounded.

7.—La Vergne, Tenn. *Union,* Palmer's Brigade; *Confed.,* Outposts of Bragg's

THE ABANDONED STRONGHOLD

Maryland Heights, in the rear of Harper's Ferry. The Federal retreat from this position on September 13, 1862, sealed the fate of Harper's Ferry. Colonel Ford was dismissed from the service for yielding it so easily. From this commanding hill and from Loudon Heights (on the Virginia side of the Potomac) the Confederate artillery could enfilade the Federal rifle-pits on Bolivar Heights. These can be seen in the opposite picture, rising amid the houses. McClellan had urged that the garrison be withdrawn, as the position could be easily reoccupied. But when one of Lee's despatches fell into his hands, acquainting him with Jackson's daring movement to capture it, he pushed forward rapidly two divisions under Franklin to prevent its fall—but in vain. Jackson's haul of more than twelve thousand prisoners had been equaled only at Fort Donelson.

Engagements of the Civil War

Army. Losses: *Union,* 5 killed, 9 wounded; *C o n f e d.,* 80 killed and wounded, 175 missing.

8.—Perryville, Ky. *Union,* First Corps, Army of the Ohio, Maj.-Gen. McCook, and Third Corps, Brig.-Gen. Gilbert; *Confed.,* Gen. Braxton Bragg's Army, Gen. B. F. Cheatham's and Simon B. Buckner's Divisions, Gen. J o s e p h Wheeler's Cav. Losses: *Union,* 916 killed, 2943 wounded, 489 missing; *Confed.,* 2500 killed, wounded, and missing. *Union,* Brig.-Gens. J. S. Jackson and Terrill killed; *Confed.,* Brig.-Gens. Cleburne, Wood, and Brown wounded.

10.—Harrodsburg, Ky. *Union,* Troops commanded by Lieut.-Col. Boyle, 9th Ky. Cav.; *Confed.,* same as at Perryville. Losses: *Confed.,* 1600 captured.

17.—Lexington, Ky. *Union,* Detach. 3d and 4th Ohio Cav.; *Confed.,* Gen. J. H. Morgan's Cav. Losses: *Union,* 4 killed, 24 wounded, 350 missing.

22.—Pocotaligo or Yemassee, S. C. *Union,* 47th, 55th, and 76th Penna., 48th N. Y., 6th and 7th Conn., 3d and 4th N. H., 3d R. I., 1st N. Y. Engineers, 1st Mass. Cav., Batteries B, D, and M 1st U. S. Artil. and E 3d U. S. Artil.; *Confed.,* Gen. W. S. Walker's Command. Losses: *Union,* 43 killed, 258 wounded; *Confed.,* 14 killed, 102 wounded.

NOVEMBER, 1862.

1.—Philomont, Va. *Union,* Pleasonton's Cav.; *Confed.,* Stuart's Cav. Losses: *Union,* 1 killed, 14 wounded; *Confed.,* 5 killed, 10 wounded.

2 and 3.—Bloomfield and Union, Loudon Co., Va. *Union,* Pleasonton's Cav.; *Confed.,* Stuart's Cav. Losses: *Union,* 2 killed, 10 wounded; *Confed.,* 3 killed, 15 wounded.

5.—Barbee's Cross Roads and Chester Gap, Va. *Union,* Pleasonton's Cav.; *Confed.,* Gen. J. E. B. Stuart's Cav. Losses, *Union,* 5 killed, 16 wounded; *Confed.,* 36 killed.

—Nashville, Tenn. *Union,* 16th and 51st Ill., 69th Ohio, 14th Mich., 78th Pa., 5th Tenn. Cav., 7th Pa. Cav.; *Confed.,* Cheatham's Division, Wheeler's Cav. Losses: *Union,* 26 wounded; *Confed.,* 23 captured.

7.—Big Beaver Creek, Mo. 10th Ill., two Cos. Mo. Militia Cav.; *Confed.* Losses: *Union,* 300 captured.

—Marianna, Ark. *Union,* 3d and 4th Iowa, 9th Ill. Cav.; *Confed.* Losses: *Union,* 3 killed, 20 wounded; *Confed.,* 50 killed and wounded.

8.—Hudsonville, Miss. *Union,* 7th Kan. Cav., 2d Iowa Cav.; *Confed.* Losses: *Confed.,* 16 killed, 185 captured.

24.—Beaver Creek, Mo. *Union,* 21st Iowa, 3d Mo. Cav.; *Confed.,* Campbell's Cav. Losses: *Union,* 6 killed, 10 wounded; *Confed.,* 5 killed, 20 wounded.

28.—Cane Hill, Boston Mountain, and Boonsboro', Ark. *Union,* 1st Division Army of the Frontier; *Confed.,* Gen. Jno. S. Marmaduke's Cav. Losses: *Union,* 4 killed, 36 wounded; *Confed.,* 75 killed, 300 wounded.

—Hartwood Church, Va. *Union,* 3d Pa. Cav.; *Confed.,* Gen. Hampton's Cav. Losses: *Union,* 4 killed, 9 wounded, 200 missing.

DECEMBER, 1862.

5.—Coffeeville, Miss. *Union,* 1st, 2d, and 3d Cav. Brigades, Army of the Tennessee; *Confed.,* Gen. John C. Pemberton, Army of Vicksburg defense. Losses: *Union,* 10 killed, 54 wounded; *Confed.,* 7 killed, 43 wounded.

7.—Prairie Grove or Fayetteville, Ark. *Union,* 1st, 2d, and 3d Divisions Army of the Frontier; *Confed.,* Gen. T. C. Hindman's command, and Gen. Marmaduke's Cav. Losses: *Union,* 167 killed, 798 wounded, 183 missing; *Confed.,* 300 killed, 1200 wounded and missing.

—Hartsville, Tenn. *Union,* 106th and 108th Ohio, 104th Ill., 2d Ind. Cav., 11th Ky. Cav., 13th Ind. Battery; *Confed.,* Gen. Basil Duke's Cav. Brigade, Hanson's Kentucky Infantry, Cobb's Battery. Losses: *Union,* 58 killed, 204 wounded, 1834 captured; *Confed.,* 21 killed, 114 wounded.

9.—Dobbin's Ferry, Tenn. *Union,* 35th Ind., 51st Ohio, 8th and 21st Ky., 7th Ind. Battery; *Confed.,* Wheeler's Cav. Losses: *Union,* 5 killed, 48 wounded.

12 to 18.—Foster's expedition to G o l d s-boro', N. C. *Union,* 1st, 2d, and 3d Brigades of First Division and Wessell's

* No record found.

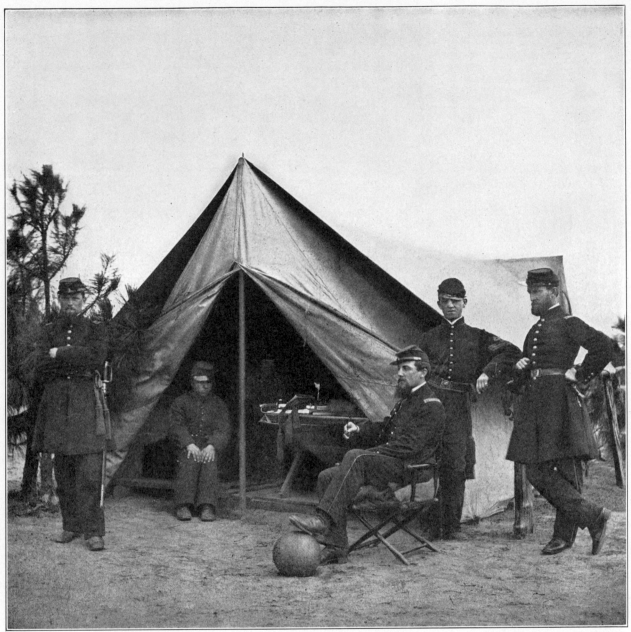

IN SOUTH CAROLINA

With his foot on the cannon-ball sits Captain Michael J. Donohoe, commanding at the time—1862—Company C of the Third New Hampshire. On the left is Lieutenant Allen, and on the right Lieutenant Cody. At the battle of Secessionville, Captain Donohoe's company was stationed on the left and received the first fire of the Confederate reënforcements. Both lieutenants were wounded. Thus in June, 1862, these gallant officers first came into notice, and Captain Donohoe rose rapidly to the rank of colonel, commanding the Tenth New Hampshire. At Fredericksburg, on December 17, 1862, the Tenth New Hampshire (organized September, 1862) was under fire for the first time and acquitted itself creditably for raw troops. Colonel Donohoe and his regiment were transferred to the Army of the James, where his old regiment, the Third New Hampshire, was distinguishing itself. On September 29, 1864, Colonel Donohoe was wounded while leading his troops at Fort Harrison, near Richmond. His gallantry was mentioned by General Ord in despatches, and he was brevetted brigadier-general September 27, 1864.

Engagements of the Civil War

Brigade of Peck's Division, Dep't of North Carolina; *Confed.,* Robertson's, Clingman's and Evans' brigades. Losses: *Union,* 90 killed, 478 wounded; *Confed.,* 71 killed, 268 wounded, 400 missing.

13.—Fredericksburg, Va. *Union,* Army of the Potomac, Maj.-Gen. Burnside; Right Grand Div., Maj.-Gen. Sumner; Second Corps, Maj.-Gen. Couch; Ninth Corps, Maj.-Gen. Wilcox. Left Grand Div., Maj.-Gen. Franklin; First Corps, Gen. Reynolds; Sixth Corps, Maj.-Gen. W. F. Smith. Center Grand Div., Maj.-Gen. Hooker. Third Corps, Maj.-Gen. Stoneman; Fifth Corps, Maj.-Gen. Butterfield. *Confed.,* Army of Northern Virginia, Gen. Robert E. Lee; First Corps, Gen. Longstreet; Second Corps, "Stonewall" Jackson; Artillery Reserve, Gen. W. N. Pendleton; Gen. Stuart's Cavalry. Losses: *Union,* 1180 killed, 9028 wounded, 2145 missing; *Confed.,* 579 killed, 3870 wounded, 127 missing. *Union,* Brig.-Gens. Jackson and Bayard killed and Gibbon and Vinton wounded; *Confed.,* Brig.-Gen. T. R. R. Cobb killed and Maxcy Gregg wounded.

14.—Kingston, N. C. *Union,* 1st, 2d, and 3d Brigades 1st Div. and Wessell's Brigade of Peck's Division, Dep't of North Carolina; *Confed.,* Gen. N. G. Evans' Command. Losses: *Union,* 40 killed, 120 wounded; *Confed.,* 50 killed, 75 wounded, 400 missing.

18.—Lexington, Tenn. *Union,* 11th Ill. Cav., 5th Ohio Cav., 2d Tenn. Cav.; *Confed.,* Forrest's Cav. Losses: *Union,* 7 killed, 10 wounded, 124 missing. *Confed.,* 7 killed, 28 wounded.

20.—Holly Springs, Miss. *Union,* 2d Ill. Cav. (6 co's), 8th Wis., part of 62d Ill.; *Confed.,* Earl Van Dorn's Cav. Losses: *Union,* 9 killed, 39 wounded, 1500 captured.
—Trenton, Tenn. *Union,* Detachments 122d Ill., 7th Tenn. Cav., and convalescents; *Confed.,* Forrest's Cav. Losses: *Union,* 1 killed, 250 prisoners; *Confed.,* 17 killed, 50 wounded.

21.—Davis' Mills, Miss. *Union,* Six Cos. 25th Ind., two Cos. 5th Ohio Cav.; *Confed.,* Earl Van Dorn's Cav. Losses: *Union,* 3 wounded; *Confed.,* 22 killed, 50 wounded, 20 missing.

24.—Middleburg, Tenn. *Union,* 115 men of 12th Mich.; *Confed.,* Griffith's Texas Brigade. Losses: *Union,* 9 wounded; *Confed.,* 9 killed, 11 wounded.

25.—Green's Chapel, Ky. *Union,* Detachment of 4th and 5th Ind. Cav.; *Confed.,* Morgan's Cav. Losses: *Union,* 1 killed; *Confed.,* 9 killed, 22 wounded.

26.—Bacon Creek, Ky. *Union,* 91st Ill.; *Confed.,* Morgan's Cav. Losses: *Union,* 3 wounded, 93 captured.

27.—Elizabethtown, Ky. *Union,* 91st Ill. 500 men captured by Morgan.
—Dumfries, Va. *Union,* 5th, 7th, and 66th Ohio, 12th Ill. Cav., 1st Md. Cav., 6th Maine Battery; *Confed.,* Stuart's Cav. Losses: *Union,* 3 killed, 8 wounded; *Confed.,* 25 killed, 40 wounded.

28.—Bacon Creek, Ky. *Union,* 91st Ill.; Ky. Cav.; *Confed.* Losses: *Confed.,* 30 killed, 176 wounded, 51 missing.

28 and 29.—Chickasaw Bayou, Vicksburg, Miss. *Union,* Thirteenth Army Corps, Maj.-Gen. W. T. Sherman, Brig.-Gens. G. W. Morgan's, Frederick Steele's, M. L. Smith's, and A. J. Smith's Divisions; *Confed.,* Gen. Pemberton's Army, M. L. Smith's and S. D. Lee's Divisions. Losses: *Union,* 191 killed, 982 wounded, 756 missing; *Confed.,* 63 killed, 134 wounded, 10 missing; *Union,* Maj.-Gen. M. L. Smith wounded.

30.—Wautauga Bridge and Carter's Station, Tenn. *Union,* 7th Ohio Cav., 9th Pa. Cav.; *Confed.,* Gen. Humphrey Marshall's command. Losses: *Union,* 1 killed, 2 wounded; *Confed.,* 7 killed, 15 wounded, 273 missing.
—Jefferson, Tenn. *Union,* Second Brigade 1st Division Thomas' corps; *Confed.,* Wheeler's Cav. Losses: *Union,* 20 killed, 40 wounded; *Confed.,* 15 killed, 50 wounded.
—Parker's Cross Roads or Red Mound, Tenn. *Union,* 18th, 106th, 119th, and 122d Ill., 27th, 39th, and 63d Ohio, 50th Ind., 39th Iowa, 7th Tenn., 7th Wis. Battery; *Confed.,* Forrest's Cav. Losses: *Union,* 23 killed, 139 wounded, 58 missing; *Confed.,* 50 killed, 150 wounded, 300 missing.

31 to Jan. 2.—Murfreesboro' or Stone's River, Tenn. *Union,* Army of the Cumberland, Maj.-Gen. Rosecrans; Right

* No record found.

[328]

A NEW ENGLAND REGIMENT IN THE SOUTH

Company F, Third New Hampshire Volunteers. Organized in August, 1861, this regiment first saw active service in South Carolina. Accompanying the famous Port Royal Expedition, by which a Federal foothold was first gained in Southern territory, the regiment was stationed at Hilton Head, November 4, 1861. While Port Royal was being elaborately equipped as a naval and military base, the troops were constantly coöperating with the gunboats in reconnaissances, the ultimate object being operations against Savannah and Charleston. At the beginning of 1862 Confederate troops were found to be massing for the purpose of shutting up the Federals on Port Royal Island, and General Stevens, determining to nip the attempt in the bud, began active operations which were pushed close to both Savannah and Charleston. The Federals succeeded in occupying the southwestern portion of James' Island on the Stono River, after skirmishes at Pocotaglio, St. John's Island, and James' Island. On June 16th a battle took place at Secessionville, within five or six miles of Charleston, in which the Federals were defeated, and in this the Third New Hampshire, under command of Colonel John H. Jackson, established its reputation for gallantry, losing 104 men.

Engagements of the Civil War

Wing, McCook's Corps; C e n t e r, Thomas' Corps; Left Wing, Crittenden's Corps; *Confed.*, Army of the Tennessee, Gen. Braxton Bragg; L. K. Polk's Corps, W. J. Hardee's Corps, Wheeler's Cav. Losses: *Union*, 1,533 killed, 7245 wounded, 2800 missing; *Confed.*, 1294 killed, 7945 wounded, 1027 missing. *Union*, Brig.-Gens. Sill killed and Kirk wounded; *Confed.*, Brig.-Gens. Rains and Hanson killed and Chalmers and Davis wounded.

JANUARY, 1863.

1.—Galveston, Tex. *Union*, Three Cos. 42d Mass., U. S. Gunboats *Westfield, Harriet Lane, Owasco, Sachem, Clifton* and *Coryphæus; Confed.*, Gen. J. B. Magruder's Command, Gunboats *Bayou City* and *Neptune.* Losses: *Union*, 600 killed, wounded, and missing; *Confed.*, 50 killed and wounded.

7. and 8.—Springfield, Mo. *Union*, Mo. Militia, convalescents and citizens; *Confed.*, Marmaduke's Cav. Losses: *Union*, 14 killed, 144 wounded; *Confed.*, 40 killed, 206 wounded and missing. *Union*, Brig.-Gen. Brown wounded.

11.—Fort Hindman, Ark. *Union*, Thirteenth Corps, Maj.-Gen. McClernand; Fifteenth Corps, Maj.-Gen. Sherman and gunboats Mississippi squadron; *Confed.*, Brig.-Gen. T. J. Churchill's command. Losses: *Union*, 129 killed, 831 wounded; *Confed.*, 100 killed, 400 wounded, 5000 prisoners.
—Hartsville or Wood's Fork, Mo. *Union*, 21st Iowa, 99th Ill., 3d Iowa Cav., 3d Mo. Cav., Battery L, 2d Mo. Artil.; *Confed.*, Marmaduke's C a v. Losses: *Union*, 7 killed, 64 wounded; *Confed.*, Brig.-Gen. McDonald killed.

14.—Bayou Teche, La. *Union*, 8th Vt., 16th and 75th N. Y., 12th Conn., 6th Mich., 21st Ind., 1st La. Cav., 4th and 6th Mass. Battery, 1st Maine Battery, and U. S. Gunboats *Calhoun, Diana, Kinsman,* and *Estrella; Confed.*, Gen. Magruder's Command, Gunboat *Cotton.* Losses: *Union*, 10 killed, 27 wounded; *Confed.*, 15 killed. *Union*, Commodore Buchanan killed. *Confed.*, Gunboat *Cotton* destroyed.

24.—Woodbury, Tenn. *Union*, Second Division Crittenden's Corps; *Confed.*, Gen.

Bragg's Command. Losses: *Union*, 2 killed, 1 wounded; *Confed.*, 35 killed, 100 missing.

30.—Deserted House or Kelly's Store, near Suffolk, Va. *Union*, portion of Maj.-Gen. Peck's forces; *Confed.*, 1st S. C. Losses: *Union*, 24 killed, 80 wounded; *Confed.*, 50 wounded.

31.—Rover, Tenn. *Union*, 4th Ohio Cav.; *Confed.*, 51st Ala., 8th Confed. Losses: *Confed.*, 12 killed, 12 wounded, 300 captured.
—Charleston, S. C. Raid of the *Confed.* Gunboats *Palmetto State* and *Chicora* on the *Union* blockading fleet; *Union*, Mercidita, Quaker City,* and *Keystone State, Ottawa, Unadilla, Augusta,* and *Memphis.* Losses: *Union*, 30 killed and wounded.

FEBRUARY, 1863.

3.—Fort Donelson or Cumberland Iron Works, Tenn. *Union*, 83d Ill., 2d Ill. Artil., one battalion 5th Iowa Cav.; *Confed.*, Wheeler's, Forrest's, and Wharton's Cav. Losses: *Union*, 16 killed, 60 wounded, 50 missing; *Confed.*, 140 killed, 400 wounded, 130 missing.

24.—Mississippi River below Vicksburg. *Union*, U. S. Gunboat *Indianola; Confed., The Webb* and *Queen of the West.* Losses: *Union*, 1 killed, 1 wounded; *Confed.*, 35 killed.

MARCH, 1863.

4 and 5.—T h o m p s o n ' s Station, also called Spring Hill and Unionville, Tenn. *Union*, 33d and 85th Ind., 22d Wis., 19th Mich., 124th Ohio, 18th Ohio Battery, 2d Mich. Cav., 9th Pa. Cav., 4th Ky. Cav.; *Confed.*, Earl Van Dorn's Cav. Corps, Forrest's, Martin's, and Jackson's Divisions. Losses: *Union*, 100 killed, 300 wounded, 1306 captured; *Confed.*, 150 killed, 450 wounded.

8.—Fairfax C. H., Va. *Union*, Brig.-Gen. Stoughton and thirty-three men captured by Capt. John S. Mosby (*Confed.*) in a midnight raid.

13 to April 5.—Fort Pemberton, Miss. *Union*, Thirteenth Corps, Brig.-Gen. Ross; Seventeenth Corps, Brig.-Gen. Quimby, U. S. Gunboats *Chillicothe* and

WHERE NEW ORLEANS WAS SAVED, JUNE 28, 1863

Donaldsonville, Louisiana. Within the little Fort Butler (the lower picture), Major J. D. Mullen, at half-past one in the morning of June 28th, with 180 men of the Twenty-eighth Maine, gallantly withstood the assault of 14,000 Confederates sent against the place by General Taylor. By daylight the little garrison, assisted by three gun-boats in the river, completed the repulse. The Confederates retired, leaving behind them, according to Major Mullen's report, 69 dead and 120 prisoners. This prevented Taylor from capturing New Orleans before the capitulation of Port Hudson would permit Banks to detach a sufficient force to drive off the Confederates, who were threatening his communications down the river. New Orleans would undoubtedly have been retaken had Taylor's request for reënforcements not been overruled by Kirby Smith. As it was, Taylor recruited his own forces to about 3,000 and moved against New Orleans in two detachments, getting within twenty-five miles of New Orleans two weeks before Port Hudson surrendered.

DeKalb; Confed., Garrison under Gen. W. W. Loring. Casualties not recorded.

14.—Port Hudson, La. *Union,* Maj.-Gen. Banks' troops and Admiral Farragut's fleet; *Confed.,* Gen. Frank Gardner's Command. Losses: *Union,* 65 wounded.

16 to 22.—Expedition up Steele's Bayou, and at Deer Creek, Miss. *Union,* 2d Division Fifteenth Corps, Maj.-Gen. Sherman, Gunboat fleet, Admiral Porter; *Confed.,* Troops of Gen. Maury's and Gen. S. D. Lee's commands. Casualties not recorded.

17.—Kelly's Ford, Va. *Union,* 1st and 5th U. S. Regulars, 3d, 4th, and 16th Pa., 1st R. I., 6th Ohio, 4th N. Y. Cav., 6th N. Y. Battery; *Confed.,* Stuart's Cav. Losses: *Union,* 9 killed, 35 wounded; *Confed.,* 11 killed, 88 wounded.

20.—Vaught's Hill, near Milton, Tenn. *Union,* 105th Ohio, 101st Ind., 80th and 123d Ill., 1st Tenn. Cav., 9th Ind. Battery; *Confed.,* Morgan's Cav. Losses: *Union,* 7 killed, 48 wounded; *Confed.,* 63 killed, 300 wounded.

22.—Mt. Sterling, Ky. *Union,* 10th Ky. Cav.; *Confed.,* Morgan's Cav. Losses: *Union,* 4 killed, 10 wounded; *Confed.,* 8 killed, 13 wounded.

24.—Danville, Ky. *Union,* 18th and 22d Mich., 1st Ky. Cav., 2d Tenn. Cav., 1st Ind. Battery; *Confed.,* Morgan's Cav.

25.—Brentwood, Tenn. *Union,* Detachment 22d Wis. and 19th Mich.; *Confed.,* Forrest's Cav. Losses: *Union,* 1 killed, 4 wounded, 300 captured; *Confed.,* 1 killed, 5 wounded.

—Franklin and Little Harpeth, Tenn. *Union,* 4th and 6th Ky. Cav., 9th Pa. Cav., 2d Mich. Cav.; *Confed.,* Forrest's Cav. Losses: *Union,* 4 killed, 19 wounded, 40 missing.

28.—Pattersonville, La. *Union,* Gunboat *Diana* with Detachment of 12th Conn. and 160th N. Y. on board; *Confed.,* Gen. Richard Taylor's Command. Losses: *Union,* 4 killed, 14 wounded, 99 missing.

30.—Dutton's Hill or Somerset, Ky. *Union,* 1st Ky. Cav., 7th Ohio Cav., 44th and 45th Ohio Mounted Vol.; *Confed.,* Gen. John Pegram's Command. Losses: *Union,* 10 killed, 25 wounded; *Confed.,* 290 killed, wounded, and missing.

APRIL, 1863.

2 and 3.—Woodbury and Snow Hill, Tenn. *Union,* 3d and 4th Ohio Cav.; *Confed.,* Morgan's Cav. Losses: *Union,* 1 killed, 8 wounded; *Confed.,* 50 killed and wounded.

7.—Bombardment Fort Sumter, S. C. *Union,* South Atlantic squadron; *Keokuk, Weehawken, Passaic, Montauk, Patapsco, New Ironsides, Catskill, Nantucket,* and *Nahant; Confed.,* S. C. Art. in Batteries Beauregard, Wagner, and Bee, Fort Sumter and Fort Moultrie. Losses: *Union,* 2 killed, 20 wounded; *Confed.,* 4 killed, 10 wounded.

10.—Franklin and Harpeth River, Tenn. *Union,* 40th Ohio and portion of Granger's Cav.; *Confed.,* Forrest's Cav. Losses: *Union,* 100 killed and wounded; *Confed.,* 19 killed, 35 wounded, 83 missing.

12 to 14.—Irish Bend and Bisland, La., also called Indian Ridge and Centreville. *Union,* Nineteenth Corps, Grover's, Emory's, and Weitzel's Divisions; *Confed.,* Gen. Richard Taylor's Command, Gunboat *Diana.* Losses: *Union,* 89 killed, 458 wounded, 30 missing; *Confed.***

12 to May 4.—Siege of Suffolk, Va. *Union,* Troops of the Army of Virginia and Department of North Carolina; *Confed.,* Gen. James Longstreet's Command. Losses: *Union,* 44 killed, 202 wounded; *Confed.,* 500 killed and wounded, 400 captured.

17 to May 2.—Grierson's expedition from La Grange, Tenn., to Baton Rouge, La. *Union,* 6th and 7th Ill. Cav., 2d Iowa Cav.; *Confed.,* detachments of Cav. and Home Guards. Losses: *Union,* 3 killed, 7 wounded, 9 missing; *Confed.,* 100 killed and wounded, 1600 captured (estimated).

26.—Cape Girardeau, Mo. *Union,* 32d Iowa, 1st Wis. Cav., 2d Mo. Cav., Batteries D and L 1st Mo. Lt. Artil.; *Confed.,* Marmaduke's Cav. Losses: *Union,* 6 killed, 6 wounded; *Confed.,* 60 killed, 275 wounded and missing.

27 to May 3.—Streight's Raid, Tuscumbia, Ala., to Rome, Ga., including skirmishes at Day's Gap, April 30th; Black Warrior Creek, May 1, and Blount's Farm,

* No record found.

SUMTER

Searching all history for a parallel, it is impossible to find any defenses of a beleaguered city that stood so severe a bombardment as did this bravely defended and never conquered fortress of Sumter, in Charleston Harbor. It is estimated that about eighty thousand projectiles were discharged from the fleet and the marsh batteries, and yet Charleston, with its battered water-front, was not abandoned until all other Confederate positions along the Atlantic Coast were in Federal hands and Sherman's triumphant army was sweeping in from the West and South. The picture shows Sumter from the Confederate Fort Johnson. The powerful batteries in the foreground played havoc with the Federal fleet whenever it came down the main ship-channel to engage the forts. Protected by almost impassable swamps, morasses, and a network of creeks to the eastward, Fort Johnson held an almost impregnable position; and from its protection by Cummings' Point, on which was Battery Gregg, the Federal fleet could not approach nearer than two miles. Could it have been taken by land assault or reduced by gun-fire, Charleston would have fallen.

May 2. *Union*, 3d Ohio, 51st and 73d Ind., 80th Ill., Mounted Inft., two Cos. 1st Ala. Cav.; *Confed.*, Forrest's *Cav.* Losses: *Union*, 12 killed, 69 wounded. 1466 missing and captured; *Confed.*, 12 killed, 73 wounded.

27 to May 8.—Cavalry Raid in Virginia. *Union*, Gen. Stoneman's Corps; *Confed.*, Stuart's Cav., Home Guards and local garrisons. Losses.*

—Grand Gulf, Miss. *Union*, Gunboat fleet; *Confed.*, Gen. Bowen's Command. Losses: *Union*, 26 killed, 54 wounded.

30.—Spottsylvania C. H., Va. *Union*, 6th N. Y. Cav.; *Confed.*, Stuart's Cav. *Union*, 58 killed and wounded.

MAY, 1863.

1.—Port Gibson, Miss. (the first engagement in Grant's Campaign against Vicksburg). *Union*, Thirteenth Corps, Maj.-Gen. McClernand, and 3d Division Seventeenth Corps, Maj.-Gen. McPherson; *Confed.*, Gen. Bowen's Command. Losses: *Union*, 130 killed, 718 wounded; *Confed.*, 68 killed, 380 wounded, 384 missing. *Confed.* Brig.-Gen. Tracy killed.

1 to 4.—Chancellorsville, Va., including battles of Sixth Corps at Fredericksburg and Salem Heights. *Union*, Army of the Potomac, Maj.-Gen. Hooker; First Corps, Maj.-Gen. Reynolds; Second Corps, Maj.-Gen. Couch; Third Corps, Maj.-Gen. Sickles; Fifth Corps, Maj.-Gen. Meade; Sixth Corps, Maj.-Gen. Sedgwick; Eleventh Corps, Maj.-Gen. Howard; Twelfth Corps, Maj.-Gen. Slocum; *Confed.*, Army of Northern Virginia, Gen. R. E. Lee; Second Corps, " Stonewall " Jackson; R. H. Anderson's and McLaws' divisions of Longstreet's First Corps; Pendleton's Art. Battalion; Stuart's Cav. Losses: *Union*, 1512 killed, 9518 wounded, 5000 missing; *Confed.*, 1581 killed, 8700 wounded, 2000 missing. *Union*, Maj.-Gen. Berry and Brig.-Gen. Whipple killed, Devens and Kirby wounded. *Confed.*, Brig.-Gen. Paxton killed, Lieut.-Gen. Jackson, Maj.-Gen. A. P. Hill, Brig.-Gens. Hoke, Nichols, Ramseur, McGowan, Heth, and Pender wounded. Jackson's wound was mortal.

3.—Warrenton Junction, Va. *Union*, 1st W. Va. Cav., 5th N. Y. Cav.; *Confed.*, Stuart's Cav. Losses: *Union*, 1 killed, 16 wounded; *Confed.*, 15 wounded.

4.—Siege of Suffolk, Va., raised. (See April 12.)

11.—Horse Shoe Bend, Ky. *Union*, Detachment commanded by Col. R. T. Jacobs; *Confed.*, Morgan's Cav. Losses: *Union*, 10 killed, 20 wounded, 40 missing; *Confed.*, 100 killed, wounded, and missing.

12.—Raymond, Miss. *Union*, Seventeenth Corps, Maj.-Gen. McPherson. *Union*, 66 killed, 339 wounded, 37 missing; *Confed.*, Gen. Gregg's Command. Losses: *Confed.*, 969 killed and wounded.

14.—Jackson, Miss. *Union*, Fifteenth Corps, Maj.-Gen. Sherman; Seventeenth Corps, Maj.-Gen. McPherson; *Confed.*, Gen. Jos. E. Johnston's Command. Losses: *Union*, 42 killed, 251 wounded, 7 missing; *Confed.*, 450 killed and wounded.

16.—Champion's Hill, Miss. *Union*, Hovey's Div. Thirteenth Corps and Seventeenth Corps; *Confed.*, Army of Defense, commanded by Gen. J. C. Pemberton. Losses: *Union*, 410 killed, 1844 wounded, 187 missing; *Confed.*, 2500 killed and wounded, 1800 missing (estimate). *Confed.*, Gen. Tilghman killed.

17.—Big Black River, Miss. *Union*, Carr's and Osterhaus' divisions, Thirteenth Corps, Maj.-Gen. McClernand; *Confed.*, same as at Champion's Hill on the 16th. Losses: *Union*, 39 killed, 237 wounded, 3 missing; *Confed.*, 600 killed and wounded (estimate), 1751 captured.

18 to July 4.—Siege of Vicksburg, Miss. *Union*, Army of the Tennessee, commanded by Maj.-Gen. U. S. Grant; Ninth Corps, Thirteenth Corps, Fifteenth Corps, Sixteenth Corps (detachment), and Seventeenth Corps, and gunboat fleet, commanded by Admiral D. D. Porter; *Confed.*, Army of Defense, Gen. J. C. Pemberton. Assault on Fort Hill on May 19th and general assault on the 20th, in which *Confed.* Brig.-Gen. Green was killed; Loring's (portion), Bowen's, Stevenson's, Forney's, Smith's divisions, forces under Gen. J. E. Johnston and 7 river batteries. Losses: Included in the table for July 4.

* No record found.

THE NEVER–SURRENDERED FORT MOULTRIE, BESIEGED APRIL 10–SEPTEMBER 6, 1863

This is no hastily constructed battery, but the remains of a fort older than Sumter itself, as is shown by the brick walls and the permanent emplacement of the guns. It may be that this was the very piece of ordnance from which was fired the first shot that staggered humanity in 1861. Like Sumter, Fort Moultrie never surrendered. Protected by the encroaching sand-banks, it presented no such target as the high brick walls of the more historic fortress. Yet it had its place in history. Eighty-five years before, guns placed here had helped to repel the British fleet, and Sergeant Jasper had nailed to the flagstaff the banner of the new republic. Farther down the harbor the Confederates held permanent positions, the efforts to capture which were costly to the blockading fleet and besieging army. Before Fort Wagner there fell more than two thousand Federal soldiers. On Morris Island, to the south, the Federals had effected lodgment and turned their guns upon Sumter, Moultrie, and Wagner. The breaching batteries they erected in the swamps helped to complete the ruin. Tons of iron and exploding shells rained for months upon the bravely defended positions. The Confederate flags at Moultrie and Sumter, shot away a dozen times, were always replaced; and they waved proudly and defiantly until Charleston was threatened from the rear.

20 to 28.—Clendenin's raid, below Fredericksburg, Va. *Union,* 8th Ill. Cav.; *Confed.,* Outposts of Lee's Army. Losses: *Confed.,* 100 prisoners.

23 to July 8.—Siege of Port Hudson, La. Losses: *Union,* 708 killed, 3336 wounded, 319 missing; *Confed.,* 176 killed, 447 wounded, 5500 (estimate) captured.

JUNE, 1863.

4.—Franklin, Tenn. *Union,* 85th Ind., 7th Ky. Cav., 4th and 6th Ky. Cav., 9th Pa. Cav., 2d Mich. Cav.; *Confed.** Losses: *Union,* 25 killed and wounded; *Confed.,* 200 killed and wounded.

5.—Franklin's Crossing, Rappahannock River, Va. *Union,* 26th N. J., 5th Vt., 15th and 50th N. Y. Engineers, supported by 6th Corps; *Confed.,* Outposts of Gen. R. E. Lee's Army. Losses: *Union,* 6 killed, 35 wounded.

6 to 8.—Milliken's Bend, La. *Union,* 23d Iowa and three regts. colored troops, gunboat *Choctaw; Confed.,* Gen. Richard Taylor's Command. Losses: *Union,* 154 killed, 223 wounded, 115 missing; *Confed.,* 125 killed, 400 wounded, 200 missing.

9.—Monticello and Rocky Gap, Ky. *Union,* 2d and 7th Ohio Cav., 1st Ky. Cav., 45th Ohio and 2d Tenn. Mounted Inft.; *Confed.,* Morgan's Cav. Losses: *Union,* 4 killed, 26 wounded; *Confed.,* 20 killed, 80 wounded.

—Beverly Ford and Brandy Station, Va. *Union,* Cavalry Corps, Brig.-Gen. Pleasonton, 2d, 3d, and 7th Wis., 2d and 33d Mass., 6th Maine, 86th and 124th N. Y., 1st, 2d, 5th, and 6th U. S. Cav., 2d, 6th, 8th, 9th, and 10th N. Y. Cav., 1st, 3d, 4th, 6th, 11th, and 17th Pa. Cav., 1st Md., 8th Ill., 3d Ind., 1st N. J., 1st Maine Cav., 1st R. I. Cav., and 3d W. Va. Cav., 8th and 12th Ill.* Cav., 1st Mass. Cav., 6th O. Cav., Batteries B and L, 2d U. S. Art., K, 1st U. S. Art., E, 4th U. S. Art., 6th Bat. N. Y. Light Art.; *Confed.,* Stuart's Cav. Losses: *Union,* 421 killed and wounded, 486 missing; *Confed.,* 301 killed and wounded, 184 missing. First true cavalry battle in the East.

11.—Middletown, Va. *Union,* 87th Pa., 13th Pa. Cav., Battery L, 5th U. S. Artil.; *Confed.,* Gen. Ewell's Command. Losses: *Confed.,* 8 killed, 42 wounded.

13 and 15.—Winchester, Va. *Union,* 2d, 67th and 87th Pa., 18th Conn., 12th W. Va., 110th, 116th, 122d, and 123d Ohio, 3d, 5th, and 6th Md., 12th and 13th Pa. Cav., 1st N. Y. Cav., 1st and 3d W. Va. Cav., Battery L 5th U. S. Artil., 1st W. Va. Battery, Baltimore Battery, one Co. 14th Mass. Heavy Artil.; *Confed.,* Gen. R. S. Ewell's Corps. Losses: *Union,* 95 killed, 443 wounded, and 4443 missing; *Confed.,* 42 killed and 210 wounded.

14.—Martinsburg, Va. *Union,* 106th N. Y., 126th Ohio, W. Va. Battery; *Confed.,* Gen. Ewell's Command. Losses: *Union,* 200 missing; *Confed.,* 1 killed, 2 wounded.

16.—Triplett's Bridge, Ky. *Union,* 15th Mich., 10th and 14th Ky. Cav., 7th and 9th Mich. Cav., 11th Mich. Battery; *Confed.,* Morgan's Cav. Losses: *Union,* 15 killed, 30 wounded.

17.—Aldie, Va. *Union,* Kilpatrick's Cav.; *Confed.,* Stuart's Cav. Losses: *Union,* 24 killed, 41 wounded, 89 missing; *Confed.,* 100 wounded.

—Wassau Sound, Ga. Capture of *Confederate* gunboat *Atlanta* by U. S. ironclad *Weehawken.* Losses: *Confed.,* 1 killed, 17 wounded, 145 prisoners.

20 and 21.—La Fourche Crossing, La. *Union,* Detachments 23d Conn., 176th N. Y., 26th, 42d, and 47th Mass., 21st Ind.; *Confed.,* Gen. Richard Taylor's Command. Losses: *Union,* 8 killed, 40 wounded; *Confed.,* 53 killed, 150 wounded.

21.—Upperville, Va. *Union,* Pleasonton's Cav.; *Confed.,* Stuart's Cav. Losses: *Union,* 94 wounded; *Confed.,* 20 killed, 100 wounded, 60 missing.

22.—Hill's Plantation, Miss. Detachment of 4th Iowa Cav.; *Confed.** Losses: *Union,* 4 killed, 10 wounded, 28 missing.

23.—Brashear City, La. *Union,* Detachments of 114th and 176th N. Y., 23d Conn., 42d Mass., 21st Ind.; *Confed.,* Gen. Taylor's Command. Losses: *Union,* 46 killed, 40 wounded, 300 missing; *Confed.,* 3 killed, 18 wounded.

* No record found.

The lower picture was taken after the war, when relic-hunters had removed the shells, and a beacon light had been erected where once stood the parapet. On September 8, 1863, at the very position in these photographs, the garrison repelled a bold assault with musketry fire alone, causing the Federals severe loss. The flag of the Confederacy floated triumphantly over the position during the whole of the long struggle. Every effort of the Federals to reduce the crumbling ruins into submission was unavailing. It stood the continual bombardment of ironclads until it was nothing but a mass of brickdust, but still the gallant garrison held it.

SCENE OF THE NIGHT ATTACK ON SUMTER,
SEPTEMBER 8, 1863

It is strange that despite the awful destruction the loss of lives within the fort was few. For weeks the bombardment, assisted by the guns of the fleet, tore great chasms in the parapet. Fort Sumter never fell, but was abandoned only on the approach of Sherman's army. It had withstood continuous efforts against it for 587 days. From April, 1863, to September of the same year, the fortress was garrisoned by the First South Carolina Artillery, enlisted as regulars. Afterward the garrison was made up of detachments of infantry from Georgia, North Carolina, and South Carolina. Artillerists also served turns of duty during this period.

WHERE BURNSIDE HELD KNOXVILLE, NOVEMBER 17th TO DECEMBER 4, 1863

This high ground, commanding Fort Sanders across the Holston River, had just been captured by the Confederates when Longstreet learned of Bragg's defeat at Chattanooga and was compelled to abandon the siege of Knoxville. He had bottled up Burnside. In Fort Sanders the Army of the Ohio was bravely holding on till help should come from Grant; they were eating bread made of pure bran, and their sustenance was almost exhausted. Before dawn on November 29, 1863, they repulsed the second assault which Longstreet's superior numbers made upon them. Longstreet, disheartened by constant disagreements with Bragg and without faith in the generalship of his superior, led the expedition, contrary to his judgment, as a forlorn hope, and his officers prosecuted the movement but half-heartedly. Longstreet himself admits that he was not as energetic as was his wont. Delay and misinformation as to the strength of the Federals cost him a thousand men before Fort Sanders. Baffled and discouraged, he finally abandoned the siege.

FORT SANDERS, KNOXVILLE, WHERE LONGSTREET ATTACKED, NOVEMBER 29, 1863

KNOXVILLE, AND TWO BRIDGES IN THE SIEGE. THE LOWER ONE, AT STRAWBERRY PLAINS, WAS DESTROYED FOUR TIMES DURING THE WAR

Engagements of the Civil War

23 to July 7.—Rosecrans' Campaign. Murfreesboro to Tullahoma, Tenn., including Middleton, Hoover's Gap, Beech Grove, Liberty Gap, and Guy's Gap. Army of the Cumberland: Fourteenth, Twentieth, and Twenty-first Corps, Granger's Reserve Corps, and Stanley's Cavalry; *Confed.*, Army of Tennessee, Gen. Braxton Bragg. Losses: *Union*, 84 killed, 473 wounded, 13 missing; *Confed.*, 1634 (estimate) killed, wounded, and captured.

28.—Donaldsonville, La., and Fort Butler. *Union*, 28th Maine and convalescents, assisted by gunboats; *Confed.*, Gen. Taylor's Command. Losses: *Confed.*, 39 killed, 112 wounded, 150 missing.

30.—Hanover, Pa. *Union*, Kilpatrick's Cavalry Division; *Confed.*, Stuart's Cav. Losses: *Union*, 12 killed, 43 wounded; *Confed.*, 75 wounded, 60 missing.

JULY, 1863.

1 to 3.—Gellysburg, Pa. *Union*, Army of the Potomac, Maj.-Gen. Geo. G. Meade; First Corps, Maj.-Gen. Reynolds; Second Corps, Maj.-Gen. Hancock; Third Corps, Maj.-Gen. Sickles; Fifth Corps, Maj.-Gen. Sykes; Sixth Corps, Maj.-Gen. Sedgwick; Eleventh Corps, Maj.-Gen. Howard; Twelfth Corps, Maj.-Gen. Slocum; Cavalry Corps, Maj.-Gen. Pleasonton, Artillery Reserve under Brig.-Gen. Tyler; *Confed.*, Army of Northern Virginia, Gen. R. E. Lee; First Corps, Gen. Longstreet; Second Corps, Gen. Ewell; Third Corps, Gen. A. P. Hill; Gen. Stuart's Cav., Reserve Artillery under Cols. Walton, Walker, and Brown. Losses: *Union*, 3155 killed, 14529 wounded, 5365 missing; *Confed.*, 3500 killed, 14500 wounded, 13621 missing.

2 to 26.—Morgan's raid into Kentucky, Indiana, and Ohio. At Blennerhasset Island, Ohio River (July 19th), the larger part of Morgan's force was killed, wounded, and captured—820 in all. The remainder, with Morgan himself, surrendered July 26th, near New Lisbon, Ohio. *Union*, Detachments of Rosecrans' Army of the Cumberland, Hobson's and Shackleford's Cav., Home Guard, and Militia; *Confed.*, Gen. John H. Morgan's Cav. Corps. Losses: *Union*, 33 killed, 97 wounded, 805 missing; *Confed.*,

about 2500 killed, wounded, and captured.

4.—Helena, Ark. *Union*, Maj.-Gen. Prentiss' Division of Sixteenth Corps and gunboat *Tyler; Confed.*, Gen. T. H. Holmes' Command, Price's Mo. and Ark. brigades, Marmaduke's and Shelby's Cav. Losses: *Union*, 57 killed, 117 wounded, 32 missing; *Confed.*, 173 killed, 687 wounded, 776 missing.

—Surrender of Vicksburg to Maj.-Gen. U. S. Grant; end of the siege. Losses, during the campaign and including Port Gibson, Raymond, Jackson, Champion's Hill, Big Black River, assaults May 19th and 22d, siege operations and skirmishes: *Union*, 1514 killed, 1395 wounded, 453 missing; *Confed.* (Incomplete) 1260 killed, 3572 wounded, 4227 captured or missing in action, surrendered (including non-combatants attached to the army) 29941.

4 and 5.—Bolton and Birdsong Ferry, Miss. *Union*, Maj.-Gen. Sherman's forces; *Confed.*, Gen. Johnston's Command. Losses: *Confed.*, 2000 captured.

—Monterey Gap and Fairfield Pa., and Smithsburg, Md. *Union*, Kilpatrick Cav.; *Confed.*, Hampton's Cav. Losses: *Union*, 30 killed and wounded; *Confed.*, 30 killed and wounded, 100 captured.

5.—Lebanon, Ky. *Union*, 20th Ky.; *Confed.*, Morgan's Cav. Losses: *Union*, 9 killed, 15 wounded, 400 missing; *Confed.*, 3 killed, 6 wounded.

6.—Hagerstown and Williamsport, Md. *Union*, Buford's and Kilpatrick's Cav., *Confed.*, Stuart's Cav. Losses: *Union*, 33 killed, 87 wounded, 293 missing; *Confed.*, 125 killed, wounded, and missing.

7 to 9.—Boonsboro, Md. *Union*, Buford's and Kilpatrick's Cav.; *Confed.*, Gen. Fitzhugh Lee's Cav. Losses: *Union*, 9 killed, 45 wounded.

8.—Port Hudson, La. Surrendered by Confederates to Maj.-Gen. Banks. (See May 23.)

9 to 16.—Jackson, Miss., including engagements at Rienzi, Bolton Depot, Canton, and Clinton. *Union*, 9th, 13th, 15th, and part of 16th Corps; *Confed.*, Gen. Jos. E. Johnston's Army. Losses: *Union*, 100 killed, 800 wounded, 100 missing; *Confed.*, 71 killed, 504 wounded, 764 missing.

MISSOURI ARTILLERY IN SHERMAN'S RAID, FEBRUARY, 1864

Battery M, First Missouri Light Artillery, originally in Colonel Frank P. Blair's infantry regiment, marched with Sherman from Vicksburg through Mississippi to Meridian during February, 1864. Sherman, with twenty thousand men and sixty pieces of artillery, was to break up all the railroad communications, so that small Federal garrisons would be able to hold important positions along the Mississippi. The advance corps under the intrepid McPherson left Vicksburg on February 3d and arrived at Meridian on the 8th. It was a precursor of the famous "March to the Sea," but on a smaller scale. The troops destroyed whatever would be of service to the Confederates, who fell back before Sherman, burning provisions and laying waste the country. At Meridian, the great railway center of the Southwest at the time, Sherman accomplished "the most complete destruction of railroads ever beheld." Meantime, General W. S. Smith, with the Federal cavalry force from Memphis, was unable to reach Meridian. Escaping in the night from a dangerous predicament at Okolona on February 22d, he managed to return safely to Memphis by February 25th, after having destroyed a million bushels of corn and many miles of railroad.

10 to Sept. 6.—Siege of Fort Wagner, Morris Island, S. C. *Union,* Troops of the Department of the South, under command of Maj.-Gen. Gillmore, and U. S. Navy under Admiral Dahlgren; *Confed.,* Garrison commanded by Gen. W. B. Taliaferro. Losses: *Union,* 1757 killed, wounded, and missing; *Confed.,* 561 killed, wounded, and missing.

—Falling Waters, Md. *Union,* 3d Cav. Division Army of the Potomac; *Confed.,* Army of Northern Virginia, Gen. R. E. Lee. Losses: *Union,* 29 killed, 36 wounded; *Confed.,* 125 killed and wounded, 1500 prisoners. C o n f e d., Maj.-Gen. Pettigrew killed.

13.—Yazoo City, Miss. *Union,* Maj.-Gen. Herron's Division and three gunboats; *Confed.,* Detachments of Capt. I. N. Brown. Losses: *Confed.,* 250 captured.

—Jackson, Tenn. *Union,* 9th Ill., 3d Mich. Cav., 2d Iowa Cav., and 1st Tenn. Cav.; *Confed.,* Gen. N. B. Forrest's Cav. Losses: *Union,* 2 killed, 20 wounded; *Confed.,* 38 killed, 150 wounded.

—Donaldsonville, La. *Union,* Advance of Gen. Weitzel's command; *Confed.,* Gen. Green's brigade, Col. Taylor's Cav. Losses: *Union,* 465 killed, wounded, and missing; *Confed.,* 3 killed, 30 wounded.

13 to 15.—Draft riots in New York City, in which over 1000 rioters were killed.

14.—Elk River, Tenn. *Union,* Advance of the Fourteenth Corps Army of the Cumberland; *Confed.,* Rear Guard of Gen. Bragg's Army in retreat. Losses: *Union,* 10 killed, 30 wounded; *Confed.,* 60 killed, 24 wounded, 100 missing.

—Halltown, Va. *Union,* 16th Pa. and 1st Maine Cav.; *Confed.,* Gen. J. D. Imboden's command. Losses: *Union,* 25 killed and wounded; *Confed.,* 20 killed and wounded.

16.—Shepherdstown, Va. *Union,* 1st, 4th, and 16th Pa., 10th N. Y. and 1st Maine Cav.; *Confed.,* Stuart's Cav. Losses: *Confed.,* 25 killed, 75 wounded.

17.—Honey Springs, Ind. Ter. *Union,* 2d, 6th, and 9th Kan. Cav., 2d and 3d Kan. Batteries, 2d and 3d Kan. Indian Home Guards; *Confed.,* Col. Cooper's Indians and Tex. Cav. Losses: *Union,* 17 killed, 60 wounded; *Confed.,* 150 killed, 400 wounded.

—Wytheville, W. Va. *Union,* 34th Ohio, 1st and 2d W. Va. Cav.; *Confed.** Losses: *Union,* 17 killed, 61 wounded; *Confed.,* 75 killed, 125 missing.

21 to 23.—Manassas Gap and Chester Gap, Va. *Union,* Cavalry advance and Third Corps Army of the Potomac; *Confed.,* Stuart's Cav. Losses: *Union,* 35 killed, 102 wounded; *Confed.,* 300 killed and wounded.

AUGUST, 1863.

1 to 3.—Rappahannock Station, B r a n d y Station, and Kelly's Ford, Va. *Union,* Brig.-Gen. Buford's Cav.; *Confed.,* Stuart's Cav. Losses: *Union,* 16 killed, 134 wounded.

21.—Quantrill's plunder and massacre of Lawrence, Kan., in which 140 citizens were killed and 24 wounded. Quantrill's loss, 40 killed.

25 to 30.—Averell's Raid in W. Va. Losses: *Union,* 3 killed, 10 wounded, 60 missing.

25 to 31.—Brownsville, Bayou Metoe, and Austin, Ark. *Union,* Davidson's Cav.; *Confed.,* Marmaduke's Cav. Losses: *Union,* 13 killed, 72 wounded.

26 and 27.—Rocky Gap, near White Sulphur Springs, W. Va. *Union,* 3d and 8th W. Va., 2d and 3d W. Va. Cav., 14th Pa. Cav.; *Confed.,* Gen. Samuel Jones' command. Losses: *Union,* 16 killed, 113 wounded; *Confed.,* 156 killed and wounded.

SEPTEMBER, 1863.

1.—Devil's Back Bone, Ark. *Union,* 1st Ark. 6th Mo. Militia, 2d Kan. Cav., 2d Ind. Battery; *Confed.,* Part of Gen. Price's command. Losses: *Union,* 4 killed, 12 wounded; *Confed.,* 25 killed, 40 wounded.

8.—Night attack on Fort Sumter, S. C. *Union,* 413 marines and sailors from the South Atlantic Blockading Squadron, led by Commander Stevens, U. S. N. *Confed.,* Garrison of Fort Sumter. Losses: *Union,* 124 killed, wounded, and missing.

9.—C u m b e r l a n d Gap, Tenn. *Union,* Shackleford's Cav.; *Confed.,* Gen. J. W. Frazer's brigade. Losses: *Confed.,* 2000 captured.

* No record found.

HOLDING THE WESTERN FRONTIER IN '63

Two regiments of fighting men from the Northwest that participated in the rough campaigning of the frontier across the Mississippi in Arkansas in 1863. In the upper picture is the camp of the Twenty-eighth Wisconsin Infantry at Little Rock, and in the lower view the Third Minnesota Infantry, Colonel C. C. Andrews commanding, is drawn up on dress parade in front of the State Capitol. Both organizations fought in the expedition which Major-General Frederick Steele organized at Helena, August 5, 1863, to break up the Confederate army under Price in Arkansas. On the very day that Vicksburg surrendered, July 4th, the Confederate General T. H. Holmes appeared before Helena with a force of over eight thousand. He had telegraphed to his superior, E. K. Smith, on June 15th, "I believe we can take Helena; please let me do it." To which Smith had replied, "Most certainly do it." Holmes hoped to make a new Vicksburg to keep the Mississippi closed from the west bank. Helena was garrisoned by a force less than half as great as that which came against it. Among the defenders were the Twenty-eighth Wisconsin. On the morning of July 4, 1863, under command of Major-General B. M. Prentiss, these Federals repulsed two vigorous assaults, and Holmes, giving up hope of success, returned to Little Rock. This aroused the Federals to the importance of holding Arkansas, and General Frederick Steele collected about twelve thousand men at Helena early in August. The troops left Helena on August 10th, and pushed back the Confederates under General Marmaduke.

THE THIRD MINNESOTA

10.—Little Rock, Ark. Evacuation by Confederates under Gen. Price. *Union*, Maj.-Gen. .Steele's troops and Davidson's Cav.; *Confed.*, Price's Division, L. M. Walker's and J. S. Marmaduke's Cav.

13.—Culpeper, Va. *Union*, Cavalry Corps, Army of the Potomac; *Confed.*, Stuart's Cav. Losses: *Union*, 3 killed, 40 wounded; *Confed.*, 10 killed, 40 wounded, 75 missing.

—Leet's Tan Yard, near Chickamauga, Ga. *Union*, Wider's mounted brigade; *Confed.*, Outposts of Gen. Bragg's Army. Losses: *Union*, 50 killed and wounded; *Confed.*, 10 killed, 40 wounded.

19 and 20.—Chickamauga, Ga. Army of the Cumberland, Maj.-Gen. Rosecrans; Fourteenth Corps, Maj.-Gen. Thomas; Twentieth Corps, Maj.-Gen. McCook; Twenty-first Corps, Maj.-Gen. Crittenden; Reserve Corps, Maj.-Gen. Granger; *Confed.*, Army of Tennesseee, Gen. Braxton Bragg; Gen. Polk's Corps, Longstreet's Corps (Army of Northern Virginia); D. H. Hill's Corps, Buckner's Corps, Gen. W. H. T. Walker's Reserve Corps, Forrest's and Wheeler's Cav. Losses: *Union*, 1644 killed, 9262 wounded, 4945 missing; *Confed.*, 2389 killed, 13412 wounded, 2003 missing.

—Blountsville, Tenn. *Union*, Foster's 2d Brigade Cav.; *Confed.*, 1st Tenn. Cav. Losses: *Union*, 5 killed, 22 wounded; *Confed.*, 15 killed, 50 wounded, 100 missing.

—Rockville, Md. *Union*, 11th N. Y. Cav.; *Confed.*, Stuart's Cav. Losses: *Confed.*, 34 killed and wounded.

OCTOBER, 1863.

3.—McMinnville, Tenn. *Union*, 4th Tenn.; *Confed.*, Detachment of Gen. Bragg's Army. Losses: *Union*, 7 killed, 31 wounded, 350 missing; *Confed.*, 23 killed and wounded.

7.—Near Farmington, Tenn. *Union*, 1st, 3d, and 4th Ohio Cav., 2d Ky. Cav., Long's 2d Cav. Division, and Wilder's Brigade Mounted Inft.; *Confed.*, Wheeler's Cav. Losses: *Union*, 15 killed, 60 wounded; *Confed.*, 10 killed, 60 wounded, 240 missing.

—Blue Springs, Tenn. *Union*, Ninth Corps, Army of the Ohio, and Shackleford's Cav.; *Confed.*, Gen. J. S. Williams' command. Losses: *Union*, 100 killed, wounded, and missing; *Confed.*, 66 killed and wounded, 150 missing.

12 and 13.—Ingham's Mills and Wyatts, Miss. *Union*, 2d Iowa Cav.; *Confed.*, Chalmers' Cav. Losses: *Union*, 45 killed and wounded; *Confed.*, 50 killed and wounded.

—Culpeper and White Sulphur Springs, Va. *Union*, Cavalry Corps Army of the Potomac; *Confed.*, Stuart's Cav. Losses: *Union*, 8 killed, 46 wounded.

—Merrill's Crossing on La Mine Bridge, Mo. *Union*, Mo. Enrolled Militia, 1st Mo. Militia Battery, 1st, 4th, and 7th Mo. Militia Cav.; *Confed.*, Shelby's Cav. Losses: *Union*, 16 killed; *Confed.*, 53 killed, 70 wounded.

14.—Bristoe Station, Va. *Union*, Second Corps, portion of Fifth Corps, 2d Cav. Division, Army of the Potomac; *Confed.*, Divisions of Heth, R. H. Anderson, and A. P. Hill. Losses: *Union*, 51 killed, 329 wounded; *Confed.*, 750 killed and wounded, 450 missing.

15.—McLean's Ford or Liberty Mills, Va. *Union*, 5th, 6th, 7th, and 8th N. J., 151st N. Y., 115th Pa., 4th Bat. Me. Art. and Bat. K. 4th U. S. Art. *Confed.*, Gen. L. L. Lomax's Cav. Brigade. Losses: *Union*, 2 killed, 25 wounded; *Confed.*, 60 killed and wounded.

15 to 18.—Canton, Brownsville, and Clinton, Miss. *Union*, Portion of Fifteenth and Seventeenth Corps; *Confed.*, Gen. W. H. Jackson's command. Losses: *Confed.*, 200 killed and wounded.

18.—Charleston, W. Va. *Union*, 9th Md.; *Confed.*, Gen. Imboden's command. Losses: *Union*, 12 killed, 13 wounded, 379 missing.

19.—Buckland Mills, Va. *Union*, 3d Division of Kilpatrick's Cav.; *Confed.*, Stuart's Cav. Losses: *Union*, 20 killed, 60 wounded, 100 missing; *Confed.*, 10 killed, 40 wounded.

20 and 22.—Philadelphia, Tenn. *Union*, 45th Ohio Mounted Inft., 1st, 11th, and 12th Ky. Cav., 24th Ind. Battery; *Confed.*, Gen. J. S. Williams' command. Losses: *Union*, 20 killed, 80 wounded, 354 missing; *Confed.*, 15 killed, 82 wounded, 111 missing.

THE MONTH BEFORE MINE RUN, OCTOBER, 1863

Meade's Headquarters at Culpeper, Virginia.   In the vicinity of Culpeper Court House, ten miles from the banks of the Rappahannock and thirty miles northwest of Fredericksburg, the Army of the Potomac was encamped after Gettysburg.   Meade had followed Lee southward throughout the summer in the hope of striking his army before it had recovered from the blow dealt it in Pennsylvania.   But Lee, in great depression and wishing to retire, remained on the defensive; the departure of Longstreet for Chickamauga in September had made him still more wary.   Meade's forces had been reduced also by the despatching of two corps, under Hooker, into Tennessee, so he in turn was urged to caution.   The fall of 1863 was spent in skilful maneuvers with the flash of battle at Bristoe Station, October 14th, where Warren worsted A. P. Hill, and at Rappahannock Station on November 7th, where the Sixth Corps distinguished itself. At Mine Run, near the old Chancellorsville battle-ground, Lee was strongly entrenched and here the opposing forces came near a general engagement on November 30th, but the moment passed and both sides went into winter quarters.   By March, 1864, all was activity at Culpeper; the army awaited its new commander, Grant, who was to lead it again toward Chancellorsville and The Wilderness.

25.—Pine Bluff, Ark. *Union,* 5th Kan. and 1st Ind. Cav.; *Confed.,* Gen. Price's command. Losses: *Union,* 11 killed, 27 wounded; *Confed.,* 53 killed, 164 wounded.

28 and 29.—Wauhatchie, Tenn. *Union,* Eleventh Corps and 2d Division of Twelfth Corps; *Confed.,* Gen. James Longstreet's Corps. Losses: *Union,* 78 killed, 327 wounded, 15 missing. *Confed.* (estimated) 300 killed, 1200 wounded.

NOVEMBER, 1863.

3.—Grand Coteau, La. *Union,* 3d and 4th Divisions, Thirteenth Corps; *Confed.,* Gen. Green's Cav. Division. Losses: *Union,* 26 killed, 124 wounded, 576 missing; *Confed.,* 60 killed, 320 wounded, 65 missing.

6.—Rogersville, Tenn. *Union,* 7th Ohio Cav., 2d Tenn. Mounted Inft., 2d Ill. Battery; *Confed.,* Gens. W. E. Jones and H. L. Giltner's Brigades. Losses: *Union,* 5 killed, 12 wounded, 650 missing; *Confed.,* 10 killed, 20 wounded.
—Droop Mountain, Va. *Union,* 10th W. Va., 28th Ohio, 14th Pa. Cav., 2d and 5th W. Va. Cav., Battery B, W. Va. Artil.; *Confed.,* Gen. Echol's Brigade. Losses: *Union,* 31 killed, 94 wounded; *Confed.,* 50 killed, 250 wounded, 100 missing.

7.—Rappahannock Station, Va. *Union,* 5th Wis., 5th, 6th Maine, 49th, 119th Pa., 121st N. Y.; *Confed.,* Two brigades of Gen. Jubal Early's command. Losses: *Union,* 419 killed and wounded; *Confed.,* 6 killed, 39 wounded, 1,629 captured or missing.
—Kelly's Ford, Va. *Union,* 1st U. S. Sharpshooters, 40th N. Y., 1st and 20th Ind., 3d and 5th Mich., 110th Pa., supported by remainder of Third Corps; *Confed.,* Stuart's Cav. Losses: *Union,* 70 killed and wounded; *Confed.,* 5 killed, 59 wounded, 295 missing.

14.—Huff's Ferry, Tenn. *Union,* 111th Ohio, 107th Ill., 11th and 13th Ky., 23d Mich., 24th Mich. Battery; *Confed.,* Wheeler's Cav. Losses: *Union,* 100 killed and wounded.

16.—Campbell's Station, Tenn. *Union,* Ninth Corps, 2d Division of Twenty-third Corps, Sanders' Cav.; *Confed.,*

Longstreet's Corps. Losses: *Union,* 31 killed, 211 wounded, and 76 missing; *Confed.,* 570 killed and wounded.

17 to Dec. 4.—Siege of Knoxville, Tenn. *Union,* Army of the Ohio, commanded by Maj.-Gen. Burnside; *Confed.,* Gen. Longstreet's Corps, Alexander's Art., Wheeler's Cav. Losses: Complete casualties not recorded. *Union,* 94 killed, 394 wounded, and 207 missing; *Confed.,* (minus the cavalry *) 182 killed, 768 wounded, 192 missing.

23 to 25.—Chattanooga, Lookout Mountain, Orchard Knob and Missionary Ridge, Tenn. *Union,* Forces commanded by Maj.-Gen. U. S. Grant, as follows: Fourth and Fourteenth Corps, Army of the Cumberland; Maj.-Gen. Geo. H. Thomas, Eleventh Corps; Geary's Division of the Twelfth Corps; Fifteenth Corps; Smith's Division, Seventeenth Corps, Army of the Tennessee, Maj.-Gen. W. T. Sherman; *Confed.,* Gen. Bragg's command; W. J. Hardee's Corps; Breckinridge's Corps; Art. Reserve, detachments of Cav. Losses: *Union,* 757 killed, 4529 wounded, 330 missing; *Confed.,* 361 killed, 2181 wounded, 6142 missing.

26 to 28.—Operations at Mine Run, Va., including Raccoon Ford, New Hope, Robertson's Tavern, Bartlett's Mills, and Locust Grove. *Union,* First Corps, Second Corps, Third Corps, Fifth Corps, Sixth Corps, and 1st and 2d Cav. Divisions Army of the Potomac; *Confed.,* Army of Northern Virginia, Gen. Robert E. Lee. Losses: *Union,* 173 killed, 1099 wounded, 381 missing; *Confed.,* 98 killed, 610 wounded, 1104 missing.

27.—Ringgold and Taylor's Ridge, Ga. *Union,* Portions of Twelfth, Fourteenth, and Fifteenth Corps; *Confed.,* Rear Guard of Gen. Bragg's Army on retreat from Chattanooga. Losses: *Union,* 68 killed, 351 wounded; *Confed.,* 50 killed, 200 wounded, 230 missing.

DECEMBER, 1863.

1 to 4.—Ripley and Moscow Station, Miss., and Salisbury, Tenn. *Union,* 2d Brigade Cav. Division of Sixteenth Corps; *Confed.,* Gen. S. D. Lee's command. Losses: *Union,* 175 killed and

* No record found.

THE ANCIENT SALLY PORT

Civil War Garrison at the Gate of Fort Marion, St. Augustine, Florida. American guns were first turned against it when Oglethorpe led his expedition from South Carolina against St. Augustine in May, 1740. Its style of architecture tells plainly of its origin and antiquity; it was called by the Spaniards "Castle St. Marcus." When Commander Rodgers brought his flag of truce to St. Augustine, the mayor proposed to turn over the fort to him, but Rodgers instructed him to establish a patrol and guard at the fort and make careful inventories of what it contained. Several good guns had been taken from it by the Confederates, but there still remained three fine army 32-pounders and two 8-inch seacoast howitzers, with a quantity of ammunition. About a fifth of the inhabitants of St. Augustine had fled at the coming of the Federals, but of the 1,500 that remained Commander Rodgers reported that they were "many citizens who are earnestly attached to the Union, a large number who are silently opposed to it, and a still larger number who care very little about the matter."

wounded; *Confed.*, 15 killed, 40 wounded.

2.—Walker's Ford, Tenn. *Union*, 65th, 116th, and 118th Ind., 21st Ohio Battery, 5th Ind. Cav., 14th Ill. Cav.; *Confed.*, Wheeler's Cav. Losses: *Union*, 9 killed, 39 wounded; *Confed.*, 25 killed, 50 wounded.

8 to 21.—Averell's raid in South-western Va.; *Confed.*, Gen. Jno. D. Imboden's command. Losses: *Union*, 6 killed, 5 wounded; *Confed.*, 200 captured.

10 to 14.—Bean's Station and Morristown, Tenn. *Union*, Shackleford's Cav.; *Confed.*, Longstreet's Corps, Martin's Cav. Losses: *Union*, 700 killed and wounded; *Confed.*, 932 killed and wounded, 150 captured.

19.—Barren Fork, Ind. Ter. *Union*, 1st and 3d Kan., Indian Home Guards; *Confed.** Losses: *Confed.*, 50 killed.

28.—Charleston, Tenn. *Union*, Detachments of the 2d Mo. and 4th Ohio Cav. guarding wagon train; *Confed.*, Wheeler's Cav. Losses: *Union*, 2 killed, 15 wounded; *Confed.*, 8 killed, 89 wounded, 121 captured.

30.—St. Augustine, Fla. *Union*, 10th Conn., 24th Mass.; *Confed.*, 2d Fla. Cav. Losses: *Union*, 4 killed.

—Waldron, Ark. *Union*, 2d Kan. Cav.; *Confed.*, Maj. Gibson's command. Losses: *Union*, 2 killed, 6 wounded; *Confed.*, 1 killed, 8 wounded.

JANUARY, 1864.

1 to 10.—Rectortown and Loudon Heights, Va. *Union*, 1st Md. Cav., Potomac Home Brigade; *Confed.*, Col. J. S. Mosby's command. Losses: *Union*, 29 killed and wounded, 41 missing; *Confed.*, 4 killed, 10 wounded.

3.—Jonesville, Va. *Union*, Detachment 16th Ill. Cav., 22d Ohio Battery; *Confed.*, Jones' Cavalry. Losses: *Union*, 12 killed, 48 wounded, 300 missing; *Confed.*, 4 killed, 12 wounded.

16 and 17.—D a n d r i d g e, Tenn. *Union*, Fourth Corps and Cav. Division of Army of the Ohio; *Confed.*, Longstreet's command. Losses: *Union*, 150 wounded.

19 and 24.—Tazewell, Tenn. *Union*, 34th Ky., 116th and 118th Ind., 11th Tenn. Cav., 11th Mich. Bat'y.; *Confed.*, Longstreet's command. Losses: *Confed.*, 31 killed.

27.—Fair Gardens or Kelly's Ford, Tenn. *Union*, Sturgis's Cavalry; *Confed.*, Martin's and Morgan's Cavalry. Losses: *Union*, 100 killed and wounded; *Confed.*, 65 killed, 100 captured.

28.—Tunnel Hill, Ga. *Union*, part of Fourteenth Corps; *Confed.*, Outposts of the Army of the Tennessee. Losses: *Union*, 2 wounded; *Confed.*, 32 wounded.

31.—Smithfield, Va. *Union*, Detachments 99th N. Y., 21st Conn., 20th N. Y. Cav., 3d Pa. Artil., and marines from U. S. Gunboats *Minnesota* and *Smith Briggs*; *Confed.** Losses: *Union*, 90 missing.

29 to Feb. 1.—Medley, W. Va. *Union*, 1st and 14th W. Va., 23d Ill., 2d Md., Potomac Home Brigade, 4th W. Va. Cav., Ringgold (Pa.) Cav.; *Confed.*, Col. T. L. Rosser's Cav. Losses: *Union*, 10 killed, 70 wounded.

FEBRUARY, 1864.

1 to 3.—Bachelor Creek, Newport Barracks, and New Berne, N. C. *Union*, 132d N. Y., 9th Vt., 17th Mass., 2d N. C., 12th N. Y. Cav., 3d N. Y. Artil.; *Confed.*, Expedition commanded by Gen. Geo. E. Pickett. Losses: *Union*, 16 killed, 50 wounded, 280 missing; *Confed.*, 5 killed, 30 wounded.

1 to March 8.—Expedition up the Yazoo River, Miss. *Union*, 11th Ill., 47th U. S. Colored, 3d U. S. Colored Cav., and a portion of Porter's Fleet of gunboats; *Confed.*, Gen. J. E. Johnston's command. Losses: *Union*, 35 killed, 121 wounded. *Confed.*, 35 killed, 90 wounded.

3 to March 5.—Expedition from Vicksburg to Meridian, Miss. *Union*, Two Divisions of the Sixteenth and three of the Seventeenth Corps, with the 5th Ill., 4th Iowa, 10th Mo. and Foster's (Ohio) Cav.; *Confed.*, Gen. Polk's command; Loring's and French's divisions, Forrest's and Armstrong's Cav. Losses: *Union*, 56 killed, 138 wounded, 105 miss-

* No record found.

[348]

FIGHTING IN FLORIDA—DECEMBER, 1863

A Civil War skirmish took place at St. Augustine, Florida, December 30, 1863, before the quaint old bastions of Fort Marion —the oldest Spanish fort in the Western Hemisphere, and the oldest anywhere outside of Spain. St. Augustine, however, was not disturbed by the one serious attempt that was made to penetrate the interior of Florida. If this could be done, it was throught at Washington that many citizens of the State would flock to the Union cause and could be reconstructed into a State whose electoral vote would be extremely valuable in retaining the Lincoln Administration in power. On February 5, 1864, under orders from General Gillmore, an expedition left Hilton Head and, arriving at Jacksonville, Florida, pushed forward across the State. Rapidly collecting reënforcements from Savannah and Charleston, the Confederate General Finegan met the Federals at Clustee and sharply defeated them February 20, 1864. This put an end to the only effort to invade the State of Florida.

ARTILLERY INSIDE THE FORT

ing; *Confed.*, 503 killed and wounded, 212 captured.

5.—Quallatown, N. C. *Union*, Detachment of 14th Ill. Cav.; *Confed.*, 26th N. C. Losses: *Union*, 3 killed, 6 wounded; *Confed.*, 50 captured.

6.—Morton's Ford, Va. *Union*, Portion of Second Corps; *Confed.*, Wade Hampton's Cav. Losses: *Union*, 14 killed, 218 wounded, 391 missing; *Confed.*, 100 killed, wounded, and missing.

9 to 14.—Barber's Place, St. Mary's River, Lake City, and Gainesville, Fla. *Union*, 40th Mass. Mounted Inft. and Independent (Mass.) Cav.; *Confed.*, Gen. Joseph Finnegan's command. Losses: *Union*, 4 killed, 16 wounded; *Confed.*, 4 killed, 48 wounded.

10 to 25.—Gen. Wm. Sooy Smith's Raid from Memphis, Tenn., into Mississippi. *Union*, Smith's Division; *Confed.*, Forrest's Cav. Losses: *Union*, 47 killed, 152 wounded, 120 missing; *Confed.*, 50 wounded, 300 captured.

14 and 15.—Waterproof, La. *Union*, 49th U. S. Colored and U. S. Gunboat *Forest Rose*; *Confed.*, Col. Harrison's command. Losses: *Union*, 8 killed, 14 wounded; *Confed.*, 15 killed.

20.—Olustee or Silver Lake, Fla. *Union*, 47th, 48th, and 115th N. Y., 7th Conn., 7th N. H., 40th Mass., 8th and 54th U. S. Colored, 1st N. C. Colored, 1st Mass. Cav., 1st and 3d U. S. Artil., 3d R. I. Artil.; *Confed.*, Colquitt's and Harrison's brigades under Gen. Joseph Finnegan. Losses: *Union*, 193 killed, 1175 wounded, 460 missing; *Confed.*, 940 killed and wounded.

22.—Okolona, Miss. *Union*, Smith's Cav.; *Confed.*, Forrest's Cav. Losses: *Union*, 47 killed, 152 wounded, 120 missing; *Confed.**

25 to 27.—Buzzard Roost, Tunnel Hill, and Rocky Face, Ga. *Union*, Fourth and Fourteenth Corps and Cavalry Corps Army of the Cumberland; *Confed.*, Troops of Gen. Jos. E. Johnston's command. Losses: *Union*, 17 killed, 272 wounded; *Confed.*, 20 killed, 120 wounded.

28 to March 4.— Kilpatrick's and Dahlgren's Raid from Stevensburg, Va., to Richmond. *Union*, Kilpatrick's Cavalry; *Confed.*, Cavalry commanded by Gens. G. W. C. Lee, Bradley T. Johnson, and Wade Hampton and Home Guards. Losses: *Union*, 330 killed, wounded, and captured; *Confed.*, 308 killed, wounded, and captured.

MARCH, 1864.

14.—Fort De Russy, La. *Union*, Detachments of Sixteenth and Seventeenth Corps and Porter's Miss. Squadron; *Confed.*, Troops under Gen. Walker's command. Losses: *Union*, 7 killed, 41 wounded; *Confed.*, 5 killed, 4 wounded, 260 prisoners.

21.—Henderson Hills, La. *Union*, Detachments of Sixteenth Corps and Cavalry Division Nineteenth Corps; *Confed.*, 2d La. Cav. Losses: *Union*, 1 wounded; *Confed.*, 8 killed, 250 captured.

24.—Union City, Tenn. *Union*, 7th Tenn. Cav.; *Confed.*, Forrest's Cav. Losses: *Union*, 450 captured.

25.—Fort Anderson, Paducah, Ky. *Union*, 122d Ill., 16th Ky. Cav., 8th U. S. Colored Artil.; *Confed.*, Forrest's Cav. Losses: *Union*, 14 killed, 46 wounded; *Confed.*, 10 killed, 40 wounded.

26 to 30.—Longview and Mt. Elba, Ark. *Union*, 28th Wis., 5th Kan. Cav., 7th Mo. Cav.; *Confed.*, Gen. Price's command. Losses: *Union*, 4 killed, 18 wounded; *Confed.*, 12 killed, 35 wounded, 300 captured.

30.—Snyder's Bluff, Miss. *Union*, 3d U. S. Colored Cav.; *Confed.*, 3d, 9th Tex. Cav. Losses: *Union*, 16 killed, 3 wounded; *Confed.*, 3 killed, 7 wounded.

April, 1864.

1.—Augusta, Ark. *Union*, 3d Minn., 8th Mo. Cav.; *Confed.*, Gen. Price's command. Losses: *Union*, 8 killed, 16 wounded; *Confed.*, 15 killed, 45 wounded.

—Crump's Hill or Piney Woods, La. *Union*, 14th N. Y. Cav., 2d La., 2d Ill., and 16th Mo. Cav., 5th U. S. Colored Artil.; *Confed.*, Gen. Richard Taylor's command. Losses: *Union*, 20 wounded; *Confed.*, 10 killed, 25 wounded.

* No record found.

THE BASTIONS OF FORT MARION

On one of the bastions of Fort Marion, St. Augustine, a white flag was raised on the evening of March 8, 1862, as Commander C. R. P. Rodgers sailed up the harbor. He had been detached from the expedition sent from the North under command of Flag-Officer Du Pont to recover control of the whole line of seacoast of Georgia, Florida, and Alabama. Florida troops had been the first to seize a Federal fortification, taking possession of Fort Barrancas and the navy yard at Pensacola, January 13, 1861, and Fort Marion, at St. Augustine, was the first fortification in Florida to be surrendered to Federal authority, Flag-Officer Du Pont having seized and garrisoned the abandoned Fort Clinch, at Fernandina, on March 4, 1862. The Confederate troops in Florida abandoned their fortifications

as Du Pont's expedition approached, and at St. Augustine were found the first inhabitants who had remained in their homes.

The citizens of St. Augustine raised the white flag on Fort Marion in answer to the one which Commander Rodgers was bearing as he approached to assure them of pacific intentions. Landing at the wharf, he was soon joined by the mayor and conducted to the city hall, where the municipal authorities were assembled. Rodgers assured them that so long as St. Augustine respected the Federal authority its government would be left in the hands of its citizens, and recommended that the flag of the Union be at once displayed at the fort. The night before a party of women had assembled in front of the barracks in Fort Marion and cut down the flagstaff to prevent its being used to again support the old flag. By order of the mayor, however, the Stars and Stripes were at once hoisted over Fort Marion.

THE OLDEST CHURCH IN AMERICA, 1864

Engagements of the Civil War

3.—Okalona, Ark. *Union,* 27th Wis., 40th Iowa, 77th Ohio, 43d Ill., 1st Mo. Cav., 13th Ill. Cav.; *Confed.,* Gen. Sterling Price's command. Losses: *Union,* 16 killed, 74 wounded; *Confed.,* 75 killed and wounded.

4.—Campti, La. 35th Iowa, 5th Minn., 2d and 18th N. Y. Cav., 3d R. I. Cav. Losses: *Union,* 10 killed, 18 wounded; *Confed.,* 3 killed, 12 wounded.
—Elkins' Ferry, Ark. *Union,* 43d Ind., 29th and 36th Iowa, 1st Iowa Cav., Battery E 2d Mo. Light Artil.; *Confed.,* Gen. Sterling Price's command. Losses: *Union,* 5 killed, 33 wounded; *Confed.,* 18 killed, 30 wounded.

5.—Roseville, Ark. Seventy-five men of 2d and 6th Kan. Cav. (*Union*) in engagement with guerrillas. Losses: *Union,* 4 killed, 10 wounded; *Confed.,* 6 killed, 20 wounded, 11 captured.

7.—Wilson's Farm, La. *Union,* Cavalry of Nineteenth Corps; *Confed.,* Gen. Richard Taylor's command. Losses: *Union,* 14 killed, 39 wounded; *Confed.,* 15 killed, 40 wounded, 100 captured.

8 and 9.—Sabine Cross Roads and Pleasant Hill, La. *Union,* Portions of Thirteenth, Sixteenth, and Nineteenth Corps and Cavalry Division of Gen. Banks; *Confed.,* Walker's, Mouton's, and Green's Divisions of Gen. Richard Taylor's command. Losses: *Union,* 300 killed, 1600 wounded, 2100 missing; *Confed.,* 600 killed, 2400 wounded, 500 missing. *Union,* Maj.-Gen. Franklin and Brig.-Gen. Ransom wounded. *Confed.,* Maj.-Gen. Mouton and Brig.-Gen. Parsons killed.

10 to 13.—Prairie D'Ann, Ark. *Union,* 3d Division Seventh Corps; *Confed.,* Gen. Price's command. Losses: *Union,* 100 killed and wounded; *Confed.,* 50 killed and wounded.

12.—Blair's Landing, La. *Union,* Gen. Kilby Smith's command, Gunboats *Osage* and *Lexington; Confed.,* Gen. Green's Division of Taylor's command. Losses: *Union,* 7 wounded; *Confed.,* 200 killed and wounded.

13.—Moscow, Ark. *Union,* 18th Iowa, 6th Kan. Cav., 2d Ind. Battery; *Confed.,* Gen. Price's command. Losses: *Union,* 5 killed, 17 wounded; *Confed.,* 30 killed and wounded.

13 and 14.—Paintsville and Half-Mountain, Ky. *Union,* Ky. Volunteers; *Confed.,* Johnson's brigade Ky. Cav. Losses: *Union,* 4 wounded; *Confed.,* 25 killed, 25 wounded.

15 and 16.—Liberty P. O., and occupation of Camden, Ark. *Union,* 29th Iowa, 50th Ind., 9th Wis.; *Confed.,* Gen. Sterling Price's command. Losses: *Union,* 255 killed and wounded.

17 to 20.—Plymouth, N. C. *Union,* 85th N. Y., 103d Pa., 16th Conn., Gunboats *Southfield* and *Miami; Confed.,* Gen. Hoke's command, iron-clad ram *Albemarle.* Losses: *Union,* 20 killed, 80 wounded, 1500 missing; *Confed.,* 500 killed, wounded, and missing. *Union,* Lieut.-Com. Flusser killed.

18.—Poison Springs, eight miles from Camden, Ark. *Union,* 18th Iowa, 79th U. S. Colored, 6th Kan. Cav.; *Confed.,* Shelby's Cav. Losses: *Union,* 204 killed and missing, 97 wounded. *Confed.,* 16 killed, 88 wounded, 10 missing.

22 and 24.—Monette's Ferry, Cane River, and Cloutersville, La. *Union,* Portion of Thirteenth, Seventeenth, and Nineteenth Corps; *Confed.,* Gen. Richard Taylor's command. Losses: *Union* (estimate), 350 killed and wounded; *Confed.,* 400 killed and wounded.

25.—Marks' Mills, Ark. *Union,* 36th Iowa, 77th Ohio, 43d Ill., 1st Ind. Cav., 7th Mo. Cav., Battery E 2d Mo. Light Artil.; *Confed.,* Troops of Gen. Kirby Smith's command. Losses: *Union,* 100 killed, 250 wounded, 1100 captured; *Confed.,* 41 killed, 108 wounded, 44 missing.

26.—Moro Creek, Ark. *Union,* 33d and 40th Iowa, 5th Kan., 2d and 4th Mo., 1st Iowa Cav.; *Confed.,* Troops of Gen. Kirby Smith's command. Losses: *Union,* 5 killed, 14 wounded.

30.—Jenkins' Ferry, Saline River, Ark. *Union,* 3d Division of Seventeenth Corps; *Confed.,* Texas, Missouri, and Arkansas troops under Gens. Kirby Smith and Sterling Price. Losses: *Union,* 200 killed, 955 wounded; *Confed.,* 86 killed, 356 wounded.

From Col. Theodore A. Dodge's "Bird's-Eye View of the Civil War," by permission of Houghton, Mifflin & Co.

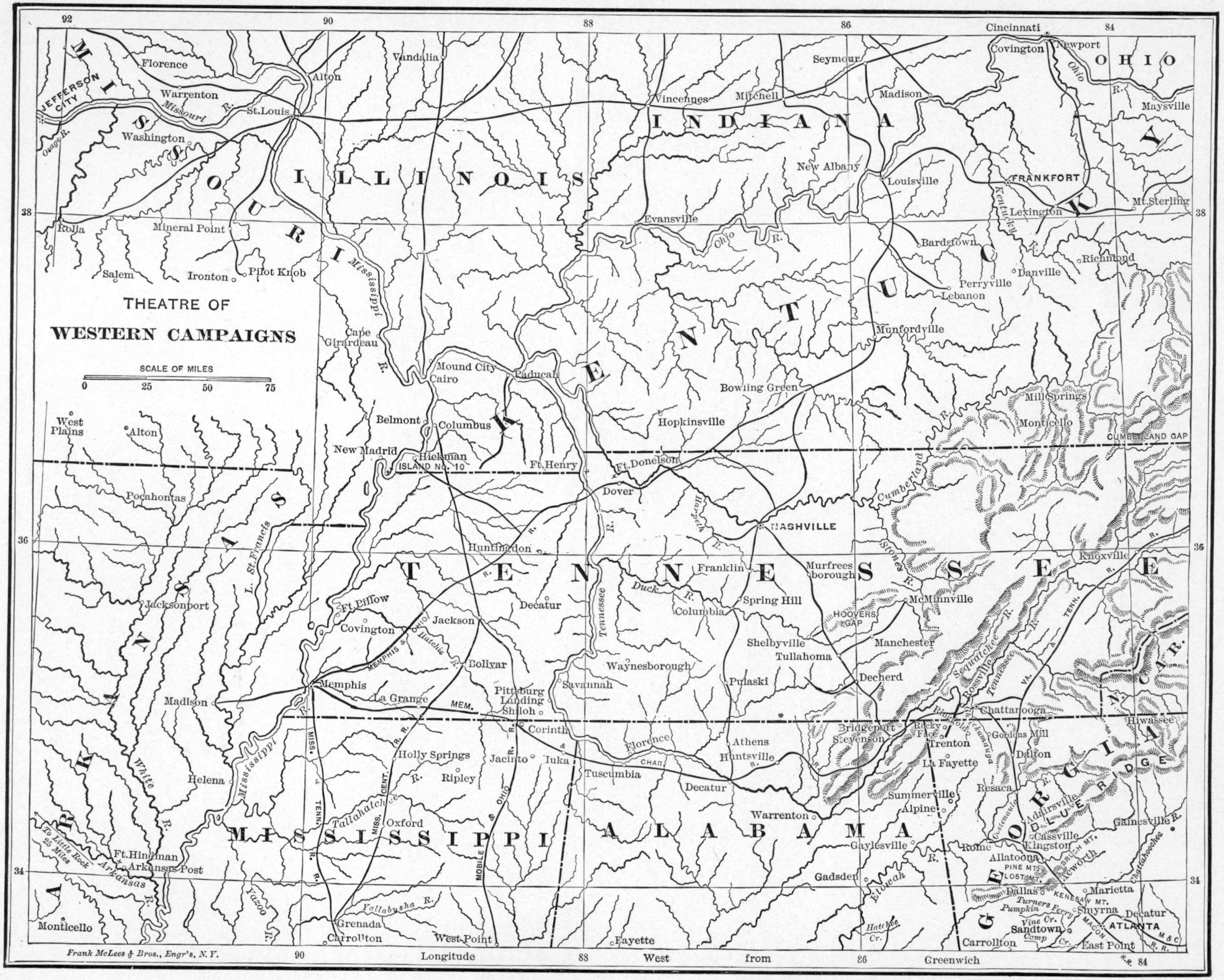

THEATRE OF
WESTERN CAMPAIGNS

SCALE OF MILES

0   25   50   75

Frank McLees & Bros, Engr's, N.Y.

Date Due

JUN 31 1972		
NOV 19 1973		
PRINTED IN U. S. A.